Popular Theater and Society in Tsarist Russia

STUDIES ON THE HISTORY OF SOCIETY AND CULTURE

Victoria E. Bonnell and Lynn Hunt, Editors

Popular Theater and Society in Tsarist Russia

E. ANTHONY SWIFT

University of California Press

BERKELEY · LOS ANGELES · LONDON

University of California Press
Berkeley and Los Angeles, California

University of California Press, Ltd.
London, England

© 2002 by the Regents of the University of California

Library of Congress Cataloging-in-Publication Data
Swift, Eugene Anthony.
    Popular theater and society in Tsarist Russia / E. Anthony Swift.
        p.   cm. —(Studies on the history of society and culture ; 44)
    Includes bibliographical references and index.
    ISBN 0–520-22594-5 (cloth : alk. paper).
        1. Theater—Russia—History.   2. Popular culture—Russia.
I. Title.   II. Series
PN2721.5 .S89   2002
792'.0947—dc21   2001005087

Manufactured in the United States of America
11   10   09   08   07   06   05   04   03   02
10   9   8   7   6   5   4   3   2   1

The paper used in this publication is both acid-free and totally chlorine-
free (TCF). It meets the minimum requirements of ANSI/NISO Z39.48–
1992 (R 1997) (Permanence of Paper).

This book is dedicated to the memory of my mother,
Glenda Shehee Swift

One fears for the future of mankind. The most ominous sign is not the fact that the cook, the servant girl and lackey want the same pleasures which not long ago were the monopoly of the rich alone, but the fact that all, . . . rich and idle as well as poor and industrious, seek and demand it all as something without which life is impossible.

Novoe vremia, December 1900,
cited in Asa Briggs, "Towards 1900:
The Nineteenth Century Faces the Future,"
in *The Collected Essays of Asa Briggs*,
vol. 2 (Brighton, 1984), 291

Contents

Illustrations

Acknowledgments

Many people in many places have assisted me in writing this book. Simon Karlinsky, Martin Malia, and Nicholas Riasanovsky gave me their encouragement and guidance at the beginning of my interest in popular theater. Reginald Zelnik has been a generous mentor and a valued friend from start to finish, and a model of the kind of scholarship that most of us can only try to emulate. I also want to thank Victoria Bonnell, Jeffrey Brooks, Mikhail Iunisov, Catriona Kelly, Lynn Mally, Boris Mironov, James von Geldern, and Mark von Hagen for their careful readings of the manuscript in various stages, and the generous criticism and advice they offered. Al'bin Konechnyi, Nikolai Khrenov, Anna Nekrylova, Liudmilla Starikova, Richard Stites, and Neia Zorkaia have shared with me many valuable insights into Russian cultural history. Raisa Ostrovskaia welcomed me into her home and aided me many times in tracking down sources. My friend and colleague Steve Smith has given me guidance, encouragement, and support at several critical junctures.

Financial support for my research has come from International Research and Exchanges Board (IREX), the Fulbright-Hays program, the Social Science Research Council, the Kennan Institute for Advanced Russian Studies of the Smithsonian Institution's Woodrow Wilson Center, and the University of Essex. I also want to thank the staffs of the Russian State Historical Archive, the Russian State Archive of Literature and Art, the State Archive of the Russian Federation, the Central State Archive of the City of Moscow, the Lunacharksy Theater Library, the Russian National Library, the Saltykov-Shchedrin Public Library, the Bakhrushin Theater Museum, the Library of the Union of Theater People, the Slavonic Library of the University of Helsinki, the Bibliothèque nationale de France, the Library of Congress, the New York Public Library, the Library of University of California, Berkeley, the Library of the School of Slavonic and East European Studies, and the Library of the University of Essex for their assistance. Sheila Levine of the University of California Press has been an encouraging and patient editor. I owe another kind of debt to the staffs of the National Hospital for Neurology and Neurosurgery, the Colchester Head Injury Rehabilitation Unit, and to Dr. Steven Lovett.

Friends and colleagues have contributed to this book in various ways. I wish to give special thanks to Jean-Nicolas Beuze, Robert Blobaum, Hugh Brogan, Cathy Crawford, Catherine Evtuhov, Ann Fagan, Brian Hamnett, Sergei Konkin, Jeremy Krikler, the late Simen Landa, Sergei Ostrovsky, Philippe Paquotte, Stuart Pinches, Alison Rowlands, Beryl Satter, and Gabor Vermes. My father, Gene Swift, my sister, Charis Swift, and my brother, Michael Swift, have encouraged and supported me in all of my efforts. Most of all, I thank my mother, Glenda Shehee Swift, who took an avid interest in my work until her untimely death in the final stages of the manuscript's preparation. This book is dedicated to her.

Wivenhoe, England
August 2000

Note on Transliteration and Dates

Throughout the text unfamiliar titles of Russian books, journals, organizations, and so forth have been given in English translation, with the original Russian in the notes. Titles of all Russian and most foreign plays are given in English translation, with the Russian titles of the plays in the Appendix of Titles. In the Bibliography and Notes I have adhered to the Library of Congress system of transliteration. In the text, for reasons of custom and convenience, I have rendered names familiar to English-speaking readers in their anglicized forms (e.g., Leo Tolstoy, not Lev Tolstoi; Alexander Ostrovsky, not Aleksandr Ostrovskii), and have dropped hard and soft signs in names (e.g., Kugel, not Kugel'; Kleigels, not Kleigel's). Dates before February 1918 follow the Julian (old style) calendar in use in Russia at the time. In the nineteenth century it was twelve days behind the Gregorian (new style) calendar used in Western Europe and the United States, and thirteen days behind in the twentieth century.

Introduction

Early in 1899, Vladimir Nemirovich-Danchenko was summoned to the office of Moscow Police Chief Dmitrii Trepov. The policeman wanted to discuss the new Moscow Accessible Art Theater, for he had learned that Nemirovich and his partner Konstantin Stanislavsky were trying to cultivate a working-class audience by holding matinees at reduced prices and distributing discounted tickets to local factories. Most of the plays performed for workers, however, were not permitted under the stringent censorship regulations governing performances before popular audiences. Trepov was affable but adamant. Under no circumstances, he told the well-known playwright and aspiring director, could the theater continue exposing workers to plays that were not approved for popular audiences. It would have to change either its repertoire or its audience; otherwise, the authorities would shut down the fledgling enterprise. Forced to choose between their twin goals of developing a new, innovative repertoire and of broadening the theater's audience, Nemirovich and Stanislavsky made a difficult decision. Art prevailed over accessibility, and the Moscow Accessible Art Theater became the Moscow Art Theater, a name under which it achieved world renown as one of the most influential theaters of the early twentieth century.[1]

The Moscow Art Theater is well remembered for its attempt to transform Russian theater by creating an entirely new style of performance, yet it is often forgotten that its founders' original goals were social as well as aesthetic. Ever since their first famous meeting in a Moscow restaurant, Stanislavsky and Nemirovich had envisioned their theater as more than an artistic endeavor; they wanted it to be an agent of enlightenment and social transformation, a "people's theater" that would bring art to audiences hitherto excluded from the mainstream of Russian cultural life. Stanislavsky emphasized the social importance of this undertaking in a speech to the troupe a few months before the theater opened, reminding his actors not to forget that their task was to "illuminate the benighted life of the poor, to give them happy, aesthetic minutes amidst the darkness that covers them." The Art Theater even attempted, without success, to persuade the Moscow city fathers to grant it a subsidy, on the grounds that the theater would serve the city's poorer inhabitants.[2]

In forbidding the Art Theater to hold performances for workers, Trepov was carrying out a state policy aimed at controlling popular theaters by subjecting them to special censorship restrictions that were more stringent than those for other, more elite, theaters. In Europe the censorship of most forms of theater has usually been more restrictive and longer-lived than that of literature, due to the assumption that theater's visual impressions are especially persuasive.[3] In the Russian case, a two-tiered censorship structure was introduced for the theater in 1888. Afraid that popular theaters would become hotbeds of subversion and infect the common folk with dangerous political and social ideas, the authorities allowed them to stage only plays that the censors had specifically approved for viewing by lower-class audiences, regardless of whether they had been approved for other theaters. By calling his theater an "accessible" theater rather than a "people's" theater, Nemirovich had hoped to avoid the onerous censorship rules that applied to the latter, but Trepov was deaf to his protests.

This encounter between the tsarist official and the playwright is more than a curious anecdote or footnote in the long saga of confrontations between Russian artists and the state. It allows us a brief glimpse at a forgotten side of the cultural ferment that Russia was experiencing in the autumn years of the Old Regime and reminds us that artists were concerned not only with finding new modes of expression but also with finding new audiences for their work. The middle-class actor Stanislavsky and the aristocratic dramatist Nemirovich were by no means alone in dreaming of a new kind of theater that would serve Russians of all social classes. By the turn of the century, *narodnye teatry,* or "people's theaters," were springing up all over Russia; there were more than ten in St. Petersburg alone, and many more in the provinces. They were organized by industrialists, liberal educators, temperance societies, cooperatives, and factory workers themselves. Leo Tolstoy wrote plays for the people's theaters, Aleksandr Blok went slumming in them, Vsevolod Meyerhold made his stage debut in one, and Maxim Gorky helped found one.

The proliferating people's theaters were a vital part of the new urban culture that was developing as Russia made its turbulent entrance into the twentieth century. Decades of industrialization, urban migration, and primary schooling had produced profound changes in Russian society, as was reflected in the opening of new public spaces exemplified by the tremendous expansion of the penny press, boulevard literature, pleasure gardens, people's theaters—in short, the cultural manifestations of civil society. An increasingly literate urban lower class was participating in Russian cultural life to a degree unthinkable in Pushkin's day, consuming a diverse offering of cultural products geared specifically toward a mass market. To be sure, many contemporaries were less than overjoyed at the profusion of popular literatures and entertainments. Government officials, liberal enlighteners, churchmen, socialists, and radical workers all added their voices to the chorus decrying the people's apparently insatiable appetite for trashy tearjerkers and heartrending melodramas, and the unscrupulous writers, publishers, and impresarios who catered to it. Others hailed the people's growing interest in literature and theater as a sign that Russian society and culture were becoming democratized. The mere fact that Russians of all classes rubbed shoulders in the St. Petersburg people's theaters, exclaimed a leading theater critic in 1908, was "a vivid, living example of the equalization of social groups."[4]

The expansion of the reading public and theater audiences had major consequences for Russian cultural life. From at least the time of Catherine the Great, Russian high culture had been imbued with tremendous social and political significance, serving as a forum for debates and criticisms that had no other outlet in an autocratic state. But until the late nineteenth century, cultural authority had remained in the grip of a thin stratum of educated society, the intelligentsia. Now the growing cultural market appeared to be challenging this authority, threatening to overwhelm the masses with vulgarity instead of contributing to their intellectual development. The intelligentsia of the early nineteenth century had seen itself as the critical intelligence and voice of the Russian nation, most of whose members were enserfed, illiterate, and unable to speak for themselves. As education and literacy expanded, however, "intelligentsia" gradually began to be used in another, looser sense, to describe Russians differentiated from the common people by their higher level of education and their adherence to the values of elite culture. By the turn of the century, terms like "people's intelligentsia" (*narodnaia intelligentsiia*) and "workers' intelligentsia" (*rabochaia intelligentsiia*) had gained currency to describe a small yet significant number of people from the subordinate classes whose intellectual achievements enabled them to take some part in Russia's cultural life, by reading elite literature, writing poetry and fiction, staging or attending theater performances. If a few representatives of the popular classes showed signs that they could be integrated into a national high culture, many educated Russians feared that unless active steps were taken to combat the pernicious influence of commercial popular culture, most of the common people would be lost to the dubious pleasures of chapbooks and fairground shows. Popular theater became one of the major arenas in which a cultural contest was fought for the minds of the Russian people.

. . .

One of the fundamental problems that confronted late imperial Russia was the widespread perception of a cultural divide, originating in the reforms of Peter the Great, that separated the Westernized intelligentsia from the *narod*, the educated elite from the common people. United by a shared hostility toward the existing social and political order, many members of the intelligentsia also shared a sense of debt to the people. After all, they felt, it was the labor of the people, enserfed until 1861, that had made possible Russia's intellectual and cultural achievements. The history of post-emancipation Russia was marked by a variety of attempts by educated society to bridge the cultural chasm separating it from the masses, to repay its perceived debt to the people by sharing the fruits of knowledge and enlightenment. Those educated Russians who embraced the civilizing mission of spreading popular enlightenment were sometimes called *kul'turtregery*, from the German *Kulturträger*. Their ultimate goal was, as Jeffrey Brooks has argued, "to bring the common people into a consensus of values shared by educated Russians."[5]

The Russian people's theater movement is sometimes identified with the theoretical works of the French socialist author Romain Rolland and the Russian symbolist Viacheslav Ivanov.[6] They, in turn, were influenced by Richard Wagner's *Art and Revolution*, in which the composer dreamed of a cathartic theater that would unite society by breaking down the barriers between the audience and the stage. Rolland, who was instrumental in shaping the people's theater movement in France, wanted to bring the people and the theater together by reviving the mass festivals of the French Revolution and staging populist historical dramas that glorified the heroism of the masses. Ivanov envisioned a mystical people's theater that would restore unity to Russian society and achieve *sobornost'*, a collective social body embracing individuals of all classes. No serious attempt was ever made, however, to establish Ivanov's symbolist people's theater.[7] Rolland and Ivanov did have some influence on advocates of proletarian culture and mass festivals after the October Revolution,[8] but had almost no impact on the prerevolutionary people's theater movement. On the whole, the Russian people's theater movement was little influenced by contemporary Western ideas, and its origins must be located in a specifically Russian historical context.

The idea of a people's theater (*narodnyi teatr*), that is, a theater that would serve to democratize the intelligentsia's cultural heritage by making it accessible to the broad masses of the population, took shape during the decade following the emancipation of the serfs in 1861. With the end of serfdom, the problem of bridging the intellectual and cultural gap took on a new urgency for representatives of the intelligentsia, who embarked on a series of efforts to lift the "simple folk" out of their darkness and acquaint them with the moral and cultural values of educated society. Like grammar schools and libraries, theatrical performances became a key component in educated Russia's "civilizing mission." By bringing drama to popular audiences at a price they could afford, the people's theater, it was hoped, would overcome commercial popular culture and contribute to the formation of a new national culture that all Russians could share.

Civilizing the people entailed more, however, than merely integrating them into a democratized national culture. The disorderly crowds of peasant migrants who increasingly filled the streets, slums, tearooms, and taverns of Moscow and St. Petersburg in search of jobs were the cause of great anxiety for both the state and urban elites. Conceived as an alternative to the tavern, the traditional fairground shows, and the growing range of commercial popular entertainments, the people's theaters were also meant to discipline the masses, to teach them to behave respectably, and to entice them to use their leisure for self-improvement.

Michel Foucault has argued that in the early nineteenth century there was a shift in Western Europe from using culture to manifest and symbolize power to using it to transform social behavior, a shift he ties to the rise of the bourgeoisie.[9] In his work on museums and exhibitions, Tony Bennett, influenced by Gramsci's theory of hegemony, relates Foucault's analysis to the emergence of new pedagogical relations between the state and the people. He shows how the people were incorporated into cultural institutions that exercised state power indirectly, instilling new codes of public behavior and making the people self-regulating.[10] In Russia, the people's theater, imagined as a new public space where the people would civilize themselves by consuming didactic cultural products and learning to emulate respectable society's codes of behavior, was envisioned as just such a disciplinary and integrative institution. The question was, however, who would use its power, and for what purposes? In works of cultural history that focus on the historical experience of England and France, with their powerful middle classes, representative institutions, and constitutional politics, scholars sometimes conflate the interests of the state and privileged society, implying that they acted in concert to impose order on the lower classes in the nineteenth century. While this may have been the case in some areas of Western Europe, no such unity of interests existed in Russia, where a weak and fragmented middle class, the absence of representative national political institutions, and the autocracy's determination to minimize society's voice in public affairs meant that the state and a large portion of privileged society regarded one another with suspicion. Often as not, the autocracy and its bureaucracy obstructed middle-class efforts to instill self-restraint in the lower classes. The people's theaters thus became one of the disputed terrains on which various groups sought to assert their interests: the state, industrialists, liberal *Kulturträger*, temperance societies, socialists, and workers aspiring to respectability.

Yet the people's theaters were not only instruments for disciplining bodies and asserting hegemony. Nor were they merely second-rate versions of the elite theaters. Rather, they were a grab bag of elite and popular cultures that produced a distinctive urban culture of year-round entertainments almost anyone could afford to enjoy. The people's theaters brought culture to the people, but the people brought to the theaters their own expectations of what constitutes entertainment; they did not always interpret or respond to what they saw on the stage as their would-be enlighteners hoped.

For Russian intellectuals, the people's theaters offered a means of preserving their position as cultural arbiters in the face of rapid social and cultural changes that threatened to undermine their authority to define what constituted "good" art. Taking a more pragmatic approach, factory owners and temperance societies embraced theater as a "rational recreation" that would combat the attractions of the tavern (and raise productivity) by luring workers away from the source of their Monday morning hangovers. Workers striving to forge new urban social identities organized and attended theater performances in order to assert their claim to respect as cultivated people who shared the cultural values of educated society. In socialist circles, the concept of "workers' theaters," which would combat the opiate of mass culture, raise class consciousness, and lay the groundwork for a future "proletarian culture," was grafted onto the people's theater idea. The people's theaters became part of a discourse that illuminates the deep conflicts in late imperial Russia over cultural power: the state's power to regulate culture and society's ability to contest that power; the intelligentsia's power to impose its cultural program on the lower classes; the common people's power to negotiate and redefine the terms of their encounter with elite culture; culture's power either to obstruct or to promote the political awareness of the masses.

• • •

Among the most striking developments of the post-Emancipation period in Russia was the rapid spread of literacy, generally held to be an indicator of "modernization." In his path-breaking study of the cheap commercial literature that catered to Russia's newly literate reading public, Jeffrey Brooks has set forth the provocative thesis that literacy was producing a modern, individualistic world-view among the common people, which he contends was reflected in popular reading tastes.[11] In contrast, Ben Eklof has argued that schooling and literacy did little to change the outlook of Russian peasants, who countered educators' attempts to civilize them by adapting education to their own limited needs. According to Eklof, "the study of peasant education reinforces the conclusion that to the very end of the Old Regime there remained a significant 'psychological gulf' between the folk and the educated public (*narod* and *obshchestvennost'*) and that the arrival of literacy, the school, and the teacher did little to bridge that gulf."[12] Both Brooks and Eklof have brought new insights to the old debate as to whether Russian society was becoming "more modern" on the eve of the revolution or whether "traditional" peasant attitudes prevailed.

Yet popular culture and the politics surrounding it can also be studied from other perspectives. Modernization in Russia, as in other countries before and since, marched hand in hand with a tremendous expansion in the number and variety of consumer goods available to the population. Popular entertainments and recreations like theater, sports, movies, cycling, and roller-skating were a vital part of Russia's developing consumer culture, a phenomenon that Russia's revolutions have eclipsed. The people's theater movement is a source of insights not only into Russia's social and cultural transformations but also into how contemporaries constructed the categories through which they viewed those transformations. After all, to create a people's theater was to construct "the people," to define who they were, what they wanted, and what they should have in the way of culture and entertainment. At the same time, the people's theaters offer an excellent opportunity to examine the difficult and often overlooked question of popular reception of cultural products, on which new light can be shed by analyzing audience surveys, contemporary observations of popular taste, and descriptions of audiences and their reactions.

The question of popular theaters' impact on audiences is fundamental yet problematic. Were they "vehicles of acculturation," introducing the people to "civilization" and an individualistic ethos?[13] In a study of the Russian popular theater movement in a wide variety of rural and urban settings, Gary Thurston argues that by 1917 the popular theaters were "beginning to make a significant contribution to the civilizing process."[14] This broad approach to popular culture is in some ways a weakness when looking at cultural change, which moves at different paces in different places. Rural theaters for peasants, which were seldom long-lived and served audiences that often had no other access to theatrical entertainments apart from folk plays or temporary fairground theaters, were quite different from urban popular theaters, most of which functioned for years and attracted much larger audiences who were already exposed to the consumption-oriented urban culture of literacy, advertising, and fashion. At times, Thurston overestimates the theaters' psychological impact on audiences, for his analysis tends to rely on the enthusiastic reports of intelligentsia *Kulturträger*, who were themselves convinced of theater's civilizing power.

The relationship between the theaters and their audiences is more complex. The urban people's theaters did not function simply as transmission belts of elite values, nor did they necessarily promote a more individualistic outlook. Rather, they became a kind of cultural crossroads where Russia's working classes encountered and tried to interpret the artistic values of the intelligentsia, defining in the process a new urban popular culture in which entertainment was a commodity separated from the routine of work and workers were consumers of cultural products.

. . .

In the chapters that follow, I examine the people's theater movement from three main perspectives. First, I approach it as a field of discourse, charged with political significance, that reveals assumptions about culture and its relationship to the common people that were widespread among the intelligentsia in late imperial Russia. By "discourse" I mean the process of constructing, defining, and using cultural images, concepts, and oppositions (for example, intelligentsia and *narod*, elite and popular, high and low, respectability and backwardness, the "people" and the "crowd") so as to include some things or people but not others, which is a form of power in that it establishes the terms in which a subject can be discussed.[15] One underlying theme in this study is how the ostensibly homogeneous category *narod*, the common people or "folk," constructed in the days of serfs and landlords, was proving increasingly incompatible with the social and cultural realities of turn-of-the-century urban Russia. Another is that the boundaries between elite and popular cultures are porous, imprecise, and ever shifting.

Second, I attempt to situate specific theaters, performances, and audiences in the social, cultural, and political context of the rapid urbanization and industrialization that transformed Russia's urban landscape from the emancipation of the serfs to the revolutions of 1917. The focus will be on people's theaters in the distinctively urban and industrial setting of Russia's two largest cities, the "two capitals," St. Petersburg and Moscow. It was here that the transformations of Russian culture and society were thrown into sharpest relief and where we can view most clearly the people's theaters in their relationship to both older forms of urban popular theatrical culture and the elite culture represented by the imperial and metropolitan theaters. Although people's theaters existed throughout the rural areas and provincial cities of the Russian empire, it is difficult to generalize about their impact and reception because of the paucity of detailed evidence about their repertoires and audiences, their often short lives, and the closer links between provincial popular and elite cultures. In the capitals, people's theaters existed over a longer time span, attracted larger audiences, played a greater and more permanent role in cultural life, and received more sustained attention from contemporaries than did their counterparts in the provinces. Moreover, urbanization gave rise in Russia as elsewhere to the commodification of secular entertainments and the separation of working time from leisure time in everyday life. In rural areas, by contrast, entertainments continued to preserve the character of special events of a celebratory nature, closely linked to the church calendar and the rhythms of agricultural labor. This, then, is a study of theater's place in the dynamics of urban cultural change and the emergence of a consumer culture.

Finally, I emphasize audiences' consumption of performances much more than the texts that were performed. In theater, and indeed in most forms of popular culture, texts acquire their meanings primarily in the context in which they are "read" by their consumers, and the significance of the people's theaters for the lower-class audiences who attended them is one of my chief concerns. By "popular culture" I mean cultural products that, on the one hand, are consumed by too many people to confer any special status on their consumers (in contrast to elite culture) and, on the other hand, are made meaningful not only by their creators and their critics but also by the people who actively consume them and adapt them to their needs and understanding. As John Fiske, reflecting on contemporary popular culture, has observed: "Popular culture is always in process; its meanings can never be identified in a text, for texts are activated, or made meaningful, only in social relations and in intertextual relations."[16] In other words, popular culture is not a discrete and eternal category with fixed meanings but an unstable terrain where dominant and subordinate classes and cultures interact, continually negotiating the terms of their encounter. The significance of urban people's theaters can be found not in textual analysis but rather in the audiences' responses to performances. By analyzing the impact of the people's theaters on the lives of the urban lower classes, I hope to bring new insights to our understanding of the interaction between elite and popular cultures during the decades of rapid social and political change that preceded the fall of Russia's Old Regime.

A Note on Terminology

The cultural discourse of late imperial Russia employed a handful of terms that need clarification at the outset. The first, *narod*, can mean the folk, the people, or the nation, depending on the context. In the context of the intended audience of the people's theaters, *narod* corresponds best to the German *Volk* or the French *le peuple*; I have rendered it here as "the common people." *Narodnyi teatr* also has several meanings. It may be translated as "folk theater," "popular theater," "people's theater," "national theater," or a combination thereof. Again, context is crucial. Here and in the discussions that follow, I use "peoples' theater" to refer to theaters with didactic aims, created for the common people by industrialists, temperance societies, liberal *Kulturträger*, or government organizations. In this usage, which first appeared in the late 1850s, the term implies a theater that aims not merely to provide entertainment but also to civilize, acculturate, edify, or discipline the common people. People's theaters were more than theaters attended by popular audiences; they were created for the express purpose of transforming the common people, and in opposition to the existing commercial popular theaters. "Popular theater," by contrast, I use in a broader sense to describe any theater that was mainly patronized by lower-class audiences, whether it aimed to enlighten or simply to entertain, including both the didactic people's theaters and the purely commercial theaters of fairgrounds and some pleasure gardens. When treating censorship and other official policies toward theaters serving the common people, I will refer to all such theaters as "popular," since the authorities classified theaters according to the social composition of their audiences and not their proclaimed goals.

Closely related to *narodnyi teatr* is *obshchedostupnyi teatr* (accessible theater), a term that came into widespread usage in the late 1880s as a response to the introduction of a special, more stringent censorship policy for *narodnye teatry*, which the government defined as theaters with low ticket prices. Some theaters that aimed to attract popular audiences tried to avoid the more burdensome censorship restrictions by calling themselves *obshchedostupnye teatry* and selling a portion of their tickets at higher prices. They were thereby able to perform a wider variety of plays than were theaters classified as *narodnye*, although this ruse did not always succeed, as in the case of Stanislavsky and Nemirovich's Moscow Accessible Art Theater. To confuse matters, in the minds of many people *obshchedostupnyi* was also associated with the idea of a theater that would serve the entire population and further the emergence of a consensual national culture shared by all Russians, in which the distinction between the common people and educated society would at last vanish.

Any entertainments or leisure activities, including theater, that were meant to combine pleasure with enlightenment were called *razumnye razvlecheniia*, or "rational recreations." They supposedly brought benefit to the mind and were contrasted to recreations that were not deemed rational, such as drinking, fighting, and fairground shows. Widely used in England from the early nineteenth century on by middle-class reformers in their battles to improve popular recreations, the term "rational recreations" probably passed into Russian from the English; the usage and meaning of the term in both languages is identical.[17]

Another Russian term used in the text requires comment: *narodnoe gulian'e* (pl. *narodnye gulian'ia*), which I have rendered variously as "carnival" and "fairground." The literal meaning of *narodnoe gulian'e* is a "people's promenade," in the sense that people generally walk about in a designated area, singing, drinking, sipping tea, and perhaps watching shows and enjoying various rides. The great *narodnye gulian'ia* held at Shrovetide (*maslenitsa*) were the Russian equivalent of the Lenten carnivals of Western Europe, but the term was used more broadly to refer to almost any outdoor holiday festivity featuring rides and entertainments. In the late nineteenth century, factory owners and temperance societies began calling the outdoor entertainments they organized for the common people *narodnye gulian'ia*. The term has several possible translations, depending on the context in which it is used, such as the British "funfair," "carnival" in American usage, "festivity," or even "amusement park" (the French *fête foraine* is another close equivalent). In the interests of simplicity and clarity, the English words "carnival" and "fairground" have been used interchangeably for *narodnoe gulian'e* in all its guises.

1 The Urban Theatrical Landscape

People's theater had deep roots in post-Petrine Russian culture. These roots were nourished from different sources, some of which were, and still are, usually thought to be antagonistic: an authoritarian state, an emerging civil society, high culture, commercial popular culture, folk culture. Understanding the origins and development of people's theater in Russia entails understanding the diverse currents in Russian cultural, social, and political history that came together, not without tension and never quite merging, to shape the idea of a theater that would both serve and transform the common people.

From the end of the seventeenth century, when Peter the Great (1682–1725) made Westernization an official policy, the state played a preponderant role in initiating, promoting, and regulating the development in Russia of a European-inspired culture, one of whose key elements was theater. The state founded the first public theater in Russia, established a network of state-subsidized imperial theaters, opened schools for actors, and zealously censored the texts performed on the nation's stages. It also alternately encouraged and obstructed efforts to democratize theater by making performances accessible to the masses, a stop-and-start attitude that reflected official Russia's highly ambivalent attitude toward the theater's potential impact on the common people.

Yet the state was not alone in shaping the development of Russian people's theaters; other forces were also at work. Commercial popular theatrical enterprises from fairgrounds, pleasure gardens, and city streets left their imprint on the form and content of performances in the people's theaters, as did the imperial theaters, which catered primarily to elite audiences. Popular theatrical traditions, such as the oral folk plays passed back and forth among factories, barracks, and rural villages, also influenced audiences' expectations and attitudes toward what they saw and heard in the people's theaters. The expansion of civil society that followed the Great Reforms of the 1860s brought new actors onto the stage, those educated Russians who began to promote people's theaters in order to take a more active role in public affairs and contest the state's power to regulate cultural and political life.

Muscovy had no secular theater performances or professional actors until the late seventeenth century, although elements of drama were a part of Russian folk culture and had a place in the festivities associated with the harvest, marriage, Yuletide, and Shrovetide.[1] *Skomorokhi*, a caste of itinerant minstrels, entertained villagers as well as courtiers with songs, performances by trained animals, buffoonery, and puppet shows, sometimes lascivious in content. Wealthy boyars often recruited troupes of *skomorokhi* for their private entertainment, for the line between elite and popular cultures was not sharply drawn in pre-Petrine Russia.[2]

The Orthodox church was generally hostile toward the *skomorokhi* and their entertainments. It condemned them as pagan sorcerers who sought to corrupt the faithful with their secular and therefore sinful merrymaking. According to the *Domostroi*, a mid sixteenth-century guide to household management and morality, both the *skomorokhi* and their audiences were destined to burn in hell. Responding to pressure from the Church, the government enacted various measures to repress the *skomorokhi* beginning in the sixteenth century, culminating in their proscription by the law code of 1649.[3] Although the Orthodox church did make some use of theater for religious instruction, its antipathy toward secular theatrical entertainments remained strong even down to the twentieth century, for it saw them as rivaling its own highly theatrical ritual.[4]

The origins of both elite and popular Russian theater lie not, however, in these rudimentary dramatic traditions, but in the state's encouragement of Westernization, which began in the late seventeenth century. Theater was an important part of the autocracy's program for transforming Russian society by cultivating Western culture, and it was state patronage that promoted the growth of theater. In the eighteenth century, not only were the imperial theaters established to serve the increasingly Westernized elite, but the state also made some attempts to inculcate a taste for theater among the urban lower classes. More significantly for the evolution of Russian popular culture, the eighteenth century saw growing numbers of foreigners coming to Russia to seek their fortunes, including troupes of artists who began performing interludes, farces, and short skits at fairs and popular holiday celebrations in St. Petersburg and Moscow. Russian acting companies also appeared, performing Russian comedies and translations before socially diverse urban audiences. In the nineteenth century, the temporary fairground theater, or *balagan*, became the focus of urban popular theatrical culture, drawing thousands to its short productions, which emphasized the exotic, the supernatural, Russia's past and present military victories, as well as traditional themes from Russian and Western European folklore.

THE STATE, THEATER, AND SOCIETY
IN THE AGE OF ENLIGHTENMENT

Although the credit for bringing professional, secular theater and literary drama to Russia is usually given to Tsar Alexis (1645–76), who made drama performances a regular part of court life,[5] it was his son Peter the Great who made the first serious attempts to promote a taste for theater among his subjects. As part of his program of Westernization, Peter was determined to change the way Russians spent their leisure hours. He imported actors from abroad, had young Russians schooled in acting, and ordered the construction on Red Square of a wooden theater *(komediinaia khramina)*, which opened in 1702.[6] Peter also encouraged drama performances at ecclesiastical schools and the Slavic-Greek-Latin Academy, where secular didactic and patriotic plays joined the existing repertoire of religious school dramas.[7]

Peter's interest in theater was motivated by practical political considerations. Unlike his father Alexis, he saw theater as more than an exotic pleasure to be enjoyed as pure entertainment. One nineteenth-century historian observed, "Theater was to serve Peter like the ardent, sincere sermons of [his panegyrist] Feofan Prokopovich: it was meant to explain to the nation's multitude the true meaning of the transformer's acts."[8] Theater was an instrument of state policy, to be used in furthering Peter's reforms by propagandizing his military victories and introducing Russians to contemporary Western culture. Public performances commemorated the capture of the Shlisselburg fortress from Sweden in 1702 and the occupation of Narva in 1704, while the theater on Red Square offered Moscow audiences translations and adaptations of works by Molière, Corneille, Calderón, Lohenstein, and other prominent Western European playwrights.[9]

Peter's *komediinaia khramina*, which held about 450 persons, was Russia's first public theater. Since the tsar intended it to civilize the common people and introduce them to new cultural forms and models of public behavior, it was also, arguably, Russia's first people's theater. Whereas under Alexis performances had been given only for the tsar, his family, and a small circle of courtiers and foreigners, Peter wanted his theater to be patronized by a broad spectrum of the population. Audiences were predominately from the urban lower and middle classes.[10] To encourage attendance, admission was inexpensive or free, the city gates were kept open late on performance nights, and spectators were exempted from gate tolls and road taxes. Performances were in Russian as well as German; the task of translating foreign plays was given to the scribes of the Office of Foreign Affairs, who struggled to find a suitable Russian literary language into which to render European drama.[11]

Like Peter's introduction of Western dress and recreations among the nobility and his promotion of the printing press and education, the theater on Red Square was intended to inculcate the tsar's subjects with the civilization of Western Europe. Behind the theater and so many of Peter's other cultural innovations was the idea, widespread during the Enlightenment, that one could transform people by altering the way they spent their leisure hours. Yet the theater was not very successful at transforming Muscovites into appreciative theatergoers: performances were noisy, and violence sometimes broke out among the spectators, who freely smoked tobacco (another Petrine import) and were often more interested in the luxury of the decorations and costumes than in the content of the works presented. Attendance was good on holidays or when the tsar was present, but at other times the theater found it difficult to attract audiences. Associating public entertainments with holidays, Muscovites never fully adapted to the concept of entertainment as a part of everyday life. The theater was partially dismantled in 1707, and Peter's sister Natalia took all of the costumes, decorations, texts, and some of the actors for her own private theater on her estate outside of Moscow. Soon afterward the tsar abandoned Moscow for good, moving the court to St. Petersburg, his new, second capital on the Gulf of Finland.[12]

It was in St. Petersburg that Peter and his successors had the most visible success in weaving new forms of culture into the fabric of everyday life. Here traditional celebrations and recreations were transformed and given new meanings as Peter put them to work in the service of his new order. Major events of state, which in Muscovy had been marked by masses and religious processions, were now also celebrated with secular entertainments. Russia's victory over Sweden in the Northern War, for example, was feted in 1721 with a carnival, a grand masquerade, processions through the streets of the new capital, and an enormous fireworks display with allegorical representations of Russia's triumph over its enemies. To popularize Peter's beloved navy among the population, public festivities invariably accompanied the launchings of new battleships.[13]

As part of his efforts to accustom the upper classes to Western European forms of sociability, Peter used recreations "to polish people."[14] He ordered society women to attend parties known as *assemblées*, where nobles mingled with rich merchants, engineers, and bureaucrats. Guests danced the polonaise and minuet, conversed, and played table games. In contrast to Muscovite custom, women and men mixed freely and, instead of sitting at a common table, people wandered from room to room as they pleased.[15]

Peter's transformation of social and recreational customs at first had its greatest impact on the gentry and a relatively small number of military officers, bureaucrats, professionals, merchants, and master artisans. The new forms of entertainment that the tsar promoted in St. Petersburg sometimes even widened the gulf between the Westernized segment of society and the common people. The festivals held at the parks of wealthy nobles on Elagin Island, for example, were open only to people in Western attire, thus excluding those who could not afford such clothing. The common people continued to enjoy the traditional winter holiday recreations, such as sledding and fist combats, which attracted huge crowds and were regulated by the police.[16]

Nevertheless, the Western influences that continued to reshape Russian society throughout the eighteenth century also had an impact on the entertainments of the common people, at least in the two capitals. Petty officials, clerks, lackeys, soldiers, and other *raznochintsy* (people of various classes who did not fit neatly into any social category) organized theater shows in Moscow that combined elements of the new European-style dramas with the old comic techniques of the *skomorokhi*.[17] The influx of foreign entertainers into Russia that had begun under Peter transformed the holiday carnivals, or *narodnye gulian'ia*, held at Yuletide and Shrovetide, as Italian, French, and German troupes began offering comic sketches, dramatic interludes, and circus acts alongside the traditional swings, ice hills, and minstrel acts. The foreign troupes recruited natives for their shows, while independent groups of Russian actors also appeared, performing before audiences of all social ranks.[18]

For most of the eighteenth century, the boundaries between elite and popular theatrical cultures were fairly fluid, as illustrated by the story of Fedor Volkov, the Kostroma merchant's son who is generally considered to be the father of the Russian theater. In the 1740s, Volkov put together a troupe of amateur Russian actors in Yaroslavl and organized small performances for the local gentry. When after his father's death in 1750 he took over the family sulfur and nitric acid factory, Volkov began staging plays for his employees in a converted warehouse. The factory workers were not only spectators but also participated in the performances along with Volkov and his brothers. In 1752, Empress Elizabeth (1741–62) commanded Volkov and his troupe to come to St. Petersburg, where, impressed by their talent, she enrolled him and the other most promising actors in the Infantry Corps of Nobles for further education. When Elizabeth founded the first Imperial Russian Theater in 1756, Volkov and his fellows formed the nucleus of its acting company.[19]

From its modest origins, the theater gradually expanded under Elizabeth's successors into a sizable network of imperial theaters in St. Petersburg and Moscow, generously subsidized by the tsars and attached to the court. Native Russian dramatists began to provide original Russian plays to supplement imports from the West. The imperial theaters were the high temples of the Westernized culture of Russia's privileged classes, and by the late eighteenth century they had become symbols of the expanding cultural gap between the elite and the common people.

Under Catherine the Great (1762–96), the state made a second attempt to bring theater to the popular masses. Like Peter, to whom she was fond of comparing herself, Catherine was well aware of the propaganda value of theatrical spectacles. During Shrovetide of 1763, shortly after wresting the throne from her husband Peter III, the usurper organized a series of allegorical entertainments that culminated in a street masquerade in which she adapted popular performance styles to celebrate her qualities as Russia's newly crowned monarch, "Minerva Triumphant."[20] To mark the successful conclusion of the First Turkish War (1768–74), Catherine had mock fortresses and towns erected for an enormous fair on Khodynka Field, just outside Moscow, where thousands were treated to free food and drink, stage shows, and a grandiose fireworks display depicting the sinking of the Ottoman fleet at Chesme.[21] Khodynka Field would remain a favorite spot for state celebrations until 1896, when several hundred people were trampled to death during the festivities held to mark the coronation of Nicholas II (1894–1917).

In 1765 Catherine, to whom are attributed the remarks, "Theater is the school of the people, and it should be directly under my supervision" and "A people who sing and dance think no evil,"[22] instructed the police to construct open-air stages on Moscow's Deviche Field (the site of popular holiday carnivals in the mid-eighteenth century) and on St. Petersburg's Brumbergova Square, near the Moika Canal. Little is known about Catherine's motivations in establishing the theaters, but they fit well with the image she wished to promote as an enlightened monarch attentive to her subjects' needs. Troupes of Russian actors gave free performances of Russian and foreign comedies on Sundays and holidays from Easter until autumn. The police not only paid the actors, but also monitored every show to ensure that nothing obscene found its way onto the stage. The St. Petersburg troupe included factory workers, typographers, bookbinders, and other artisans. The Moscow theater must have been very poorly constructed, as by 1770 it was falling apart and had to be restored. The next year an outbreak of plague in the city forced its closure, and performances were never revived. The St. Petersburg theater came to an end at about the same time, for unknown reasons.[23] In any event, in 1775 a massive popular uprising in the south of Russia, led by the Cossack Emilian Pugachev, put an end to any ideas Catherine may have had about enlightening the common people.[24]

The idea that the theater can be a vehicle for popular enlightenment, which dates back at least to Aristotle's *Poetics* and was expounded more than once in Diderot's compilation of Enlightenment thought, the *Encylopédie* (1751–59), became embedded in Russian thought in the course of the eighteenth century. Although the attempts by Peter and Catherine to create state-funded theaters for the common people did not bear fruit, they nonetheless established a tradition of using theater for educational purposes that could later be invoked to bolster arguments for a people's theater. Time and again, the proponents of the people's theater would cite Peter's *komedi-inaia khramina* or Catherine's remark that "theater is the school of the people" as proof that it was in the state's interest to allow them to bring theater to the people.[25]

THE IMPERIAL THEATERS

The imperial theater network in St. Petersburg and Moscow was the dominant force in Russian theatrical life throughout most of the nineteenth century. The imperial theaters indirectly influenced the repertoire available to popular theaters, since most of the plays the popular theaters could choose to produce had first appeared on the imperial stages. Run by a department of the Ministry of Court, the Directorate of Imperial Theaters, they had the status of official state theaters and received large subsidies. Potent symbols of tsarist authority and its patronage of elite culture, the imposing buildings of the imperial theaters grandly occupied commanding positions in the centers of the two capitals. In St. Petersburg there were three imperial theaters. The neoclassical Aleksandrinskii Theater, used for drama productions, faced Nevskii Prospekt across the Catherine Garden. The Mariinskii Theater, opened in 1860 on Theater Square, was the home of the imperial ballet and opera companies, while the Mikhailovskii Theater, on Mikhailovskii Square, produced mainly French plays. Moscow's Malyi Theater, sometimes called the city's "second university," housed a drama troupe next door to the Bolshoi Theater, where ballet and opera were performed. A third imperial theater, the Novyi, existed from 1898 to 1907 in Moscow, staging a mixed repertoire of both drama and opera.[26]

The imperial theaters had a monopoly on public theater performances in St. Petersburg and Moscow from the beginning of the nineteenth century until 1882, an advantage that enabled them to maintain their position as Russia's leading theaters with little competition until the end of the century. Their repertoires set the tone for theaters throughout the empire, and their actors enjoyed salaries and pensions that were the envy of their less fortunate brethren working in the provinces. For playwrights and actors, the imperial stage offered public recognition, reviews by leading critics, and the key to professional success. Although they were often accused of conservatism and favoritism, and certainly many plays served primarily as vehicles for leading actors to display their talents, the imperial theaters' repertoires were extremely diverse, for they staged dozens of plays, operas, and ballets every year. Works performed in the imperial theaters circulated outward from the center to the provincial theaters and sometimes made their way onto the stages of the fairground theaters, where entertainers adapted them to popular tastes and expectations.

In the first half of the nineteenth century the imperial stage was dominated by historical patriotic plays and French and Russian melodramas and vaudevilles. During this period it was not uncommon for magic shows to be a part of the entertainment offered. In the second half of the century a growing number of works by Russian dramatists such as Ivan Turgenev, Alexei Pisemsky, Nikolai Gogol, Aleksandr Griboedov, and especially the prolific Alexander Ostrovsky, were established as classics of the Russian repertoire and were performed together with light comedies, translations of French and German playwrights, and plays written especially for one or another actor. By the turn of the century, the imperial theaters were shedding some of their old-fashioned reputation, as modernist influences infiltrated them and they began staging the works of Chekhov, Gorky, Ibsen, and other playwrights considered socially progressive, but the staples of the imperial stage remained Russian classics, light comedies, and contemporary plays that offered its stars a chance to shine.[27]

The audiences of the imperial theaters represented the various social elites of the capitals: nobles, officials, military officers, merchants, the intelligentsia, and, usually occupying seats in the gods, students. By the beginning of the twentieth century, however, at least a few workers were also attending the imperial theaters. To be sure, the imperial theaters remained a socially exclusive public space, and a sense of social unease often accompanied workers' forays into the cultural world of the privileged classes. Yet tickets in the gods could be had for as little as twenty or thirty kopeks, and some workers took advantage of them to enter the glittering citadels of elite culture. N. A. Sakharov, a Moscow typesetter, went to the opera at the Bolshoi Theater more than two hundred times between 1898 and 1910, but was still occasionally embarrassed by his modest attire when he arrived directly from work.[28]

POPULAR THEATERS AT THE FAIRGROUNDS

By the early nineteenth century, the carnival theaters that appeared in the eighteenth century had become an integral part of the popular holiday culture of St. Petersburg and Moscow, providing a striking contrast to the imperial theaters in the simplicity and impermanence of their construction, their market orientation, and the social diversity of their audiences. These temporary wooden theaters, called *balagany*, were put up for the duration of the carnivals and taken down afterward. They offered a wide variety of entertainments, including comic sketches, puppet shows, trick riders, acrobatics, magic shows, and displays of wild animals and other curiosities.[29] Until mid-century, performances in Russian were prohibited and pantomimes dominated the repertoire, with foreigners running most of the large *balagany*. The French showman Christian Leman arrived in Russia in 1818 to thrill Petersburgers with his pantomime-harlequinades, which became the favorite spectacle of the fairground theaters for many years to come.[30]

For most of the nineteenth century, the great holiday carnivals, or *narodnye gulian'ia*, were held at Shrovetide and again during Easter week on St. Petersburg's Admiralty Square, within sight of the Winter Palace. In 1872, following a fire that consumed two of the large theaters at the Easter carnival, the city government decided to transform the dusty square into a public park, and the carnivals were moved a short distance away to the Field of Mars, the imperial parade ground. The Moscow carnivals were usually held at Novinskii Wall, but in 1874, when a boulevard was constructed on the site, they were relocated to Deviche Field on the western side of the city.[31] Some of the St. Petersburg showmen also operated *balagany* in Moscow, but these shows were not usually as lavish as those in the imperial capital.[32]

The carnivals and their theaters were attended by almost everyone, including aristocrats and wealthy merchants. According to an observer writing in 1822, "In the morning the best of the aristocracy, fashionable society, and the merchantry go sledding on the ice hills and visit the shows, and in the afternoon our simple, good folk [do the same]."[33] Even Tsar Nicholas I and his family visited Leman's *balagan* several times.[34] For members of high society and their imitators, the *narodnye gulian'ia* were also an opportunity to show off their fine carriages and clothing while circling the perimeter of the fairground.[35] Still, most of the spectators at the fairground theaters belonged to the popular classes—of the 127 persons killed or injured during a fire that consumed Leman's *balagan* in 1836, the overwhelming majority were clerks, serfs, artisans, and students from poor families.[36]

Run by entrepreneurs who vied to outdo one another in delighting their public, the holiday *balagany* and puppet theaters were the genuinely popular theaters of Moscow and St. Petersburg in the nineteenth century.[37] According to a journalist who described the show in 1834, the press of the crowd before the entrances to Leman's *balagan* was unforgettable, as were the sights within: "Leman shows you devils, skeletons, hell, fire, murder, but he has a good nature. If he kills someone, then in a minute he resurrects him; if he tears off Pierrot's head, then out of pity he soon returns it to his torso; if he cuts Harlequin up into pieces, then he quickly puts them back together; if devils put Pantalon behind bars, then Leman sets him free. None of his murders are distressing, but rather make you laugh."[38]

As with the antics of Petrushka, the Russian Punch, a comic kind of violence was part of the fun at the fairground theaters, where everything on stage was calculated to evoke laughter and amazement. Audiences expressed their approval through laughter or rapt attention, never by applause.[39] The pantomime spectacles were constructed around the mishaps suffered by Harlequin (who was usually killed, cut into pieces, and then resurrected), his tricks in escaping his pursuers (such as vanishing into thin air), and transformations of people into animals and vice versa. The fairground shows sometimes related Harlequin's adventures to topical events, sending him by train to an *exposition universelle* in Paris, for example, and having him make an ascent in a hot air balloon.[40]

There was no distinct line between popular and elite cultures in the fairground theaters. The *balagan* shows acquainted the common people with the new technologies that were appearing in Russia, and even with works of art from the realm of contemporary high culture. In 1835, for example, Leman presented a *tableau vivant* depicting "The Last Day of Pompeii," recreating the painting by Karl Briullov that had caused a sensation only a few months earlier at the Academy of Arts. In 1836, one year prior to the opening of Russia's first railway line, Leman put on a harlequinade in which a moving train with passengers crossed the stage. Contemporary military campaigns also found their way to the fairground stage: during the Crimean War audiences were treated to an enactment of the Russian navy's destruction of a Turkish fleet off Sinope.[41]

Toward the end of the 1830s, themes from Russian folklore and the cheap popular woodblock prints known as *lubki* began to appear in the shows, bringing folk characters such as heroic Bova the King's Son, Solovei the Bandit, miserly Kashchei the Deathless, the Serpent Gorynych, the evil witch Baba-Iaga, and the Firebird to life on the stage. Once the authorities lifted the ban on Russian-language performances at the *balagany* in the mid-1860s, the impresarios rushed to take advantage of their new freedom by staging "talking plays," recruiting amateurs and provincial actors. The repertoire began to change, borrowing and adapting texts from high culture, and the old pantomimes made way for new works based not only on folk tales and *lubki* but also on adaptations of literary classics, operas, melodramas, science fiction, and patriotic episodes from Russian history.[42] In 1870 a St. Petersburg newspaper remarked the appearance of entire historical plays, such as *Peter the Great at the Battle of Poltava, Dmitrii the Pretender,* and *Ermak Timofeevich or The Conquest of Siberia,* some of which had made their first appearance years before on the imperial stages.[43] Both Peter and Ermak, a Cossack bandit leader who led an expedition to conquer Siberia in the 1580s, were among the favorite historical heroes of popular literature in the late nineteenth century.[44]

Vasilii Malafeev, a St. Petersburg timber merchant, was one of the new breed of entrepreneurs who excelled in producing the historical-patriotic genre. Every drama was concocted from a standard recipe: scenes in the Russian and enemy camps were followed by a massive battle scene with special effects such as explosions and fires, and an apotheosis glorifying the Russia's victory concluded the show. Little effort was made at achieving historical accuracy in uniforms, arms, or the portrayal of events.[45] The Russian victory over the Turks in 1878 spawned a new generation of contemporary patriotic works for the *balagan* stage, such as *Russians Across the Balkans in 1878* (1879 and 1883), *The Taking of the Fortress Geok-Tepe* (1880), and *The Heroic Feats of the White General, or the Liberation of the Slavs* (1890), but the exploits of Russian arms during the Time of Troubles, under Peter the Great, and in the Napoleonic Wars remained the mainstay of the popular patriotic repertoire until 1917 and were resurrected under Stalin.[46]

By the last quarter of the century, the fairground spectacles had become incredibly lavish, akin to the spectaculars popular in Victorian England in the same period.[47] During Shrovetide of 1890, the biggest hit of the fairground was Malafeev's Crimean War saga *Russian Heroes at Sevastopol*, which featured a cast of more than three hundred persons and twenty horses and complemented the usual battle scenes, naval gun duels, and explosions with fires, large *tableaux vivants*, singing and dancing soldiers, Turkish dances, and an apotheosis, all in five acts and ten scenes.[48] Painted panoramic backdrops on rollers were slowly scrolled across the stage to give the illusion of movement in journey scenes. Special effects became increasingly complex, creating onstage the illusion of flight, sunrise and sunset, the reflection and play of light on water, wind, waterfalls, the roar of thunder, and the flash of lightning. Along with special effects, costumes were among the most important elements of the shows; in bright, vivid colors, they were made of fabrics calculated to produce an effect of luxury, like satin, velveteen, moleskin, and wool, trimmed in gold and silver and adorned with jewels, sequins, and beads. Some costumes were even on strings, to facilitate transformation scenes.

Style was all-important in the fairground theaters. At the core of the show was the visual impact it made on audiences rather than the content of the text performed. Given the short duration of performances, which lasted only thirty or forty minutes and were repeated as many as twelve times in seven or eight hours, there was little time for developing complex characterizations; impresarios sought instead to stun audiences with breathtaking special effects and fast-paced action.[49] Alluring posters advertised the shows, illustrating the most sensational scenes, describing the special effects, songs, and dances, and listing the characters but not the names of the actors. Titles were long and explanatory, helping the prospective spectator to visualize what was in store: *Fighting the Indians, or Around the World in Eighty Days*, or *Ivan the Simpleton and the Power of the Enchanted Pike, or The Volga Bandits*.[50] In a sense, the *balagany* resembled early cinemas in that they functioned as factories of mass culture, repeatedly selling an identical product, easily recognizable and consumable, to an ever-changing stream of new spectators.

Even at Entertainment and Benefit (Razvlechenie i pol'za), a St. Petersburg *balagan* where in the 1880s and 1890s Abram Leifert and Aleksei Alekseev-Iakovlev pioneered longer adaptations of classics by Pushkin, Ostrovsky, Gogol, and other "highbrow" writers, the emphasis was on action rather than words:

> The plays were usually arranged so that the actors had to express the plot largely through action and *say as little as possible*. For this reason the mass scenes, choruses, dances, various special effects and in general the whole decor were of primary importance. The performances were

spectacles and had to make a vivid impression on audiences, who were not at all in a thoughtful or serious mood. Audiences wanted things to be magical, pleasant, vivid, and not dull—they might not listen to long dialogues, or even understand them.[51]

Although Alekseev-Iakovlev and Leifert were successful in bringing adaptations of works from the realm of high culture to the *balagan* stage, they quickly learned that the shows had to be adapted to the festive atmosphere of the *narodnoe gulian'e.*

In 1882 Alekseev-Iakovlev decided to produce an adaptation of Alexander Ostrovsky's melodrama *You Can't Live as You Please,* about a newcomer to Moscow who drinks heavily, mistreats his wife, and begins an affair on the sly. When the object of his adulterous affections learns that he is married, she breaks off the affair. Enraged and inebriated, the young man decides to free himself by murdering his wife but is brought to his senses by the sound of church bells. The play met with an indifferent reception: audiences found the scenes long, depressing, and too "realistic," in contrast to the cheerful holiday mood of the fairground, and these negative evaluations discouraged others from attending.[52]

Alekseev-Iakovlev took measure of the reasons for the flop, however, and found a way to adapt the play to the taste of the fairground audience:

> Without giving up on the texts, which were predominantly in verse, I began to present them in small doses, so that the actors had to express the plot primarily by their actions. I appreciated the importance of beautiful, elegant sets, understood the value of changes in tempo, rhythm, and color, and chose the path of vivid, festive shows. I strove for romantic animation, and as a director, gave first place to the moral element in the fate of the characters.[53]

This formula proved to be a success, and other St. Petersburg showmen soon followed Alekseev-Iakovlev's example. Adaptations of classics and literary plays became a regular feature of the *balagan* repertoire, leading an observer to conclude in 1890 that popular tastes were changing and the fairgrounds were giving birth to "a genuine people's theater, capable of giving the people edifying spectacles and serving them as a school."[54]

The so-called respectable public (*chistaia publika*) continued to patronize the shows until the end of the century, although newspaper journalists periodically lamented that the better-off classes were beginning to desert the *balagany* for more cultivated entertainments. In 1857, for example, a columnist for *Son of the Fatherland* claimed that many of the people who once sought entertainment at St. Petersburg's Shrovetide fairgrounds were now going to the imperial theaters instead, and he confidently predicted that soon the fairground's amusements and shows would cease to be the center of the holiday festivities. Five years later, however, columnists in the same paper observed that the *narodnoe gulian'e* was still bringing together all strata of urban society and that tickets to the largest *balagany* were in great demand even among "the very important." In the 1860s and 1870s, it was still fashionable for socialites to attend the fairground shows. As late as 1891, the theaters were the main attraction of the fairground, and a St. Petersburg journalist reported that the big ones "draw both highbrow and lowbrow audiences."[55]

The fairgrounds, for all their social mixing, did not undermine ordinary status distinctions but merely adapted them to the holiday environment. The fairgrounds' spatial organization was strongly hierarchical, consisting of two to four rows of temporary structures. The first concourse was lined with the largest *balagany*, which were built of wood and resembled huge barns, with many entrances and exits along their sides. They were festooned with flags and decorated with paintings and posters depicting scenes from the shows. These theaters attracted a diverse public, but they preserved class distinctions in their seating arrangements. There were usually three interior seating sections, each with its own separate entry: boxes and chairs, which might cost as much as several rubles, and a large standing section for people of more modest means, where tickets could be had for as little as twenty kopeks. The big theaters held 1,200–2,000 people and presented eight to ten shows daily for some 40,000–60,000 spectators during the eight days of the carnivals.[56]

The back rows were occupied by theaters of a more modest size and appearance, which offered less sumptuous but still exotic fare and were patronized almost exclusively by the common people: factory workers, maids, cooks, small-time merchants, and clerks. Here one could see a two-headed or five-legged calf, an Egyptian mummy, a wild man from Africa who ate live birds, a bearded woman, a fire-eating American Hercules, and other "monstrous, inexplicable natural phenomena." Some of the small *balagany* staged short plays, like *Tsar Nebuchadnezzar*, in which the title character "struts in wide Turkish trousers, a red cloak and an Indian turban, with a police whistle around his neck, which he blows to signal the change of set."[57] Others featured the pugnacious puppet Petrushka, whose boisterous antics were not limited to the fairground, for they could be seen year-round at street performances put on by itinerant puppeteers.[58] The attractions of the fairground also included the traditional ice hills and swings, as well as merry-go-rounds, some of which were enclosed and presented dancers and short skits. Roller coasters, or "American moun-

Figure 1. Roller coaster at the carnival on the Field of Mars, 1895. Courtesy of the Central State Archive of Documentary Films and Photographs, St. Petersburg.

tains," as they were called, made their appearance in the 1890s, in a wonderful synthesis of new technology and the centuries-old custom of sledding on Shrovetide.[59]

The urban *narodnye gulian'ia* of the nineteenth century were festive, noisy, and rowdy, bringing with them a relaxation of everyday standards of public order. A German actor who lived and worked in St. Petersburg in the 1840s, Edward Jerrman, left this account of a Shrovetide carnival:

Figure 2. Ferris wheel and *balagan* theater at an Easter carnival at Ekateringof Garden. St. Petersburg, 1895. Courtesy of the Central State Archive of Documentary Films and Photographs, St. Petersburg.

> Early on the morning of the first day of the Maslinizza [*sic*], the vast place is crowded with people;—all Petersburg is on its legs, hastening to and from the carnival. All business is suspended; for these eight days are exclusively devoted to popular diversions. So long as they last, there reigns pure and unlimited social democracy; no drunkenness is punished; no nocturnal rovers are taken up; even detected thieves are rarely given up to the police, but, instead, often receive upon the spot some slight punishment.[60]

Although Jerrman may be exaggerating the licentious atmosphere of the fairgrounds, his comments are surely nearer the truth than those of the showman Abram Leifert, who in his nostalgic reminiscences of the St. Petersburg *balagany* of bygone days claimed that "drunks seldom came to the Field of Mars."[61]

It was precisely the unsavory aspects of the fairground and *balagan* that attracted the attention of the radical Russian writers of the 1860s, who saw them as symptoms of the poverty of urban popular culture. Under the influence of the radical publicists Nikolai Dobroliubov and Nikolai Chernyshevsky, who held that it was literature's duty to depict society realistically, with all its warts, to draw attention to social ills, and to suggest solutions to them, progressive writers turned out a large number of novels and sketches that focused on the daily life and customs of the peasants and urban lower classes. In their hands, the fairgrounds and their entertainments became metaphors for the moral degradation of the common people.[62]

While intrigued by the folksy humor of the fairground barkers, whose doggerel they often recorded in detail in their sketches, radical publicists also deplored the drunkenness and disorder of the popular carnivals. Describing a *narodnoe gulian'e* at a village just outside of Moscow, Gleb Uspenskii focused on the inebriation of the celebrants, dourly observing that "the overall appearance of the field and the drunks could serve as the subject of a portrayal of a battlefield."[63] Vasilii Sleptsov struck an equally disapproving tone in his ironic depiction of a Yuletide carnival in St. Petersburg, emphasizing the drunkenness, vulgarity, and violence of the scene:

> Inebriated muzhiks walked arm in arm or embracing, and if one fell into the mud he dragged the other with him. As a result all kinds of quarrels took place, the people gathered around the fallen men, laughter erupted, witty remarks were heard, and everyone had fun. . . . Painted on one *balagan* were a naked woman and a devil, with the inscription "Chinese Conjurers from Peking, Also Showing Sleeping Beauty and the House-Demon in the Moonlight." On the Italian theater a dead woman was depicted rising from the grave, together with a clown in a three-cornered hat. Underneath was written "Harlequin, Faust's Master in Hell's Darkness." On the balcony, the same clown, his face smeared with soot, beat on the back of Harlequin, who in turn kicked a Spaniard in the head.[64]

In another feuilleton, Sleptsov chided "speculators and entrepreneurs" for trying to distract the people from the hardships of everyday life with *balagan* spectacles.[65]

On the one hand, Sleptsov was using the *gulian'ia* and *balagany* to criticize the state and its attitude toward society in Aesopian language, equating the government ministers with the fairground performers.[66] On the other hand, he is also blaming the market for the ostensible coarseness of popular entertainments, a common refrain of educated Russian detractors of the fairground entertainments.[67] The pervasive prejudice against commercial popular entertainments of all kinds led many middle-class observers to focus on those aspects of the *balagan* that they considered to be tawdry and vulgar, exaggerating the low quality of the fairground shows and thereby distancing them from legitimate art. At the same time, the imagined link between the fairground and urban degeneracy fit neatly with the populist view of urban civilization as a corrupting influence on the morals of a virtuous peasantry.

A journalist writing for the middlebrow newspaper *The Petersburg Sheet*, D. Danchin, went even further than the radical writers in attacking the *balagan* theaters, arguing that they mirrored the common people's "low level of intellectual development" and contained nothing intelligent, only "vulgar escapades and cynical spectacles." Accusing the performers of drunkenness and sexual immorality, Danchin surmised that the people went to the taverns because they were not satisfied by the battle scenes and devils of the fairground stages. He called on the fairground theaters to stage "comedies or simply scenes, but with plenty of sense, adapted to the comprehension of the masses and taken from the life of the common people."[68] Whereas Danchin believed that the dancers in the merry-go-round shows came from brothels, others claimed that they were poor working girls who fell into moral turpitude under the influence of the vodka they were given to ward off the cold.[69] The association of moral corruption with *balagan* entertainments was a commonplace in literary and journalistic descriptions of the fairground. Sergei Semenov, a self-educated peasant writer, made the fairground theaters the first step along the road to ruin in his short story "The Soldier's Wife," published in 1889. In the story, a peasant migrant woman's descent into adultery and prostitution begins with a visit to the *balagany* of Moscow's Deviche Field in the company of a fellow laundress, who introduces her to the urban world of easy morals.[70]

By the end of the century, *balagan* had become a derogatory appellation, commonly employed as the antonym of real theater and art, or to refer to worthless or inferior culture in general—"something primitive," as one journalist put it.[71] Recalling the preparations for the Moscow Accessible Art Theater's first season in the rented theater of the Hermitage pleasure garden, previously the home of spectaculars and variety shows, Stanislavsky described the new theater he wanted to create. He envisioned a theater that would bring to life the psychological truth of the drama, and as such it was the polar opposite of the commercially oriented *balagan*, with its emphasis on showy special effects and superficial impressions. "I can create a temple instead of a marketplace," he wrote. "But what was my disappointment when I entered the same Punch and Judy house [*balagan*] on which we had declared war."[72] In *What Is To Be Done?* (1902), Lenin used *balagan* to describe the sort of popular literature that was simply too lowbrow to be of any value, even for "especially backward workers."[73]

For all the negative connotations that the *balagan* acquired in Russian cultural discourse and the imagined distance between the fairground and the "legitimate" stage, it was hardly the tawdry den of inferior, primitive culture that its critics made it out to be. In the second half of the nineteenth century, actors from the imperial theaters sometimes directed or performed in the shows, and professional decorators were hired to design the stage sets. Some *balagany*, such as Leifert's, created entirely new sets and costumes for every production, long before Stanislavsky introduced this "reform" in the Moscow Art Theater. Leifert's costumes were so esteemed that he branched out into the theatrical costume business, supplying theaters and amateur troupes all over Russia from his vast inventory.[74] The special effects created in the *balagany* often excelled anything that could be seen even in the imperial theaters' most spectacular productions. The fairground theaters did not exist in isolation from the influence of elite culture but took from and manipulated it; they frequently based their shows on classical Russian literature and plays that had run on the legitimate stage, adapting and simplifying them to meet the needs of their short, rapidly paced productions, much as folk plays and chapbooks had long borrowed from literary sources.[75] Popular theater, in the *balagany*, picked and mixed, molding the canon to fit the demands of its audience.

COMMERCIAL THEATERS AND PLEASURE GARDENS

The numbers of commercial theatrical establishments in Russia's largest cities steadily increased during the second half of the nineteenth century. Russia's first pleasure garden, the Artificial Mineral Water Gardens, opened in 1834, amusing well-to-do Petersburgers with opulent spectacles featuring Gypsy singers, circus acts, puppet shows, *tableaux vivants*, and fireworks. From the 1860s more moderately priced pleasure gardens began springing up in both St. Petersburg and Moscow, offering entertainment to broader audiences of middle-class townspeople, tradesmen, and artisans, as well as aristocrats, officers, and fashionable society. Often bearing names redolent of the foreign and exotic—Monplaisir, Hermitage, Arcadia, Fantasia, Alhambra, Tivoli, Chicago, Aquarium—as well as more prosaic names—

Russian Family Garden, Zoological Garden, Saks's Garden—they hosted an eclectic assortment of spectacles. The end of the imperial theater monopoly in 1882 meant that the gardens could now put on operas and dramas, which shared the stages with professional concerts, variety shows, French chansons, operettas, pantomimes, stunt artists, Gypsy musicians, acrobats, fantasy extravaganzas (*féeries*), and spectacular reenactments of battles, train wrecks, and volcanic eruptions.[76]

The entertainments featured in the summer pleasure gardens were a synthesis of high and low cultures, drawing their inspiration from the imperial theaters, European cabaret, the circus, and the *balagan* shows. A number of entertainers at the pleasure gardens also worked in the imperial or *balagan* theaters, facilitating a process of cultural cross-fertilization among venues. Petr Medvedev, who later became a star and director at the Imperial Aleksandrinskii Theater, managed Moscow's Family Garden in the late 1860s. Several of the most famous fairground showmen, such as Vasilii Egarev, Wilhelm Berg, and Alekseev-Iakovlev, also ran or directed pleasure gardens and brought with them the experience they had gained in the *balagany*. Alekseev made his stage debut performing humorous couplets in the late 1860s at the entrepreneur Vasilii Egarev's Ekateringof Vauxhall and Russian Family Garden. Wilhelm Berg conducted hot air balloon flights at Iusupov Park in the 1840s, 1850s, and 1860s, and operated a *balagan* from the 1850s through the 1880s, where he recruited Alekseev from the Egarev's Family Garden to help him stage plays that included Alexei Tolstoy's historical drama *Prince Serebrianyi*. Over the years, Alekseev worked at St. Petersburg's Livadia, Arcadia, Krestovskii Garden, and Zoological Garden, thrilling the public with the spectacular reenactments of battles that won him fame on the fairgrounds. Mikhail Lentovskii, the impresario who organized the popular festivities celebrating Alexander III's coronation in 1883, also directed operettas and military pantomimes at St. Petersburg's fashionable Arcadia and Moscow's renowned Hermitage in the 1880s. Yearning to put his talents at the service of the common people, Lentovskii later opened a low-priced people's theater in Moscow.[77]

A few pleasure gardens targeted the lower end of the entertainment market. St. Petersburg's Ekateringof Garden became increasingly popular among workers at factories in the adjoining Narva and Kolomenskii districts from the 1860s. While workers came in droves on Sundays to listen to military bands and choirs, the respectable public avoided the Ekateringof Garden, preferring to visit the neighboring Ekateringof Vauxhall, which was more upmarket and charged an entrance fee. Krestovskii Island and Aleksandrovskii Park were also frequented by St. Petersburg's lower classes on Sundays and holidays, while the Zoological Gardens, opened in the 1870s, attracted citizens of every rank to see its vaudevilles, circus acts, variety shows, fireworks, and spectaculars. Moscow's workers, servants, and clerks favored the summertime variety stages in the fresh air of Sokolniki and Petrovskii parks.[78]

Circus, another entertainment that crossed class boundaries, was a permanent feature of the urban scene after 1853. Although clowns, acrobats, and trained animal acts were the main attractions at the circus, variety shows, Gypsy singers, magic shows, ballets, and pantomimes were also an important part of the circus repertoire. Circus performers often appeared at the fairground theaters, where many stars began their careers, while circuses sometimes engaged *balagan* variety acts.[79]

The pleasure gardens and circuses and the diverse public they served were part of the mass commercial entertainment culture that was evolving in urban Russia during the second half of the nineteenth century, a culture consumed by Russians of all classes. To be sure, the commercialization of entertainments was not new, for the holiday *balagany* had always been commercial enterprises and had played an important role in urban culture since the late eighteenth century. What was new was the variety of middle-brow everyday entertainments that appeared on the market in the nineteenth century, as the state's tutelage over Russian culture weakened and it gradually lost its aristocratic stamp. The heroes of the songs, operettas, melodramas, and vaudevilles performed on the stages of the pleasure gardens often pursued material and sexual gratification (with varying degrees of success) in the hedonistic setting of the big city. Audiences heard songs celebrating peasants who had made it rich in the city and improved their social status by patronizing the right tailors; they also wept at the misfortunes of poor, honest heroines in Adolphe Dennery's imported French tearjerkers, which had been a mainstay of the imperial theater repertoire in the 1840s and 1850s. Historical works extolling Russian patriotism and military valor remained popular through the end of the century, weathering the disastrous Russo-Japanese War to enjoy their last revival at the outbreak of World War I.[80]

If the end of the imperial theater monopoly opened the door to commercial drama theaters for the growing middle-class public of the capitals, only a handful were able to make enough profit to stay afloat for long. The actress Anna Brenko founded her semi-legal Pushkin Theater in Moscow shortly before the monopoly was abolished, but the venture failed after two years when her millionaire patron withdrew his support.[81] The city's most important commercial theater was founded by the lawyer and translator

Fedor Korsh in 1882. Korsh was a superb entrepreneur who cultivated audiences by holding Sunday discount matinees and distributing free tickets to students. In addition to promoting new plays by Dumas, Sardou, Sudermann, and Chekhov, he spiced up the repertoire with farces, comedies, and topical works that ensured commercial success. The Korsh Theater flourished until 1932, when it was abolished and its building handed over to a branch of the officially sanctioned Moscow Art Theater. In St. Petersburg, several drama theaters opened after 1882, but not until the appearance of the Theater of the Literary-Drama Society in 1895 did the city have a stable commercial drama theater. Run by Aleksei Suvorin, a conservative newspaper publisher and close friend of Chekhov, the Suvorin Theater, as it was usually called, used its owner's political connections to obtain permission to stage a number of previously banned plays. Its relatively daring repertoire sparked a flurry of critical interest in its first season, but the theater soon shifted toward a more conventional blend of classics, melodramas, and light comedies, sprinkled with a few sensational plays on topical issues.[82]

The appearance in 1898 of the Moscow Art Theater, with its emphasis on lifelike sets, historically accurate costumes, a socially progressive repertoire, and a realistic ensemble of actors who did not strive to outshine one another, brought a new kind of theater onto the scene. Producing only a few carefully chosen plays each season, the Art Theater held countless rehearsals to ensure that each production was honed to perfection. It quickly became the darling of the liberal intelligentsia, yet despite its sold-out performances and critical acclaim it was not a commercial success for several years and relied heavily on the financial backing of Savva Morozov, a Moscow industrialist who shared Stanislavsky's vision. The Moscow Art Theater's new approach to staging inspired imitators all over Russia and had some influence on the Korsh, Suvorin, and imperial theaters, which also began incorporating modernist dramas into their repertoires. Its relatively high-priced tickets meant that, despite the hopes of its founders to make it accessible to a broad public, the theater generally catered to the well-heeled.[83]

If people from the lower classes could occasionally be seen among the urban middle-class and provincial visitors who frequented the Korsh, Suvorin, and Moscow Art theaters, it was usually at the discounted Sunday matinees for students. During the "days of freedom" that accompanied the brief breakdown of tsarist authority when the 1905 Revolution engulfed Russia, both the Korsh and Moscow Art theaters made a democratic gesture by distributing discounted tickets through workers' organizations, but the initiative did not outlive the revolution.[84] Until the appearance of people's theaters, workers, servants, shop clerks, and seamstresses more commonly went to the *balagany* or modest commercial theaters in outlying districts. There is little record of the latter, which were deemed too "lowbrow" to warrant critical attention.

A visitor to one such venue, A. A. Cherepanov's Family Park and Theater, located in 1903 in an industrial area of Moscow known as Zamoskvoreche, likened the appearance of the theater and its public to what one would come across in some distant provincial backwater. He found the sets and costumes primitive and the actors difficult to hear above the shouts of the prompter. Nevertheless, the undemanding working-class audience was delighted by the lachrymose melodrama and was indifferent to the production's flaws.[85] Old melodramas, a staple of the legitimate theater repertoire until the 1880s, found a new audience in the commercial popular theaters at the turn of the century. Entertaining the common people with moralistic stories about the tribulations of poor but honest folk saved by the hand of Providence, the melodramas were often disparaged by educated observers, who accused popular theater impresarios of pandering to the uncultivated tastes of the crowd for the sake of profit.

FOLK THEATER IN THE FACTORY AND THE BARRACKS

Performances of folk plays were an important part of the orally transmitted culture of Russian peasants, migrant factory workers, and soldiers in the nineteenth century. The folk dramas may have originated among the peasants who provided seasonal labor for the factories of the nation's industrial centers. The ethnographer V. Iu. Krupianskaia has made a convincing case that *The Boat*, one of the best-known folk plays of the nineteenth century, first appeared in the textile regions surrounding Moscow.[86] Folk dramas combined elements of traditional folk songs and borrowings from literary works that circulated in the form of inexpensive publications and woodblock prints (*lubki*).[87] Carried back and forth between factory and village, continually transformed and adapted in each milieu, the folk dramas testify to the difficulty of distinguishing between "traditional" and "urban" cultural forms. N. E. Onchukov, who went to the Russian North at the turn of the century to gather examples of folk dramas, found that many of the plays had first been brought to the villages by peasants who had learned them while working in St. Petersburg factories or Archangel sawmills, or during military service.[88]

The folk dramas had no written scripts and were constantly changing as actors improvised on the basic framework of the plot. The dramas often contained elements of social justice, and banditry was a favorite theme, as it was in woodblock prints, chapbooks, and folksongs. *The Boat*, for example, is a dramatization of the folk song "Down Along the Mother Volga" (Vniz po matiushke po Volge), into which verses from several of Pushkin's poems (in particular "The Brigand Brothers" [Brat'ia razboiniki]) have been incorporated.[89] *The Boat* centers on the adventures of a free-living band of robbers and their leader, and some versions feature scenes of an attack on a noble estate. Social satire is the predominant motif in the folk dramas *The Master* and *The Would-be Master,* where a cruel or greedy gentleman is outwitted by his social inferiors and presented as a figure of ridicule.[90] Historical characters familiar to audiences from songs and chapbooks, such as the Cossack rebel Stenka Razin and the criminal hero Vanka Kain, were sometimes inserted into the plays.[91] At least one patriotic folk drama existed in the nineteenth and early twentieth centuries, *How the Frenchman Took Moscow,* inspired by Napoleon's invasion of Russia. It includes scenes in which a Russian general chooses to die rather than betray the tsar and Napoleon poisons his wounded soldiers rather than sending them home to France, and it ends with Napoleon in flight from peasant women armed with pitchforks.[92]

It is difficult to determine to what extent folk dramas were performed by urban factory workers, since ethnographers preferred to seek out "authentic" folk culture in rural areas rather than in urban settlements, but there is evidence to suggest that workers were often familiar with them. Nikolai Popov, a playwright and director who was interested in the potential of theater for popular enlightenment, saw workers at the Tsindel cotton mill perform the folk drama *Tsar Maximilian* in 1896. Popov's account of the performance is of particular interest in that it documents the enduring importance of the folk drama in the lives of workers at one of Moscow's largest and most modern factories at the very end of the nineteenth century.[93] Like other large, highly mechanized textile factories, the Tsindel mill employed hundreds of unskilled and semi-skilled workers, most of whom retained ties to the villages of their birth.[94] Since peasant migrants and army recruits were the medium by which the folk plays circulated between village, regiment, and factory, it was only natural that some of the Tsindel workers were familiar with *Tsar Maximilian.*

One of the best-known and most widespread folk dramas, *Tsar Maximilian,* as Elizabeth Warner points out in her study of the Russian folk theater, "is not a single unified drama but, rather, an amorphous collection of scenes, only tenuously linked together, the number and content of which vary considerably from one text to another."[95] As with many folk dramas, there are numerous recorded variations of the text, but the play's basic theme is a religious conflict between the pagan Maximilian and his son Adolf, who refuses to honor his father's gods and is finally executed for his recalcitrance. There then follows a series of scenes in which the warrior Anika successfully defends the tsar against various enemies, only to be cut down in the end by Death.[96]

According to Popov, the workers had already staged the play several times, at their own initiative and with no outside help. Although they performed on the same stage where intelligentsia amateurs sometimes put on literary plays for the factory's workers, their acting was ritualistic and stylized, employing various conventional techniques that bore no trace of professional influence. The actors, apparently all male, wore their everyday clothing, with only a few costume accessories made from paper or bast matting.

The version that Popov saw performed by the Tsindel factory workers is unusual in that it contains an outcome not found in any other known variant: when Maximilian orders Adolf's execution, the tsar's retinue rises up against him and kills him. The tsar's murder is followed by a highly comical and parodical funeral service. As Popov described it: "No intellectual would have risked teaching those fellows all that they were doing in that 'requiem'—the youths reveled in their acting, performing all that 'blasphemy' with completely straight faces. . . . There were so many risqué places [in the performance], so much 'explosive material,' that we, the spectators [Popov and his friends], glanced at the entrance from time to time to see whether some policeman or uninvited visitor might be standing there, especially during the requiem."[97] The workers, of course, performed their play without the permission of either the censors or the police; under no circumstances would the depiction of the murder of a reigning monarch or the parody of a religious service have been permitted on a factory stage.[98] The factory administration seems to have known about the performance, however, for Popov was invited by one of its directors. In any case, there was no written text that could be submitted to the censors.

In "killing the tsar," the workers may have been acting out a fantasy of rebellion against the oppressive patriarchal authority of fathers or employers. It seems unlikely that the staged murder of Tsar Maximilian was an expression of the workers' hostility toward the tsar himself. After all, Popov notes that in this as in most versions of the play, Maximilian introduces himself by making it clear that he is a foreign ruler, and there are hints of the demonic in the foreigner who comes from no known land ("I'm not the Russian tsar, not the French Napoleon, not the Swedish king, not the Turkish sultan, but the terrible Tsar Maximilian from faraway lands!").[99] Moreover, he is a pagan who tries to impose his faith on his Christian subjects. Certainly, the workers' parody of priests and their rituals does not in itself indicate any rejection of religion, for such scenes had long been a component of folk drama in Russia as in other European countries.[100] More probably, it was merely a reflection of widespread popular disrespect for the clergy.[101] Semen Kanatchikov, who worked at a machine-building factory not far from the Tsindel mill during the year 1895–96, later remembered that while "even the older workers listened indulgently to tales about the adventures of priests," they were deeply offended by any mockery of the saints or God.[102]

It is impossible to know for certain whether performances of *Tsar Maximilian* and other works from the folk repertoire were common at other Moscow and St. Petersburg factories, but it seems likely that they were, especially during Yuletide and Shrovetide. In her notes on her youth in the St. Petersburg suburb Tsarskoe Selo, Anna Akhmatova remembers seeing a Shrovetide performance of *Tsar Maximilian* by workers from a local wallpaper factory.[103] Moscow district police records reveal that peasant workers at a textile factory in the outlying village of Vladykino staged the play shortly before Christmas in 1911. The factory administration and the police gave their approval to the performance, believing it would encourage holiday sobriety.[104] A temperance activist reported in 1916 that *Tsar Maximilian* was still popular among workers at a sugar factory in Chernigov province. They staged the play at Christmas from memory, and it was repeated each year with slight changes and additions.[105] Workers who, like those at the Tsindel cotton mill, had important ties with the village were probably acquainted with folk plays, which were widely known in rural areas.

Popov's account of the performance of *Tsar Maximilian* at the Tsindel factory is an important reminder that Russian peasant migrant workers had a theatrical culture of their own. It was there long before the people's theaters set out to acquaint the workers with literary theater, and it continued to flourish until after the revolution. Although intellectuals who sought to "raise" the cultural level of the working classes routinely assumed that workers had no culture, or at least none worth preserving, the performers described by Popov still possessed the rich dramatic heritage of the Russian folk theater as late as 1896. If, as a 1900 survey found, almost 90 percent of the Tsindel workers had never set foot in a Moscow theater, they nonetheless enjoyed drama.[106]

• • •

Russian urban popular theater was vibrant and varied before the Emancipation of the serfs put the issue of people's theaters on the agenda of educated Russian society's plans for transforming the culture of the lower classes. If the imperial theaters and, later, the legitimate commercial theaters, were largely out of reach, the *balagany*, pleasure gardens, and circuses offered theatrical entertainment at prices that most workers, servants, clerks, waiters, and seamstresses could afford. Nor were the common people entirely isolated from the products of elite theatrical culture, for the shifting frontiers separating folk culture, popular culture, and elite culture were often quite porous. Themes and characters from folklore made their way to the stages of both the fairgrounds and the imperial theaters. *Tsar Maximilian*, for example, was performed at Malafeev's St. Petersburg *balagan* at Shrovetide 1886.[107] Several of the enduring historical romantic dramas of the early nineteenth century, such as Nikolai Polevoi's *Ermak Timofeevich, or Volga and Siberia* and Aleksandr Shakhovskoi's *The Bigamous Wife*, originally performed in the imperial theaters and later staples of the fairground and commercial popular theaters, contained elements of the banditry theme borrowed and adapted from chapbooks, folk songs, and dramas.[108] The melodramas that flourished in the imperial theaters for most of the century eventually became a part of the popular repertoire in the *balagany*, pleasure gardens, and cheap theaters on the city outskirts, along with adaptations of Russian and foreign classics, while some *balagany* introduced the fairground public to versions of Russian classics by Pushkin, Ostrovsky, Gogol, and others.

For educated Russians who began to take an interest in the intellectual and moral improvement of the common people in the 1860s, however, the *balagany* and other commercial theatrical entertainments accessible to the people were of dubious value. Hostility toward the profit-oriented values of commercial culture was endemic among Russian intellectuals,[109] who yearned for a didactic theater that would not merely entertain but also uplift the people by exposing them to art and broadening their mental horizons. The movement to create theaters for the people was an elite attempt to civilize the people by offering them an improved substitute for commercial fare: a people's theater with a systematic repertoire oriented toward art rather than profit. Once given a choice, the influential playwright Alexander Ostrovsky reasoned, "the majority of the common audience will desire real, healthy art" and turn its back on the inferior likes of melodrama and operetta.[110] People's theater was also a way for members of Russia's budding civil society to push the boundaries of public activity outward, to exert pressure on the state to allow society a greater role in shaping the nation's social and political development. The difficulty lay, on one hand, in overcoming the state's determination to maintain control over the influences to which the people were exposed, and, on the other hand, in enticing the people away from the pleasures of the fairgrounds and other commercial popular entertainments.

2 People's Theater and Cultural Politics

The concept of a theater that would serve as an instrument of popular enlightenment first attracted widespread attention in the 1860s, a decade of unprecedented social and political change in Russia. Alexander II (1855–81), who ascended the throne in the midst of Russia's humiliating defeat in the Crimean War, soon embarked on a series of "Great Reforms" that fundamentally transformed Russian society. To mobilize public support behind his reform initiatives, Alexander introduced a policy of *glasnost'*, encouraging, within limits, more open discussion of social and political issues in the press and unleashing a flood of public interest in improving almost every aspect of Russian life.

The keystone of the reform program was the Emancipation Manifesto of 1861, which liberated millions of peasants from serfdom and paved the way for further reforms. A new system of local government was set up beginning in 1864, creating first rural zemstvos and then urban dumas, whose elected representatives were given authority to attend to various local needs, including education, roads, and medical services. Legal reforms, introduced in 1864, separated the judiciary from the executive and established the principle that all Russian citizens, regardless of social rank, were equal under the law. Alexander made a partial retreat from his early reformist ambitions in the wake of the 1863 Polish Revolt and an attempt by a student to assassinate him in 1866, but the reforms begun were carried through. In 1874 the reform era came to an end with the last of the Great Reforms, when the Russian military introduced universal eligibility for conscription irrespective of social status.[1]

Alexander's reforms failed to satisfy the high expectations *glasnost'* had aroused. The peasants received only about half of the land they tilled and were saddled with redemption payments to the government. The authority of local government institutions was carefully circumscribed to prevent them from becoming a voice in national politics, which remained the exclusive prerogative of the tsar and imperial bureaucracy. By the end of the 1860s rough political positions had crystallized around different attitudes toward the reform legacy and the desirability of further reform. Conservatives felt that the reforms had gone far enough or even too far, liberals wanted to push the government further in the direction of constitutionalism, while radicals wanted to abolish the autocracy altogether and introduce some form of popular democracy. In the absence of national representative institutions and with the press constrained by censorship, cultural and educational issues became substitute political battlefields. Liberals and radicals called for initiatives to serve the people by raising their cultural and educational level and saw realistic art and literature dealing with social questions as a force for progress. Conservatives, on the defensive, rejected attempts to enlighten the people and criticized the subversive tendencies of artistic and literary realism.

The emancipation of the peasantry and the other reforms put the spotlight on the issue of popular education, which had received scant attention under previous tsars. Peter the Great, while making education a key element of his Westernizing reforms, had focused on training people to serve the state rather than educating the general population. Catherine the Great toyed with the idea of making some education compulsory for the entire male population, but the Pugachev uprising dampened her enthusiasm for popular education, and her educational reforms were largely directed at the upper classes. During the reigns of Alexander I (1801–25) and Nicholas I (1825–55) there was talk of creating parish schools and offering basic education to the common people, yet these discussions were not translated into concrete measures. So long as the overwhelming majority of the common people remained enserfed and under the direct authority of landowners, the issue of popular education remained on the back burner. In 1864, however, having freed the peasants and transformed them from serfs into citizens, Alexander II's government enacted a new Education Statute, which made various state and local institutions responsible for ensuring that the common people had access to primary schooling.[2]

The cause of popular enlightenment was taken up with enthusiasm by educated Russian society. The *glasnost'* of Alexander II's early reign, together with the establishment of elected local government institutions, aroused society's hopes that it would be permitted to take a more active role in public affairs and sparked interest in the establishment of grammar schools, evening courses, libraries, theaters, and other measures designed to improve the common people intellectually and morally. By the mid-nine-teenth century, many educated Russians felt that the process of Westerniza-tion initiated by Peter the Great had effectively created two Russias: that of the Westernized elite, or intelligentsia, with its education and European high culture; and that of the common people, or *narod*, who remained out-side Russian intellectual life in poverty and ignorance. The enormously influential populist ideas of Alexander Herzen, Nikolai Chernyshevsky, Nikolai Nekrasov, and many other publicists and authors called for the intelligentsia to reach out to the common people and, in their liberal variant, lent support to the idea that the intelligentsia should serve the people by raising their educational and cultural level.

This binary system of opposite categories, the "intelligentsia" and the "people," had first been elucidated by the Slavophiles in the 1840s in their debates with the Westernizers over whether Russia should follow Peter the Great's path of Western-style political, social, and economic development or its own distinctly Russian path rooted in the traditions of the *narod*. The intelligentsia-*narod* opposition became an underlying assumption in much prerevolutionary Russian political, social, and cultural discourse. It was pre-sent in the Populists' debates of the 1860s and 1870s over whether the intel-ligentsia should teach the people or learn from them, in the 1880s idea that the intelligentsia should undertake "small deeds" aimed at improving the lot of the common people, and in Lenin's conflict with the Mensheviks in the 1900s over his belief that the proletariat could not achieve class con-sciousness without the tutelage of Marxist intellectuals.

As descriptive terms, both words could be employed in various senses. For example, "intelligentsia" was often used to denote people who adhered to "progressive" ideas that opposed, in varying degrees, the existing autocratic order. *Narod* could be used to refer to the Russian people as a whole or, much more narrowly, to distinguish the rural agricultural peasantry, uncontami-nated by exposure to urban or industrial civilization, from "factory people" (*fabrichnyi liud*). Most often, however, the terms were used to broadly desig-nate, and differentiate, on the one hand, the stratum of society that had some education and was acquainted with high culture and national socio-political issues (the intelligentsia) and, on the other hand, the peasant or semi-peasant masses who had little or no formal education or contact with high culture and whose political awareness was limited to local, communal issues (the *narod*). With some education and effort, some members of the *narod* could advance into the intelligentsia, yet the terms that emerged by the turn of the century to describe these cultural migrants—"people's intelligentsia," "workers' intel-ligentsia"—still underlined their special, liminal position.[3]

THE CULTURIST AGENDA

Educated Russians, who often felt a strong sense of obligation to help the *narod*, dreamed of ending the perceived separation of the intelligentsia and the common people by creating a unified society in which all Russian citizens would have access to culture and enlightenment. The intelligentsia's efforts to disseminate its cultural values among the people were shaped by an attitude that Jeffrey Brooks has described as "culturism," that is, a "cultural idea of national unity" based on the adherence of all members of the nation to a common culture. For the Russian intelligentsia, as Brooks observes, "the term 'culture' was conceived in the broadest sense of shared values, but these values were expressed primarily through the Russian literary tradition, which consisted of a pantheon of respected authors and critics and of the judgment that the true function of belles lettres was to illuminate social reality and transform readers." Although Brooks's comments refer specifically to the intelligentsia's attitude toward literature, they also describe its attitude toward the arts in general, including theater and drama.[4]

Educated society initiated many efforts to serve the common people during the Great Reform era, often in the form of cultural philanthropy. The "Sunday School movement" of 1859–62 brought together educators, university students, enlightened industrialists, and others with a penchant for social activism to promote literacy among urban workers by holding free classes on Sundays.[5] In 1861 a group of intellectuals founded the St. Petersburg Literacy Committee to encourage primary schooling and the spread of basic literacy among the common people. The committee's activities attracted the support of prominent literary figures such as Leo Tolstoy and Ivan Turgenev, and in the 1880s it began publishing inexpensive editions of the Russian classics in a not terribly successful bid to wean the common people away from the adventure stories and romances turned out by commercial publishers. The Society for the Dissemination of Useful Books, by which was meant works of popular science and moralistic stories written especially for the common people, was also founded in 1861; it published over 2 million copies of these "useful books" over the next twenty-five years. Some commercial publishers, most notably Aleksei Suvorin and Ivan Sytin, began publishing relatively inexpensive volumes of Russian and foreign literature for the popular market in the 1870s and 1880s.[6]

As a means of reaching the common people and introducing them to the cultural heritage of educated Russia, the printed word had its limits, for in 1859 only 6 percent of the empire's population was literate.[7] Levels of literacy were higher in the cities; in St. Petersburg they ranged from 29 percent among woodworkers to 49 percent among metalworkers in 1862.[8] Educational projects were intended to remedy the situation, and literacy spread phenomenally in the decades prior to World War I, but the acquisition of the ability to read even relatively simple texts takes time and effort.[9] Faced with the enormous task of enlightening a largely illiterate population, educated Russians also turned to cultural forms, such as theater, that could be understood by anyone, at least in theory. As a St. Petersburg journalist put it, theater would "introduce the people to the treasures of the intelligentsia and of art" and "awaken their spiritual forces with ever newer impressions."[10] People's theaters also offered a potential means of overcoming the cultural barriers between the intelligentsia and *narod*.

The movement to establish people's theaters engendered numerous projects and attracted wide support in the years following Emancipation. By 1868, the influential journal *Fatherland Notes*, edited by the populist poet Nikolai Nekrasov, noted that "the desire to have [a people's theater] has been expressed so insistently of late that it threatens to become an *idée fixe* among many people."[11] The imperial theaters' monopoly on public performances in the capitals obstructed the establishment of permanent people's theaters, however, while the second half of Alexander II's reign was marked by increasing conservatism and suspicion of cultural and social initiatives independent of the state. This conservatism was even more pronounced under Alexander III (1881–94), who inherited the throne in the wake of his father's assassination by a terrorist on the streets of St. Petersburg, and under his son, Nicholas II. Still, interest in people's theaters did not abate. In 1881 Russia's most famous playwright, Alexander Ostrovsky, submitted a lengthy memorandum to the new tsar calling on him to establish a national people's theater in Moscow.[12] In 1887 a rural schoolteacher, K. D. Alchevskaia, published an enormously influential book describing the educational value of reading Ostrovsky's plays to peasant pupils.[13] Leo Tolstoy also lent his backing to the concept of a people's theater as a civilizing force, writing two plays for popular audiences about the dangers of alcohol and another about the consequences of adultery in a rural village. Anton Chekhov was sympathetic to the idea, and Konstantin Stanislavsky and Vladimir Nemirovich-Danchenko made several proposals to establish a network of people's theaters. Although the people's theater project sometimes met with opposition in conservative and ecclesiastical circles, it nevertheless attracted widespread support from police officials, industrialists, actors, writers, directors, and temperance societies. By the 1890s, the Finance Ministry had come out in favor of people's theaters, lending moral and financial support as part of its efforts to promote temperance.

Aside from bureaucratic impediments, the government's fear that the people's theaters would foment sedition, and chronic funding difficulties, the people's theater movement was also hampered by its supporters' lack of consensus on fundamental issues. The proliferation of people's theaters in the 1880s and 1890s gave rise to sharp disagreements over what bringing theater to the people entailed, disagreements that emerged in debates over the identity of the theaters' projected audience, the appropriate repertoire, and the precise meaning of "civilizing" the people. The diverse promoters of people's theaters had different, even rival, agendas. Liberal educators and enlighteners wanted to use people's theaters to educate the people, while *Kulturträger* regarded them as a means of democratizing elite culture and combating commercial popular theaters. Factory owners saw theater as a "rational recreation" that would lead to increased labor productivity by luring workers away from the taverns. The Finance Ministry's temperance societies, too, believed that there was a strong link between theater attendance and sobriety, while also subscribing to the view that the right kind of theater would have an ennobling effect. To attract the people to their theaters, however, the temperance societies had to compete with the commercial popular theaters, and that meant finding the right mixture of classics and entertaining spectacles. To some socialist workers, theater was an instrument for raising class consciousness (of which sobriety was thought to be an attribute) and encouraging the formation of a "proletarian culture," while for other workers theater was primarily a symbol of the culture and social respectability they wanted to appropriate. All of these contrasting visions came to be embodied in the idea of a people's theater as it took shape in late imperial Russia.

PEOPLE'S THEATER AS A CIVILIZING FORCE

The 1860s marked the beginning of ever more rapid and far-reaching urbanization in Russia, the effects of which were especially pronounced in St. Petersburg and Moscow. Freed of their bondage to the land by the Emancipation Manifesto, peasants flocked to urban centers in hopes of finding employment and escaping rural poverty. Between 1863 and 1869, the number of peasants living in St. Petersburg rose by over 46,000, reaching a total of 207,000—some 31 percent of the city's total population, which itself rose from 539,481 to 667,207 during the same period.[14] Moscow grew at an equally impressive rate, from 462,500 inhabitants in 1863 to 602,700 in 1871.[15] Both educated society and the authorities regarded the flood of peasant migrants with an uneasy eye, and not without cause. In St. Petersburg,

drunkenness and crime rose even more rapidly than did the population during the 1860s, while prostitution, venereal disease, and illegitimate births
were also on the increase.[16] The apparent deterioration of popular morality
aroused widespread concern and gave new urgency to discussions of raising
the cultural level of the common people.[17]

It is in the context of the post-Emancipation enthusiasm among the intelligentsia for taking a more active role in public affairs, the sense of obligation
to serve the common people by enlightening them felt by so many educated
Russians, and the anxieties about urban disorder and lower-class immorality
that the emergence of the people's theater movement must be understood.
The vision of a free citizenry encouraged by the Emancipation underlined the
need to educate the masses, while the social disruption that accompanied it
pointed to the need to "civilize" them. It was assumed that once exposed to
the culture and life of educated Russia, the common people would behave in
a more respectable manner. The people's theater came to be seen as at least a
partial solution to all of these problems, since it offered educated society a
way to assert its independence from the tutelage of the state, contribute to
the intellectual progress of the common people, and at the same time create
an alternative to the existing popular recreations.

This was quite an agenda, to say the least. But if we remember that it was
the introduction by Peter the Great and his successors of Western cultural
forms such as theater that initiated the very "civilizing process" that gave
birth to the intelligentsia, then the faith that the intelligentsia placed in
theater's power to act as an agent of social and cultural transformation is
more understandable. Just as the Russian nobility had learned about
Western manners and morals by attending theater performances and oblig-
atory parties, the people were supposed to absorb the manners and morals
of educated society through exposure to the refining influence of theater.

In 1862, on the occasion of the celebration of Russia's official millen-
nium, the St. Petersburg newspaper *Son of the Fatherland* issued a call for
the establishment of a people's theater with tickets priced within the reach
of the people, in order to lure them away from "coarse pleasures" and exert
a "civilizing influence." Since Russia had chosen the "path of progress" (i.e.,
the liberation of the serfs), art should serve the common people, and theater
was the art form most accessible to them. It is worth citing the article at
length, for it clearly summarizes the hopes invested in the people's theater:

> Theater in particular has an undoubted effect on the development of the
> common people. It is a school in which the people learn more willingly,
> because here learning is united with pleasure, it is more vivid and com-
> prehensible and consequently reaches anyone. Theater by its very struc-

ture engraves itself on the memory more powerfully [than does school], leaving behind an indelible impression.

Thus we should not look upon theater as mere pleasure and entertainment, but as a primary school, and only then will its real purpose be achieved. But for this to happen we need a people's theater, accessible to the simple folk, and plays that they can understand. In general we need to accustom the people to theater, and then it can do them all kinds of good. Theater will divert the people from those vile pleasures which, in the absence of alternatives, are now the only source of entertainment for our common folk. It will also teach them to think and to understand, and, most important, it will ennoble their senses and soften their mores.[18]

In presenting his case, the author of this article employed all of the arguments that were to become orthodoxy for the people's theater movement. First, theater was equated with school. Indeed, it was deemed a more powerful and effective means of teaching the common people than was the classroom, due to its visual impact and its combination of entertainment and enlightenment. Second, if it was going to educate the common people, it had to be accessible to their minds as well as their pockets. Therefore, its repertoire must consist of plays that the people could comprehend. Third, theater would civilize, even "ennoble," the people by luring them away from crude and dissolute entertainments and affording them an alternative, cultivated recreation.

These arguments were to be used again and again by the most diverse and even mutually hostile groups, in dozens of books, articles, reports, projects, and congresses celebrating the benefits of people's theaters. For over a half century, until the demise of the Old Regime in 1917 and even beyond, liberal and radical intellectuals, government officials, temperance advocates, factory owners, and socialist workers would come to embrace the cause of theater for the people as a means of variously enlightening, acculturating, disciplining, sobering, and/or radicalizing the subordinate classes.

All of these attempts pitted Russia's nascent civil society against the traditional powers of the state to regulate activity in the public sphere. Popular leisure became one of the battlefields where the Russian middle classes sought, on the one hand, to overcome the autocracy's resistance to public initiative in addressing socio-cultural issues, and, on the other hand, to supplant popular culture with an alternative culture of "rational recreations" imposed from above. The movement to create theaters for the people combined elements of a distinctly Russian conflict between the state and civil society, a pervasive elite sense of paternalistic obligation to serve the *narod*, and a typically Victorian approach to remedying social disorder through cultural self-improvement.

PEOPLE'S THEATER VERSUS THE IMPERIAL THEATER MONOPOLY

There were some isolated instances of theater performances organized for workers and peasants in the 1860s and even earlier, but these efforts were sporadic and uninfluential, receiving little or no publicity at the time. They were essentially cultural charity affairs, financially dependent on the interest of paternalistic industrialists, landowners, or amateur actors, vanishing as suddenly as they had appeared when that interest waned. From the 1820s until his death in 1859, the Moscow industrialist Timofei Prokhorov organized a theater on the premises of his textile factory, where workers staged plays under his direction. The director of Moscow's imperial theaters opened a summer theater just outside the city in 1830, in a short-lived attempt to acquaint the common people with history and inculcate national patriotism. In 1862, the noted liberal drama critic and translator Sergei Iurev staged Alexander Ostrovsky's *You Can't Live as You Please* for the peasants on his estate, with a cast made up of family members, servants, and peasants. This melodrama, about a disobedient son and unfaithful husband who repents his misdeeds in a moment of spiritual inspiration, was to become a favorite repertoire choice in the people's theaters due to its powerful and blunt moral message. A group of Moscow amateurs, among them Alexander Ostrovsky and the radical poet Aleksei Pleshcheev, are known to have held a few low-priced charity performances in an industrial district for a brief time in 1863.[19]

Efforts to create people's theaters in St. Petersburg and Moscow were stymied for years by the imperial theater monopoly, which prohibited the establishment of privately owned public theaters in those cities. The monopoly, existing de facto since the beginning of the nineteenth century, was formalized in 1854 and remained in effect until 1882. While it protected the imperial theaters from competition, the monopoly also ensured that public performances in the capitals remained under government supervision, unless they were held in private clubs. Clubs multiplied to get around the monopoly, especially during the reign of Alexander II, when educated society began to push against the restrictions autocracy imposed on public life, and usually admitted anyone willing to pay the entrance fee. At the authorities' discretion, a few theaters specializing in innocuous genres such as light comedy and operetta were sometimes permitted to open.[20]

The first projects for people's theaters all ran aground on the monopoly. Indeed, in the 1860s and 1870s, the cause of the people's theater, widely embraced in progressive circles, was seen as much as a way to break the imperial theater monopoly as a way to serve the people. An early proposal to allow privately owned public theaters in the capitals was rejected in 1858 due to the government's fear of being unable to control theater's impact on the people, coupled with its deep suspicion of any participation in public affairs on the part of educated society. Minister of Court V. F. Adlerberg, whose ministry was in charge of the imperial theaters, chaired the committee that examined the proposal. Seeing political ramifications in the issue, Adlerberg questioned "whether it is timely to give such freedom to private enterprise." Alluding to a recent spate of fictional works treating the injustices of serfdom,[21] as well as to the outpouring of discussion in the press that the proposed Emancipation had elicited, Adlerberg argued that recent literature often contained "harmful ideas" in disguise, a tendency evident in journals, novels, stories, and drama—even the imperial theaters had occasionally staged plays that were openly hostile toward the government.[22]

Even though Adlerberg exaggerated the subversive intentions of the literature to which he refers, his remarks were not entirely groundless. Until the 1905 Revolution wrested some civil liberties from the autocracy, literature and literary criticism often served in Russia as a substitute arena for Aesopian political discussions that could not be broached directly due to stringencies of preliminary press censorship. "For us, plays and theaters are the same thing as, for example, parliamentary events and political speeches are for a Western European," observed a drama critic in 1899.[23] The discussions of reform that began shortly after Alexander took the throne unleashed an avalanche of literature and drama critical of the shortcomings of the Russian state and society. N. M. Lvov's comedy *The World Is Not Without Good People*, which premiered on the imperial stage in 1857, unmasked hypocrisy and corruption in the St. Petersburg bureaucracy, with the actors made up to resemble recognizable government officials. The censors banned it after twenty-four performances.[24] Another example of the use of drama to comment on political questions in the reform era is the critical reception of Ostrovsky's play *The Storm*, first performed in the imperial theaters in 1859, in which a young wife, Katerina, is driven to adultery and suicide by the coarseness and cruelty of her husband's provincial merchant family. In a famous piece of literary criticism, "A Ray of Light in the Kingdom of Darkness" (1860), the influential radical critic Nikolai Dobroliubov used the play to criticize the servile order and the autocracy, interpreting Katerina as a symbol of the masses' aspiration for freedom and equating her suicide with an act of rebellion against the existing social and political order.[25]

If sedition could be fomented from the stages of the imperial theaters, which were under the government's direct control and monitored by a special censorship committee attached to Adlerberg's own ministry, then what could be expected from privately owned theaters? For the minister, the answer was clear enough: they would become a weapon in the hands of the radical opposition. In his report to the tsar, he raised the specter of revolution and linked it directly to theater's potential for influencing the common people:

> Those who desire a revolution will discover in [theater] a reliable means to have a powerful and rapid effect on all classes, especially the common people. Those who think that in these theaters the government will acquire a means for the moral education of the people are mistaken. . . . Even at the beginning the government will be unable to protect itself from works that are hostile, if not in their entirety, then in particular episodes, one of which will be enough to refute everything written in the spirit of the government. No censorship and no police measures will prevent this. It should not be forgotten that in all revolutions privately owned theaters served as a means for arousing passions, and that their proliferation in France and Germany is the fruit of revolutions.[26]

As for the idea of creating a people's theater, Adlerberg dismissed it by claiming that there were no plays suitable for performance before the common people. The existing repertoires of Russian theaters consisted entirely of works that were "either incomprehensible to the common people or alien to them by virtue of their spirit and content." Without an appropriate repertoire, the people's theaters would be able to stage only vaudevilles and farces, and these, he asserted, were even worse than the pantomimes and harlequinades of the *balagany* because they were of foreign origin and more likely to corrupt the morals of the common people.[27]

In his vehement attack on privately owned theaters in general and people's theaters in particular, Adlerberg was motivated as much by the desire to preserve his ministry's monopoly on theater productions in the capitals as by concern over the theater's potentially harmful impact on the common people. By linking theater to revolutionary unrest, he adroitly played on apprehensions within ruling circles about the possibility of a jacquerie, or *pugachevshchina*, fears that were widespread during the early part Alexander II's reign.[28] Adlerberg's arguments won the day, for Alexander II found them persuasive, writing in the margin of the report, "I share your opinion entirely."[29]

Proposals to create people's theaters in St. Petersburg in 1862 and 1865 met with the same fate, as did an attempt by a Moscow joint-stock company in 1864.[30] As *Fatherland Notes* lamented in 1868, although "the public has long decided unanimously that it is useful, necessary, and should exist," there was still no people's theater, as the government remained steadfast in refusing to permit one. There was one ray of hope, however, for the journal reported that rumors were circulating of a new project for a people's theater, backed by none other than the St. Petersburg chief of police, General F. F. Trepov.[31]

In the wake of Dmitrii Karakozov's attempt on the tsar's life in April 1866 and the cholera epidemic that struck St. Petersburg two months later, the authorities became increasingly anxious about the potential for unrest among the population of former serfs in the imperial capital. They were also worried that revolutionaries might try to muster support among factory workers in the city and its suburbs, for Karakozov had put up a proclamation justifying the assassination attempt, addressed "To Our Worker Friends," at the gates of one of the city's largest factories.[32] In June 1866, the tsar himself ordered the police to curb the growing "debauchery, depravity, and especially drunkenness" of the city's lower classes.[33]

The police responded with a series of measures that included the restriction of public drinking. Among the targets of their campaign were the *narodnye gulian'ia*, where the police prohibited the sale of alcohol, though this measure failed to prevent people from bringing their own supply of spirits or imbibing before setting off for the fairgrounds. The police also attempted to have a positive influence on the urban lower classes, calling upon the clergy to encourage sobriety and morality from the pulpit, and even sponsoring their own dry carnival on the Field of Mars.[34] Claiming the problem of public drunkenness was under control, Trepov decided it was now time to raise "the moral level of the common folk."[35]

Trepov's project, submitted to Alexander II in April 1868, presented people's theater as a disciplinary instrument designed to preserve public order and inculcate virtue in the common people. Having limited the opportunities of the "uneducated milieu" to indulge in "crude pleasures," he argued, the police were now obliged to provide them with "the opportunity for a different, more sublime means of satisfying their need for amusement." In the minds of police officials, drunkenness and immorality were cultural rather than social problems: the people drank because they had no alternative way to spend their leisure hours, not because they were poor and sought escape from the hardships of daily life. Employing the discourse of "rational recreations," Trepov offered didactic people's theaters as a means of combating popular immorality:

> Not only practical sense, but also the centuries-old experience of history points to this institution as one of the most effective measures for

morally and intellectually influencing the masses. Affordable theatrical performances, adapted to the comprehension of the crowd, will inevitably draw the common folk away from the revelry and debauch that are inseparable from crude pleasures and drunkenness. At the same time, by presenting them with edifying examples, it will imperceptibly inculcate in them an aversion to vice and an understanding of honest labor, thrift and so on.[36]

The proposal succeeded in arousing the interest of the tsar, who ordered Minister of Internal Affairs A. E. Timashev to discuss the matter with Minister of Court Adlerberg and Count Petr Shuvalov, chief of the Third Section, the political police force charged with fighting subversion.

Shuvalov, who had taken command of the Third Section in the wake of the assassination attempt, was an opponent of the Great Reforms who used Alexander's fear of subversion to gain control of the offices responsible for public order and to limit the reforms as much as possible. Timashev, one of his former assistants, had recently been appointed Minister of Internal Affairs at Shuvalov's suggestion. Both men, arch-conservatives, sought to use their power and influence to strengthen police powers and censorship and were highly suspicious of any attempts to enlighten the common people that were not under the strictest control of the state.[37]

In May Trepov produced a second, more detailed project, calling for a privately owned and operated network of people's theaters, which the government would regulate, censoring their repertoires and imposing limits on their number. There was an element of interministerial rivalry in the plan, for it recommended giving the responsibility of supervising the theaters to the Ministry of Internal Affairs, thereby circumventing the Ministry of Court and in effect abolishing the imperial theater monopoly.[38] Trepov worked out his plan with the assistance of the noted writer and playwright Vladimir Sollogub, who underlined the disciplinary potential he saw in the people's theater.[39] Sollogub had earlier been involved in a reorganization of the Moscow prisons and now suggested that theaters and prisons were institutions that similarly aimed to reform. Theater, he claimed, "like the prison, can have as its goal the civilization of the people," if it were run by the state and not abandoned to "speculators."[40] Sollogub's comparison is significant, for it expresses bluntly the idea behind his and Trepov's proposal as well as most conceptions of the people's theater: that it was an instrument of power that could be used to reform and impose order on the unruly population by influencing the common people to regulate and monitor their behavior. In this case, the power of theater would be wielded by the state, which would ensure that the people received morally uplifting entertainment under its watchful eye in a regulated environment, and teach them to abandon dissolute pleasures and discipline their bodies for "honest labor."

Other government officials were not so sure that the state would be able to fully control the people's theaters and make them serve its interests. Count Shuvalov approved in theory of the suggestion that the police should take part in the "moral education" of the people, but only on condition that the government exercise the firmest control and supervision over any people's theaters, since the common people were intellectually immature and extremely susceptible to any bad impressions transmitted from the stage. Private enterprise could not be entrusted with raising popular morality, he maintained, pointing to the example of the *balagany* and provincial commercial theaters, whose stages in the past season had been packed with racy songs and couplets, foreign comedians, "scandalous dances," and women in immodest attire. The reactionary state official was no less hostile toward the commercial entertainments than were the liberal and radical critics of popular amusements. In his opinion, a theater operated by private interests could be of no benefit to the common people, since it would be concerned with making money rather than doing good and only "indulge the people's disposition for debauchery."[41]

Although Shuvalov was at least sympathetic to the idea that the state could use theater to foster morality among the common people, Adlerberg remained adamantly opposed to the very concept that any theater could be of benefit to the people. Determined to protect his imperial theaters from competition, Adlerberg criticized Shuvalov for supporting people's theaters under the aegis of the state, arguing that theater was a product, not a means, of civilization.[42] The minister thus took the arguments of the proponents of people's theaters and turned them on their head—in his view it was precisely because the common people were so backward, ignorant, and poor that they had no need of any theater other than the existing *balagany*. Adlerberg elaborated his position in a lengthy report to Minister of Internal Affairs Timashev, reiterating the fears he had expressed ten years earlier about the danger that the people's theater would fall into the hands of the radicals, who would find it to be "the most powerful and easiest means to cultivate in the people ideas hostile to the existing order."[43] Once again, Adlerberg's arguments linking theater to subversion proved persuasive, and Trepov's project was rejected.

Despite these setbacks, calls for the establishment of people's theaters continued to be used to challenge the imperial monopoly. Aleksandr Fedotov, an actor at the Imperial Malyi Theater, unsuccessfully petitioned in 1870 for permission to open a people's theater in Moscow.[44] That same year, the St. Petersburg Literacy Committee published a report concluding that (1) the need for theater had indeed arisen among the common people, (2) the existing "crude and immoral" popular entertainments should be replaced by "rational recreations" that would advance the cause of popular education, and (3) the people's theater should serve members of all classes who were of "low intellectual development due to habit or poverty" and draw them away from the taverns. The literacy committee called for the construction of a privately owned people's theater in St. Petersburg, which would stage only Russian-language plays of moral and educational value, at prices affordable to the poorer classes. To curry favor with the government and assuage its concerns about the propaganda potential of such a theater, the report claimed that it would benefit the state by promoting patriotic sentiment.[45]

Some headway was made in the summer of 1870, when the *balagan* showman Vasilii Malafeev was granted permission to stage the historical drama *Ermak Timofeevich, Conqueror of Siberia*, during the All-Russian Manufacturing Exposition in St. Petersburg. In the same year, a provincial actor opened a people's theater in Odessa, but the venture collapsed after only a few months due to financial problems.[46] In 1872, the zemstvo board of St. Petersburg province vainly requested authorization for a people's theater in a densely populated industrial district.[47] That year, however, the movement to bring theater to the people scored its first major success, with the opening of the People's Theater at the Moscow Polytechnic Exposition.

PEOPLE'S THEATER AT THE POLYTECHNIC EXPOSITION

The Moscow Polytechnic Exposition of 1872, held in conjunction with the celebration of the bicentennial of Peter the Great's birth, was planned as a showcase of Russian industrial progress and a demonstration of the country's modernity. Not only did the exposition afford Moscow's recently established duma the chance to have a voice in a national event, it also enabled middle-class professionals and industrialists to take part in public discussions about the planned exhibitions and to participate in the commissions responsible for them. The idea for a people's theater, supported by several prominent Muscovites and the city duma, surfaced during the exposition's planning stages.

In late 1871, a group of Moscow industrialists, professors, and writers had tried to form a society for the moral and educational betterment of the working classes but had been unable to get the requisite official approval.

Seeing the forthcoming exposition as an opportunity to put their ideas into action, they now organized a Commission for the Care of Workers and Artisans to participate in the exposition and enlisted the support of Moscow Governor-General V. A. Dolgorukov, Prince Vladimir Cherkasskii, the mayor and one of the architects of the Emancipation, and Modest Kittary, a Moscow University chemistry professor devoted to the cause of popular enlightenment. The commission proposed to establish a people's theater at the exposition, in addition to organizing choral groups, public readings, libraries, and inexpensive tearooms.[48]

The Moscow actor Aleksandr Fedotov was invited to join the commission and to work out a plan for the theater. After his expulsion from St. Petersburg University for his part in student protests in the early 1860s, Fedotov had established himself as a leading talent in the Imperial Malyi Theater. Dissatisfied with the routine that reigned there and eager to find a way to realize his dream of a theater in which an ensemble of actors would perform the classics in a simple, lifelike way, he had been taking part in private amateur drama productions. For Fedotov, the proposed People's Theater at the Moscow Polytechnic Exposition was a golden opportunity to combine his professional aspirations with social service.[49]

The young actor sent a petition to the exposition's chairman, General Nikolai Isakov, asking for his support and elaborating the merits of the project. In keeping with the interests of the industrialists on the committee, who included Timofei Morozov, owner of one of Russia's largest textile concerns, Fedotov portrayed the People's Theater as a disciplinary instrument for the reform of the urban working classes. He argued that as the exposition aimed to further the development of Russian industry, it had to concern itself with the intellectual and spiritual development of the working classes, in which respect the Russian workers lagged far behind their foreign counterparts. The main problem, according to Fedotov, was that the working classes had access only to entertainments that led to debauchery and wasteful spending, such as taverns, card games, heads-or-tails, and singing. He warned of the negative influence of urban life, pointing out that the urban lower classes' "corrupted taste and developing sensual instincts are not content with folk songs and demand reworked romances of a vulgar character and often of an entirely depraved content." The most useful form of recreation for the working classes was theater, he concluded, because it was ideally suited for "introducing in the people the rules of morality and a modest, steady, and industrious life."[50]

The claim that theater could serve to produce a more disciplined, hardworking labor force for Russian industry was thus wedded to earlier arguments about the power of theater to introduce the common people to the culture of educated society and teach them to spend their free time in pursuits other than drinking and carousing. Thanks to the strenuous efforts of Kittary, who enjoyed the confidence of official circles, this time both Timashev and Shuvalov were persuaded to throw their support behind the People's Theater, overcoming the opposition of Adlerberg, who remained anxious to maintain the imperial theaters' monopoly on performances. The tsar granted his permission for a theater to be constructed as part of the exposition.[51]

Funded in part by voluntary contributions and a hefty subsidy from the Moscow duma, the People's Theater opened its doors on 4 June 1872, the 170th anniversary of the opening of Peter the Great's theater on Red Square. In Peter's honor, the program for the first performance included Nikolai Polevoi's *The Grandfather of the Russian Fleet*, which celebrated Peter's role as the founder of the Russian navy and had been popular on imperial stages in the 1830s and 1840s. Designed in the neo-Russian style by V. A. Gartman, who had also drawn up plans for the theater proposed by the St. Petersburg Literacy Committee, the theater was located on Varvarskaia Square, near the center of the city. Constructed entirely of wood, it held 1,625 spectators, offering 1,056 tickets for each performance at prices ranging from five to forty kopeks, to ensure it would be affordable to all. The acting troupe, under Fedotov's direction, was made up of leading actors from the provincial stages, including Modest Pisarev, Nikolai Rybakov, Aleksandra Strelkova, and Konstantin Berg, some of whom went on to successful careers in the imperial theaters.[52]

Because popular audiences would be attending the theater, the Ministry of Internal Affairs insisted on approving the repertoire, even though all of the proposed works had previously been staged in the imperial theaters. The question of what repertoire was most appropriate for the common people was discussed at several public meetings at Moscow University, provoking long disputes between Fedotov, who championed the classics and contemporary plays dealing with social issues, and the officials, who preferred patriotic, morally edifying plays and light vaudevilles. Some censors did throw their support behind the classics, however, arguing that the theater must be educational. Besides, they claimed, the common people would be eager to see the upper-class characters that peopled most of the classics. In the end, Fedotov obtained permission to stage plays and operas by such noted Russian authors as Ostrovsky, Pushkin, Gogol, Glinka, and Potekhin, translations of plays by Molière and Shakespeare, together with vaudevilles, light comedies, and patriotic works.[53]

Unfortunately, contemporary accounts say only that large numbers of the "simple folk" attended and enjoyed the performances but give no clear sense of how they responded to the plays. The journal *Discussion*, for example, reported that Glinka's opera *A Life for the Tsar* was a big hit with popular audiences but said nothing about whether the source of its appeal lay in its patriotism, heroism, folk melodies, or plot, in which a clever peasant outwits foreign invaders by leading them deep into the forest.[54] Fedotov later remembered that the audiences appreciated Russian classics and found Gogol's comedy about corrupt small-town officialdom, *The Government Inspector*, and Fonvizin's satire on the provincial gentry, *The Minor*, hilarious but were bored by old vaudevilles. This judgment, sometimes cited as proof of popular audiences' preference for high quality drama and disdain of inferior works, may well simply reflect the prejudices against vaudeville of Fedotov himself.[55] A reviewer in *The Russian Gazette* had another explanation for the cool reception of one of the vaudevilles that supposedly bored the common people, Nikolai Kulikov's *A Crow in Peacock's Feathers*, reporting that it was poorly staged, with the actors wearing primitive makeup as if in a mystery play.[56] Popular audiences quite possibly did not expect to be greeted with stylized allusions to folk drama when they entered a real theater for the first time.

The press devoted most of its coverage of the theater to the performances and repertoire, and most reviews expressed admiration for the troupe and Fedotov's directing, although individual actors received their share of criticism. *The Russian Gazette* reported that in *The Government Inspector* the People's Theater's troupe far outshone that of the Imperial Malyi Theater in their ensemble acting, the depth to which they entered into their parts, and their attention to every detail of even secondary roles. Author and critic Dmitrii Averkiev was less impressed, pointing out that the troupe achieved a fully ensemble performance only in certain scenes, and finding fault with some actors' understanding of their roles. One critic objected to the decision to stage Ostrovsky's *Poverty Is No Vice*, in which the drunkard Liubim Tortsov saves his niece from an unhappy marriage, voicing the opinion that Tortsov's heroism would give the common people the impression that drunkenness was no vice. He also condemned the choice of some vaudevilles, equating them with "*balagan* amusements."[57] Political interference from Minister of Internal Affairs Timashev, who visited the theater in the company of Alexander II in July, resulted in the eventual withdrawal of *The Government Inspector* from the repertoire, on the grounds that the play's depiction of corrupt officials would not further the "softening and ennoblement of mores."[58]

In October 1872, one month after the end of the Moscow Polytechnic Exposition, the brief history of the People's Theater came to end. Although the Commission for the Care of Workers and Artisans attempted to get the government's approval to continue performances on a permanent basis, and both Timashev and Shuvalov expressed their support, Adlerberg took the matter out of their hands by giving two Moscow state officials, Prince F. M. Urusov and S. V. Taneev, permission to operate the theater. They purchased the building from the municipal government and reopened it as a commercial enterprise, the Accessible Theater.[59]

The new theater was of a very different character from Fedotov's People's Theater. It labored under severe handicaps imposed by the government, which, to protect the imperial theaters from competition, allowed it to stage only scenes from plays and forbade actors to appear in costume. Some of Fedotov's actors stayed on, but the new managers had no expertise in running a theater and attendance fell, partly because Urusov and Taneev raised ticket prices and eliminated the cheap seats to increase their profits. The Accessible Theater struggled on for three years, closing in 1876.[60]

As for Fedotov, he went to St. Petersburg, where he continued to struggle unsuccessfully against the imperial theater monopoly for a few years, pleading the case for "rational, sober, and moral recreations" like the People's Theater.[61] He eventually began working in Moscow semi-professional theater, where he met Konstantin Stanislavsky, then a young industrialist with a passion for amateur theatricals. Fedotov became one of Stanislavsky's teachers and a co-founder of the Society of Art and Literature, which laid the foundations for the Moscow Art Theater. Both Fedotov's dream of reaching out to popular audiences and his vision of a theater where actors would eschew declamation and exaggerated gestures to create a realistic ensemble under the firm guidance of the director were to exert a profound influence on Stanislavsky's work.[62]

The People's Theater at the Moscow Polytechnic Exposition was a short-lived experiment, yet it was the first breach in the imperial theater monopoly, and its success was taken as a demonstration of the possibilities theater offered for exerting a positive moral and intellectual influence on the people. Textile magnate Aleksandr Sapozhnikov even claimed that drunkenness almost vanished among his workers, who had deserted the taverns for the People's Theater.[63] *The Russian Herald* praised the inclusion of a theater in the exposition and argued that the experience demonstrated that people's theaters could play a vital role in the urgent task of uniting the intelligentsia and the *narod* in one community of Russian citizens:

It is about time, by the way, that we put all our efforts into the moral and intellectual uplifting of our people. It was possible for the people to stagnate in ignorance when they were slaves, enserfed. But since twenty million former serfs have become full members of our civic and political life it is impossible to let them remain at the former level of ignorance. It is impossible to remain at that chasm which divides our educated classes from the common folk. The progress of science is communicated more slowly than that of art. Let us bring our people into the realm of art as much as possible. With living speech and images we will acquaint them with ourselves and with our ideals, and, at least in part, with our common past.[64]

The *Russian Gazette* hailed Russia's "first attempt at free theater," calling its closure a great disappointment for Muscovites, while other papers said it demonstrated the contribution that private theater could make to Russian art by bringing in new blood and competition to refresh the "swamp" of the imperial theaters.[65] For the liberal intelligentsia, the People's Theater had proved that private initiative, freed from the constraints imposed by the state, could be a potent force for both artistic renewal and popular enlightenment.

OSTROVSKY CALLS FOR A NATIONAL
RUSSIAN THEATER

Rumors about plans to rescind the imperial theater monopoly started circulating shortly after Alexander II's assassination in March 1881. Although his successor, Alexander III, was an arch-conservative whose reign was marked by efforts to curtail his father's educational and local government reforms, the new ruler apparently recognized the futility of the imperial theater monopoly and the need for additional drama theaters to serve the rapidly expanding populations of Moscow and St. Petersburg. Besides, private amateur drama circles and club theaters had multiplied during the 1860s and 1870s, as had musical theaters and pleasure gardens (to which the restrictions did not apply), so in ending the monopoly the government was to some extent legalizing what already existed.[66]

A few months after Alexander III ascended the throne, Alexander Ostrovsky proposed the establishment of a model national people's theater in Moscow. The dramatist laid out his arguments in a lengthy "Note on the Situation of Dramatic Art in Russia at the Present Time," which he presented to the new tsar in late 1881. Ostrovsky called attention to the fact that the one existing dramatic theater, the Imperial Malyi Theater, could scarcely meet the needs of Moscow's population, and he underlined the importance of theater for the intellectual and moral well-being of society. What he had in mind was not a special theater catering only to the common people but a "Russian national theater for all of Russia" (*russkii teatr, natsional'nyi, vserossiiskii*) that would serve every class and become a showcase of Russian dramatic art. His "Note" is worth examining in some detail, as it reveals how the concept of a didactic theater was intertwined with hopes for theatrical reform and the protection of art from commercial degradation, as well as the transformation of the common people into a civilized citizenry.[67]

In Ostrovsky's view, the benefits of a noncommercial national theater were fourfold. First, it would be educational, helping the peasants pouring into Moscow "to become humanized" (*ochelovechivat'sia*). Artistic plays about everyday life would demonstrate to audiences "what is good and kind in a Russian person, what he should guard in himself and nurture, and what in him is wild and coarse, with which he should struggle." Historical plays would promote popular patriotism, by fostering a sense of citizenship and membership in a national community. Second, the proposed theater would bolster Russia's self-esteem and pride in its cultural achievements. Like academies, universities, and museums, a national theater was "a sign of a nation's adulthood."[68]

Third, Ostrovsky claimed that a national theater would nourish and support the development of Russian drama. In a chauvinistic vein, he rejected foreign models, alluding to the popularity of adaptations of French operettas and melodramas on the Russian stage. "The Russian nation is still taking shape, fresh forces are entering it; why should we rest content with the vulgarities that gratify the bourgeoisie's lack of taste?" he asked. The notion that Russia was a young nation that drew its strength from the healthy forces of the people was central to his arguments for the creation of a democratic national theater, in which a vital and unspoiled audience would provide playwrights with fertile soil to nourish their talents: "Russian authors wish to try their powers before a fresh audience, whose nerves are not too sensitive, who require powerful dramatic effects, grand comedy, ardent, sincere sentiments, lively and powerful characters. Dramatic poetry is closer to the people than all other branches of literature. All other works are written for educated people, but drama and comedy are written for all of the people."[69]

Finally, a national theater would save both art and the *narod* from corruption by commercial interests after the abolition of the imperial theater monopoly. In his youth, Ostrovsky had been drawn to the ideas of the Slavophiles, and his arguments reflected their idealization of the Russian

people and view of the West as a source of moral contamination. He warned
of the dire consequences that would ensue if the tender minds of the common people were exposed to commercial theater:

> Without a model Russian theater art will be sacrificed to speculation;
> without a model repertoire audiences will go astray, they will have no
> beacon to indicate where and what is real art. Among the intellectually
> immature, uneducated common people there are those with serious
> intentions, and with aesthetic instinct, if not taste.
>
> They need to know that on the one hand stands real, eternal art,
> and on the other, temporary digressions from it, provided to us by an
> advanced but anti-artistic nation [i.e., France]. This is melodrama, with
> impossible events and inhuman passions; this is operetta, where pagan
> gods and priests, kings and ministers, armies and nations dance the can-
> can; this is a fantasy extravaganza, where the sets change twenty-four
> times, and in the course of an evening the spectator manages to visit
> every corner of the earth and the moon besides, and where in all
> twenty-four scenes there are the same naked women.
>
> If such a choice is afforded them, then we can hope that the majority
> of the common audience will desire real, healthy art, and this is extremely
> likely, if we take into account the freshness of feeling and serious cast of
> mind with which the Russian is endowed. But if there is no model theater,
> then the common audience could take the operettas and melodramas that
> inflame the curiosity or sensuality for real, genuine art.

The common people thus had to be protected from the foreign influence of
commercial theaters and their sensational trash, which would only reduce
art to an "empty amusement" and discredit it in the eyes of "people only
beginning to live an intellectual life."[70]

Ostrovsky readily admitted that the model Russian national theater he
envisioned would never be achieved by reliance on private enterprise, for he
was convinced that entrepreneurs were interested in profits rather than art.
Ideally, the Moscow duma would take on the project, but it was unlikely the
city could find the money for such an endeavor. Ostrovsky was confident,
however, that the educated Moscow merchantry would come up with the
necessary funds for the theater, as it had for other cultural institutions like
the Moscow Conservatory and the Russian Music Society. Were his idea to
meet with the government's approval, he expressed his willingness to take
on the task of organizing the theater.

Although Ostrovsky succeeded in convincing Alexander III, who wrote
on the margin of the "Note" that "it would be highly desirable to realize
this idea, which I share entirely,"[71] he was not so fortunate in attracting
financial backing for a national people's theater. Commercial theaters began

to sprout up in the capitals after the imperial theater monopoly was at last abolished in 1882, but Ostrovsky's grand project remained only a dream. Nevertheless, his arguments for a theater that would unite art and the people were extremely influential. While the idea that theater would civilize and enlighten the common people was hardly new, Ostrovsky was the first to suggest that the theater needed the people as much as the people needed the theater. In the people he had discovered a new, fresh audience that would enable Russian drama to flourish despite competition from "anti-artistic" French imports. People's theaters thus took on a new hue. Not only could they serve as a school and an alternative to the existing popular recreations, they could be refuges where art could flourish free from the constraints of profit.

Like many of his contemporaries, Ostrovsky assumed that the tastes of the common people were healthy and unspoiled, and required only exposure to "real, eternal art" to awaken them. Given a choice, the people would intuitively distinguish art from vulgar trash and cast their votes for the former. Still, there were two obstacles to be overcome. Art had to reach the people before commercial entertainments had corrupted their taste. And a way had to be found to pay for it, since, as even Ostrovsky recognized, no theater that catered to the budgets of the common people could possibly maintain high production standards and still make a profit. Mistrustful of private enterprise, he looked to local government or private sponsorship to fund his scheme, as did most supporters of the people's theater. So long as the people's theater lived only in the minds of the intelligentsia and the pages of the periodical press, however, the potential conflict between artistic ideals and financial realities remained purely academic.

COMMERCIAL PEOPLE'S THEATER: THE SKOMOROKH

A few months after the repeal of the imperial theater monopoly, the impresario Mikhail Lentovskii opened the Skomorokh Accessible Theater in Moscow. An actor who had studied under the great Mikhail Shchepkin, Lentovskii was renowned throughout Russia for the lavish costumes and dazzling special effects of the melodramas, operettas, and fantasy extravaganzas he produced at up-scale entertainment meccas like Moscow's Hermitage summer garden. Hoping "to do something really useful for art" by bringing it to the people, Lentovskii had attempted to get permission to open a popular theater in Moscow in 1879, but was thwarted by the imperial theater monopoly.[72] Now freed from this constraint, he got financial backing from a millionaire, refurbished an old circus in central Moscow, and assembled a troupe of well-known provincial actors. The Skomorokh Accessible Theater debuted in November 1882 with a performance of Dmitrii Averkiev's *Frol Skabeev*, an 1860s comedy about the romantic escapades of a poor but clever nobleman, based on a late seventeenth-century manuscript tale.[73]

Tickets were priced low, starting at fifteen kopeks on weekdays, five kopeks on Sundays and holidays. Visitors did not have to remove their overcoats on entering the theater, sparing them an additional expense at the cloakroom. The repertoire was a mélange of comedy, melodrama, and the classics, composed with little regard for contemporary distinctions between "real art" and sensational entertainment. Alongside works from the contemporary dramatic canon, such as Ostrovsky's *Poverty Is No Vice* and Alexei Tolstoy's *Prince Serebrianyi*, Lentovskii staged thrillers like A. S. Liutetskii's *Stenka Razin, the Volga Bandit,* which combined fast-paced action with themes and characters from folklore. Lentovskii was an entertainer, not an educator, and, like the fairground showmen, he understood the importance of spectacle. In many of his productions he sought to awe and delight popular audiences with the special effects that were such a hit at the more elite venues where he usually worked. One performance featured a railroad complete with telegraph poles and a train that crossed the stage puffing artificial clouds of steam.[74]

Lentovskii's style of popular theater was not to everyone's taste, however, for he was too much of a showman and not enough of an enlightener to conform to the pervasive view of people's theater as a didactic conveyor belt. The 1883 Moscow District Teachers' Congress passed a resolution condemning the Skomorokh, comparing it to the hucksters who sold cheap popular literature and woodcut prints at the infamous Nikolskii Market.[75] The repertoire's inclusion of a play with a criminal hero, *The Bandit Churkin* (adapted by I. I. Miasnitskii and M. G. Iaron from a tremendously popular serial novel of the same title), provoked a manufacturer to complain that the theater was inciting workers to "burn out their bosses or even cut their throats." The Moscow theatrical journal that published his letter seconded the opinion and caustically commented that "the Skomorokh stage, in Lentovskii's hands, does the people more harm than good."[76] The young journalist Anton Chekhov gave a more sympathetic evaluation of the theater after a visit in January 1883:

> The corridors are dark and eerie, as in the dungeons of the Inquisition. It wouldn't hurt to install a few extra lamps. Prices are moderate, everyone can see [the stage], the ticket-takers don't pester you, and the audience applauds when it's pleased. But it's devilishly cold. . . .

> We saw Gedeonov's *The Death of Liapunov*. It's an old play, cold, high-faluting, and as slow as molasses, but we have almost nothing against its production at the Skomorokh. Let the unlearned audience learn some history for only twenty-five kopeks. That's in the first place, and in the second place, such plays can be understood by anyone, they're not tendentious and treat issues that are far from unimportant. And that may well be enough.[77]

Cold and uncomfortable, the Skomorokh was nonetheless a hit with the audiences who filled the cheap seats in the balconies, cheering heroes and booing villains with little regard for the skill with which they were portrayed: "an actor who played, even though badly, a noble, heroic role could count on a noisy success, while a talented actor who performed a negative character would even get howls of indignation from the upper rows."[78] Still, the receipts were not enough to cover expenses, and the Skomorokh was a financial failure.[79] Unable to break even, unwilling to make cutbacks in order to reduce overhead, and unsuccessful in his efforts to get a subsidy from the city duma, Lentovskii was forced to close the Skomorokh in February 1883. Moscow's first commercial people's theater had lasted only four months. Its closure, wrote a workman in a letter to a theatrical weekly, "left the crowd or mass of artisans, workers, and all of the poor working class without a theater."[80]

Undaunted by his commercial failure, Lentovskii resurrected the Skomorokh in late 1886, this time in a refurbished panorama on Sretenskii Boulevard. With 2,600 seats or standing places priced from ten kopeks to one ruble, the new Skomorokh had luxuries like electric lighting and gas heating. In a gesture to the theater's associations with popular enlightenment, the interior was decorated with portraits of great writers, while in an attempt to discipline the sometimes unruly audiences, signs were posted instructing spectators to remove their hats and refrain from making comments to the actors during performances. Lentovskii's second venture into people's theater was as successful as the first had been in drawing popular audiences to see its well-staged mixture of classics, comedies, and melodramas. Still, he was unable to reconcile his love of lavish productions with the limited income the low-priced tickets generated. Financial problems continued to dog the enterprise, and in 1888 ownership was assumed by the troupe. In 1891 one of Lentovskii's creditors turned management of the theater over to the actor and experienced *balagan* showman A. A. Cherepanov, who was able to make enough profit to continue running the Skomorokh for several years.[81]

Under Cherepanov's management the theater continued to produce a wide variety of plays ranging across the spectrum from Shakespeare and Pushkin to vaudevilles, melodramas, and contemporary farces, and even the occasional opera. The 1892–93 season featured Shakespeare's *Othello* and *Hamlet*, Pushkin's *Boris Godunov*, Ostrovsky's historical drama *Dmitrii the Pretender and Vasilii Shuiskii*, Aleksei Verstovskii's romantic opera *Askold's Tomb*, Adolph Dennery's adaptation of Jules Verne's *Around the World in Eighty Days*, and the spectacular *Christopher Columbus and the Discovery of America*. In 1893 Lentovskii returned for a last performance on the stage of Skomorokh, starring in *Hamlet* to the audience's delight but to the consternation of a reviewer, who accused him of distorting Shakespeare's text with his enthusiastic ad-libbing. Skomorokh was the first theater to produce Tolstoy's didactic drama *The First Distiller*, a tale of how peasants were introduced to alcohol by a devil and as a result became lazy and quarrelsome. Tolstoy's greatest drama, *The Power of Darkness*, prohibited for years because of its controversial depiction of adultery, murder, and infanticide among Russian peasants, received its premiere before popular audiences in 1895 thanks to Cherepanov's prolonged negotiations with the censors.[82]

Despite the theater's efforts to produce recognized classics and other fare deemed appropriate for the edification of the *narod*, it was constantly criticized in the press for lowering itself to the level of the crowd in the interests of commerce. The main targets of the critics were the Skomorokh's production standards, its use of sensationalistic advertising posters, and, especially, its eclectic repertoire.[83] Moscow's leading theatrical monthly, *The Artist*, deplored Skomorokh's "complete lack of effort to give healthy mental nourishment to the masses."[84]

Nikolai Popov, a young director who had staged a few plays for factory workers, acted with Stanislavsky in his Society of Art and Literature, and helped organize an exhibit on people's theaters at the Fourth All-Russian Agricultural Exposition in 1895, was scathing in his criticism of Cherepanov's Skomorokh. According to Popov, Skomorokh had never been an "artistic-educational institution." Even when Lentovskii was in charge the theater had "spoiled the repertoire and with it the tastes of the audience," he claimed, but admitted that it had at least given "the less well-off inhabitants of the capital and students an opportunity for rational recreation." If under Lentovskii things had been unsatisfactory but tolerable, Cherepanov had "reduced his theater to the level of a bad *balagan*," attracting to it an audience "that yields little to the fairground public in its ignorance and uncontrollable behavior." Forced to constantly perform new roles due to the theater's emphasis on novelty, actors did not know their lines and either mumbled their way through or relied constantly on prompters for assistance. Sets were shoddy, the orchestra pitiful.

Worst of all, Cherepanov used gaudy posters and spiced up the titles of staid classics in order to attract audiences:

> It is difficult to imagine more illiterate advertising, a cruder indulgence of the public's base instincts. Double and triple titles, invented with a special relish for every possible horror, have become the indispensable adornment of the Skomorokh's placards. The shamelessness of the advertising has reached the point where the performances are billed as *The Robber's Bride, or The Terrible Stranger and Fiery Death of the Robber Band,* drama in 3 acts by Schiller, and *The Water-Sprite, Queen of the Dnepr,* epic folk poem by Pushkin. And such a play: *Mazepa: The Battle of Poltava under Tsar Peter the Great and the Execution of Kochubei,* drama in 5 acts by A. Sokolov. This drama used to play simply under the title *Mazepa,* and now they add these enticing extras about battle and execution. Obviously, the most important consideration is to somehow lure in an audience.

The use of explanatory titles was, of course, an old advertising technique in the fairground theaters, used to attract audiences who might not be familiar with a play by letting them know what was in store, and filling seats was a major consideration if a theater was to stay afloat. Popov, in real or feigned ignorance of marketing's importance for any commercial enterprise, complained puritanically that every year, in an apparent attempt to improve its repertoire, the Skomorokh opened the season with a good play and scarcely made use of advertising, only to return to its former bad ways within a week. He dismissed the idea that a commercial theater could serve the people and called on the municipal government, private philanthropy, or, best of all, the state to take matters in hand and assume the guardianship of popular morals and taste.[85]

Popov's comments and language reveal more about his ambivalent image of the *narod* than they do about Skomorokh's repertoire, actors, or public. He accuses the theater of having "spoiled" the taste of the audience, implying that it was fresh and pure before exposure to the theater. Yet he describes the instincts of the common people as "base," and he excoriates the theater for degrading itself by indulging those instincts with crude gimmicks. Popov's attack on the theater is in part a condemnation of the "uncontrollable" and "ignorant" people, for his *narod* is a Janus-faced figure, simultaneously innocent, requiring protection, and primitive and irrational, needing discipline.

What was ultimately wrong with the Skomorokh in the eyes of critics like Popov? All theaters are sometimes guilty of low production standards, and no actor succeeds in every role, especially when he or she acts in the dozens of plays typically staged seasonally in most Russian theaters (with rare exceptions after 1898 like the Moscow Art Theater). As for the repertoire, it was not terribly different from that of a provincial theater, made up of some plays that were running in the Imperial Malyi or Korsh theaters, a broad selection of vaudevilles, operettas, and farces, together with a hefty dose of recognized classics. By ordinary standards, the Skomorokh was a successful enterprise—it attracted popular audiences *and* was commercially viable, raking in the more than respectable sum of 45,000 rubles in the 1894–95 winter season.[86]

Skomorokh's flaw, in the view of the *Kulturträger*, if not of the public, lay in its failure to pursue the task of enlightenment single-mindedly. It resembled a provincial theater, rather than conforming to the ideal of a didactic people's theater, and promoted a pluralistic entertainment culture that threatened to infect the putatively unspoiled common people with the tastes of the urban middle-class habitués of legitimate theaters and pleasure gardens. Ivan Shcheglov, a tireless advocate of the benefits of people's theater, came away from a visit to the Skomorokh in the mid-1890s with mixed feelings. On the one hand, he was thrilled to see a performance of Gogol's *The Government Inspector* before a popular audience, and the reaction of the public confirmed his belief that the *narod* need only be exposed to good performances of good plays to develop an appreciation for the classic works of Russian drama. On the other hand, he was chagrined to find that the same audiences who enjoyed Gogol equally enjoyed an operetta-extravaganza, *The Devil's Wife*, in which dancing girls revealed their undergarments as well as their legs. To make matter worse, during intermission tickets to a "You Can't Lose" lottery were being sold along with vodka in the buffet. Shcheglov's disappointment with the theater and, implicitly, its public can be attributed to his inability to accept the seeming contradiction that what were for him the sacred and the profane could exist side by side, apparently undifferentiated by the spectators. The very people who loved *The Government Inspector* also liked to listen to "vulgar" ditties and to see a bit of anatomy, too. Shcheglov ended by citing a respected critic who, after seeing *The Power of Darkness* at Skomorokh, which he contrasted with the usual "disgraceful repertoire," asked rhetorically, "How useful this theater could be. And it does not want to. Why?" The unstated but implied answer was that commerce and enlightenment were incompatible.[87]

THE SPREAD OF PEOPLE'S THEATERS

The Skomorokh was a bitter disappointment to those who hoped that theater would have a civilizing influence on the common people and introduce them to the culture of the intelligentsia, for its experience seemed to prove that the sacred task of bringing wholesome, artistic theater to the people could not be entrusted to commerce. From where, then, would the necessary financial support come? Popov and Shcheglov, like Ostrovsky and most proponents of popular cultural enlightenment, felt that the people's theater should be in the hands of philanthropists, municipal governments, or the state. Philanthropy, however, played only a minor role in establishing people's theaters in the capitals, in part due to the autocracy's suspicious attitude to public initiative in matters relating to popular education. A notable exception was work of the liberal, wealthy, and well-connected Countess Sofiia Panina, who succeeded in overcoming bureaucratic impediments to create an excellent people's theater at her People's House in St. Petersburg in 1903.[88] Although city dumas recognized the need for "rational recreations" and provided small amounts of money for holiday entertainments, plans for permanent municipal people's theaters tended to get stuck in their finance committees, where they languished for years.

The St. Petersburg city duma first raised the question of funding "rational recreations" for the common people in 1884, and during the next several years a number of reports were prepared on the subject. Finally, in 1893, the city executive board approved a recommendation by its own Committee on Popular Education that the city sponsor popular recreations, but the idea remained buried in the duma's finance committee, which failed to find the required funds. An 1896 project for a municipal people's theater met the same fate. Anatolii Kremlev, whose plan for a people's theater was approved by the First All-Russian Congress of Theater People in 1897, tried in vain for years to get the city to underwrite it. The more liberal Moscow duma started sponsoring summer open-air concerts in 1892 but was slow to give financial backing to theaters. The duma began considering a project for a network of ten people's theaters in the late 1890s, but only one was ever constructed, and it did not open until late 1904, although the city workhouse got a theater in 1902. Stanislavsky and Nemirovich-Danchenko attempted to get a municipal subsidy for their original Moscow Accessible Art Theater, on the grounds that it would serve the lower classes, but were turned down. The duma refused to consider a second proposal for a people's theater submitted by Stanislavsky and Nemirovich in 1908. At last, in 1915, the duma approved a plan to construct a network of "people's houses" with theaters, libraries, and tea rooms, but the financial strains of World War I prevented its realization.[89] Municipal governments, perennially short of funds and restricted in their ability to raise revenues, were loath to commit themselves to financing costly cultural initiatives, no matter how worthy of support in principle.[90]

In St. Petersburg and Moscow, the first noncommercial theaters for the people were established not by local governments, intelligentsia *Kulturträger* eager to enlighten the masses, or theater people seeking a new audience, but by pragmatic industrialists who wanted a more disciplined workforce and believed "rational recreations" such as theater were the answer. Looking for ways to combat working-class drinking habits and to increase labor productivity, factory owners started founding theaters for their workers during the 1880s and 1890s. They were followed onto the stage at the turn of the century by the Guardianships of Popular Temperance, state-funded temperance societies operating under the auspices of the Finance Ministry, which soon became the leading force behind people's theaters in the Russian empire.

In 1898 Aleksandr Kugel, theater critic and editor of Russia's leading theatrical weekly, *Theater and Art*, wryly observed in an article entitled "Theatrical Populism" that "the enthusiasm for the people's theater that fills 'the best part of our society' is indescribable." If in the past long hair was a sign of love for the common people (*narodoliubstvo*), he added, it had now been supplanted by the clean-shaven face and short hair of an actor.[91] Although Kugel's remarks were made tongue-in-cheek, there was indeed an explosion of interest in bringing theater to the people in the 1890s.

Several factors lay behind the intense fascination with people's theaters at this time. The well-publicized activities of factory theaters appeared to confirm the idea that theater could have a positive effect on the common people by luring them away from the tavern and acquainting them with more respectable ways of passing their leisure hours. The rapid industrial growth of the late 1880s and 1890s drew ever more peasants in from the countryside to labor temporarily or permanently in the factories, homes, and shops of St. Petersburg and Moscow, intensifying the social problems linked to urbanization that had first become evident following Emancipation. By the 1890s there was what Ben Eklof has called "a confluence of forces promoting education as a solution to the core problems often associated with the transitional phases of modernization."[92] Theater joined ranks with the primary school, library, reading room, and magic-lantern lecture as a force for intellectual and moral progress.[93] Finally, the 1890s were marked

Figure 3. Open-air summer stage sponsored by the Guardianship of Popular Temperance in Petrovskii Park. St. Petersburg, early 1900s. Courtesy of the Central State Archive of Documentary Films and Photographs, St. Petersburg.

by increased attention to the problem of alcoholism, which led, beginning in 1895, to the introduction of a state liquor monopoly and the establishment of officially backed temperance societies to promote sobriety among the lower classes.[94] Russian industrialists and the Guardianships of Popular Temperance both quickly embraced the people's theater as a valuable ally in the war on drunkenness.

During the 1890s and 1900s the number of people's theaters grew enormously. In 1896 the catalog of an exhibit on people's theaters at the Fourth All-Russian Agricultural Exposition listed more than thirty localities scattered throughout the Empire where "people's performances" (*narodnye spektakli*) had been held; by 1904 they were being offered on roughly 150 stages.[95] Long before Vsevolod Meyerhold revolutionized Russian theater with his modernist experiments, he gained his first acting experience in 1897 on the prosaic stage of the people's theater in his hometown of Penza.[96] Between 1899 and 1909, the Guardianships of Popular Temperance used their generous state subsidies to spend 8,551,255 rubles on some 47,245 theater performances that were attended by over 18 million people.[97] By 1914, there was scarcely a corner of Russia where industrialists, temperance societies, local governments, educators, and amateur and professional actors were not organizing theater performances for workers and peasants. The largest networks of people's theaters, drawing not only the common people but also middle-class audiences to their productions, were in St. Petersburg and Moscow.

THE PEOPLE BEHIND THE PEOPLE'S THEATER MOVEMENT

The growing number of people's theaters and projects for new ones were accompanied by a flood of literature and meetings on the subject of popular theater. Except on the part of industrialists and the state-subsidized temperance guardianships, however, words did not necessarily produce results. As a theater critic commented in 1899, "It is already three years since the people's theater entered, so to speak, the first rank of issues in Russian civic life. . . . Notwithstanding, it is curious that discussion has far surpassed action, and that if even half of what has been talked about had been done, then Russia would have had more people's theaters long ago."[98] Both the aforementioned Agricultural Exposition and the Second Congress of Russian Activists in Technical and Professional Education (Moscow, 1895) featured exhibits on people's theaters, while the First All-Russian Congress of Theater People (Moscow, 1897) passed resolutions calling for more affordable theaters and the abolition of the special censorship policy for popular theaters. At the theater congress, people's theaters were held up as one of the means by which actors could realize their aspirations to social recognition as being not simply entertainers but professionals who practiced a specialty that was of public benefit.[99] On the eve of the congress, Stanislavsky, Chekhov, and other theater activists met at the offices of the liberal journal *Russian Thought* to discuss a grandiose project for a people's theater drawn up by the architect Fedor Shekhtel. Chekhov was very enthusiastic about the idea at the time, but the project was never realized due to its cost.[100] Maxim Gorky, with the support of Stanislavsky and other members of the Moscow Art Theater, took part in the creation of a people's theater in his native Nizhnii Novgorod in 1903.[101] An organization of Russian artists that included Fedor Shaliapin and Ilya Repin began providing technical assistance to amateur workers' and peasants' theaters in 1910, and the educational value of theater was discussed extensively at the congress on rational popular recreations organized by the Kharkov Literacy Society in the summer of 1915.[102] The people's theater movement culminated in the First All-Russian Congress of People's Theater Activists, which opened in Moscow at the end of 1915.[103]

In addition to the many articles that filled the pages of the press, "experts" like Ivan Shcheglov and Nikolai Popov produced a number of weighty volumes with detailed information on virtually every aspect of organizing theaters for the people, such as repertoire, decorations, costuming, stage design, and fire prevention measures.[104] Interest in the people's theater was widespread in the Russian theatrical world, and a great number of writers, directors, actors, and critics either participated in theoretical discussions or assisted efforts to bring theater to the people. By the turn of the century, the people's theater idea had been endorsed by many prominent Russian cultural figures, including Alexander Ostrovsky, Leo Tolstoy, Konstantin Stanislavsky, Vladimir Nemirovich-Danchenko, Anton Chekhov, Maxim Gorky, Ivan Shcheglov, and Evtikhii Karpov, as well as a number of important but now relatively obscure writers, theater professionals and educators.

Ivan Shcheglov, whose real name was Leontev, was easily the leading figure in the people's theater movement, publishing dozens of articles and four books on the subject until his death in 1911. A talented comic writer and close friend of Chekhov, Shcheglov became interested in popular theater performances while serving in the army, where he saw soldiers putting on plays and directed at least one performance. A moderate liberal, he took a fairly broad-minded view of people's theater, often emphasizing the value of pure entertainment. Because of his attention to popular audiences and what they actually liked, as opposed to what was supposedly good for them, his publications are among the best sources of information on popular audiences' reception of theater. Like most educated witnesses, however, he tended to idealize the people and had his own prejudices as to what cultural products they should prefer.[105]

Nikolai Popov, who was so outraged by the Skomorokh theater's commercialism, was typical of the high-minded Russian intellectuals who were determined to serve the people by bringing theater to them. A member of the merchant estate, he became involved as a young man in organizing performances and writing popular dramas for the workers at his uncle's textile factory in Ivanovo. A committed *Kulturträger*, he was filled with good intentions, but later confessed in his memoirs that he had been attempting to write about themes and people he knew nothing about.[106] He joined Stanislavsky's semi-professional drama circle in the 1890s and tried to apply Stanislavsky's ideas when he was appointed director of St. Petersburg's

Vasilevskii Island Theater for Workers in 1902. Whereas critics praised his productions of classics and new literary plays, audiences preferred the melodramas to which they were accustomed. As Popov himself admitted, "my first encounter in a real theater with mass popular spectators ended in failure."[107] Popov's inability to win the common people over to the Moscow Art Theater's brand of psychological realism led him to abandon his quest for the ideal popular audience, although he continued to write about people's theaters. Subsequently he became a director in Vera Komissarzhevskaia's St. Petersburg theater, and after the revolution worked in the Theatrical Department of the Commissariat of Enlightenment (TEO Narkompros).

The director, playwright, and people's theater activist Evtikhii Karpov had been exiled to Siberia as a young man for participating in the populist movement "to the people" in the 1870s. On his return from exile Karpov worked briefly as an actor in Yaroslavl, where he began writing dramas about the lives of workers and peasants. Some of these plays, which often reflected Karpov's populist convictions about industrial capitalism's negative effects on Russian society, were performed in not only in people's theaters but also in the imperial and commercial legitimate theaters. He was hired to direct plays at the Nevskii Society for the Organization of Popular Recreations in 1892, and went on to be a director in the Aleksandrinskii Theater, staging the first production of Chekhov's *Seagull* in 1896. Karpov was an influential member of several theatrical professional organizations who published two books on the educational significance of theater for workers and chaired the repertoire committee at the Congress of People's Theater Activists in 1915–16.[108]

Nikolai Bunakov, an outspoken liberal educator and the author of several textbooks for peasant children, became a tireless advocate of people's theaters through his experiences staging plays with the pupils at his rural school near Voronezh. He published extensively on the educational uses of theater for peasants and workers and contributed to the people's theater exhibit at the Fourth All-Russian Agricultural Exposition. After his death in 1904, his wife, L. I. Bunakova, continued to champion people's theater, reporting on the subject at the People's Theater Congress.[109] Another participant in the congress was Anatolii Kremlev, a justice of the peace and later a St. Petersburg barrister who worked with the Nevskii Society and authored a number of projects for people's theaters. Kremlev combined his legal career with acting on provincial stages, in addition to finding time to publish on the subject of theater and drama.[110] The director Aleksandr Briantsev took part in the performances of the Nevskii Society as a student, eventually joining Pavel Gaideburov's theater at Countess Panina's People's

House. After the revolution, he helped to organize the theatrical division of the Petrograd Institute of Continuing Education and was one of the founders of the Soviet Children's Theater.[111] Nikolai Timkovskii, a moderately successful playwright, worked on the catalog of the people's theater exhibit at the 1895 Agricultural Exposition, authored reports and articles on the use of "rational recreations" in raising labor productivity, and played a prominent role at the Congress of People's Theater Activists.

The philanthropist Countess Sofiia Panina created the theater most successful in systematically promoting a didactic, artistic repertoire for popular audiences at her People's House in St. Petersburg's plebeian Nevskii district. The Ligovskii People's House, as it was usually called, offered evening courses and readings to workers and contained a library, tearoom, cafeteria, and theater auditorium. Panina enlisted Pavel Gaideburov and his wife Nadezhda Skarskaia to form a troupe and direct the theater. Gaideburov, who had taken up acting after his expulsion from the university for his part in a student demonstration, met Skarskaia while acting in the provinces. Skarskaia, the sister of the renowned actress Vera Komissarzhevskaia, had worked for a time with the Moscow Art Theater, and she and Gaideburov tried to acquaint provincial audiences with that theater's repertoire and production techniques, without much success at the box office. With Panina's financial backing, they eschewed crowd-pleasers like melodrama and light comedy and set about making the Ligovskii Theater into a model people's theater, cultivating a working-class audience (many of whom were also students in Panina's evening courses) for Ostrovsky, Chekhov, Gorky, Shakespeare, and other recognized masters of the drama. In 1905 they began taking their Moscow Art Theater–influenced productions on the road, touring the provinces every summer. During World War I, with the People's House requisitioned as a hospital, Gaideburov staged performances for soldiers at the front.[112]

For all the support behind the people's theaters and the talk about their potential benefits, there was little accord on how they should be run. As the people's theaters began to multiply in large urban centers like St. Petersburg and Moscow, the debates over their nature and purpose became heated and even bitter. These debates centered around four issues. First, was the people's theater necessary at all? This was a political issue, pitting conservative guardians of moral and political orthodoxy against liberal and moderate *Kulturträger*. Second, was it primarily an artistic, educational, or recreational institution? Most people agreed that it was some combination of all three, yet almost everyone promoted one of these functions at the expense of the others. Third, whom should it serve? The answer, obviously, was that it should serve the people, but who were they? The latter two questions were closely linked to the fourth, most controversial issue, repertoire: What should the people see on the stage?

What is most striking about these debates is that virtually no one was willing to leave it to the people themselves to choose what sort of theater they preferred. Some felt that the people needed a special repertoire adapted to their supposed level of comprehension, others contended that people's theaters should cultivate their audiences by offering only classics and works of "literary merit," still others advocated melodrama as the genre most suitable for popular audiences. Even those people's theater advocates who rejected the notion of a special repertoire for the people were nonetheless quick to add that they should not be exposed to anything that was "inartistic" or "vulgar" or that "indulged their baser instincts."

DO THE PEOPLE NEED THEATER?

The question of whether the people really needed theater in the first place was usually raised by conservatives and members of the clergy, wary of what they perceived to be a liberal bid for the hearts and minds of the *narod*. The end of the nineteenth century was a time of growing social and political unrest, marked by strikes, student demonstrations, assassinations, and the establishment of underground political parties. Conservatives associated people's theaters with the contemporary assault on the status quo. The reactionary *Moscow Gazette* waged a veritable war on people's theaters, claiming that they would only be used by "perfidious intellectuals" to corrupt the people, and even equating factory theaters with socialism![113] The *narod*, who in the view of the *Moscow Gazette* were still unblemished by the political aspirations of the educated classes, desired only the Church to satisfy their spiritual needs and would reject "any morality that the populists want to give them in tendentious lectures and theater [performances]."[114] A provincial landowner, commenting on performances of Ostrovsky's historical drama *Vasilisa Melenteva* for factory workers in Kostroma, was convinced that such spectacles would cause "the thorns of free-thinking, discontent, and a critical opinion of everything that Russia lives by" to germinate in the minds of the people, and called on the authorities to put a stop to them before it was too late.[115]

Some critics, while acknowledging that theater might have the potential to exert a benign influence on popular morals, contended that the contemporary theater was in such a state of decline that it was more likely to corrupt them.[116] Their comments were often permeated with chauvinism, xenophobia, and anti-Semitism, reflecting a widespread conviction among conservatives (including Nicholas II himself) that the Russian people were by nature loyal to the tsar and alien to foreign ideas like liberalism and socialism. In 1896 the conservative *Russian Herald* complained that the people's theater was becoming an obsession among journalists "'of a progressive mentality,'" and argued that the tavern would do the common people less harm than would introducing them to the theater of the intelligentsia, which was permeated with sex, adultery, socialism, anarchism, and Jewish influences.[117] Another opponent, objecting to a project before the Moscow city government for a municipal network of ten people's theaters, warned they would expose the people to baneful Western influences and undermine "patriarchal family relations."[118]

Prominent clergymen joined in attacking people's theaters. The Church historically had taken a hostile stance toward secular theater, which it viewed as a competitor of pagan origins.[119] In the eyes of some church leaders, theater was a foreign import that had already led the intelligentsia astray and undermined its religious faith; to expose the common people to its pernicious influence would be sheer folly. Bishop Aleksandr of Mozhaisk, author of numerous articles deploring the moral decadence of Russian society in the 1870s and 1880s, identified people's theaters with social degeneracy, charging that they would lure factory workers away from the Church and further corrupt their spirits, which were already becoming tainted with the values of "crude urban civilization."[120] What seems to have most aroused the clergy's ire was that popular performances were invariably organized on Sundays and holidays, when the working classes were free to attend them. Although a few clerics eventually came to sympathize with the educational goals of the people's theaters,[121] most priests continued to see them as an enemy to be fought tooth and nail from the pulpit and in the press.[122]

Other opponents of the people's theaters were more sophisticated and centered their reservations on whether it was appropriate for the intelligentsia to impose its aesthetic tastes on the common people. "The common people are neither a *tabula rasa* nor a green youth, for whom all of life's impressions are new," observed K. Medvedskii in a review of Ivan Shcheglov's *The People's Theater in Sketches and Portraits*. The people, he cautioned, had their own culture and were "enlightened in their own way." Even if the urban popular classes had lost touch with the traditional culture of the village, they still had their distinctive tastes and were interested in entertainment, not lessons. If they wanted theaters, they should be allowed to create them for themselves; when they did so, the intelligentsia should respond to their initiative by offering assistance.[123] In the same vein, another journalist proposed that instead of giving the common people theaters for which they were not "culturally prepared," traditional popular recreations such as music and dancing should be encouraged, for the only truly rational recreations were those rooted in national traditions. The *narod*, he added, had nothing in common with Shakespeare's characters and could not empathize with them.[124]

In the minds of the supporters of people's theater, the clergy's criticisms carried little weight, while arguments to the effect that the intelligentsia should not force its cultural values on the people were so rare as to go unnoticed. Nikolai Bunakov argued there were no Biblical prohibitions against such entertainments, while the theater historian and critic Ivan Inozemtsev noted that a number of priests and bishops supported the temperance societies' efforts to organize performances for the common people.[125] Responding to the *Moscow Gazette's* campaign against the people's theaters, Ivan Shcheglov swept aside the objection that they would corrupt audiences, pointing to the special censorship policy in force for popular theaters. He also sarcastically dismissed fears that people's theaters would contribute to the disappearance of "patriarchal mores," observing that "on the eve of the twentieth century it would be more prudent to be silent about that."[126]

ENTERTAINMENT OR ENLIGHTENMENT?

Disputes about what the people's theaters were to accomplish were less easy to resolve and continued to hound nearly every discussion of the issue for years to come. V. Stepanov, a contributor to *People's Theater*, the collection of articles published in conjunction with the people's theater exhibit at the 1895 agricultural exposition, was convinced that the primary mission of the people's theater should be "instruction," since the force of the impressions it produced on audiences made it "the most powerful means for bringing this or that idea to the people." Until universal literacy had been achieved, theaters for the common people should devote their efforts to education rather than art. An actor echoed this view at the First All-Russian Congress of Theater People: "For the uneducated spectator, theater is a school that teaches him to understand life, awakens his best instincts, and ennobles his soul. Theater in this form, i.e., a theater-school, is a matter of state importance."[127]

Most partisans of the people's theater, however, wanted it to be more than an adjunct to the classroom; they also hoped it would further the development of an appreciation for art among the common people. Both Ivan Bunakov and Nikolai Popov argued in their contributions to the *People's Theater* collection that theater should not preach to the people or ply them with moralistic lessons but should offer them a better quality of entertainment than that to which they were accustomed in the *balagany*. Drama critic Ivan Inozemtsev, remarking on the widespread tendency to assign educational tasks to the people's theaters, warned that "the fundamental aim of theater should never be forgotten, and that aim is to satisfy the aesthetic sense that is in every person." His view was shared by Evtikhii Karpov, who told an interviewer in 1899 that the people's theaters should provide the people with nourishment for the mind "in an entire series of truly artistic works, rather than in a dry didactic form." Karpov was confident that once the people had access to a broad, "artistic repertoire," they themselves would be able to "discern the good from the bad" and would prefer aesthetic entertainment. D. L. Talnikov, later to become a leading Soviet theater specialist, reiterated this point in 1916, rejecting didacticism in favor of inculcating in the common people an "aesthetic culture" that would awaken in them a sense of "human solidarity."[128] Those who emphasized entertainment nonetheless ascribed a didactic function to the people's theaters: they merely wanted the lesson to be aesthetic.

WHAT IS A POPULAR AUDIENCE?

The confusion over what the goals of the people's theaters should be was in large part due to a lack of agreement as to whose needs they were supposed to meet. The Nevskii Society and other groups of manufacturers created their theaters for local factory workers. The urban Guardianships of Popular Temperance intended their theatrical entertainments mainly, though not exclusively, for the urban lower classes, who were ostensibly most inclined to drink excessively. Indeed, since the origin of the idea in the 1860s, it had generally been agreed that the people's theaters in St. Petersburg and Moscow would serve the *narod*. Nonetheless, once the theaters actually began to appear, some critics were dismayed to find that they were filled not with long-bearded peasants, fresh from the village and wearing bast shoes, but with a wide cross-section of urban society. The definition of the *narod* was called into question, as the press debated the identity of the people whom the people's theaters were to serve.

In 1898, for example, the liberal daily *Stock-Exchange News* excoriated the St. Petersburg Temperance Guardianship because its theaters were not attracting peasants, who were the real Russian people, but factory workers and artisans, "that element cut off from the *narod*, in whom are monstrously combined the crudeness of the muzhik, the habits of the idle townsman, and the vices of the street."[129] In the same vein, a journalist for *The Petersburg Gazette* wrote that the people's theaters should focus their energies not on semi-skilled workers and shop assistants but on the "the masses that are entirely uneducated and untouched by any kind of culture." A shop assistant, he believed, would rather listen to "French music-hall songs that he cannot understand" than watch a play in a people's theater.[130]

At the opposite extreme from those who wished to exclude all but genuine peasants both from the ranks of the *narod* and from the halls of the people's theaters were those who welcomed the blurring of social boundaries, as Russians from all classes came together in one audience. Following a visit to the Vasilevskii Island Theater, one observer approvingly reported that it was filled with "the poorest part of the intelligentsia," which he identified as "shop clerks, milliners, petty officials, and the like," who enjoyed the performances no less than did the factory workers. Affordable theater was needed not only by the common people, he pointed out, but also by this "petty intelligentsia," and he suggested that the "people's theaters" (*narodnye teatry*) should be transformed into "accessible theaters" (*obshchedostupnye teatry*), which would present "truly artistic works" rather than a "special people's repertoire."[131]

A critic for *The New Times* pointed out that the conditions of urban life made it impossible to draw a clear distinction between people's theaters and accessible theaters or "to separate some class of society or people, put it aside, and talk only about its welfare." Large numbers of urban Russians needed affordable theater, not only the common people, and the people's theaters should serve everyone: "If it is still possible to recognize in theory the existence of a special, ignorant class of common folk, even in the big cities, there is still no reason why these common folk, some illiterate muzhik or semi-literate cabby, should enjoy theaters that are denied to people who are superior in their education, but live in the same material conditions." Ivan Shcheglov, however, felt strongly that it was desirable to maintain a firm distinction between people's theaters and those attended by the intelligentsia, at least until "true education levels the classes and the difference between the intelligentsia and the people ceases to exist."[132]

Ivan Inozemtsev shrewdly observed that the *narod* should not be considered a distinctly separate group from other classes because urbanization had broken down the old social categories. Commenting on the fact that many middle-class people attended the performances organized by the St. Petersburg Temperance Guardianship, he dismissed the very possibility of defining where the *narod* ended and the intelligentsia began in big cities. The urban population was a diverse lot and would not fit into neat binary categories:

> It is in the countryside that you can more or less set some sort of bound-ary: the teacher, the priest, the district police chief—these are the *intelligenty*, separated almost by a chasm from the illiterate common people, and even between them there can be intermediate steps such as landlords who have turned muzhik and better-educated peasants.
>
> In urban life these intermediate steps occupy the whole ladder be-tween the highest educated society and the common people. The transi-tions are imperceptible from the worker to the shop assistant and the lower-level technician, then to the clerk, the petty official and so on. The same is true with regard to the female sex. The woman factory worker imperceptibly merges with the domestic servant, who at the upper end merges with the seamstresses, who in turn merge with the wives of petty officials. In a word, no boundaries are possible, and comparative cultivation cannot be determined by attire.

In the long term, Inozemtsev predicted, there would evolve "a true people's theater . . . which all of the people will attend, without that division into two groups, '*intelligenty*' and '*narod*,' which has already cost Russia enough." He hoped that the people's theater would facilitate the cultural unification of Russian society and the transcendence of the barrier, originating in serf-dom, between the educated elite and the common people.[133]

THE REPERTOIRE QUESTION

The diverse conceptions of both the purposes of the people's theaters and their intended audiences were reflected in endless arguments over reper-toire. "If on other questions some differences of opinion exist in the press," wrote Shcheglov in 1892, "a kind of inconceivable muddle prevails on the question of a popular repertoire."[134] The debate over what the people should see in the theater resembled contemporary discussions of what they should read. In both cases, it was widely agreed that the people could and would appreciate works of artistic or literary merit, if only they were given access to these works before their tastes were corrupted by trashy commercial fare. Just as the publishers of inexpensive editions of "good" books aimed to win the common people away from chapbooks, many of the proponents of the people's theater hoped that these theaters would replace the fairground the-aters by fostering in the common people a love for "genuine art."[135]

The discussions surrounding the repertoire question were complicated by the multitude of functions that were assigned to the people's theater. If it were to be a school, then plays should be judged by their instructiveness. If it were to be a means of acquainting the people with the culture of the intelligentsia and thereby fostering cultural unity, then only plays of "artistic value" would be suitable. If, however, theater was merely a "rational recreation" and an alternative to the tavern, then it was most important that the plays be interesting and attract audiences, although even the most broad-minded commentators urged the exclusion of works that would supposedly encourage the people's "baser instincts."

The first systematic attempt to set guidelines for repertoire was made by the St. Petersburg Literacy Committee, in its 1870 report calling for the establishment of a people's theater in the capital. Even though the report stated that the theater's main goal should be not to educate but to draw customers away from the taverns, its authors' comments on the repertoire question indicate that they had more in mind than simply entertaining the people. The repertoires of the existing fairground theaters were rejected out of hand, and the report recommended "the repertoire of our theater [i.e., those theaters patronized by the intelligentsia]—with the exclusion of all that is not suitable for the people." What was "not suitable for the people" was never specified. Judging from the authors' expressed hope that the people's theaters would stimulate the existing theaters to "Russify" their repertoires and stage more plays of "moral and human value," the plays to be excluded were those "mediocre and sometimes immoral foreign operettas and shameless translations" that were attracting even educated audiences to the detriment of classic Russian works, a state of affairs the report blamed on "the market."[136] In short, the repertoire of the people's theaters was to entertain, but in an edifying way, and with preference given to works of Russian origin. Appended to the report was a list of 126 recommended works, most of which were historical dramas and plays "from Russian life," although a few operas and translations were also included.[137]

Other catalogs followed, joining those that the censorship office began publishing in 1891 to list the plays it had approved for the popular stage. The educator Viktor Ostrogorskii reprinted the Literacy Committee's recommended repertoire in an 1892 article on the people's theater.[138] Two years later the director Iurii Ozarovskii compiled his own "systematic catalog," a list that was heavily influenced by the work of the Literacy Committee, although it discarded some of the patriotic historical dramas that dated from the reign of Nicholas I, and added a number of works by Ostrovsky, Pushkin, Gogol, Shakespeare, and Molière.[139] Ozarovskii wanted the people to see only plays that had undisputed literary merits, and, in an outburst reflecting the commonly held view of Slavophiles and populists that the purity of the Russian people was endangered by foreign contamination, he condemned the inclusion of imported melodramas in the people's theater repertoire. The people's theater exhibit at the 1895 agricultural exposition featured a catalog of plays available in popularly priced editions, although the organizing committee refused to endorse them, citing the need for further study of the repertoire question.[140] Anatolii Kremlev included only classics in the model repertoire he presented to the St. Petersburg city duma in 1896.[141] In 1905, at the request of the Finance Ministry, Ivan Shcheglov drew up a list of one hundred plays that he recommended for staging before popular audiences; the ministry then published the list as a brochure and sent copies to local Guardianships of Popular Temperance throughout the empire.[142] Shcheglov, a firm advocate of melodramas and vaudevilles as well as the classics, though not of opera or operetta, published yet another catalog in 1911, this time with two hundred works, a few of which were in Ukrainian.[143]

In addition to compiling catalogs, the supporters of theaters for the people also disputed the repertoire issue in private and in the press, in arguments that were as muddled as they were numerous. Disagreements centered on whether the people needed a repertoire specially adapted for them ("dumbed down," as we would say today), or whether they could be exposed to any plays that were worthy of seeing. In a letter to Nemirovich-Danchenko in 1903, Chekhov, referring to Gorky's work in founding a people's theater in Nizhnii Novgorod, criticized special literature and plays for the people, telling him, "You must not lower Gogol to the people, but raise the people to the level of Gogol."[144] Nikolai Timkovskii, linking his hopes for the reform of the Russian stage to the emergence of a new audience, argued that popular spectators were better able to appreciate good plays than was the intelligentsia, because the people felt the emotions they evoked more strongly and were less concerned with the performances of individual actors.[145]

Leo Tolstoy, an ardent advocate of the didactic people's theater, displayed a more contradictory attitude toward the repertoire question. Discussing with an actor the upcoming production of his *The Power of Darkness* at the Skomorokh in 1895, he suggested that the theater stage Shakespeare: "Perhaps you think the common people will not understand Shakespeare. You needn't fear. They are more likely not to understand a contemporary play in an alien setting, but they will understand Shakespeare. The people will understand all that is truly great."[146] Nine years earlier, however, Tolstoy had advised P. A. Denisenko, actor-manager of the Vasilevskii Island Theater for Workers, that he should adapt and simplify plays so that they could be understood "by all those audiences who go to the fairground theaters."[147] And despite his professed conviction that the common people would understand "all that is truly great," Tolstoy's own plays for popular audiences were moralistic in tone and written in a pseudo-folk language. Two, *The First Distiller* (1886) and *The Cause of It All* (1910), warn of the dangers of alcohol consumption, while the third, *The Power of Darkness* (1886), is a gripping portrayal of the consequences of adultery in a peasant milieu.

Tolstoy was not alone in oscillating between the poles of art and edification. V. Stepanov, who felt that the people's theater should be first and foremost an educational institution, advocated "a repertoire adapted for the 'simple folk,' that is, for spectators who have little or no education and are unprepared [for theater]"; it should be made up exclusively of plays that would raise the people's "intellectual and moral level." He especially recommended melodramas (so long as the moral was clear) and historical plays. Translations of foreign classics, like Molière's *The Miser*, were also acceptable, providing the characters and situations were Russified. Stepanov was against plays about everyday life, which he feared the people would misinterpret: "A play about everyday life can be good for the people only if it illuminates some dark side of life, throwing into relief all of its ugliness, mocking superstition, exposing the people's 'benightedness,' that is, when it is 'tendentious.' There must be some idea that stands out in the play and provokes no misunderstandings, and that does not confuse the people's views, which are muddled enough already."

Despite its anti-alcohol message, Tolstoy's *The First Distiller* was rejected by Stepanov, for it contained a scene in which the devil appeared and might encourage the people to believe in demons. Molière's *Georges Dandin* could give the masses the idea that wives should rule their husbands, while Gogol's *Marriage* and *The Government Inspector* were unsuitable because "pointing out that there are people who find it difficult to marry, and that officials used to take bribes, will add very little to the intellectual or moral capital of the common people." Nor should it be taken into account whether audiences liked the plays—the only thing that mattered was whether they had the desired impact. Having laid down his criteria for selecting a popular repertoire, which were stricter than those of any censor, Stepanov concluded by adding yet another condition: "the ideal play should be both artistic and beneficial to the people."[148]

The educator Nikolai Bunakov claimed to take a broader, more tolerant approach to the repertoire issue and gave entertainment priority over edification. In his opinion, the people's theater should "give the people just what they like, and not force on them only what we consider to be wholesome and instructive for them; the business of softening mores through theater will take care of itself."[149] Bunakov, however, hardly took a laissez-faire attitude toward repertoire. In his "Reflections on the People's Theater Exhibit Organized in Moscow in 1895," he complained that even the theaters patronized by the intelligentsia had forgotten their "civic and educational significance," forsaking the classic works of Gogol, Ostrovsky, Shakespeare, and Molière for *poshlost'* (vulgarity), as he described Offenbach's *La Belle Hélène*, Puccini's *La Bohème*, and Bizet's *Carmen*.[150] Bunakov's comments reveal a fundamental dilemma for the would-be arbitrators of popular repertoire: How does one define a canon for the common people when even the "best" theaters seem to have gone off the track?

One answer was to renounce the vagaries of contemporary tastes and retreat behind the walls of the tried-and-true classics. Andrei Kremlev took this approach in the comprehensive plan for a people's theater that he submitted to the St. Petersburg duma in 1896: "Theater should serve neither recreation, nor entertainment, nor sport, nor edification. It should serve art." Art meant the classics; anything else was merely "debauchery and perversion." Melodramas, patriotic plays, ballets, fantasy extravaganzas, operettas, farces, and *tableaux vivants* were all to be barred from "the stage of a serious temple of art."[151]

The state's censorship policy was often blamed for keeping good plays off the popular stage while permitting plays of little or no artistic value, but many *Kulturträger* were no less severe in their judgments of what the people should see on the stage. Nikolai Popov, discussing in his memoirs the limitations that censorship imposed on popular theater repertoires, observed that "the most terrible censors of all, however, were those who worked most zealously to make the people's theaters flourish."[152] But Popov himself was not immune to this censorious attitude. In his report on "The Organization of Recreation for Workers," presented to the Second Congress of Activists in Technical and Professional Education in 1895, he criticized St. Petersburg's Vasilevskii Island Theater for Workers, which was self-financing, for being *too* responsive to its audiences' tastes:

> The distinctive characteristic of the Vasilevskii Island Theater is its repertoire, which depends on an audience that is not overly fond of plays from everyday life, preferring melodrama instead. It is only with great difficulty that the director manages to insert even Ostrovsky's plays into the repertoire. Financially dependent on its audiences, the Vasilevskii Island Theater is forced to accommodate their tastes, and that is its main defect. . . . If it depended less on the audiences that attend it, then it might serve as a model for other people's theaters.[153]

Figure 4. Stage of the Vasilevskii Island Theater for Workers. The curtain, which depicts an idyllic village scene, is emblazoned with the motto, "Learning is light, ignorance is darkness." St. Petersburg, 1898. *Niva*, no. 35 (29 August 1898): 692.

The great advantage of the performances funded by the Nevskii Society, he added bluntly, was that in his view the repertoire did not reflect the tastes of the audiences.[154]

WHAT DID THE PEOPLE WANT FROM THE THEATER?

Although comments like these, along with the various repertoire catalogs, may say a great deal about the tastes and opinions of their authors, they unfortunately reveal almost nothing about how popular audiences received the plays that their intellectual "betters" had determined were good for them. There were a few voices in the wilderness that called for more attention to be paid to what the people themselves wanted to see. The tendency to view the people as passive and childlike consumers of the cultural and intellectual nourishment fed them by the intelligentsia was repudiated by Aleksandr Kugel, for instance, who mocked what he described as "the populist approach to repertoire." The "populists," he suggested, would do well to devote less time to philosophical debates and pay more attention to audience preferences, as did commercial theaters: "The most mediocre commercial enterprise, with a repertoire intended for the unlearned audience, will be more capable of attracting the common people than the 'people's' theaters and 'accessible' theaters, because the entrepreneur does not bandy clever sophistries about, but judges by cash receipts, and the receipts are a reliable indicator of the tastes and interests of the popular spectator."[155]

Still, Kugel was hardly in favor of leaving the repertoire question to be decided by either popular tastes or the market. He had editorialized against the spread of commercial popular theaters like the *balagany*, warning that even though their visually exciting but "unworthy and superficial" shows appealed to the tastes of the common people, they were not in keeping with the pedagogical goals of the people's theater.[156]

Ivan Shcheglov was also critical of the intelligentsia's cultural paternalism, even if he was disappointed when he saw popular audiences enjoying risqué operettas along with Gogol at the Skomorokh Theater. He blamed the confusion over repertoire on "all that deadening pedagogical routine, the pedagogues' pusillanimous failure to decide to break out of . . . the outmoded moralistic-social framework and ill-starred pretension to teach from above, without the least consideration for what is desired from below."[157] To Popov and other would-be arbitrators of popular taste, Shcheglov recommended a trip to the fairground shows, which he idealized as an expression of native Russian entertainment: "If Mr. Popov visited the Easter *balagany* on Semenovskii Parade Ground, then he would see for himself what plays enjoy the greatest success among the people."[158]

By the turn of the century, however, the *balagan* theaters that had flourished for decades on the Shrovetide and Easter fairgrounds were on the verge of extinction, and they disappeared entirely before World War I. Their place was taken by factory theaters, temperance theaters, and workers' amateur theaters, in competition with an ever-expanding entertainment market of commercial theaters, cinemas, and miniature (or "street") theaters offering a mixture of film, variety shows, and comic skits. These theaters, seldom able to live up to the lofty ideals of the people's theater activists, were often vilified in the press for corrupting audiences and continually hampered by censorship restrictions. Yet they did attempt to satisfy the popular demand for entertainment with a surprisingly broad repertoire and, especially in the case of the temperance theaters, were very successful in doing so.

. . .

The idea of a people's theater grew out of the rising civic consciousness that accompanied Russia's Great Reforms. The people's theater movement was closely linked to nascent civil society's aspirations to play a role in the mental and moral improvement of the common people and to contest the limits the autocracy placed on public initiative regarding social and cultural issues. At the same time, people's theaters were seen as a means to foster cultural unity by introducing the *narod* to the best works of Russian drama so that they could take part in a common national culture, even if only as consumers. These theaters also had another aim, one with which at least a few state officials sympathized, that of "rational recreations" designed to supplant those popular entertainments deemed vulgar and dissolute by the respectable middle classes: the fairground theatricals and the taverns. Akin to Western European middle-class reform movements, the Russian people's theater movement was in part an attempt by educated society, fearful of social degeneration, to civilize and discipline the common people.[159]

When the autocracy rescinded the imperial theater monopoly in 1882, there were hopes that at last the way was open for a surge of public initiative to bring to life the ideal of a theater for the lower classes of St. Petersburg and Moscow. The first attempt to establish a permanent people's theater, however, the Skomorokh, proved disappointing despite its success with audiences, for it threatened to introduce the *narod* to the corrupting influence of the urban mass entertainment culture that the people's theaters were supposed to oppose. When people's theaters began to appear on a large scale, it was due to the efforts of pragmatic industrialists and temperance societies who saw them as a useful weapon in their fight against working-class moral degeneration and drunkenness. The growth of people's theaters was accompanied by constant debates over whether the people's theaters were staging the right plays and over the identity of the people they should be serving, debates that often posited an ideal repertoire and a metaphysical conception of a pure Russian *narod*, ignorant but eager to dine at the table of elite culture.

Three common threads ran through the discussions about the right kind of the people's theater. First, it had to be didactic, whether in the service of popular education, morality, or art appreciation. Second, repertoire was too important to be left up to commercial considerations; the people needed to see the "right" plays, even if there was no consensus as to what these were. Third, no one thought it appropriate simply to let the common people decide what they preferred to see in the theater—they had to be guided in their choices, lest they fall prey to the sirens of commercial culture.

Published discussions about the people's theater illuminate much about the cultural visions and hopes of educated Russians but less about the dynamics of interaction between the theaters and their audiences. To understand what happened when the *narod* went to the theater, it is necessary to examine the censorship constraints under which the people's theaters operated, the kinds of entertainments offered to the people, where and by whom, and audiences' reactions to what they saw.

3   Censorship and Repertoire

The hand of the state, in the guise of censorship, weighed heavily on the arts in Russia, and most heavily on popular theater. Art and politics were closely linked in the minds of tsarist officials, who as a result were suspicious of any initiative to bring secular art to the masses. If theater might combat drunkenness and civilize the common people, might it not also expose them to dangerous notions with unpredictable consequences? Although all writing was subject to preliminary censorship before publication or performance, only works destined for the popular stage had to undergo special scrutiny to determine whether they were suitable for popular audiences. Like the proponents of the people's theater, the state was convinced that the common people were especially susceptible to visual impressions, and it took extra care to control the content of what they saw in the theater.

The state's anxiety about the theater's potentially subversive impact on the common people was a major factor in its resistance before the 1880s to calls to lift the monopoly of imperial theaters.[1] After the monopoly was lifted in 1882, the state was faced with the problem of regulating the repertoires of the people's theaters that began to appear: the Skomorokh Theater (Moscow, 1882), the theater of the Nevskii Society for the Organization of Popular Recreations (St. Petersburg, 1885), the Vasilevskii Island Theater for Workers (St. Petersburg, 1887). Konstantin Pobedonostsev, the procurator of the Holy Synod and a notorious reactionary who was one of Alexander III's chief advisers, sounded the alarm. In 1887 he warned Minister of Internal Affairs Dmitrii Tolstoi that the Skomorokh was "catering to the bad taste and sensual instincts of the crowd and thus having a harmful influence on the morals of the poor" and was even intending to stage Leo Tolstoy's controversial drama *The Power of Darkness*.[2]

Tolstoi drew up a plan for a special censorship policy applying to works performed on the popular stage, which he submitted to Alexander III in early 1888. Noting with trepidation the recent proliferation of popular theaters, he echoed Pobedonostsev's claim that they were staging plays that had the potential to corrupt the common people. Although the censors had already approved the performance of most of the plays in question, the minister now questioned whether they were suitable for mass consumption:

> In examining plays the censor has in view the more or less educated
> public that attends theater performances, but not exclusively any one
> social class. Due to his level of mental development, his outlooks and
> conceptions, the common man will often interpret in an utterly wrong
> sense something that would present no temptation for a somewhat edu-
> cated person, and thus a play containing nothing blameworthy from a
> general point of view may be unsuitable and even harmful for him.
> Since the theater unquestionably has an important educational signifi-
> cance, it would seem necessary to ensure that the people receive from it
> sober and beneficial impressions and nothing that would promote their
> moral corruption.[3]

In other words, what was good for educated society was not necessarily good for the people, and it was the state's duty to protect them from a diet they were not equipped to digest. Theater censorship would have to be adjusted to take account of the cultural and educational differences separating the educated public from the *narod*.

Tolstoi proposed the enactment of a "temporary measure" requiring theaters attended mainly by the common people to perform only plays that had been specifically approved for popular audiences, regardless of whether the work had already been approved for other theaters. He noted that the new policy would be difficult to enforce, however, because theater owners could potentially avoid the restrictions on popular repertoire "by not calling their theaters 'popular' [*narodnyi*] and by establishing them as if on a general basis." Moscow's Skomorokh Theater, for instance, was oriented to popular audiences but bore the designation "accessible" (*obshchedostupnyi*) rather than "popular." To ensure against circumvention of the popular theater censorship, Tolstoi suggested that seat prices be considered in determining whether to classify a theater as "popular" and thereby subject to special restrictions on its repertoire, leaving it up to local officials to determine whether prices were low enough to make a theater "popular."[4] He drew no distinction between purely commercial popular theaters and the didactic people's theaters; from the state's perspective, the issue was the nature of the audience, not the aims of the theater. Tolstoi failed to define the criteria censors would apply in judging plays destined for popular audiences, confining himself instead to ominous but vague warnings about the potential danger theater posed to the people's morals. The tsar approved his proposal, and in February 1888 the office responsible for censorship, the Main Administration for Press Affairs, sent out a circular announcing the creation of a special censorship for popular theaters.[5] This "temporary measure" remained in effect until the fall of the Old Regime in 1917.

Any consideration of how tsarist censorship shaped Russia's popular theater repertoire raises several fundamental questions. What guided the censors in determining what could or could not be staged before popular audiences? How did these criteria differ from those applied to ordinary theaters? What image of the common people did the censors conjure in making their decisions? Was the censorship policy effective in preventing forbidden plays from reaching the popular stage? Did censorship in fact impose virtually unbearable restrictions on the popular theater repertoire and thereby seriously handicap the people's theaters in their mission of popular enlightenment, as many contemporaries (and later, Soviet theater historians) argued? What were the popular theaters allowed to perform?

The main source of information on popular theater censorship as a bureaucratic institution is the files of the Main Administration for Press Affairs, which contain memoranda, correspondence, circulars, reports on plays, and other evidence reflecting the viewpoint of the state.[6] The files not only shed light on the censorship process; they also illuminate the failures of censorship policy and suggest that policy was not always translated into practice. Still, the censorship files do not tell the whole story and must be supplemented with evidence about actual performances and repertoires in the popular theaters.

CENSORSHIP IN RUSSIA

Like most European states in the nineteenth century, Russia subjected theatrical works to preliminary censorship before permitting them to be staged.[7] Censorship of published literature and theater performances had existed in various guises since the eighteenth century, but there were different levels of censorship, depending on the potential audience for the work under consideration. Foreign-language works, for example, could be available to high officials on a "need-to-know" basis or to the general public on request, in unlimited circulation, or in inexpensive mass editions. To restrict their accessibility, foreign works were sometimes approved in the original language but banned in Russian translation.[8] Works in Russian were subject to the same graduated censorship policy.[9] Under the 1865 Statute on Censorship and the Press, for example, only scholarly works or periodicals with an annual subscription cost of at least seven rubles could engage in even limited social and political criticism.[10] Plays were subject to two levels of censorship, depending on whether they were to be published or performed, and theater performances were censored more strictly than publications because they were public events and comprehensible to more people.

Censorship in nineteenth-century Russia was strongly influenced by the government's fear that the common people might become infected by the ideas debated among the intelligentsia. Serfdom and censorship were closely linked in Nicholas I's mind, as Bruce Lincoln has argued, for the tsar believed that "any discussion of Russia's problems which reached the ears of the masses might spark another peasant revolt, like the Pugachev uprising."[11] Particularly worrisome from the authorities' standpoint was the circulation of chapbooks and cheap prints among the peasants and working classes, which expanded steadily throughout the nineteenth century. The government's attitude toward the spread of secular ideas among the masses was one of wariness, if not outright hostility. When Minister of Education Count Sergei Uvarov asked the censors in 1834 whether it was desirable to allow cheap popular literature similar to Britain's penny press to develop in Russia, they responded that the influence of secular literature was incompatible with the existing order in Russia, an opinion with which the tsar completely agreed. Near the end of Nicholas's reign the Ministry of Education decreed that only works of a religious nature could be published for a mass popular readership. The cheap popular prints known as *lubki* were subjected to censorship in 1839, and in 1851 all previously uncensored woodblocks and plates were ordered destroyed. Religious leaders were also disturbed by the growth of secular literature and often warned of its bad influence on the people.[12]

If during the era of Great Reforms that followed Nicholas's death the government became more willing to tolerate some public discussion of social and political questions, its fears of the negative effects these discussions could have on the masses did not diminish. The policy of *glasnost'* might be permissible within educated society, but it did not extend to the unlearned millions. In 1865 there was a proposal to create a special censorship to monitor materials published for the young and the common people. Alexander II favored the idea, but it was discarded as impractical for so large a country. A similar proposal was considered in 1899 and rejected for the same reason. Other efforts to place restrictions on the literature accessible to the masses were more successful. In 1864 the Holy Synod and the Ministry of Education began issuing lists of works approved for primary school libraries, and in 1869 the Ministry of Education decreed that henceforth only works that it had approved could be read aloud to popular audiences. This policy of distinguishing between what the people could read and what could be read to them continued until 1906, although by then the spectrum of approved works had widened considerably. Although published popular literature was never made a separate censorship category, the censors were advised in 1872 to be extra vigilant in examining cheap publications.[13]

The censorship process was reorganized in 1865, when the Main Administration for Press Affairs, attached to the Ministry of Internal Affairs, was created to censor texts for both publication and performance. Under the new rules, authors, translators, directors, and theater owners who wished to stage a work had to submit two copies of it to the Press Administration. The censors could approve for performance plays they deemed inoffensive merely by placing an official seal on the submitted text. When the censors considered it necessary to ban or make cuts in a play, or when the censors were uncertain whether the play was permissible, they sent a report explaining their opinions to the head of the administration, who made the final decision. Plays judged acceptable for the stage were entered on a list published in *The Government Herald,* which indicated the particular edition so approved. The government periodically issued booklets listing the plays approved for performance.[14]

The 1865 statute on censorship allowed any theater to stage a play once it had been "unconditionally approved for the stage." If a play was "approved with excisions" (meaning that the censors had required the deletion of portions of the text), theaters were allowed to perform only the corrected text bearing the censor's seal. Enforcement of the censorship regulations was left entirely to the local authorities, who were supposed to verify that all plays performed in the area under their jurisdiction were either on the official list of unconditionally approved plays or, if the play was approved with excisions, that the script to be used bore the censor's seal of authorization for the stage.

In making their decisions the censors were guided by a welter of laws, circulars, and instructions, some of which were never made public. Soviet theater historian Sergei Danilov aptly described the dramatic censorship regulations as "a total legislative chaos."[15] The fundamental text governing the censorship of both the press and the theater was the 1865 Statute on Censorship and the Press, according to which the censors were "to prohibit offense to the respect due to the teachings and rituals of Christian faiths, protect the inviolability of the Supreme Authority and its attributes, respect for members of the reigning house, the steadfastness of the basic laws, popular morality, honor, and the domestic life of each person." Works expounding "the harmful teachings of socialism and communism, which lead to the undermining or overthrow of the existing order and to the introduction of anarchy," were also strictly prohibited, as were those which "arouse the enmity and hatred of one class [*soslovie*] toward another" or "offensively ridicule entire classes or officials in the state or public service." In examining works dealing with history or politics, the censors were to make sure that they contained "nothing offensive to the Russian government nor to those governments friendly to Russia."[16]

The guidelines contained in the censorship statute applied equally to the press, scientific works, literature, drama, and opera. Before a work could be performed on the stage, however, it had to be specially approved by the separate theater censorship division of the Main Administration for Press Affairs, even if it had already been approved for publication. Performances were a source of special concern for two reasons. First, they were potentially accessible to a much larger audience, including illiterates, than were publications; they could thus disseminate ideas beyond the confines of the educated circles that followed the debates of the "thick journals" and influence people who might not have been exposed to them otherwise. From the viewpoint of an autocracy convinced that ideas suitable for discussion in educated society must be prevented from reaching the eyes and ears of the common people, the theater—and especially the popular theater—constituted a potentially dangerous adversary that had to be kept under firm control. Second, the process of transforming the printed word into living speech, the very essence of the theatrical art, was imbued with danger, for who could predict what effect words might have when uttered with gestures and intonations by actors in costumes and makeup, before a public able to express its reactions audibly and even demonstratively? In an effort to minimize the impact of ideas and representations deemed undesirable, the state subjected the theater to controls that were more stringent than were those applying only to publications. These special restraints on the theater were not elaborated in the censorship statute but were rather the product of various circulars, directives, and informal instructions that were issued on an ongoing basis by the Press Administration in response to the policy needs of the moment. For example, theaters were forbidden to stage works depicting members of the clergy or the Romanov dynasty, but there is no mention of this prohibition in the censorship statute.

CENSORSHIP AND POPULAR THEATER

Government policy toward what could or could not be performed in popular theaters was never set down in law. The 1888 edict provided for the separate scrutiny of all works performed in popular theaters but did not specify any of the criteria censors were to use. To understand how the censors determined what was unsuitable, suitable, or desirable for the people to see on the stage, one must rely on official memoranda and the censors' own reports on the plays they reviewed.

The first case of popular theater censorship was in 1872, when the censors were instructed to review the repertoire of the People's Theater at the Moscow Polytechnic Exposition. In the report they submitted with the approved repertoire, the censors described their approach:

> Special attention was given to works distinguished by a patriotic mood or which introduce historical events and personages, but notwithstanding it was deemed necessary to exclude those plays in which the personality of Ivan the Terrible is presented in an unattractive light, since depictions that do not at all correspond to the common man's reverent conception of the tsar's dignity would have a disagreeable effect. As concerns plays about everyday life, the list does not include one of the well-known dramas drawn from the life of the people, *A Bitter Fate*. This play, having undoubted virtues, can make an extremely powerful impression on the spectator, but it is for this very reason that it should not be allowed in the people's theater at the present time, which is still not distant enough from that epoch when events like those depicted in that drama could occur.[17]

Ostrovsky's *Vasilisa Melenteva* was forbidden because of its negative portrayal of Ivan the Terrible, while his *A Ward of the Mistress* and *A Much Frequented Spot* were probably struck from the repertoire because some of their characters are criminals who go unpunished. The works that obtained approval included not only Nikolai Polevoi's jingoistic tribute to Peter the Great, *The Grandfather of the Russian Fleet*, but also Ostrovsky's *Poverty Is No Vice*, Pushkin's *Rusalka*, Fonvizin's *The Minor*, and Molière's *Georges Dandin*, as well as some then-popular vaudevilles and melodramas.[18]

Thus, even before a formal policy of separately censoring works for the popular stage was introduced, the principle had been established that the censors should take into account the imagined reception of the plays by popular audiences, especially when they touched on rulers, history, social injustice, or official corruption. How the censors constructed the popular audience reflected the autocracy's ambivalent view of the people. If on the one hand they were perceived as "simple" (*prostye*) and in need of protection from corrupting outside influences, on the other hand they were "the crowd" (*tolpa*), dangerous and unpredictable, a view of the common people shared by most educated Russians. As Daniel Field has pointed out, "the childlike innocent and the 'uncouth half beast' were two expressions of one myth, the myth of the peasant."[19] In keeping with the myth, the censorship of popular theater justified itself in terms that were simultaneously paternalistic and repressive, claiming to seek to preserve the ostensible purity of the people's world view, to encourage moral behavior, and to prevent their incitement to violence under the impression of ideas they were supposedly not equipped to comprehend.

The idea that the "simple folk" were excessively impressionable and incapable of critical judgment was to some extent a useful fiction for the authorities, who were very aware that actors and educated audiences often "misinterpreted" plays to give them political resonance, particularly during the restless 1860s and 1870s, and again in the years leading up to the 1905 Revolution. In tsarist Russia, where freedom of speech was limited and public meetings required official permission, the theater was a relatively anonymous and safe environment for political expression, especially for the students who packed the cheap seats in the gods. In 1876, for instance, the young actress Mariia Ermolova cut out and rearranged bits of her role as the peasant girl Laurencia in Lope de Vega's *Fuenteovejuna* to heighten its theme of resistance to tyranny, provoking such storms of applause among audiences in Moscow's Imperial Malyi Theater that the government banned the play for a time. On the Moscow Art Theater's first visit to St. Petersburg in early 1901, which coincided with bloody clashes between student demonstrators and police on the city's streets, their performance of Ibsen's *An Enemy of the People* turned into an antigovernment demonstration. When Stanislavsky, playing the hero Dr. Stockman, uttered the phrase, "One must never put on a new coat when one goes out to fight for freedom and truth," students in the audience interrupted the performance with applause and cheers, rushing onto the stage to embrace the actor.[20] During the 1905 Revolution, theaters often became scenes of political protest and conflict, as actors and audiences related plays and performances to topical concerns. With applause, whistles, hissing, and booing, audiences sanctioned or condemned the texts that were being performed, turning theater auditoriums into symbolic parliaments and sometimes provoking the police to intervene.[21]

Political demonstrations at theater performances were rituals of largely symbolic protest, but the fact that the state took them so seriously only heightened their significance for the audiences who thumbed their noses at tsarist authority from the comfort of their theater seats. Even though these protests functioned not so much to politicize audiences as to preach to those already converted, the state nevertheless feared the explosive effect theater could have on popular audiences. Yet to acknowledge that the common people might react to Aesopian social and political criticism in the theater as did educated audiences was to admit that the people were not necessarily the loyal subjects of the autocracy that official mythology made them out to be. By employing a rhetoric that justified decisions to prohibit plays on the grounds that they might be wrongly interpreted by ignorant popular audiences, the censors sought to preserve the fiction that social and political discontent was limited to educated society, while at the same time implicitly acknowledging the people's potential for violent opposition. As retired State Counselor P. M. Pchelnikov, appointed to monitor Moscow performances in 1901, argued in a report to the Press Administration:

> If the repertoire of theater does exert an influence on cultured spectators, then on the spectator of a low intellectual development theatrical performances must bring to bear an irresistible influence. Only the effective and most attentive control of the performance can ensure that the theater's powerful influence is aimed at producing a benign influence on the crowd of simple folk; insufficient control or, even worse, its absence, could be the source of the most undesirable consequences, difficult to rectify, since the unprepared theater spectator is always inclined to accept as truth everything that he hears or sees in the theater, for his low level of development does not give him the means to evaluate his impressions critically.[22]

Although the official image of the loyal Orthodox Russian people, pure and unsullied by "foreign" subversive ideas, was shaken by the 1905 Revolution, when striking workers brought the autocracy to its knees and even the supposedly apolitical peasants held national congresses to press for reforms, that image lived on in right-wing discourse and in the reports of the theater censors until 1917.

The 1888 circular establishing separate censorship for popular theaters left it entirely to the discretion of the local authorities to determine what admission fee was low enough to make a theater "popular" and therefore subject to special restrictions. Plays were either "unconditionally approved," "approved with excisions," or "prohibited." Initially, the script of every work presented in a popular theater had to bear the Press Administration's seal of approval, and any excisions from the text that applied only to popular theaters were marked in blue ink, to distinguish them from the excisions that applied to all theaters and were marked in red ink.[23] Later the rules were changed to permit the popular theaters to put on any play listed as "unconditionally approved" in the *Alphabetical Lists of Dramatic Works Approved for Performance in Popular Theaters,* on presentation to the proper local authority of the published edition of the play corresponding to the one designated on the list.[24]

There were no special censors for the popular theaters. The regular theater censors examined works intended for performance on the popular stage as they were submitted, and their reports were filed together with those on plays for other theaters. The censors did not write reports on every work they examined but only to prohibit a play, reverse an earlier decision, or refer a play to the head censor for a ruling. Reports were occasionally issued on plays "approved with excisions," but the nature of these excisions was rarely specified. The reports thus tell much about why the censors prohibited plays and little about why they approved them.

An examination of the reasons behind the prohibition of plays for performance in popular theaters reveals much about the image of the *narod* in the minds of the authorities, since the imagined reception by a popular audience was the main factor in their decisions. The vast majority of the plays submitted for the popular stage had already been approved for performance in ordinary theaters. The plays most commonly prohibited for the popular theater were those which contained depictions of the tsar or other ruling figures, examined sensitive historical subjects such as rebellion or serfdom, contained unflattering portrayals of secular or religious authorities, referred to social antagonisms, condoned criminal behavior, or treated sexuality in a "vulgar" way.

Censorship practice did evolve over the years, as a number of earlier prohibitions came to be reversed. The motives for judging a play "inappropriate" for popular audiences remained essentially the same, but the range of subjects that could be treated on the popular stage did widen somewhat between 1888 and 1917. A number of works initially prohibited for the popular stage eventually obtained the censors' approval, especially after 1905.

REPRESENTATIONS OF RULERS

One of the most sensitive censorship issues was the depiction of Russian rulers on the stage, for the authorities worried that an unskillful or negative portrayal might distort and even tarnish the tsar's image in the eyes of his subjects. In 1837, at the urging of Count Uvarov, Nicholas I forbade the representation of members of the Romanov dynasty in any theater; earlier tsars could appear in dramas or tragedies if "presented with all the requirements of decorum, historical truth and taste," but not in operas without the emperor's personal approval. Uvarov based his argument on Official Nationality's idealized view of the relationship between the people and their tsar, while at the same time appealing to Nicholas's obsession with revolution. He emphasized the "special notions that are linked with the names of Ruling Persons in the eyes of Russians, notions hallowed by Religion, custom and feelings rooted in the people," and reminded the tsar that the 1830 Revolution in France had begun at a performance of Marie-Joseph Chénier's tragedy *Charles IX or St. Bartholomew's Night.*[25]

Exceptions to the policy of prohibiting the representation of Russian rulers in opera were made only when the work in question was deemed to be of considerable artistic merit and sufficiently patriotic in content. Among the operas so approved were Mikhail Glinka's *A Life for the Tsar* and *Ruslan and Liudmilla,* Modest Mussorgsky's *Boris Godunov,* and Aleksandr Serov's *Rogneda,* although permission was usually granted only to the imperial theaters, which ostensibly could be relied upon to present the person of the tsar with due reverence. The reluctance to allow the depiction of the tsar on stage attained ridiculous proportions at times, even hindering some attempts to use theater to cultivate patriotic sentiment. When, in 1910, the director of the imperial theaters announced a competition for plays on the themes of the Patriotic War of 1812 and the 1613 election of Michael Romanov (for the jubilee celebrations of these events held in 1912 and 1913), the tsar refused to make an exception to permit dramatists to portray Michael, his father Filaret, or Emperor Alexander I, despite Prime Minister Stolypin's own favorable recommendation.[26]

With the introduction of a separate censorship for the popular theaters, the censors initially tended to interdict any representation of a tsar in such theaters, believing that standards of production were not high enough for depicting royalty. "The very appearance of the tsar's person on popular stages seems to me to be absolutely impossible," wrote one censor in 1895, "especially if the acting personnel and poor decorations in theaters of this kind are taken into account."[27] Long approved for the regular stage, E. V. Aladin's *Godfather Ivan,* in which Ivan the Terrible disguises himself as a wandering musketeer, uncovering the corruption of village authorities, uniting lovers, and christening a peasant child, was prohibited for the popular stage in 1888, despite its obvious patriotism, because the censor considered it undesirable to "depict the tsar's person, albeit in a far-off time and not of the Romanov dynasty, on a *balagan* stage."[28] Anton Rubinstein's opera *The Merchant Kalashnikov,* adapted from the poem by Mikhail Lermontov, was approved for the regular stage in 1901 after years of prohibition for obscure reasons, but all petitions to perform the work in popular theaters were denied because "there is no guarantee that it would be performed with the care appropriate to the importance of the subject and that the excisions made by imperial command would be carefully observed."[29]

In the early 1900s, however, the government began to take more interest in using the stage to promote popular patriotism and national pride and allowed a few of the people's theaters, usually those run by the Guardianships of Popular Temperance, to stage works in which historical tsars made an appearance. Plays featuring Peter the Great as a modernizing empire-builder were particularly well received by the censors.[30] In 1901, for example, the St. Petersburg Temperance Guardianship succeeded in obtaining permission to produce Viktor Krylov's *Peter the Great,* a chronological series of scenes from the monarch's life that depicted his youthful boat building, the Poltava victory, his wise rule and role as father and enlightener of his subjects, his assumption of the imperial title, and the celebration of the Peace of Nystadt. "All these patriotic scenes produce a deep impression and will undoubtedly be greeted with gratitude and emotion by the audiences of the people's theater," the censor observed in recommending that the guardianship's petition be granted. The play was subsequently performed before Nicholas II, who gave his approval for it to be staged at the theater of the guardianship's Emperor Nicholas II People's House. A few months later, due to its "great success on the stage of the guardianship's theater, maintaining patriotic feelings among the spectators," it was sanctioned for performance in all popular theaters, on the condition that the local authorities ensure that "the production of the dramatic chronicle *Peter the Great* and the quality of the actors performing the role of Russia's Great Transformer entirely correspond to the importance of the subject and maintain the appropriate mood."[31]

Peter's exploits became a favorite subject for the propagandists of autocracy on the popular stage. To commemorate the 1903 bicentennial of the founding of St. Petersburg, the city's temperance guardianship held a competition for a play "which would acquaint the city's population with the historical significance of the event." Although none of the ten works submitted was found to be satisfactory, the guardianship decided to rework Lev Zhdanov's *St. Petersburg* to suit its needs. The resulting play included scenes of the storming of a Swedish fortress under Peter's command and the first Russian naval victory over the Swedes, with Peter directing the battle in a captain's uniform, first to board the enemy ship with a bomb in hand. It concluded in an apotheosis in which Peter falls asleep after his numerous labors and has a dream in which he sees the city he has created two hundred years later, in 1903. Before the spectators appears an aerial view of St. Petersburg, in which St. Isaac's Cathedral, the parade ground, and the Bronze Horseman monument are visible. An allegorical figure of Fame rises radiantly over Peter to the sound of music and the ringing of bells. In petitioning for approval to present Peter on the stage, the guardianship pointed out that he would be depicted as "a fearless military genius" and that numerous scenes would be devoted to his work in building the new capital. The work was indeed a model of a eulogistic portrayal of the autocrat; as the reactionary Minister of Internal Affairs Viacheslav Plehve commented, it "entirely satisfies the requirements of a historical play whose hero is the Russian tsar."[32]

Another work whose flattering portrayal of Peter won it Nicholas's approval for performance at the Nicholas II People's House was Albert Lortzing's comic opera *Tsar and Carpenter*. This celebration of the tsar's humanity and love for the "little man" told the story of Peter's stint working incognito as a carpenter in Holland. The French and English ambassadors learn of his presence and come to Zaandam to find him and negotiate a treaty. The French ambassador recognizes Peter, but his English colleague has the bad luck to mistake the Russian deserter Ivanov for the tsar. The French get their treaty, and Peter reveals his identity before his departure, forgiving the deserter Ivanov and arranging his marriage to his beloved, the burgermeister's niece.

"Emperor Peter the Great is portrayed as ardently loving his homeland, devoting all his strength and thoughts to increasing its greatness, merciful to those who err, like the repentant Ivanov, and formidable to enemies like the mutinous *streltsy*—that is, in exactly those strong traits which have made of Tsar Peter an almost mythical hero in the mind of the people," wrote Stolypin in his report to the tsar in 1906. Two years later a dramatic adaptation of *Tsar and Carpenter* was approved for performance on all popular stages.[33] Although Richard Wortman has argued that after 1905 Peter's importance diminished in official literature, which began emphasizing the seventeenth century as "the most important period in the foundation of the Russian autocracy," Nicholas's approval of plays glorifying Peter on the popular stage suggests that the image of the tsar as reformer and state-builder retained much of its appeal.[34] Nicholas refused to allow the portrayal of the dynasty's founder, Michael (1613–45), on the stages of even the imperial theaters during the celebration of the Romanov tercentenary in 1913, but Peter was prominently featured the year before in *The Taking of Azov*, a mass open-air spectacle in St. Petersburg's Petrovskii Park that was approved without hesitation.[35]

Some aspects of Peter's rule could prove embarrassing at times. Petr

Figure 5. The Emperor Nicholas II People's House decorated for the celebrations of the tercentenary of the Romanov dynasty. St. Petersburg, 1913. Courtesy of the Central State Archive of Documentary Films and Photographs, St. Petersburg.

Gnedich's play *Assemblée*, which dealt with Peter's introduction of Western manners and customs, was banned in popular theaters at the outbreak of World War I because it emphasized the tsar's reliance on Germans in achieving his program of modernization.[36] The unspoken assumption was, of course, that the common people might be reminded that Nicholas II himself was closely linked to Germany by ties of blood and marriage. *Assemblée* was performed on the imperial stages, however, right up until the autocracy's collapse.[37]

If the exploits of Peter the Great sometimes did find their way to the popular stage by virtue of their patriotic merits, the reign of Ivan the Terrible often remained off limits. *Prince Serebrianyi*, adapted for the popular stage from Alexei Tolstoy's novel of the same title by N. I. Sobolshchikov-Samarin, was prohibited in 1897 because the censor felt that the work would give uneducated audiences a one-sided impression of Ivan the Terrible by focusing on his "bestiality and insanity."[38] An adaptation of the play by S. F. Mikhailov was finally approved "with excisions" in 1911.[39] Alexander Ostrovsky's *Vasilisa Melenteva*, first judged unsuitable for popular audiences at the People's Theater at the Moscow Polytechnic Exposition in 1872, suffered prohibition for a second time in 1905; the censor claimed that "in this drama acts of Ivan the Terrible are depicted which are capable of arousing in the ignorant clientele of popular theaters a false impression of tsarist authority."[40] Later that year, another censor reversed the earlier decisions and approved the play with excisions, presumably of those acts deemed to cast a negative light on tsarist authority.[41] Yet the censors did not succeed in keeping *Vasilisa Melenteva* off the popular stage entirely before 1905, for the Vasilevskii Island Theater had staged it in the 1890s.[42]

Sometimes the authorities were unable to agree in their evaluations of how the common people would interpret a work's depiction of the tsar, as was the case with Aleksandr Navrotskii's tragedy *Tsar Ivan III*, which opened at the Nicholas II People's House in early 1903. The production was patriotic in tone and the program contained a four-page description of Ivan's life and significance in Russian history, but the play had been approved only for the regular stage. A police official, who found the play "gloomy" in tone and unsympathetic in its portrayal of the autocrat, informed the municipal governor. The report was passed on to the Press Administration, where the censor decided that *Tsar Ivan III* was an excellent choice for the popular stage, since it would educate the people about their history by visual means. The play had already been passed for performance in regular theaters; the issue now at stake was its reception by popular audiences. The censor argued that even the common people would be able to properly evaluate Navrotskii's portrayal of Ivan III: "One should hope that the spectators of the People's House, though considered to be semi-literate and uneducated, would be able to appreciate the sublime traits of the tsar's character. It could not strike anyone that Navrotskii's Ivan III is cruel by nature and is drawn to punishing people. The idea of the state is put forward too consistently, and leaves no room for false impressions." But the head of the Press Administration disagreed, and the People's House was forced to remove *Tsar Ivan III* from its repertoire.[43]

Works about foreign rulers were also frequently prohibited for the popular theaters if the censors felt that they could possibly discredit the monarchical principle in the eyes of the people. Schiller's *Don Carlos*, approved unconditionally for the regular theaters, was prohibited for the popular stage in 1906. "From the standpoint of the popular theaters," reasoned the censor, "this play is scarcely desirable: the cruel reign of Philip of Spain and his favorite the Duke of Alba undermine the meaning of monarchism, and the heir to the throne's protest and indignation against his father increases the play's harmful meaning for the people."[44] In 1905 Byron's *Sardanapalus* was banned despite its positive portrayal of the Assyrian king because "the representation of an uprising against the tsar is hardly good for popular theaters, even if the person of the tsar is ideally portrayed." Given the rash of uprisings sweeping Russia in 1905, the censor's caution is certainly understandable. The Ligovskii People's House was eventually permitted to stage the play, in the calmer political atmosphere of 1909.[45]

The depiction of reigning monarchs, Russian or foreign, was off limits for all theaters, although some exceptions were made in the case of Kaiser Wilhelm during the world war. This policy sometimes hindered attempts to use the popular stage to inspire patriotism, for patriotic works could fail to win approval for "purely formal reasons," as was the case with *To the Far East*, a jingoistic play written especially for the popular theater in 1904. Although ultra-patriotic in content, the play contained a scene in which a portrait of Nicholas II was brought onto the stage and representatives of the peoples of the empire laid wreaths at its foot. The stage was deemed an inappropriate setting for displaying the tsar's likeness, and the work was prohibited.[46]

During World War I, the policy prohibiting the depiction of reigning monarchs sometimes prevented popular theaters from staging even works that ridiculed the rulers of enemy powers. Konstantin Shitorli's *The Bloody Kaiser* and Mamont Dalskii's *The Shame of Germany*, chauvinistic plays that included satirical portrayals of Wilhelm II and Franz-Joseph, were among the works prohibited for the popular stage, although *The Shame of Germany* was approved for more upscale venues like the Suvorin Theater, where it played to packed houses in the patriotic enthusiasm of late 1914. In 1916, with the war going badly and popular dissatisfaction on the rise, the Press Administration raised the possibility of revising censorship policy to allow the depiction of reigning foreign monarchs in patriotic plays, but the Ministry of Internal Affairs rejected the idea. In contrast, the cinema was able to turn out a number of anti-German films featuring the kaiser.[47]

PORTRAYALS OF THE PAST

When it came to reviewing historical plays, the censors' decisions reflected the government's ambivalence toward acquainting the common people with their past. Although ostensibly in favor of providing the *narod* with a basic knowledge of Russian history, the authorities simultaneously feared the impact portrayals of sensitive historical events might have on the people.

Censors found the Time of Troubles (1598–1613), with its political instability, foreign usurpers, and succession of pretenders to the throne, especially problematic. If works glorifying resistance to Polish invaders, such as Glinka's opera, *A Life for the Tsar*, and Nestor Kukolnik's patriotic tragedy in blank verse, *The Hand of the Almighty Has Saved the Fatherland*, were generally encouraged,[48] those touching on the social and political struggles of the Time of Troubles were seldom deemed fit for presentation to popular audiences. In 1893 one censor even went so far as to argue that "for the uneducated mob, scenes from the Time of Troubles are utterly inappropriate on the theater stages."[49] *Dmitrii the Pretender and Prince Vasilii Shuiskii*, a *balagan* spectacular with processions, dancing, battle scenes, and an apotheosis glorifying Russia, failed to receive approval in 1888 because the censor felt that the common people were too ignorant about history to distinguish between rebellion against a false tsar and rebellion against a legitimate ruler.[50]

The argument that the people could not be trusted to give the "correct" interpretation to historical events was commonly evoked to justify the prohibition of plays set in the Russia's distant past. *Ataman Ustinia Fedorovna*, set among the Volga Cossacks in the seventeenth century, had been approved in 1887 for the regular theaters, yet it was banned for the popular theaters in 1888 out of fear that audiences would find the Cossacks' lifestyle all too appealing: "The common people cannot comprehend the distance between the seventeenth and nineteenth centuries. Neither clothing nor speech, in a word, nothing can indicate to uneducated spectators, the majority of whom are illiterate, that these times are forever past. For such spectators all this could have taken place yesterday, and among many of them could and probably will arise the desire that such a free and rich lifestyle would come tomorrow."[51]

The social and political turmoil that erupted during the 1905 Revolution and the early period of semiparliamentary government that followed made the censors even stricter in their evaluations of historical works destined for the popular stage. They were quick to discern any themes that could be construed to refer to contemporary events, and not without reason, for all over Russia audiences used performances of plays dealing with rebellion against monarchy as an occasion to express support for the oppositional Liberation Movement. For example, Schiller's romantic drama *William Tell,* with its stirring tale of resistance to foreign tyranny, ignited demonstrations of anti-tsarist sentiment at theaters in Kiev and St. Petersburg when it was staged in 1905.[52]

The censors' verdict on an operatic version of *William Tell* not only illustrates their concerns about theater's potential for subversive propaganda among the masses but also reveals that their often repeated statements about the people's inability to properly evaluate what they saw on the stage were really a formula, which enabled them to prohibit genuinely subversive works while keeping up the pretense that the subversive content was only a question of misinterpretation. In September 1905, S. N. Melnikov requested approval for his translation of Rossini's opera *William Tell*. Melnikov gave it the more innocuous title *Charles the Bold*, possibly hoping that it would thus slip past unnoticed, but given the reception of Schiller's version of the tale in the regular theaters, the censors were anxious about the opera's potentially provocative impact and prohibited its performance before popular audiences. In late 1906, after order had been restored by a combination of political concessions and military force, the translator resubmitted the opera under its real title, having attempted to cut out the offensive passages. The opera was again rejected because, according to the censor, popular audiences were unfamiliar with the story and would not realize that Tell was revolting not against "the legal rule of the German emperor" but against the usurper Gessler. Of course, the issue was not whether popular audiences would be able to comprehend the opera but whether they would interpret it just as educated audiences had interpreted Schiller's *William Tell*, as a paean to the struggle against tyranny. The censor was simply employing a rhetoric that confirmed the official myth that the common people were loyal subjects and could only embrace antimonarchical sentiment by error. Having been sufficiently revised to ensure it would be clear that the Swiss did not rise up against the German emperor, the opera was finally approved on its third submission, but only for the Nicholas II People's House.[53]

For years, the Press Administration was reluctant to allow plays treating the lives of the peasants under serfdom to appear on the popular stage, fearing that they might exacerbate existing social tensions by reminding audiences of old injustices that were best forgotten. In 1888, for example, two plays written for the popular stage, D. S. Dmitriev's *Welcome News* and V. A. Nikolaev-Sokolovskii's *19 February 1861 or The Liberation of the Peasants*, were banned due to their depiction of the peasants' harsh life under serfdom, despite both plays' emphasis on the peasants' gratitude to the "Tsar Liberator," Alexander II.[54] By the early 1900s, however, some works that dealt with social relations under serfdom began to receive approval, such as Pisemsky's *A Bitter Fate*, which had been barred from the popular stage since the days of the Moscow Polytechnic Exposition.[55] In

November 1905 the Moscow duma resubmitted the play to the Press Administration in hope of receiving permission to stage it in the municipal People's House. Censor Oskar Lamkert, whose pronouncements on other plays do not reveal any liberal sympathies, gave the play unconditional approval. His explanation of his reversal of the earlier prohibition suggests the gradual evolution of a somewhat more liberal attitude on the part of the Press Administration in deciding what kinds of history were suitable for the popular stage:

> Taking into consideration the fact that the main reason for the prohibition of *A Bitter Fate* was the notion that it was undesirable to remind the people of serfdom, a concern hardly relevant today, forty-five years after the liberation of the peasants, and also in view of the absence of any tendentiousness in the depiction of relations between peasants and landlords, I would suggest simply to satisfy the petition for permission to perform this drama on the stages of popular theaters.[56]

Since there was no specific policy regulating what kinds of history could or could not be seen by the people, this 1905 decision did not mean that henceforth plays about serfdom would be permitted on the popular stage. Everything depended on the censor's own interpretation of the text. In 1910 one censor gave approval to *19 February* and A. A. Navrotskii's *The Great Day*, two plays about the liberation of the serfs that were subsequently staged with great success at St. Petersburg's Nicholas II People's House on the fiftieth anniversary of the Emancipation, while another censor banned V. Kozlov's *The Tsar's Grace Is the Joy of the People*, citing its depiction of the mistreatment of serfs in the days before the Emancipation.[57]

RESPECT FOR AUTHORITY

Comedies and farces about government officials, often long familiar to the patrons of the regular theaters, as well as to readers of popular literature, took on dangerous hues when considered for *performance* before the common people. Ostrovsky and Solovev's farce *A Happy Day*, whose subject was the scheming of a corrupt provincial police official and his wife to marry off their two daughters, was thus deemed impermissible for popular audiences in 1891, even though the censor admitted that it was a "harmless farce on the ordinary stage." Resubmitted fourteen years later, during the 1905 Revolution, *A Happy Day* was again rejected, for the censor felt that it was "particularly unsuitable for the popular theater at present, given the current tendency to discredit without grounds representatives of the government from great to small in the eyes of the public."[58]

Not every play that cast the authorities in a negative light was kept off the popular stage. The first play in Aleksandr Sukhovo-Kobylin's classic trilogy satirizing Russia's corrupt officialdom, *Krechinskii's Wedding*, did get unconditional approval for popular theaters in 1895.[59] The other works of the trilogy did not fare so well. *Tarelkin's Death* was prohibited for all theaters; it was first performed following the February Revolution in 1917. As for *The Case*, a black comedy about bureaucratic red tape and bribe-taking submitted in early 1906, the censor felt that its harsh depiction of the shortcomings of Russian officials was far too accurate for popular consumption.[60] Plays containing unflattering portrayals of military officers were also frequent victims of the censor's veto when submitted for popular theaters, even if they were already being produced in the regular theaters.[61]

Although it was categorically prohibited to depict the Orthodox clergy, saints, icons, or religious rituals on the stage of any theater, the popular theaters were often barred from staging works containing any reference even to Roman Catholic institutions and practices. The reasoning was that the common people, who in the official myth were devoted to the Orthodox faith, could misunderstand the subject matter and become infected by foreign anticlerical attitudes. Ostrovsky's translation of Paolo Giacometti's melodrama *Civil Death*, which dealt with the Italian clergy's abuse of office, was thus prohibited in 1893. "For a public having nothing in common with the scions of the Roman Catholic church and insufficiently educated to discern the difference between the clergy's misuse of its rights and its fervent performance of its duties, such a play could only be harmful," explained the censor in his report. In 1904, a translation of the French dramatist Victorien Sardou's *The Sorceress* got approval only after the scenes involving the Inquisition were deleted because the censor argued that popular audiences would be unable to distinguish between the Inquisition and the Church as an institution. Both *Civil Death* and *The Sorceress* were, however, already approved for the regular stage.[62]

WEALTH, PRIVILEGE, AND SOCIAL DISCORD

The provisions of the censorship statute forbade works that "arouse the enmity and hatred of one class toward another" or "ridicule entire classes."[63] Applied to the regular theaters, these rules resulted mainly in the interdiction of "tendentious" works that denounced existing social structures or attempted to call public attention to industrialists' more egregious abuses of their workers. With respect to the popular theaters, works were often prohibited merely because they contained unbecoming depictions of members of the privileged classes.

A number of socially critical plays were kept off the popular stage long after they had been authorized for production in theaters attended by the educated public. Ivan Turgenev's *The Sponger*, which had shocked the censors on its appearance in 1848 and remained banned from the stage until 1861, was still considered too sharp a portrayal of the landed gentry to be seen by popular audiences over three decades later. Reviewing it together with Petr Boborykin's *The Smallholder* in 1893, the censor banned both plays for popular theaters because they "portray big landowners as heartless and corrupt tyrants, pitilessly mocking the poor." Pisemsky's *The Partition*, which focuses on the greed of the members of a noble family who gather to divide their inheritance, was also rejected as unsuitable for popular theaters in the same year. In December 1905, however, it was resubmitted and this time was approved unconditionally by censor Vereshchagin, who could not see "anything harmful for the people in the contents of *The Partition*."[64] With revolutionary ideas sweeping the country and Moscow in the throes of an armed insurrection, Pisemsky's 1853 comedy perhaps seemed relatively harmless, although the censors had used the specter of the 1905 Revolution to ban other plays.

Among the most frequent recipients of the censor's veto were plays in which representatives of the upper classes were pictured as promiscuous and morally corrupt, a commonplace subject in popular literature and folklore. F. Kareev's *The Fatal Step*, a melodrama about an impoverished young woman who is forced to become a prostitute when her lover, a rich student, jilts her for a wealthy baroness, was rejected for the popular theater in 1893. Reviewing the play for a second time in 1908, another censor recommended leaving the earlier decision in force, "since beyond all question it can only arouse in the people ill feeling toward the wealthy class." Dmitrii Lenskii's famous vaudeville, *Lev Gurych Sinichkin*, one of the most widely performed plays in Russia since its premiere in 1840, failed to win approval for the popular stage in 1905, when the censor objected to its portrayal of the sexual exploitation of actresses by wealthy theater patrons. "The depiction of the privileged class in such a ludicrous guise," he concluded, "can hardly be considered desirable for the people."[65]

The censors took a particularly dim view of works in which the common people figured as victims of the sexual advances of their social superiors. Mozart's opera based on Beaumarchais's *The Marriage of Figaro* was thus prohibited in 1904. Although the censor noted that the attacks on censorship and tyranny found in Beaumarchais's original text had been deleted from the opera's libretto, he felt that the love intrigues between aristocrats and their servants and the evocation of the lord's feudal right to possess his vassal on her wedding night still made the opera inappropriate for a popular theater. Daniel Auber's opera, *La muette de Portici*, in which a young Spanish nobleman seduces and then discards a mute Italian fisherwoman, provoking her brother to lead an uprising against Spanish rule in Naples, was prohibited in the heated atmosphere of 1905 due to its "depiction of the violence done to the lower classes by representatives of the upper classes and the mob justice which the people resort to in such cases." The censors may well have been aware that a performance of Auber's opera in Brussels on 25 August 1830 had helped to set off the Belgian revolt. In 1908, a play focusing on the consequences of syphilis was banned, despite its educational value, because the action took place in an upper-class milieu and therefore "could give the people a false opinion of the privileged class as the spreaders of that disease."[66]

The censors were not always consistent in their judgments, for not all plays that touched on social injustice were banned from the popular theaters. Evtikhii Karpov's melodrama, *The Workers' Settlement*, got the censor's unconditional approval for performance in popular theaters despite its grim depiction of factory life and graphic portrayal of the ruin brought on by a foreman's advances to the wife of one of his workers. Frustrated by his inability to stop the foreman, the worker turns to drink, and consequently his hitherto virtuous wife abandons him and moves in with the foreman. Heavily moralistic in tone, the play ends with the worker's death and his wife's disenchantment with her new lover, whose philandering continues. The censor did not explain his reasons for approving *The Workers' Settlement*, but in this case the depiction of sexual immorality appears not to have raised objections, perhaps because in the eyes of the censor both parties were from the same social milieu.[67]

The Unemployed, by Sofiia Belaia (Bogdanovskaia), was also approved and widely performed in both legitimate and popular theaters, even though it focused on the hardships of workers' lives. In the play a young worker loses his arm in a factory accident. Unable to work, he becomes dependent on his brother-in-law Egor for support and later commits suicide when the closure of the factory where Egor works threatens the family with starvation. Yet other plays were prohibited for popular audiences precisely because of their depiction of "the hopeless situation of factory workers."[68] The censors banned S. A. Palgunov's *Tornado* in 1908, despite its antistrike message:

> This drama, approved for performance on the regular stage, depicts the disastrous consequences of a strike provoked by the agitation of a

student outsider. Individual scenes and discussions, such as those treat-ing the need for solidarity among the workers in the rejection of the employer's demands . . . could be wrongly interpreted by the public of the popular theaters, on whose stages it is not at all desirable to stir up these sorts of burning questions at present.[69]

In explaining his decision, the censor maintained the official rhetorical fic-tion of an innocent common people, alien to ideas like class solidarity, despite the evidence of the urban working class's organizational capacity and strike activity in 1905 and earlier.

IMMORAL IMPRESSIONS

The government viewed the task of censoring the popular theater repertoire as more than just a police measure carried out with the aim of combating ideas that could undermine the common people's awe of their tsar, respect for authority, or contentment with the existing social order. It also claimed to be protecting the people from influences deemed to be immoral. Since the censors believed, or at least pretended to believe when writing their reports, that the common people were overly "impressionable," "poorly educated," and liable to "misinterpret" what they saw and heard on the stage, the least moral ambiguity was considered sufficient justification to find a play unac-ceptable for popular consumption. Plays featuring crime and sex were thus frequently prohibited for performance in popular theaters, although many of them had already been approved for ordinary theaters.

In the censors' opinion, not only must crime not pay, but it also had to be clearly punished. A good illustration of their attitude toward the represen-tation of crime on the popular stage is the censorship history of *Life and Death, or Hard Labor and Homecoming*, a melodrama written by N. A. Talin in the early 1890s. First submitted in 1892, it told the story of one Aleksei Doronenko, who is condemned to exile and hard labor for the mur-der of his wife, leaving behind a young son who is raised by an officer. Freed after twenty years for good behavior, he returns home just in time for his son's wedding. The censor enthusiastically approved the tale of redemption: "Talin depicts a good, honest officer, loved by all his neighbors, a repentant criminal who has atoned for his guilt with many years of physical and men-tal suffering." In 1893 Talin revised the play in an apparent attempt to give it added theatrical effect, showing that Doronenko murdered his wife because she intended to enter into a liaison with a rich young man, and adding more convicts to the cast. If in its first version it was virtually a model of the type of morally instructive play thought to be appropriate for the popular stage, the revised *Life and Death* now smacked of immorality in the view of the censor, who found it "entirely unnecessary to depict various criminals boasting of their crimes on the stage of the popular theater. A bond forger, an old tramp murderer, and a young murderer appear before the audience as some kind of heroes and not as people deserving the punishment given to them." A few months later Talin submitted yet another version of his play. He left in the scenes of the convicts recounting their exploits but added a scene where they are granted amnesty by the tsarevich Nicholas during his trip through Siberia in 1891, along with a scene of the convicts kneeling and singing "God Save the Tsar" in unison. The new patriotic overtones did not save the play from prohibition, for the censor remained persuaded that it presented the convicts in too positive a light to be tolerated on the popular stage.[70]

Plays were sometimes prohibited for the popular theaters even when they showed the negative consequences of crime, if the censors felt the wrongdoers did not receive sufficient punishment. In 1888, a vaudeville about a drunken scribe who abuses the local peasants, takes bribes, and tries to seduce his assistant's fiancée was vetoed because although the scribe is fired for his misdeeds, he is not brought to trial. According to the censor, such a treatment of crime "can only instill in uneducated spectators the conviction that it is all right to steal and booze it up, and that these vices should be forgiven."[71] Indeed, the censors appear to have feared that popular audiences were likely to find immortal behavior and crime appealing unless the miscreants were shown to suffer for their wrongdoing. Reviewing two comic sketches in 1906, one in which a young woman is unfaithful to her husband during their wedding celebration, the other in which a conductor catches a ticketless passenger but lets him go in return for a bribe, the censor reported, "Unfortunately both are common occurrences that cannot shock the public of the popular theaters, but on the contrary are capable of amusing it. But if we deem the popular stage to have an edifying and educational significance, and bear in mind that theater has a stronger impact on the educated public than on the educated, then the repertoire must be strictly guarded from representations of illegal and immoral conduct that goes unpunished."[72] If the censors often imagined the common people to be innocent and requiring protection from harmful ideas, they also imagined the people to be more prone to criminal behavior than were more educated Russians.

The double standard in theater censorship was perhaps most evident in the censors' treatment of works dealing with sex and marriage. Plays containing depictions of rape, adultery, sexual promiscuity, or free love, although common in many Russian theaters after the turn of the century, were usually found to be unfit for viewing by popular audiences.[73] Even Sophocles's *Oedipus Rex* received the censor's veto in 1899, and again in 1905, due to its treatment of parricide and incest.[74] Aleksei Vershinin's *Life Is Going By*, about the family of a retired bureaucrat whose daughter and niece are prostitutes, was banned in 1916 because "scenes of the decline of family morals are not at all acceptable for the popular stage, nor is the depiction of prostitution."[75] Z. Iu. Iakovleva's *Under His Highness's Wing*, about Prince Potemkin's love affairs and Catherine the Great's jealousy, was banned for popular audiences in 1906, while a translation of Marcel Prévost's *Virgins in Name Only* was judged "unsuitable" for presentation to the common people in 1908 because it showed the arousing effect of "society girls" on their "cavaliers."[76]

OPPOSITION TO THE CENSORSHIP OF POPULAR THEATER

Although those educated Russians who wanted to use theater to civilize the people usually agreed with the censors that theater should not arouse what was commonly referred to as "the base instincts of the crowd," they frequently attacked the existence of a special censorship for works performed in popular theaters. Liberals and radicals echoed the views of Stanislavsky, who in 1905 criticized the various censorship provisions in a report to a group of Moscow actors and writers. The worst restrictions were those governing the popular theater, he observed, adding that "under contemporary conditions the development of people's theaters must be admitted to be hopeless."[77]

The champions of didactic people's theaters saw censorship as a nearly insurmountable barrier to their efforts to acquaint the masses with the classics of the dramatic repertoire. Censorship, they contended, made it nearly impossible for low-priced theaters to stage works of true artistic value because so few were authorized for performance in the popular theaters. At the same time, people's theater advocates were dismayed by the censors' approval of plays they deemed to have no artistic merit and to pander to the tastes of the fairground *balagan* public.

The separate censorship of popular theaters was regularly protested in the theatrical press and at congresses of theater people. In 1897, the First All-Russian Congress of Theater People vainly petitioned the Ministry of Internal Affairs to allow the people's theaters to stage works in accordance with the regular dramatic censorship, leaving the special censorship in force only for the *balagany*. At the start of the 1905 Revolution, leading members of the Russian theatrical community, including people's theater supporters Evtikhii Karpov, Nikolai Popov, and Ivan Shcheglov, published a manifesto criticizing censorship in general and drawing attention to the particular hardships faced by popular theaters. After the tsar promised equal rights to all Russians in his October Manifesto, censorship policy was criticized on the grounds that it made popular audiences second-class citizens.[78]

Although censorship did ease somewhat following the 1905 Revolution, the policy of distinguishing between popular and regular theaters was vigorously attacked at the All-Russian Congress of People's Theater Activists in late 1915. A. K. Klepikov, a delegate from the Moscow Section for Assisting the Organization of Factory and Village Theaters, claimed that the censorship had proved incapable of distinguishing good plays from bad: "Lacking a guiding idea of the goals of its work, it helplessly fusses over the mass of plays that pour onto the theatrical marketplace, unsystematically approves one and rejects another, and only irritates the people with its tutelage." Klepikov contrasted the absence from the approved repertoire of works by Shakespeare, Schiller, Goethe, Ibsen, and even Ostrovsky with the presence of dozens of "empty and vulgar pieces" like *The Indian Princess's Bridegroom* and *An Adventurous Dinner*, a state of affairs that demonstrated the "uselessness" of the popular theater censorship. The censorship was often criticized for prohibiting the wrong plays, the unspoken assumption being that censorship might be useful if it were guided by artistic concerns and banned "vulgar" plays rather than classics.[79]

Critics of the censorship policy for popular theaters were legion. Even the theaters of the Guardianships of Popular Temperance, supervised by the government's own Finance Ministry, found the repertoire restrictions too confining and continually besieged the Main Administration for Press Affairs with petitions for permission to produce prohibited works. In 1904 the ministry sent the Press Administration a list of thirty-seven plays that it wanted to use in its theaters, but only a handful were approved.[80]

Moscow's mayor added his voice to the chorus of critics in 1905, when the actors at the new Municipal People's House struck for several weeks to protest the special censorship rules for popular theaters. The paucity of serious plays approved by the censors was endangering the efforts of the People's House to continue its theatrical activities, he told the Press Administration, and requested permission to add some seventy-six plays and operas to the repertoire. As it turned out, however, the mayor and the theater managers were unaware that fifty-one of these works had already been approved for performance in popular theaters, while only eleven had

Figure 6. The Moscow Municipal People's House, 1900s. Author's collection.

Figure 7. The troupe of the Moscow Municipal People's House, 1900s. Author's collection.

been prohibited! Another fourteen had never been submitted for censorship in the first place—six of these were now approved.[81]

This sort of confusion as to which plays were or were not permitted on the popular stage was mainly due to the inordinate complexity of the censorship rules. The *Alphabetical Lists of Dramatic Works Approved for Performance in Popular Theaters* could include a work only when the Press Administration had a published edition in its archives. Thus, even if the censors were to unconditionally approve a manuscript or working copy, it did not necessarily enter the *Alphabetical Lists*. If a work had been approved only on condition of deletions from its text, the theater had to send a copy to the censors, who made the necessary deletions and stamped it with their seal of approval. Given the contemporary practice of staging as many as one hundred different plays a year, it was natural that popular theaters chafed under the bureaucratic burden of censorship.

Another problem was the lack of any precise definition as to what constituted a "popular theater." The law establishing the special censorship stated only that they were those theaters with a low admission fee. What constituted a low admission fee and whether a particular theater was designated to be "popular" was left to the judgment of the local authorities, usually the police. In 1890, for example, the Moscow municipal governor criticized the city police chief for allowing a French-language operetta to be performed at the theater of the Zoological Garden, since for thirty kopeks anyone could enter the park and watch the performance from a distance without buying a ticket to the show. In 1913, however, responding to an inquiry from the Press Administration as to why two St. Petersburg theaters attended largely by the city's less privileged inhabitants were staging plays that had not been approved for popular theaters, the St. Petersburg governor-general replied that he did not consider the theaters in question to be "popular" since they charged ten to fifteen kopeks for admission, although this was unquestionably a very low price by any standard. In 1902 the official charged with monitoring theater performances in Moscow, P. M. Pchelnikov, observed that a number of theaters attended by "the common folk" were not designated "popular" and regularly produced works that were prohibited for popular audiences.[82]

In defining theaters as "popular" on the basis of their ticket prices rather than the composition of their audiences, the government failed to take into account the diversity of the vague social category it labeled "the people," indiscriminately lumping together peasant farmers, domestic servants, shop clerks, unskilled factory workers, and highly skilled artisans. In his final report to the Press Administration in May 1905, the ever vigilant

Pchelnikov attempted to draw attention to the problem. He argued that in the big cities it was impossible to draw a sharp distinction between the common people and the rest of society and called for the censorship to evaluate plays on the basis of whether they were to be presented before urban or rural audiences. Urban factory workers, he rightly pointed out, had the means to attend ordinary theaters and were increasingly organizing troupes to stage plays themselves. Furthermore, urban workers were characterized by "greater intellectual maturity" than was the rural population. Pchelnikov contended that removing the burden of the special censorship for urban popular theaters, factory theaters, and workers' dramatic circles, which often circumvented it anyway, would allow these theaters to "better answer contemporary needs and, moreover, will give more meaning to the dramatic censorship, as it will be more difficult to get around its decisions." Pchelnikov's proposal elicited no response from the Press Administration, however, and at the end of the year a government commission assigned to evaluate censorship policy recommended leaving the theater censorship virtually unchanged.[83] Only the overthrow of the autocracy in 1917 would bring an end, for a time, to all forms of theater censorship.

CENSORSHIP'S LIMITATIONS

The government's attempt to regulate what the masses could see and hear on the theater stage brought mixed results at best. As with other branches of the imperial civil service, the censorship was hampered by a lack of coordination among the agencies responsible for ensuring adherence to its decisions.[84] The censorship regulations were routinely ignored,[85] and since their enforcement depended entirely on the vigilance of the police, there was little the Press Administration could do beyond sending out innumerable circulars calling for closer adherence to the rules.[86] Even the theaters funded by the government failed to adhere to the censorship's restrictions. In 1901 the Press Administration reported to Finance Minister Sergei Witte that out of 196 plays staged recently at the Nicholas II People's House, 75 had not been approved for performance in popular theaters. On the contrary, many had been expressly prohibited, such as Schiller's *The Robbers*, Leo Tolstoy's *The Power of Darkness*, and a pantomime "of extremely scabrous content—*The Kidnapped Bride*."[87]

Censorship of both the regular and popular theaters was often rendered ineffective by the fact that while the Press Administration could censor a play, it had little control over the conditions in which it was performed. The censors, focusing on the written text rather than on its performance, were unable to cope with important elements of theater such as gesture, ad-lib, intonation, makeup, and audience response. As a result, the text-in-performance might bear little resemblance to the text-as-read-by-censor and could contain things that would have been banned had they been visible to the censor when he approved the text. In 1915, responding to complaints in the conservative press accusing them of excessive leniency, the censors noted that unless they were actually present at performances they could do little to prevent directors and actors from violating both the letter and the spirit of censorship rulings. Since there were only four censors at the time, it was of course impossible for them to monitor performances even in St. Petersburg alone.[88]

The difficulties in controlling how dramatic texts were presented on the stage was emphasized by Pchelnikov in a 1901 letter to the head of the Press Administration, Prince Shakhovskoi, where he argued that only by monitoring theater performances could the censorship office hope to fulfill its mission:

> In the continual struggle with the demands of the censorship, the theater disposes of a quite wide arsenal of weapons that are perfected from year to year. Actors have at their disposal weapons in the form of the methods by which they realize their roles: diction, mimicry, makeup, gestures and costume. . . . With this arsenal there can be no doubt in the outcome of the struggle, of course under the condition that the censorship limits itself to only monitoring the text, neglecting to control the performance.[89]

During the 1905 Revolution, when the state's authority came under assault throughout Russia, the censorship's already tenuous control over performances was further weakened, at least temporarily. Attempting to restore order in early 1906, the Press Administration demanded that theaters and actors adhere to its guidelines, noting that "by the deletion of separate expressions and whole phrases, a play is intentionally given a tendentious character that it does not actually have." Ad-libbing was another way performers could circumvent censorship, although the law could punish them if caught. It was a widespread habit among actors working in the provincial and popular theaters, who often went on stage after only two or three rehearsals and relied on improvisation when they forgot their lines.[90]

Actors at times simply ignored the censors and stuck to the original text. Censor Mikhail Tolstoi, attending the performance of a farce at a St. Petersburg theater in 1907, was shocked to find that the actors paid no heed to the censors' deletions and with their gestures "impart a pornographic sense to the most ordinary of scenes." The censors, he complained, could not possibly divine what would become of a text once it reached the theater, since all depended on the actors' "adherence to decency" in their performance. "This condition, however," he concluded, "lying entirely within the jurisdiction of the police inspectorate, is constantly violated, just as is adherence to the censored text." Aleksandr Briantsev, who worked briefly at a St. Petersburg people's theater, recounts in his memoirs that the actors never adhered to the censors' deletions and always performed the full texts of plays. According to Briantsev, the censors themselves suggested possibilities for tendentious interpretations, for their deletions drew the actors' attention to the potentially most provocative passages.[91]

If the censorship policy was not entirely successful in controlling what went on in the theaters, neither was it entirely static. Although the theater censorship was not abolished in 1905, as was the preliminary censorship of publications, it did become a bit less repressive. For the popular theater, this meant that a number of previously forbidden classics and literary plays could now be staged. Among the works approved for all popular theaters in 1905–6 were Goethe's *Faust*, Schiller's *Mary Stuart*, Shakespeare's *Hamlet* and *The Winter's Tale*, Molière's *Don Juan*, Beaumarchais's *The Barber of Seville*, Ibsen's *An Enemy of the People*, Chekhov's *Uncle Vanya*, and Gorky's *The Lower Depths*.[92]

There were two factors in the increased willingness beginning around 1905 to approve a wider variety of plays for performance in the popular theaters. First was a sense that given the social and political turmoil Russia was experiencing, and in which the "common folk" played a prominent role, at least some of the plays that had earlier been thought to contain dangerous ideas were relatively innocuous. Leo Tolstoy's *The Power of Darkness*, which so frightened Pobedonostsev when the Skomorokh Theater announced plans to stage it in 1887, no longer seemed likely to corrupt the "simple folk" in the context of the events of 1905. As a censor put it in December of that year in recommending the play's approval for the popular theaters, "at the present time it is hardly necessary anymore to consider Tolstoy a bearer of extreme ideas."[93]

Second, the distinction between what could be seen by educated society and what the people could see had become somewhat less sharp. While no circular was ever issued denoting a change in policy, the comments of the censors do reveal that their attitude toward works destined for the popular stage did undergo a change. A good example is the censorship history of Sergei Naidenov's *A Wealthy Man*. First examined in 1903, this four-act comedy was prohibited because the censor felt that its negative portrayal of a rich merchant was such that "the intellectually immature audiences of popular theaters could make undesirable generalizations."[94] In November 1906, reviewing the same play on its resubmission, another censor decided that it could now be approved. In his report to the head censor, he indicated that official policy toward the popular theaters had become more lenient since 1903:

> At that time there dominated in the dramatic censorship a tendency to limit the popular repertoire as much as possible to either purely patriotic or tendentiously moralistic plays. Plays in which types from the upper layers of society and even the merchantry are depicted in a not entirely attractive way were generally not allowed on the popular stage, and as a consequence the play by Naidenov under consideration was prohibited. At the present time Your Excellency has found it possible to widen the repertoire of the popular theaters, thus I would find it just to allow the staging of *A Wealthy Man*, as having no harmful tendentiousness, depicting both the merchant and his subordinates impartially, with all of their good and bad qualities.[95]

Thus, while the 1905 Revolution did not lead to the abolition of the popular theater censorship, it did change the context in which the censors viewed some plays.

If censorship policy toward the popular theaters did ease slightly after 1905, many subjects and themes nonetheless remained taboo. Depictions of the tsar and the clergy were still categorically impermissible, as were works that seemed to emphasize social antagonisms or undermine the authorities' prestige. But the distinction between the popular and the regular theater did ease somewhat. The assumption (or pretence) that the common people were utterly incapable of understanding and critically evaluating what they saw on the stage became less common in the censors' judgments after 1905, although it never entirely disappeared.

The main effect of censorship was to stymie the development of a distinctly popular theatrical repertoire in Russia and, with it, low-priced commercial popular theaters other than the holiday *balagany*. Authors tended not to write plays that were specifically aimed at popular audiences, for these had much more difficulty in gaining the censors' approval than did plays destined for the regular stage. As a result, the popular theaters simply recycled plays that had once been performed in more highbrow theaters and had subsequently gained the censors' approval for popular audiences. The burdens imposed by the censorship system, already baneful for ordinary theaters, was often too much for popular theaters that depended on receipts from low-priced tickets. Limited in their choice of repertoire and facing great losses if a play in rehearsal was suddenly forbidden by a local official (who might or might not understand the relevant censorship ruling), few commercial popular theaters were able to turn a profit for long. Only the people's theaters, which received subsidies from various noncommercial sources—industrialists, temperance societies, philanthropists, local governments—had the wherewithal to go through the arduous and often lengthy process of attaining permission to stage new plays and to write off their losses when the authorities forced them to withdraw productions.

THE POPULAR REPERTOIRE

The majority of the plays submitted for performance in popular theaters were in fact approved, either unconditionally or with excisions. According to Press Administration statistics, 702 (86 percent) of the 818 works submitted from 1908 through 1915 were approved. Statistics do not exist for earlier years, but the entries in the censors' registers indicate that the proportions of plays approved and prohibited were similar in the period 1888–1907.[96]

People's theater supporters often claimed that melodramas, farces, and jingoistic plays dominated the popular stage because the censorship blocked the performance of aesthetically superior works. The censors thus joined the commercial entrepreneurs as scapegoats for the many critics of the entertainments offered to popular audiences in their frequent and exaggerated claims that the people's theaters were failing in their mission of enlightenment because they were not presenting a systematic repertoire of high artistic quality. While it is certainly true that censorship made the selection of a repertoire a constant difficulty, this was due to the bureaucratic obstacles and red tape rather than to the fact that "good" plays were kept off the popular stage. It is difficult to agree with Stanislavsky's claim that the censorship made the development of people's theaters "hopeless," for the range of works legally performed on the popular stage was actually quite broad, not to mention the frequency with which prohibited works were staged.

The most common criticism of the popular theater repertoire was that it was not "systematic." That is, it was not constructed according to a coherent educational and aesthetic vision but was a hodge-podge of works approved by the censors and entertaining enough to attract audiences.[97] This criticism was valid enough from the idealistic perspective of the *Kulturträger* but was unfair in taking no account of the practical issues with which popular theaters had to cope. Staging requirements were an important factor in the choice of repertoire; the theaters of the temperance guardianships had the resources to stage operas and plays requiring large casts and complex sets, while factory theaters, especially if they primarily relied on amateur performers, often had to be content with works calling for a limited number of actors and more modest sets. Popular theaters followed the Russian custom of staging a new play each day or week, depending how often performances were held. Although there were always some repetitions, this meant that the theaters had to come up with anywhere from ten to several dozen plays a year.

In two seasons from 1892 through 1894, for example, the Vasilevskii Island Theater staged some 108 different works, the Nevskii Society 122. Moscow's leading commercial venue, the Korsh Theater, also produced a plethora of plays during the same two seasons, 79 in all. Whereas the Korsh repertoire was dominated by contemporary drama, French and Russian farces, and comedies, however, the people's theaters emphasized Russian and foreign classics together with tried-and-true Russian vaudevilles, comedies, and farces. The Nevskii Society staged some 27 works by Ostrovsky, a sprinkling of classics by Gogol, Fonvizin, Sukhovo-Kobylin, Beaumarchais, and Molière, Karpov's popular dramas, and Russian vaudevilles, while the Vasilevskii Island Theater's repertoire was much the same, with the addition of Griboedov, Pisemsky (including his still forbidden *A Bitter Fate*), and Shakespeare.[98]

The repertoires of the popular theaters were in truth no less "systematic" than those of their upmarket counterparts. Indeed, it was only with the advent of the Moscow Art Theater that Russia acquired a theater that pursued clear goals in its repertoire, offering audiences a few but painstakingly rehearsed new works by Chekhov, Gorky, Ibsen, and Maeterlinck, as well as innovative, naturalistic productions of Shakespeare, Ostrovsky, and Alexei Tolstoy. The imperial and commercial theaters of the capitals produced an eclectic mixture of classics, contemporary dramas, operettas, musical comedies, Russian and foreign operas, and translations or imitations of French and German farces. The main difference between the elite theaters and the popular theaters was that the latter tended to include a stronger dose of Ostrovsky and the classics in their repertoires, seasoned with a variety of often dated Russian historical-patriotic plays, vaudevilles, farces and comedies, which would have tasted a bit stale to experienced theatergoers but were still fresh to popular audiences. The patriotic dramas of Nikolai Polevoi and Nestor Kukolnik, officially sanctioned playwrights during the reign of Nicholas I, were seldom performed even in the imperial theaters after the 1840s, but received a new life on the popular stage, as did Luka Antropov's dramatic adaptation of the folk tale *Vanka the Steward*, P. G. Grigorev's vaudeville *The Coachmen*, Aleksandr Ablesimov's eighteenth-century comic opera *Miller, Sorcerer, Cheat, and Matchmaker*, and A. Krasovskii's matchmaking comedy *The Groom from the Cutlery Department,* all of which had been hits earlier in the nineteenth century. After the turn of the century, the various people's houses began staging more contemporary drama, including some of the authors promoted by the Moscow Art Theater, while most factory theaters continued to rely on Ostrovsky, old classics, vaudevilles, and farces.[99]

The overwhelming majority of plays staged by most elite and popular Russian theaters in the late imperial period failed to pass into the canon and have been forgotten, their titles often unfamiliar even to theater specialists. To identify some of the plays that made up the popular theater repertoire is not to set apart a body of texts that can be called "popular" as opposed to "elite." The popular theater repertoire was popular not in the sense that it was fundamentally different from the repertoires of imperial or commercial theaters but in the sense that it was the repertoire, almost entirely borrowed from the hitherto elite culture, that was offered to and consumed by the common people in the inexpensive theaters established by industrialists, temperance societies, philanthropists, and worker-amateurs. For example, some plays written especially for the common people, or "popular dramas" (*narodnye dramy*), such as those by Evtikhii Karpov or Leo Tolstoy's *The Power of Darkness,* were also staged in legitimate theaters, while works by Gogol and Pushkin, written for aristocratic audiences before the Emancipation, became a central part of the popular theater repertoire. To a certain extent, the popular theater repertoire was made up of formerly elite cultural products that had "trickled down," usually but not always filtered through the special censorship. At the same time, popular theaters did not always lag behind, staging only the classics or hits of yesteryear; by the turn of the century, some were acquainting their audiences with new plays that were right in the mainstream of contemporary Russian and European drama, including works by Chekhov, Gorky, Ibsen, Maeterlinck, and Hauptmann.

To sketch the broad contours of the popular repertoire is not to suggest that the plays that made it up necessarily found favor with audiences, or that assumptions about popular tastes, values, or perceptions can be made by analyzing the texts that were most often presented to the people from the stage. To be sure, the managers of popular theaters had to attract audiences and did so by staging the kinds of plays they believed the people wanted to see. But, in selecting the plays, managers were guided by their imaginations and prejudices as to what constituted entertainment or enlightenment for the people, and their choices cannot be simply equated with those of the audiences, for whom the popular theater was often "the only show in town." Moreover, the people's theaters pursued an agenda of enlightenment and did not depend entirely on box office receipts, which meant that to some extent they could impose their choice of repertoire, in the hope that the people would "learn to like it." There is no direct link between repertoire content and audience reception, which must be analyzed by considering how viewers consumed the cultural products they were offered, their reactions to specific performances, and the material and cultural factors that influenced them in their responses.[100]

Any discussion of what was performed for the common people has to begin with the works of Alexander Ostrovsky, which became the foundation of the prerevolutionary popular theater repertoire. One of the pioneers of Russian realistic drama, Ostrovsky depicted the lives of the merchantry and the common people in sentimental plays whose titles often expressed their moral message in the form of a Russian proverb. His colorful characters, lively colloquial dialogue, and skillful portrayals of Russian life made him a favorite of critics, actors, and audiences, a popularity that outlasted the Bolshevik Revolution and continues unabated today. Ostrovsky's *oeuvre*, comprising over fifty plays, was constantly on offer not only in the popular theaters but also in the imperial theaters (especially Moscow's Malyi Theater), Korsh's theater, and provincial theaters throughout Russia.

The Ostrovsky plays most regularly performed in the popular theaters usually have a simple plot, set in the social milieu of the urban lower and middle classes and focusing on a straightforward moral issue. The characters' psychological development is seldom complex; they are often stereotypes whose actions and comments reveal their motivations. Tyrannical patriarchs, their browbeaten families and employees, middle-aged suitors looking for a large dowry, corrupt merchants and officials, and honest but poor drunkards—such are the characters who people Ostrovsky's dramas and comedies, which often revolve around intergenerational conflicts and the pursuit of material gain. Sudden reversals of fortune and surprise revelations, the staples of melodrama, lead more often than not to happy endings in which the underdogs receive justice, the wicked are punished, and the generations reconciled.

Ostrovsky's *Poverty Is No Vice* (1853) and *You Can't Live as You Please* (1854) were among the most frequently performed works in popular theaters. *Poverty* focuses on the despotic merchant Tortsov's plans to marry his daughter Liuba to a rich industrialist, despite her love for Mitia, one of her father's clerks. Liuba's uncle, the drunkard Liubim Tortsov, comes to the aid of the lovers by insulting the industrialist, who renounces his claim to the girl and leaves her free to marry her true love, whose honest character is at last recognized by her father. The moral implications of adultery are examined in *You Can't Live as You Please,* in which the young merchant Petr's extramarital affair leads him to contemplate murdering his virtuous wife Dasha in a drunken rage. Petr is brought to his senses at the last minute by the sound of church bells, and he and Dasha are reconciled.

Among the other works by Ostrovsky that were approved by the censors and became regular features in the popular theater repertoire were *Easy Money, Sit in Your Own Sled, Even a Cat Has Lean Times, An Old Friend Is Better Than Two New Ones, A Lucrative Position, The Heart Is Not a Stone, The Forest, The Poor Bride,* and *A Much Frequented Spot.* Most of them set out a clear moral conflict, in which the weak but virtuous characters triumph over the powerful and greedy, and are technically easy to stage, as they require only one or two simple sets. Ostrovsky's great tragedy *The Storm,* whose unhappy heroine, neglected by her husband, embarks on an affair and is ultimately driven to suicide by her tyrannical mother-in-law, was less often performed, possibly because of its unrelieved gloom and depressing end. *Diary of a Scoundrel* or *Enough Stupidity for Every Wise Man,* Ostrovsky's best-known work outside of Russia, an exposé of the duplicitous conniving of a young careerist who wins the confidence of equally dishonest officials, was also neglected by most popular theaters, perhaps due to the absence of a single positive character.

The classic works of Gogol, Fonvizin, Griboedov, Pushkin, Molière, and Shakespeare were the stalwarts of the popular stage. Comedies such as Gogol's *The Government Inspector* and *Marriage,* Fonvizin's *The Brigadier* and *The Minor,* Griboedov's *Woe from Wit,* and Molière's *Georges Dandin, Tartuffe,* and *The Bourgeois Gentleman* delighted audiences and played year after year in commercial popular theaters, factory theaters, people's houses, and workers' theaters. Shakespeare's works, particularly his tragedies *Othello* and *Hamlet,* were often performed, as were Pushkin's *Rusalka,* a fairy-tale story of romantic betrayal and revenge, and his historical tragedy *Boris Godunov.* Schiller's *Mary Stuart, Love and Intrigue,* and *The Robbers* occasionally played before popular audiences, while some classics, such as Fonvizin's eighteenth-century satire of the loose morals of the provincial gentry, *The Brigadier,* became the almost exclusive property of the popular stage after the 1890s. The theaters run by the temperance guardianships, with their substantial resources, also staged a variety of operas, giving precedence to works by Russian composers such as Glinka, Mussorgsky, and Rubinstein. Aleksei Vertovskii's 1835 romantic opera *Askold's Tomb,* a now forgotten hit of the nineteenth-century Russian stage that was performed hundreds of times in imperial and provincial opera houses, charmed new audiences at popular theaters with its folk motifs and use of native Russian instruments and was sometimes staged as a drama adapted from the libretto.

Historical plays were an ever-present feature of the popular theater repertoire. Due to the censorship constraints, they were usually highly patriotic in tone, and included Polevoi's *The Grandfather of the Russian Fleet*, Gedeonov's *The Death of Liapunov*, and Kukolnik's *The Hand of the Almighty Has Saved the Fatherland*. Dmitrii Averkiev's 1872 historical drama of romantic betrayal, *The Old Days of Kashirsk*, a favorite on imperial and commercial stages all over Russia throughout the late imperial era, was also a perennial offering at the popular theaters, along with other tales of amorous intrigue and deception set in the past such as *Vanka the Steward* and Aleksandr Shakhovskoi's *The Bigamous Wife*. Historical plays and operas celebrating Russian patriotism and military heroism, long staples of the fairground *balagany*, were a distinctive characteristic of the repertoire of the Nicholas II People's House, which became renowned for its extravaganzas featuring huge casts and expensive scenery and costumes. On its capacious stage, audiences could watch Ivan Susanin sacrifice his life to save Russia from the Poles in Glinka's *A Life for the Tsar*, the Russians defeat the Swedes at Poltava in Krylov's *Peter the Great*, the heroic but ill-fated resistance to British and French invaders in Petr Olenin's *Sevastopol*, or Russia's generous assistance to their Slavic brethren during the Russo-Turkish War in A. A. Sokolov's *The White General*.

The Russo-Japanese War stimulated a brief upsurge of patriotism on the Russian stage. *Port Arthur* and *Japan's War with Russia* were hits at popular theaters in the spring and summer of 1904, before Japan's continuing victories belied their optimistic depictions of the war's course. The Moscow and St. Petersburg temperance guardianships offered a few plays about past triumphs, including Viktor Krylov's *1812* and M. V. Dandevil's *Generalissimo Suvorov*, but no new works about contemporary events, and the onset of revolution in 1905 quickly overshadowed the Far Eastern conflict.[101] World War I produced another flurry of patriotic plays, even if some anti-German hits like Konstantin Shitorli's *The Bloody Kaiser* and Mamont Dalskii's *The Shame of Germany* were kept off the popular stage by the censors because they caricatured reigning monarchs.[102] The People's House in St. Petersburg, now renamed Petrograd at the outbreak of the war, staged a handful of contemporary works that emphasized the common man's deep love for his homeland and the newfound unity of Russians of all classes and ethnicities in opposing German aggression. In *Rebirth*, by an anonymous author, a Jewish student gains the respect of his Orthodox fellow citizens by joining the army to fight for Russia, while K. A. Davydovskii's *The Blaze of*

War showed Russians of different political stripes coming together to defend the motherland.[103]

Even in wartime, however, historical works remained the chief vehicle for patriotic expression in the temperance theaters. In August 1914 the People's House opened the season with a new and spectacular dramatization of Suvorov's exploits in the Napoleonic wars, before going on to stage Nikolai Tamarin's *Love and the Motherland,* a melodrama about the cruelty of the fourteenth-century Teutonic Knights, along with the operas *Taras Bulba* and *William Tell.* The 1915–16 season began with that old patriotic warhorse, *A Life for the Tsar.*[104]

Melodrama, light comedy, and vaudeville were central components of the repertoires of all popular theaters. French melodramas, with their poor but virtuous heroines, treacherous upper-class villains, improbable coincidences, and surprise endings, played to packed houses at factory and temperance theaters and commercial popular theaters. Adolphe Dennery's 1874 tearjerker, *The Two Orphans,* a model of the genre written in collaboration with Eugène Cormon, moved audiences with its tale of the misfortunes, separation, and reunion of Henrietta and the blind Louisa. Other imported melodramas that reigned on the popular stage long after they had disappeared from the footlights of the legitimate theaters were Dennery's *The Grace of God,* Victor Ducange's *Thirty Years, or the Life of a Gambler,* Brisbarre and Nus's *The Poor of Paris,* Eduard Schenk's *Belisarius,* and Pierre Decourcelle's *Two Youngsters.* Luigi Camoletti's Italian melodrama *Sister Teresa or Elizabeth Soarez* never achieved much success in the legitimate theaters, but its exposure of the seamy side of convent life and celebration of love's victory over lucre titillated popular audiences for years.

Light comedies and vaudevilles about matchmaking, courtship, and marriage, which packed lots of laughs into one or two acts with few characters and modest staging requirements, like Gogol's *Marriage* and Chekhov's *The Bear, Jubilee, The Proposal,* and *The Wedding,* were often performed in pleasure gardens, factory theaters, people's houses, and by workers' amateur troupes. Old Russian vaudevilles, such as the Petr Karatygin's 1845 *The Uniform* and Dmitrii Lenskii's 1855 *The Simple Girl and the Refined Girl,* which had enjoyed popularity on the imperial stages in the mid-nineteenth century, were revived decades later for new audiences in the popular theaters. P. G. Grigorev's vaudeville *The Coachmen,* first performed at the Aleksandrinskii Theater in 1844, humorously recounts the struggles of a young coachman to win the hand of his beloved, despite attempts by his rival, the village postmaster, to spread ill rumors and discredit him in the eyes of the girl's father. The lies are eventually exposed, and the lovers marry. In Nikolai Kulikov's 1853 comedy *A Crow in Peacock's Feathers*, the young man Anton wins a huge sum of money and begins to lead a spend-thrift and dissolute life, abandoning his betrothed, Parasha, because she is not worthy of his new status. Parasha's mother works for a doctor who steps in and, knowing that Anton is terrified of death, convinces him that he is ill and will soon die if he does not give up his wild behavior. The trick has the desired effect, and Anton returns to the forgiving Parasha.

One comedy was staged so often that it became an example for *Kulturträger* as the antipode of the high culture they wanted to bring to the people: Viktor Krylov's *Matrena the General's Wife*. The heroine, a serf, marries her owner General Kurliatev and does her best to improve the lot of his serfs. Andrei, the general's cruel nephew, is counterpoised to the big-hearted Matrena, imposing ever heavier burdens on the peasants and even buying a married serf couple in order to sell the wife to a prince for his harem. The pair run away and find refuge with Matrena. Andrei's wife leaves him when she learns of his behavior, causing him to do a comic about-face, giving the couple their freedom in order to entice his wife to return. The manager of the Moscow Municipal People's House, Aleksei Bakhrushin, gave a back-handed complement to the play's drawing power when he sadly admitted to a journalist that staging more plays like *Matrena the General's Wife* would bring in more money than the classic and literary plays he was determined to bring to the common people, although he was quick to point out that his theater was not a commercial enterprise.[105]

Farce, imported from France and Germany and reworked by prolific hacks such as Ivan Miasnitskii (Baryshev), D. A. Mansfeld, and S. F. Rassokhin, first gained a following at the Korsh Theater in the 1880s, but soon spread to the provincial stage and the popular theaters. Miasnitskii's works often poked fun at the mores of the Moscow merchantry, as in *The Hare*, a favorite of middle- and working-class amateur actors at factory the-aters and other popular venues. The lawyer Spishnev, living with his jealous wife Olga and her suspicious mother, receives a letter from Kokoshkina, an old girlfriend who intends to pay him a visit. The resulting antics of Spishnev as he tries, with the assistance of his friend Krasnopolskii, to get his wife and mother-in-law out of the house before his old flame arrives, lead to a hilarious series of events in which he is exposed and Krasnopolskii is tricked into betrothing himself to Olga's sister, Liubochka. All ends well for Spishnev, however, for Liubochka is his mother-in-law's favorite daugh-ter, and he rejoices in the knowledge that he will be rid of his nagging mother-in-law now that she will go to live with Liubochka and Krasno-polskii. The crude comic effects of Rassokhin's *On Maneuvers*, a lightly reworked translation of a Berlin farce first performed at the Korsh Theater in 1896, in which characters fall into ponds and climb through windows, were a tremendous commercial success and migrated easily to the popular stage.[106]

Naturalistic dramas, such as Pisemsky's *A Bitter Fate*, that focused on the hardships of working-class and peasant life occupied a prominent place in the popular theater repertoire, especially those by Evtikhii Karpov and Sofiia Belaia. Karpov wrote several "popular dramas" that graphically dramatized the social transformations that accompanied industrialization, urbanization, and peasant migration in the late nineteenth and early twentieth centuries: *The Workers' Settlement, The Free and Easy Life, The George Mine, The Village Widow*, and *A Hard Lot*. Tinged with Karpov's populist convictions, his popular dramas posed clear moral dilemmas, offered audiences positive heroes, and upheld ideals of social justice. Although they were written for popular audiences, Karpov's plays were performed by leading actors and enjoyed considerable success on the imperial and commercial stages, especially in the politically agitated years preceding the 1905 Revolution. *The Village Widow* portrays the struggle between an honest widow and a rapacious rural tavern keeper, ending in the victory of justice when the village council unmasks the tavern keeper as an arsonist. It was a hit in the Aleksandrinskii Theater in 1897, with the great Mariia Savina in the title role, and was produced to great acclaim in Moscow's Malyi Theater in 1898, this time starring the renowned Mariia Ermolova.[107] In *The George Mine*, staged by Karpov himself in the Suvorin Theater in 1901–02, the coalminer Egor, a notorious ladies' man, has an affair with his best friend Petr's wife. Petr learns of the liaison and sets out to revenge himself upon Egor, but finds him near death after an explosion in the mine. Petr forgives his friend, carries him out of the mine to die, and abandons his wife and the mine forever to seek his fortune in the vast expanse of Russia.

Karpov's popular dramas were a "crossover" phenomenon, enjoying success in both elite and popular theaters. Their melodramatic devices and superficially developed characters were outweighed for many contemporaries by their engagement with the problems faced by ordinary people in a fast-changing society. Nikolai Efros, a leading drama critic, commended Karpov's works for their sense of social justice, calling *The George Mine* a "huge collective drama." The plays also had resonance for workers, who praised his plays for depicting their lives and addressing the issues they confronted daily.[108] In contrast, with the exception of his masterpiece *The Power of Darkness*, originally written for Lentovskii's Skomorokh, Leo Tolstoy's popular dramas seldom appeared in legitimate theaters, nor were

they often staged even in temperance and factory theaters, despite their edifying messages about the consequences of drink and adultery. After the censors lifted the ban on *The Power of Darkness* in 1905, it was widely produced in popular theaters, although it had appeared as early as 1895 at the
Skomorokh, where it enjoyed a run of eighty performances.[109]

The Unemployed, a contemporary naturalistic drama by Sofiia Belaia,
inscribed itself in the popular repertoire after its publication in 1909. It was
often staged by worker's amateur theaters, perhaps because its grim depiction of the hardships of working-class life could be used to unmask capitalism's exploitation of the proletariat.[110] Belaia, a provincial actress and theatrical entrepreneur who managed to produce a prodigious dramatic output
while touring across the Russian empire, is a shadowy figure whose contemporary importance is belied by her absence from most histories of prerevolutionary Russian drama. After 1917 Belaia adapted her work to the
new socialist environment, reworking her earlier plots, which tend to focus
on romantic love and social injustice, to introduce themes like class struggle
and women's changing status.[111] Her plays were so popular with peasant
drama circles in the 1920s that a Soviet theater journal declared Belaia to be
"the prophet of the new spectator."[112]

In the 1900s some people's theaters began to branch out beyond the clas-
sics, melodrama, and comic genres to produce more contemporary works
borrowed from the repertoires of legitimate theaters. In addition to
Chekhov, people's theaters staged Gorky's *The Lower Depths* and
Philistines, Naidenov's *A Wealthy Man,* and *Vaniushin's Children,* Ibsen's
Enemy of the People, Hauptmann's *The Sunken Bell,* and Maeterlinck's *The
Blue Bird.* Symbolist drama, in vogue at the turn of the century, never
gained a foothold in the popular theater repertoire, although some symbolist productions were attempted at Countess Panina's Ligovskii People's
House. As for the spate of plays dealing with the "sexual question" (*polevoi
vopros*) that appeared after the 1905 Revolution, they were kept off the
popular stage by the censors, even if they did make their way into fashionable pleasure gardens and onto cinema screens.[113]

• • •

That the state's censorship policy hampered the development of Russian
popular theater is beyond dispute. Since the common people were assumed
to be ignorant, credulous, and easily aroused to violence, plays that were
acceptable on regular stages took on dangerous hues when evaluated for
popular audiences. The censorship policy for popular theaters reflected the

fundamental contradiction in the regime's view of the common people. On one hand, they were seen to be the naive, unlettered, but loyal mainstay of the autocracy, to be shielded from the harmful ideas that had made the intelligentsia into an enemy. On the other hand, the common people were regarded as the dangerous classes whose capacity for violent disorder had to be contained. Behind the censors' rhetoric about the common people's inability to correctly interpret what they saw on stage lay official Russia's apprehensions of a massive popular uprising, like the Pugachev rebellion that had threatened to topple Catherine the Great. The street fighting and rural rebellions that accompanied the 1905 Revolution did nothing to allay those fears, but the censors did allow a wider variety of plays to be performed on the popular stage after 1905, particularly in the officially sanctioned temperance theaters.

Yet popular theaters were able to stage numerous plays from the classical Russian and European repertoire, along with many of the same melodramas, comedies, and contemporary dramas that entertained audiences in more elite theaters in the capitals and the provinces. In spite of the obstacles posed by the censorship, the popular theater repertoire was actually quite broad, even if some works were banned or suffered from censors' deletions. As for the didactic people's theaters, they may have offered less enlightenment due to the censorship but nonetheless succeeded in finding plenty of fare to entertain their audiences, even if from the perspective of Russia's cultural missionaries some of it was not all that nourishing.

4 Theater, Temperance, and Popular Culture

Russia underwent a period of unprecedented industrial expansion during the last two decades of the nineteenth century that culminated in the industrial boom of the 1890s, which the state supported through high tariffs and orders for manufactured goods. The number of factories rose from 30,888 in 1887 to 39,029 in 1897, an increase of over 25 percent. Rapid industrial growth was accompanied by even more rapid urbanization, as peasants were drawn into the cash economy and increasingly sought temporary or permanent employment in large cities and factory towns. Migrants swelled St. Petersburg's population from 1,033,600 in 1890 to 1,439,600 in 1900. Moscow grew at a similar pace, experiencing a 38 percent population increase between 1882 and 1897, when it counted just over 1 million inhabitants.[1]

Of course, not all newcomers to the city became factory workers. At the turn of the century, only 25 percent of St. Petersburg's hired labor force were employed in factories; for Moscow, the figure was 21 percent. Other migrants found work as day laborers, domestic servants, waiters, seamstresses, and shop clerks. Nonetheless, the factory workforce increased significantly in absolute terms. The number of industrial workers in Moscow, for example, rose from 67,400 in 1890 to 99,300 in 1900, a 47.4 percent increase for the decade. In some factories the workforce expanded even more rapidly: by 1901 St. Petersburg's Putilov metalworking plant employed 12,441 workers, up from only 2,306 five years earlier.[2]

Many factory workers lived, both literally and figuratively, on the margins of urban society. Crowded into industrial districts on the peripheries of St. Petersburg and Moscow, they often had little contact with other social classes. Working long hours for low wages, few workers had the time or money to enjoy the cultural and recreational opportunities that urban life could offer. Illiteracy exacerbated the cultural isolation of many workers.

Although basic literacy rates rose steadily from the 1860s, nearly half of Russia's factory workers could neither read nor write, according to the census of 1897. To be sure, literacy levels were much higher in large cities like St. Petersburg and Moscow, especially among skilled, younger male workers.[3] Less skilled or female workers were less likely to be literate, and also less likely to take advantage of the cultural opportunities offered by urban life. At Moscow's Tsindel cotton mill, which employed large numbers of unskilled and semi-skilled workers, a 1900 survey of over 1,400 workers found that only 2 percent had ever been to a public lecture, 9 percent to a circus, and 11 percent to a performance at one of the city's theaters. Even though both the Tretiakov Gallery and the Rumiantsev Museum were but a short walk from the factory, few workers had visited either. Only the Polytechnic Museum had attracted a significant percentage of the Tsindel workers (43 percent), because, they explained, it was located near the flea market where they purchased clothing, shoes, and other necessities. Among skilled workers, who were more likely to be literate, participation in urban cultural life was more common—a third of the metal workers employed at the Tsindel factory had attended a performance at a city theater, and half had visited the Tretiakov Gallery.[4]

The focal points of workers' existence were the factory, the dormitory or communal apartment (*artel'*), and the tavern. Many factories resembled self-contained towns, with shops and lodgings on the premises. Workers found respite from hard work and overcrowded living conditions in the taverns; usually in close proximity to the workplace, they were a central part of male working-class sociability.[5] Among male workers, the most common form of recreation was heavy drinking, which frequently led to violent brawls:

> Twice a month, on Saturday paydays, our artel indulged in wild carousing. Some, as soon as they had collected their pay, would go directly from the factory to beerhalls, taverns, or to some grassy spot, whereas others, the somewhat more dandified types, first went back to the apartment to change clothes. Somber, cross, often bruised, and in some cases still in a state of undiluted intoxication, the inhabitants of our artel would return home late at night or on Sunday morning.[6]

Russia's industrialists viewed their workers' drinking customs with dismay, as a symptom of their low cultural level and lack of self-control. As early as 1867, Ludwig Nobel, owner of an important St. Petersburg metalworks, told the Imperial Russian Technical Society that the excessive alcohol consumption that accompanied workers' holiday celebrations was having a harmful effect on productivity, "diminishing the quantity of manufactured items and raising the cost of labor." The large number of religious holidays in the Orthodox calendar only aggravated the problems resulting from holiday drinking binges, but, not surprisingly, attempts to reduce the number of holidays usually met with stiff resistance from workers.[7]

One industrialist, Timofei Prokhorov, had employed theater to raise his workers' educational and cultural level in the early nineteenth century, when he established Moscow's first recorded factory theater at his family's Trekhgornaia textile mill. Prokhorov took a paternalistic interest in his employees' spiritual and moral well-being, founding Russia's first factory technical school in 1816. Seeing theater as an educational tool, he directed pupils from the school in performances held at the factory. Few details are known about the productions, but among the plays staged was Denis Fonvizin's *The Minor*, later to become a regular feature in the people's theater repertoire. The theater vanished upon Prokhorov's death, yet it is significant as one of the first attempts by a factory owner to put the dramatic arts to use as "a means of assisting our younger brother in his moral education and mental development," to cite the populist language of its chronicler, the critic and theater historian Aleksei Iartsev. Most other factory owners were much less concerned with the spiritual welfare of their workers, and some even ridiculed Prokhorov's ideas about providing workers with educational opportunities.[8]

As Russia's industrial drive intensified in the 1880s, however, educational and cultural initiatives directed at the working class attracted support from many industrialists, who embraced them as a way to increase productivity. In an effort to reduce holiday drunkenness and raise the cultural level of their workers, factory owners began organizing lectures, readings, Sunday schools, magic lantern shows, and other "rational recreations" at their factories. Theater performances, believed to be especially persuasive due to the powerful visual impressions they made on audiences, became a key element in these attempts to inculcate in workers a taste for sober, moral recreations. The passage in 1897 of legislation limiting the workday to eleven and a half hours highlighted the problem of working-class leisure pursuits, and by the end of the 1890s most of the larger factories in St. Petersburg, Moscow, and other Russian cities were sponsoring theater performances on a regular basis. Combining a paternalistic sense of obligation to their "younger brothers" with motives of material self-interest, industrialists hoped that "rational recreations" like theater would help the peasants who flocked to their factories to acquire the rudiments of knowledge and self-discipline required of industrial workers.

Theater performances gradually became an integral part of factory life in urban Russia. Industrialists often built theaters and auditoriums on their factories' premises, some of which can still be seen today. Like Peter the Great, they saw theater as a potentially powerful ally in their "civilizing mission," which wedded elements of a modern, progressive approach to workers' welfare to an older patriarchal tradition of proprietorial dispensation. Although most performances were amateur efforts, it was not uncommon for professional and even imperial actors to be invited to appear before factory audiences—a practice that continued into the Soviet period.

Paradoxically, given the regime's anxieties about theater's potential to corrupt the common people morally and politically, the people's theater movement got its biggest boost from an agency of the state. While the Ministry of Internal Affairs, charged with domestic policing and censorship, tried to keep popular theaters under strict surveillance, its perennial rival the Finance Ministry sponsored them. Theater was enlisted in the campaign it began waging in the 1890s to reduce workers' alcohol consumption, part of Finance Minister Sergei Witte's ambitious program to increase Russian industrial productivity. A state liquor monopoly was introduced between 1895 and 1904 to limit where and when alcoholic beverages could be sold while simultaneously assuring the government of an enormous new source of indirect tax revenues. Guardianships of Popular Temperance, established in localities throughout the empire, were entrusted with the dual task of monitoring adherence to the liquor laws and encouraging more moderate drinking habits among the population. The liquor monopoly provided the state with the income it needed to pay for Witte's industrial policies, while the temperance campaign aimed to produce a more sober and productive labor force. In Russia, unlike Victorian England or the United States, the goal of the official temperance movement was not to stop people from drinking entirely (in part because the government relied so heavily on alcohol sales for revenue) but to reduce their excessive intake of hard spirits like vodka in holiday binges.[9]

According to the instructions issued by the Finance Ministry in December 1894, the temperance guardianships were to "unite all the best local powers to aid the government in attaining its set goal." Composed of state and local officials, together with professionals, the clergy, and other prominent citizens, the guardianships' duty was to ensure that alcohol sales conformed to the law, disseminate information on the dangers of excessive drinking, and establish facilities for the treatment of alcoholism. They were also instructed to "organize popular readings [*narodnye chteniia*], publish suitable brochures, and open reading rooms, tea rooms, and similar institutions where the population can find recreation or healthy relaxation during its free time."[10]

In 1897, the Finance Ministry added theater to its list of suggested measures for promoting sobriety among the population:

> Accessible to the illiterate as well as the literate, and presenting more varied impressions than can even public readings with magic lantern slides, theater performances will doubtlessly attract the common people most. Their relative length will be beneficial in that on a given day they will occupy the entire evening's leisure time and will leave no free time for visiting the taverns.
>
> At the same time it must be kept in mind that people's theaters can serve not only as entertainment but also as a means of moral influence on the popular masses. In particular, with a suitable selection of plays, the guardianships can use theater performances to spread the idea of the danger of abusing strong drink.[11]

The Guardianships of Popular Temperance quickly became the leading sponsors of people's theaters in the Russian empire. Already in 1899 they organized 1,332 theater performances and 1,356 *narodnye gulian'ia*, which usually included plays performed on outdoor stages. In 1904 5,139 theater performances were held under the auspices of the guardianships, together with 4,238 *gulian'ia*. According to the records of the Finance Ministry, some 47,245 theater performances and 32,031 *gulian'ia* were held from 1899 through 1909.[12] Enthusiasm for people's theaters reached such proportions that Witte began to suspect that the guardianships were devoting too much energy to popular entertainments, and he cautioned them against excessive preoccupation with theater in 1900 and again in 1902.[13]

By 1898, St. Petersburg boasted several theaters that catered to popular audiences. The Vasilevskii Island Theater, founded in 1885 by a group of local manufacturers and now run by the Society of Inexpensive Cafeterias, Tearooms, and Workhouses offered theatergoers a variety of year-round entertainments. The society sponsored another people's theater across town in the Okhta district. Just south of the city, on the Shlisselburg Road, the Nevskii Society for the Organization of Popular Recreations ran a winter theater and summer open-air performances for local factory workers. During the summer months, the Guardianship of Popular Temperance organized *narodnye gulian'ia* and staged plays at the Tauride Gardens, not far from the city center, as well as at suburban Ekateringof and Poliustrovo. Altogether there were some twelve public popular theaters or summer *gulian'ia* in St. Petersburg, all but two of which were nonprofit enterprises.[14] Theaters also existed at the Putilov armaments works, the Baltic shipyards, and the Zhukov meat-processing factory. In 1899 there was even an abortive project for a "floating people's theater," which, in addition to holding daily performances at a quay in the city, would be periodically towed up and down the Neva in search of new audiences.[15] In 1900 the temperance guardianship opened the huge Emperor Nicholas II People's House, with a theater that could hold up to 3,000 spectators.

The appearance of the factory and temperance theaters marked a tremendous change in the urban cultural landscape. To be sure, there had always been holiday *balagany* where the lower classes could see elaborate spectacles and, from the 1880s, adaptations of Russian theater classics. A few pleasure gardens catered to people with little money to spare, the imperial theaters had a few cheap seats in the upper balconies, and they and the legitimate theaters staged discount matinees. But it was relatively expensive for all but the best-paid to attend most performances: at the turn of the century the very cheapest tickets to the Bolshoi Theater started at 60 kopeks, to the Malyi Theater at 37 kopeks, while the average annual wage of a Moscow blue-collar worker was 264 rubles, or 22 rubles a month, rising to 400–600 rubles (35–50 rubles a month) for a highly skilled machinist.[16] Women and nonfactory workers earned even less. The more fashionable summer pleasure gardens, although not out of reach to workers fortunate enough to earn 20–40 rubles per month, still cost too much to frequent regularly. Entry into St. Petersburg's Arcadia or Moscow's Aquarium gardens, for example, cost 40 or 50 kopeks, with an additional charge to enter the enclosed theaters. The factory and temperance theaters, however, offered low-priced entertainments for 5 or 10 kopeks year-round and opened the door for working people to see a stunning variety of drama, vaudeville, farce, operetta, and sometimes opera and ballet, as well as the folk singers, comedians, acrobats, clowns, and magicians that were familiar from the fairgrounds and pleasure gardens. Nor were these theaters, even those in industrial suburbs, exclusively patronized by the urban poor. Factory managers and their families, officers, petty officials, students, shopkeepers, and even professionals also attended the people's theaters, making them a rare public space where all classes of urban society rubbed shoulders, at least in the lobbies, buffets, and surrounding parks, if not in the seats.

The factory and temperance theaters ushered in a new era in urban popular culture, in which low-priced entertainment became a commodity regularly available to the urban subordinate classes. Of course, the mass market entertainment *par excellence* appeared at the turn of the century—the cinema, or *kinemo*, as it was known in popular parlance. The "moving photographs" came to Russia in May 1896, when the Lumière brothers' famous train pulled into the station on screens at St. Petersburg's Aquarium and Moscow's Hermitage pleasure gardens, before going on to amaze visitors to the Nizhnii Novgorod Exposition. At first films were usually shown in pleasure gardens and on fairgrounds, but in 1903 two "electric theaters" opened in Moscow, showing hour-long programs of short newsreels and "scenes from life." Not until after the 1905 Revolution did cinema cast off its association with fairground entertainments, when purpose-built cinemas showing feature films spread to cities and towns throughout the empire—by 1913 there were 134 cinemas in St. Petersburg, 107 in Moscow.[17]

Although the first Russian feature film, the seven-and-a-half-minute *Stenka Razin*, was released in 1908, the Russian market was dominated by French and other foreign imports until World War I. Melodramas, detective stories, and historical dramas were the mainstays of the prewar cinema repertoire. Russian directors also adapted folktales like *Stenka Razin* and classics of Russian literature like Tolstoy's *War and Peace* to the screen. Even after the advent of feature films, however, movies usually ran for only about fifteen to thirty minutes, and a cinema program often consisted of four or five titles. Longer films became common only after 1913, with the phenomenal success of *The Keys to Happiness*, a melodrama about a woman's search for fame, love, and sexual satisfaction, adapted from Anastasiia Verbitskaia's blockbuster into a two-part film (each segment ran for over an hour).[18]

Cinema was often hailed as the new democratic entertainment, and it is true that, as Denise Youngblood observes, "cinema going was a pastime primarily identified with the 'middling classes' in the cities, including the literate proletariat."[19] Different cinemas, however, usually had different clienteles. The cinemas located in city centers were often quite luxurious "movie palaces" and catered to middle-class audiences, while those in working-class districts were usually modest structures resembling long barns and served a more lowbrow public. In some of the larger cinemas with socially mixed audiences, there was segregation by seating, as in theaters, with the cheapest seats in the front or in the upper gallery.[20]

The line between cinema and theater was sometimes blurred. The Nicholas II People's House showed movies, and many cinemas included live variety acts in their programs.[21] At the end of the 1900s a new type of urban popular theater made its appearance, a spin-off from the cabarets or intimate theaters that were usually called "miniature theaters." Miniature theaters like the Crooked Mirror and the Bat, established in 1908, were elite venues for an in-crowd, where the cream of Russian artistic bohemia and their hangers-on enjoyed theatrical improvisations and parodies.[22] But they were soon emulated by commercial enterprises eager to cash in on the fashion for miniature theater, and by 1912 there were some 125 operating in Moscow and St. Petersburg, having lost both their elite cachet and their intimate atmosphere (some held a thousand people). Many of them, known as "theaters of the streets" (*teatry ulits*), were small operations located on alleys in working-class districts or the city outskirts and specialized in the variety show format familiar to audiences from the cheap pleasure gardens and the fairgrounds—operettas, farces, vaudevilles, circus acts, comic routines, and sentimental ballads, together with short films.[23] Sparsely attended on weekdays but packed on holidays, the miniature theaters of the streets ran six to twelve shows a day for a public that a journalist contemptuously described as "from the very lowest depths" of the population.[24] They were a sort of condensed version of the bigger *balagan* theaters, selling working-class consumers a series of short entertainments without the carnival atmosphere.

The factory theaters, temperance theaters, cinemas, and miniature theaters had come to occupy roughly the same territory in the urban cultural landscape by 1914. Yet they were very different social spaces. In the temperance theaters and some of the factory theaters the variety and scale of entertainments surpassed anything that could be seen in the cinemas or miniatures. The cheap cinema or miniature "theater of the streets" offered an hour- or hour-and-a-half–long experience, consumed in the relative anonymity (and darkness, in the case of the cinema) of a small interior that had no foyer, buffet, or park. In the cinema, the classes might come together, but they did not see much of one another, even if they did sense each other's presence in the darkness.

DRY CARNIVALS IN A WORKERS' SUBURB

In April 1885 a group of manufacturers, officials, and residents on the Shlisselburg Road, a thoroughfare running through the industrial suburbs of St. Petersburg that stretched for miles along the right bank of the Neva from the Obvodnyi Canal to the village of Slavianka, founded a circle to organize holiday carnivals for the area's factory workers. They elected as their president the paper manufacturer and advocate of popular education Vladimir Vargunin. Raising 1,375 rubles by subscription, the circle fenced off a vacant lot, lent free of charge by the Nevskii Suburban Railway Society, and constructed an orchestra pavilion, swings, a climbing mast, and other modest attractions. In May 1885 the first of their dry *narodnye gulian'ia* was held in the factory village of Aleksandrovskoe, just southeast of St. Petersburg. Admission was only ten kopeks for adults (three kopeks for children), and entertainment consisted of a military band, a soldiers' chorus, and a fairground barker, or *balagannyi ded*.[25] Despite the modesty of its recreational offerings, the *narodnoe gulian'e* was a success, attracting a couple of thousand people and depriving the neighborhood taverns of nearly half their customers. In July an outdoor stage was completed, and performances by clowns, acrobats, and storytellers were added to the entertainments, along with pantomimes, short comedies, and one-act vaudevilles. Twenty-five carnivals were held the first year, attended by some 64,000 people.[26]

The "Vargunin" *gulian'ia*, as they were popularly known, were intended as an answer to the problem of holiday disorder and drunkenness among the thousands of workers who inhabited the area along the Shlisselburg Road, the site of some of St. Petersburg's largest and most technically advanced factories. A pamphlet published by Evtikhii Karpov to commemorate the decennial of the carnivals described the situation from the factory owners' point of view:

> Until the opening of the *narodnye gulian'ia* in the village of Aleksandrovskoe, the tens of thousands of workers living beyond the Nevskii Gate had no rational recreations. Working folk . . . poured onto the streets on holidays, crowding the taverns and drinking away their hard-earned kopeks. The young people gathered on the bank and in the fields, organizing fistfights and games of heads or tails and cards, which often ended in quarrels and blows. The local police always had to struggle with this disorder.[27]

The area's workers did have other ways of passing their leisure time besides drinking and fighting. Though taverns were indeed a place to drink on credit, they were also a focal point of community life, where singing was a favorite pastime and newspapers were available to peruse or read aloud to others. According to Konstantin Skorobogatov, who grew up in the neighborhood and began working at the Obukhov machine-building factory as a boy, some traditional rural holiday celebrations endured in the area, reflecting the endurance of peasant customs among migrant workers living on the fringes of urban culture:

> Before Whitsunday, in the great courtyard of the Imperial Card Factory's "outbuildings," the workers from the Obukhov, Baird, and Card factories would dance around a birch tree decorated with multicolored ribbons and sing "Lipen'ka." This was a popular round-dancing song. The fellows were not admitted into the round dance. They played *gorodki* [a game] and waited to see who would be taken into the circle. Finally the girls picked one fellow, pushed him into the circle, teased him, and then pushed him out of the circle. At the end they went dancing and singing down to the Neva to drown the birch-*lipen'ka*.[28]

However, as Karpov suggests, other pastimes were less innocuous. Fighting often broke out around the taverns, especially between the local residents and the peasants who came from Riazan to seek temporary work unloading coal shipments for the Obukhov factory. Organized mass fist combats, a common recreation in rural Russian villages, were a favorite "spectator sport" on the Shlisselburg Road: "Sometimes they were regarded as an entertaining, gripping spectacle. They did not arise spontaneously but were organized. The combats took place on Sundays and holidays. In the narrow, shallow gully between two hills, the inhabitants of the villages of Aleksandrovskoe and Farforovskoe would arrange a savage fistfight [between members of the two villages]. A great number of people would gather to watch the renowned strong men, the Zaitsev brothers."[29]

Middle-class Russians saw the very existence of the organized fist combats, when as many as a thousand men sometimes took part in the fun, as proof of "popular backwardness and crudeness" and argued that any alternative entertainment would be an improvement.[30] Russian factory owners shared this appraisal but also worried about the disruptive influence and debilitating effect of holiday drinking and violence on the workforce. In sponsoring the *narodnye gulian'ia*, the Shlisselburg Road manufacturers hoped to bring a civilizing influence to bear on the recreational behavior of their employees.

By calling their entertainments *narodnye gulian'ia*, Vargunin and his collaborators were associating them with the carnivals traditionally held in Russian towns at Shrovetide, Easter, and other holidays.[31] Unlike their namesakes, however, the Vargunin *gulian'ia* were held not only on religious holidays but lasted throughout the summer. They took place not in a fairground open to all but in an enclosed park with access restricted to those who paid the ten-kopeck entrance fee. Once inside the gates, visitors had unlimited and free access to all the shows, whose form and content depended on the judgment of the park's organizers rather than on the commercial instincts of theatrical entrepreneurs. The emphasis on temperance and orderly behavior was a far cry from the atmosphere of the traditional *gulian'e*, which was permeated with the alcohol that formed an integral part of any Russian holiday celebration. The noun *gulian'e* itself has connotations of carousing and getting drunk, particularly in its diminutive form, *gulian'ka*. In effect, the industrialists were seeking to create an ersatz, sanitized carnival, a *gulian'e* purged of any *gulian'ka*. Naturally, no hard spirits were sold; visitors were instead plied with tea from steaming samovars.

The organizers of the *narodnye gulian'ia* were pleased with the results of their efforts, which they claimed had tamed the formerly savage behavior of the workers, at least within the precincts of the park: "The absence of strong drink in the snack bar . . . made the *gulian'ia* entirely decorous. There was neither rowdiness, fighting, nor foul language. Workers came to the *gulian'ia* with their wives and children. Having listened to the music, laughed at the clowns' escapades, watched a comedy, and drunk a bit of tea as a family, they went home satisfied." The manufacturers proudly reported in 1895 that, despite the enormous crowds of visitors, during ten years of *gulian'ia* "there was not a single incident requiring the energetic intervention of the police," who were apparently sympathetic to the circle's aims. According to Nikolai Popov, who reported on the Nevskii Society's activities at the Second Congress of Activists in Technical and Professional Education in 1895, the idea for the Shlisselburg carnivals was initially suggested by a local police official.[32]

The carnivals may have been orderly, but the quality of entertainment offered was not very high at the beginning, with the repertoire limited to vaudevilles, comic sketches, and Polevoi's historical-patriotic drama, *The Grandfather of the Russian Fleet*. Ivan Shcheglov, the leading prerevolutionary expert on popular theater, drew a dismal portrait of one of the early *narodnye gulian'ia*: "The site allotted for the *gulian'e* was an utter wasteland, at the end of which rose an 'open stage' of rather wretched appearance. A little to the side of it a motley group of workers despondently drank tea under a wooden awning, and another similar group intently danced a polka on the bare sand in the company of gaunt factory girls. In particular, the performance at the open theater made a depressing impression on me." Under the energetic leadership of Vargunin and other members of his family, however, the carnivals steadily improved. A professional actor invited to take charge of organizing entertainment in 1886 added Ostrovsky's *Poverty Is No Vice* and *You Can't Live as You Please* to the repertoire of the theater's second season, as well as Leo Tolstoy's temperance tract, *The First Distiller*. Two years later the *gulian'ia* were moved to a more central location on the Shlisselburg Road, next to the Imperial porcelain factory, and in 1889 the circle took out a 44,500-ruble loan to purchase the property and its four buildings from the Kalinkin brewery. The dramatic offerings expanded greatly over the years, with Ostrovsky's works serving as the foundation of the repertoire. On a return visit to a *narodnoe gulian'e* in the early 1890s, Shcheglov found no trace of the former "wasteland," but instead "a vast and well-equipped park," which he compared to the city's better pleasure gardens.[33]

In 1891 the circle was reorganized as the Nevskii Society for the Organization of Popular Recreations, whose charter defined its reform agenda as "affording the local working population with moral, sober, and inexpensive recreations, such as *narodnye gulian'ia*, readings, concerts, and dance evenings."[34] A not-for-profit organization, the society excluded tavern owners from membership and claimed to be interested only in making its recreations as inexpensive and accessible as possible. In 1893 the society opened a library and reading room, adding a second library in 1896.[35]

Theatrical performances rapidly took the lead role in the Nevskii Society's cultural enlightenment activities, so much so that at the 1895 All-Russian Agricultural Exposition the literacy committee gave it an award for furthering the development of people's theaters.[36] In 1891 an indoor winter theater with a capacity of 250–300 was built that in its first season presented some twenty-three different plays, including seven works by Ostrovsky and Gogol's comedy, *Marriage*.[37] Evtikhii Karpov, invited in early 1892 to direct performances at the Nevskii Society, organized two amateur troupes for productions in the winter theater (professional actors were used in summer performances). One troupe was composed of intelligentsia amateurs—teachers, students, writers and their wives, university lecturers, artists, and other members of the free professions. The second troupe was made up exclusively of workingmen from the machine-building factories, women workers from the porcelain and card factories, and seamstresses. The intelligentsia troupe performed Griboedov's *Woe from Wit*, Gogol's *The Government Inspector*, Ostrovsky's *Easy Money*, and other plays set in an educated milieu, while the workers' troupe staged only plays "from the daily lives of peasants, merchants, and the lower middle class [*meshchanstvo*]," which had roles they could identify with.[38]

Karpov was one of the few people active in the people's theater movement who was intimately acquainted with the lives of workers, having worked at various times as a machinist on a Volga tugboat and a metal fitter in a Nizhnii Novgorod factory. Nikolai Skorobogatov, who participated in one of the workers' troupes organized by Karpov at the Nevskii Society, later remembered that "for me and a number of young actors who had received no methodical professional instruction, Karpov was a wonderful teacher." He continued to give advice to the workers' troupe even after leaving the society in 1895 and was instrumental in arranging guest performances by actors from the Imperial Aleksandrinskii Theater.[39]

Karpov was replaced as director by Sviatoslav Svetlov, a dentist who was also a professional actor and director. Svetlov followed in Karpov's footsteps, assembling a troupe of professional actors, often people temporarily without a seasonal contract, to stage works by Ostrovsky, Fonvizin, Pushkin, Griboedov, Leo Tolstoy, Alexei Tolstoy, Shakespeare, Schiller, Hugo, and other greats, together with melodramas, farces, and light comedies.[40] Even full-length operas, including *Faust* and *A Life for the Tsar*, were occasionally staged, to the enthusiastic response of audiences.[41] Among the public's favorite plays, according to Karpov, were Gogol's *The Government Inspector*, Fonvizin's *The Minor*, and Griboedov's *Woe from Wit*.[42] By 1900 the society could boast a 1,500-seat theater and a special children's theater where children staged plays under adult supervision. In the following years the society produced more plays by contemporary authors, such as Chekhov, Gorky, and Naidenov, but melodramas and spectacular stage effects never lost their popularity with audiences.[43]

The Nevskii Society's theater was widely considered to be a model theater for the working classes. The populist writer Nikolai Mikhailovskii characterized the recreations organized by the society as having "an educational character in the broadest sense of the word." Even the ultra-conservative *Moscow Gazette*, often vitriolic in its condemnation of people's theaters for allegedly corrupting the people, admitted that in the hands of its industrialist sponsors the Nevskii Society was "a good enterprise." Aleksandr Briantsev, who as a student worked at the theater during the 1902–03 season, credited it with staging "serious performances for worker audiences." As for the audiences, according to Skorobogatov, a socialist worker not inclined to exaggerate the munificence of the bosses, "the theater enjoyed the recognition and love of the inhabitants of the Nevskii Gate [area]."[44]

A few contemporaries took a dimmer view of the society's theatrical activities, which they criticized for emphasizing entertainment at the expense of enlightenment. Nikolai Popov looked askance at the custom of holding dances while changing the sets between acts, arguing that this gave the entire *gulian'e* "a purely recreational character" and made audiences loath to watch serious drama. He also found fault with the society for staging patriotic plays, farces, and other unedifying fare. One St. Petersburg theatrical paper praised the repertoire as "varied, adjusted to suit the tastes of the local public, consisting predominately of working folk," and acknowledged that performances almost always attracted a large crowd, but commented disapprovingly that "together with such plays as *The Cherry Orchard, Othello, Angelo, The Lower Depths,* etc., run heart-rending melodramas like *Martyrs, Belisarius,* and so on."[45]

Yet the Nevskii Society was attentive to the tastes of its clientele. In 1895, at Karpov's suggestion, it conducted a survey to determine which plays audiences liked best.[46] Opera was introduced into the repertoire in the late 1890s and proved successful, despite the sometimes uneven quality of performances.[47] On the whole, the society produced an even balance of literary plays, light comedies, vaudevilles, farces, and melodramas, even if critics did question some of the selections from an aesthetic or didactic perspective and fault it for not staging only serious drama.

The Nevskii Society's *gulian'ia* were a fascinating microcosm of the social and cultural dynamics of St. Petersburg's transformation into a booming modern industrial metropolis and the fifth largest city in Europe. A setting in which newfound tastes, roles, and identities were tried on for size, the park was a smorgasbord of genres, cultures, and social types. Gogol and Pushkin were served up together with factory ditties (*chastushki*), "Ta-ra-ra-bum-dee-ay," and café chansons imported from the pleasure gardens, to be enjoyed by dandified young men and women who peppered their speech with vocabulary lifted from the pages of the boulevard press, as well as by people who looked as though they had just stepped out of a peasant *izba*—all to the intermittent strains of the quadrilles, waltzes, and polkas that were superseding folk tunes in urban popular culture.

Audiences were predominantly made up of local workers, a heterogeneous group whose appearance reflected the great variations in degree of acculturation to urban life that were typical of St. Petersburg's working classes at the turn of the century. Shcheglov's description of the crowded dance floor at intermission, while somewhat condescending toward workers' attempts to be fashionable, gives a good sense of the sociocultural quilt:

> a fellow in an overly tight jacket dances with a lass in a sleeveless peasant dress [*sarafan*], a Russian peasant shirt whirls with a local factory girl in a stylish jacket and bustle. In one place two peasant women, in another an old man in a bowler hat bobs up and down with a girl, probably his daughter. In the crowd occasionally flashes a stylish woman's hat, the service cap of a telegraphist and even—Oh horror!—a top hat, a genuine tall German top hat.[48]

Sometimes workers discovered a new role as paid performers and took part in variety shows. In the early 1890s, waiting for the curtain to rise on Ostrovsky's *An Old Friend Is Better Than Two New Ones*, audiences were entertained by folk singers and dancers in "traditional costumes," an opera soloist in evening dress, a comic in checkered trousers, a factory girl singing romances in a silk dress and gloves, and a locally reputed accordionist, a factory worker who performed popular songs about love, betrayal, and the financial hardships of marriage.[49]

A nostalgic tone permeates Shcheglov's sketches of the entertainments, performers, and audiences, for he is uneasy with the social and cultural transformations he witnesses at the Nevskii Society. He complains about the use of "foreign" words by the factory public and in the posters advertising the shows—for example, *sekundant* (assistant), *antrakt* (intermission), *divertisment* (variety show)—and shares the disappointment of a worker, who cannot join in the dancing since he does not know the quadrille, with the disappearance of traditional dances like the Ukrainian *kazachok*. The man in checkered trousers, typically worn by the urban petit bourgeoisie according to the contemporary Russian stereotype, is amusing the public with the same "vulgar" ditties "that have made the rounds of all the pleasure gardens." He describes the appearance of the girl singing romances in detail (a silk dress with a train, evening gloves, and flowers in her hair and bodice). He ironically compares her to the French star Sarah Bernhardt, noting that the master of ceremonies introduces her as Madame (*gospozha*) Sidorova, much to the amusement of her acquaintances and the envy of one of the young women in the audience. Shcheglov also complains that a profusion of women's hats blocks the view of the stage, just as in the city's finer venues, implying that working people are imitating the fashions worn by the privileged classes. He is quick to point out that fancy dress is no guide to social status:

> It would be a mistake to assume that the ladies with palm fronds on their heads and men in stylish bowlers comprise in any way the cream of the intelligentsia, for in the event of any unpleasant misunderstanding that leads to a confrontation, the dandy who looks like a man-about-town on Nevskii Prospekt turns out to be an ordinary metalworker from a neighboring factory, while the lady in a cloak with a Spanish collar and an ostrich plume in her hat turns out to be a laundress from the nearby textile mill.[50]

Shcheglov's preoccupation with vocabulary, dances, and attire reveals his dismay at the intrusion of urban, foreign mannerisms and styles into popular culture. His sketches of the crowds are also tinged with a sense that the *narod* is transgressing social boundaries, adopting roles inappropriate to their status, and rewriting the cultural scripts that set the expectations of their comportment. He seems to discern, at least subconsciously, that people's theater on the Shlisselburg Road entails much more than merely giving the common people the gift of elite artistic culture, that "civilizing" them is a polyvalent process. Like Chekhov's peasant-cum-capitalist Ermolai Lopakhin, the workers of the St. Petersburg factory suburb are buying the gentry estate but cutting down the cherry orchard to build summer cottages.

THE SPREAD OF FACTORY THEATERS

The extensive publicity surrounding the Nevskii Society's theatrical activities and other "rational recreations" soon led factory owners in other parts of

St. Petersburg to establish their own theaters and pleasure gardens for workers. Encouraged by St. Petersburg municipal governor P. A. Gresser, a group
of manufacturers from Vasilevskii Island constructed a theater on Smolensk
Field, near the Baltic shipyards.[51] The Vasilevskii Island Theater for Workers
opened with ceremony and prayer on a Sunday in early February 1887, in
the presence of Gresser, the mayor, the director of the Baltic shipyards, and
other city dignitaries. According to newspaper accounts, the theater drew a
large and responsive working-class audience from the surrounding area:

> The opening produced quite a favorable impression. The theater looked
> festive and was decorated with flags inside and out. The auditorium,
> which is very spacious and fairly comfortable, was full. Ostrovsky's
> drama *You Can't Live as You Please* and the skit *Night Watch* were
> performed. The "gray" working folk watched the drama with great
> attention and reacted passionately and with animation to both it and
> the performers, generously rewarding the latter with applause. . . . The
> working class's sympathy for the new theater could be seen in the fact
> that not only workingmen, but also their wives and children, came to
> the performance.[52]

The theater held over seven hundred spectators and was situated on Bolshoi
Prospekt, in a small park where *narodnye gulian'ia* were organized during
the summer months, with music, attractions, and outdoor theater performances.

The Vasilevskii Island manufacturers did not manage the theater themselves but instead leased it to various theatrical entrepreneurs, who were
given a share of the profits in return for staging plays and organizing holiday entertainments. The entrepreneurs had difficulty making ends meet on
sales of the low-priced tickets, and the theater struggled for several years
under a succession of actor-managers: provincial actor P. A. Denisenko
(1887), veteran of the imperial and operetta stages A. F. Makarev-Iunev
(1889–92), and St. Petersburg actor N. I. Merianskii (1892–94). In 1894 the
Society of Inexpensive Cafeterias, Tearooms, and Workhouses took charge
and ran the theater until 1902, when it passed into the hands of the newly
organized Vasilevskii Island Society for Popular Recreations, an association
of local factory owners. The Guardianship of Popular Temperance assumed
management in 1906.[53]

At first local workers and their families predominated in the audience,
especially on Sundays and holidays, but the theater gradually attracted a
more socially varied public from other parts of the city, who were drawn by
the low-priced performances of Ostrovsky, Shakespeare, other Russian and
foreign classics, and especially melodramas. Boxing and wrestling matches

Figure 8. Children's performance at the Vasilevskii Island Theater for Workers. St. Petersburg, 1898. *Niva*, no. 35 (29 August 1898): 692.

were also big crowd-pleasers, until the city governor banned them.[54] After a visit in 1892, Ivan Shcheglov reported that, as at the Nevskii Society's entertainments, the public of the Vasilevskii Island Theater was a hodgepodge of St. Petersburg's lower and middle classes, "from officers to unskilled workers, from stylish ladies with lorgnettes to peasant women in scarves and sheepskin coats."[55]

The 1890s saw the appearance of more factory theaters in St. Petersburg, but they were more modest ventures than the Nevskii Society's theater or the Vasilevskii Island Theater. In the Vyborg district an association of factory owners established a pleasure garden called Vyborg Park, where summertime carnivals featured variety shows, vaudevilles, farces, dancing, and occasional displays of fireworks, all for an admission fee of twelve kopeks.[56] Attendance was sparse, however, due to the mud that surrounded the park during rainy weather and the proximity of a garbage dump. To make matters worse, the entrepreneur who managed the *gulian'ia* tried to cut costs by repeating the same entertainments day after day. After several seasons the *gulian'ia* ceased in 1895.[57]

In the Nevskii district, inhabited by some 10,000 factory workers, the Zhukov slaughterhouse decided in 1897 to organize holiday entertainments for its workers "to divert them from drunkenness and at the same time eradicate the so-called *ponedel'nichanie* [St. Monday, or the practice of showing up for work late or not at all after a day off], an extremely undesirable phenomenon in factory life."[58] During the winter of 1898 the firm began sponsoring readings and magic lantern shows at the slaughterhouse, distributing free tickets to employees. The readings and shows were so popular that workers from Zhukov's other factories began asking for tickets, which were sometimes resold for from three to fifteen kopeks. At Shrovetide and Easter a troupe of intelligentsia amateurs staged several vaudevilles at the factory, which for most of the audience was their first exposure to theater. Nine readings and two theater performances were held that winter, attended by over 5,000 persons.[59]

Impressed by the success of the readings and theater performances, the Zhukov factory planned a series of *narodnye gulian'ia* during the summer of 1898. The local factory inspector backed the idea, as did factories in the neighborhood, which contributed nearly 3,000 rubles to the project. On an unused parcel of land belonging to the Zhukov firm a park was laid out, with an open-air theater, a dance floor, and a refreshment counter that sold nothing stronger than kvass. From mid-June until the end of August fourteen *gulian'ia* were held at the Ligovskii Park, attended by over 26,000 people, unskilled workers for the most part. The program consisted of variety shows, dancing, fireworks, and performances of vaudevilles and comedies by an amateur troupe. The repertoire, based on that of the Nevskii Society, included Gogol's *Marriage*, Molière's *Georges Dandin*, and Ostrovsky's *A Lucrative Position*.[60]

The organizers of the Ligovskii *gulian'ia* were confident that they had made a positive impact on working-class life. "Little by little a need for rational recreations and a love for the fine arts will develop among the people, and then perhaps the tavern's coarse environment will begin to attract them less," was their optimistic assessment of the park's first season. Even the factory owners admitted, however, that workers would hardly be satisfied with entertainments when they had so many other urgent material needs. Some workers regarded the recreations with unconcealed cynicism, remarking that the bosses were amusing only themselves, for if they really wanted to help their employees they would do something about the lack of decent housing, medical facilities, sickness benefits, and affordable shops, instead of merely building a park.[61]

Labor relations grew increasingly discordant in the 1890s, for the factory theaters and other owner-sponsored recreations did nothing to avert grievances concerning wages and hours. The textile factories along the Shlisselburg Road experienced massive strikes in 1896, 1897, and 1901, as did other St. Petersburg factories. The strike of 1896–97 led to the implementation of a law limiting the workday to eleven and a half hours on weekdays and to ten and a half hours on Saturdays and the eve of holidays.[62] Interestingly, the strikes did not subdue industrialists' enthusiasm for sponsoring theatrical entertainments, while the workers' modest gains in leisure time put a spotlight on the need for "rational recreations." A performance of Molière's *Tartuffe* at the Nikolaev Railway workshops in 1898 drew so large an audience of workers that the management built a theater with space for a thousand, hired a professional troupe, and began selling tickets by subscription to determine which plays audiences were most interested in seeing.[63] During the early 1900s two dramatic troupes, one composed of white-collar employees, the other of workers, regularly performed at St. Petersburg's Obukhov factory.[64] In 1901 the Nobel mechanical factory opened a People's House for workers in St. Petersburg's Vyborg district, which organized popular science lectures, religious-ethical readings, evening courses, choral performances, a workers' orchestra, and readings of Ostrovsky's plays.[65]

As the nineteenth century drew to a close, factory owners throughout Russia were sponsoring theater performances and holiday carnivals to combat their workers' excessive alcohol consumption. In Moscow and the central industrial region, people's theaters were sprouting "like weeds," exclaimed a journalist writing in *The New Times*. Nikolai Popov characterized the trend in 1896:

> A number of facts, which have demonstrated clearly enough the significance of these entertainments for the factory owners themselves, have inspired the largest factories to set up theaters and organize *narodnye gulian'ia*, while the factory folk, having discovered the possibility of spending holidays out of the tavern, have thus lessened the number of post-holiday absences and in this manner have begun to return with interest what their employers have spent on the organization of entertainments. This mutual benefit, naturally, causes other factory owners to join the new current.[66]

The press was filled with similar stories about the miraculous effects of theater on working-class behavior. Theater critic and historian Aleksei Iartsev noted in 1900 that industrialists were reaping the benefits as theater's influence on workers made itself felt. This rosy picture was in part due to the writers' desire to promote people's theaters, and in some cases to encourage a potential growth sector for theatrical employment. *Theater and Art*, always attentive to the interests of the acting profession, even called on factory owners to build theaters in every industrial center. In any case, it seemed clear that factory theaters, as the liberal journal *The Northern Herald* observed, had become "a widespread and characteristic phenomenon of the epoch in which we are living." Although Moscow industrialists initially lagged behind their St. Petersburg counterparts, by 1899 the majority of the city's larger factories and workshops were holding theater performances for their workers, according to a report issued by the Russian Theatrical Society. As at the Nevskii Society, sometimes workers took part in the productions and even formed their own troupes.[67]

The Prokhorov dynasty's Trekhgornaia textile mill began staging plays for its workers again in 1890. Eventually a 200-seat theater was built, with 17 rows and 23 boxes. Admission was free for workers, but seating was defined by the social hierarchy of the factory: the first rows and lodges were occupied by officials, white-collar employees, and their families, while the workers filled the back rows, although everyone mingled at the refreshment counter during intermission. Several amateur troupes performed at the theater, including one made up of younger factory workers, who staged Gogol's *Marriage* and Grigorev's vaudeville *The Coachmen* in 1894 before an audience of workers and their families. Occasionally, actors from the Imperial Malyi and other Moscow theaters performed at the factory.[68]

Between 1894 and 1903 theaters appeared at the Tsindel, Till, Kuvshinskii, Balashinskii, Guzhon, Einem, and Giro factories in Moscow, as well as at the workshops of the Moscow-Kazan and Moscow-Kursk railways.[69] In the mid-1890s, the Maliutin factory at Ramensk built a two-tiered theater with gas lighting, where factory stewards and teachers performed together with a chorus of workers.[70] The Great Yaroslavl Manufactory began staging plays for employees in 1894, in the 1,500-seat auditorium of the factory's school.[71] In the Zvenigorod district near Moscow, the Ivanovskaia textile factory organized some 110 performances for workers and local peasants between 1890 and 1916.[72] The theaters and other entertainments may have been sponsored with the aim of improving working-class behavior, but they nonetheless had a festive air. Sunday evening performances were often followed by dances, which often lasted until early morning.[73]

Konstantin Stanislavsky, unable to realize his goal of establishing an "accessible theater" where a new audience could see his innovative productions, brought the theater to the people when he had one built at his Moscow ribbon mill in 1902. In addition to an auditorium, the complex included a library, reading room, and tearoom. A larger and well-equipped theater, known as the "Little Art Theater," was constructed at the factory in 1904, at a cost of 50,000 rubles. A troupe of workers and white-collar employees performed a number of works by Ostrovsky, as well as Gogol's *Marriage* and several vaudevilles. When the Little Art Theater was forced to close in 1909 to make room for an expansion of the factory, Stanislavsky convinced the other members of the board of directors to supply workers with free tickets to the Moscow Art Theater and gave all the stage sets and props to the Moscow Municipal People's House. He also continued to give assistance to the workers' troupe, which remained intact until 1917.[74]

The longevity of these theatrical efforts is difficult to determine, as they seldom attracted the attention of the periodical press after the initial wave of enthusiasm receded and the novelty wore off. Dependent on the goodwill and financial support of the factory owners and lacking permanent troupes, some of the factory theaters in St. Petersburg and Moscow were short-lived and their activities sporadic. Performances at the Nikolaev Railway workshops, for example, were ended in 1899 by a new foreman who felt that they kept workers from resting properly on holidays.[75] Still, quite a few of the theaters endured for over a decade. The archives of the Moscow district police record that workers, white-collar employees, and amateur or professional troupes were staging concerts and plays at a number of local factories in the early 1910s.[76] Performances were being held at the Guzhon, Einem, and Moscow-Kursk Railway workshop theaters at least until 1913, and at the Nevskii Society and Putilov and Obukhov factories until 1917.[77] The entertainments were welcomed by many factory workers, who told investigators examining workers' grievances after the Bloody Sunday massacre of demonstrators in January 1905 that one of their desires, along with an eight-hour day, higher wages, and respectful treatment, was for more provision of cultural activities like theater, in the absence of which they said there was little to do but drink.[78] The press's interest in factory theaters, however, peaked in the early 1900s. As the growing assertiveness of Russian workers made itself felt on the eve of the 1905 Revolution, the optimistic reports of cultural progress in the factories became yesterday's news.

CULTURAL PHILANTHROPY AND RATIONAL RECREATION

Factory owners generally took a pragmatic approach to theater, viewing it as a "rational recreation" that would raise workers' productivity. But there was also a more general interest in theater and cultural philanthropy among industrialists at the end of the nineteenth century, linked to their desire to establish their respectable credentials. This was especially true in Moscow, where Pavel Tretiakov built a public museum to house his collection of Russian art, Savva Mamontov and his wife Elizaveta founded an artists' colony at Abramtsevo and an opera in Moscow, Aleksei Bakhrushin founded Russia's first theater museum, while Savva Morozov bankrolled the Moscow Art Theater in its early years. Amateur theatricals were common among Moscow's upwardly mobile middle classes, and Stanislavsky's well-known involvement in amateur theater was far from exceptional. Middle-class industrialists and merchants also "borrowed symbols and stereotypes from other, higher estates and social groups and imitated their behavior," acquiring the attributes of an aristocratic lifestyle in the country estates they purchased.[79]

The theaters established at Russian factories, especially those in Moscow, combined elements of industrialists' old-fashioned patriarchal attitudes to workers, their attempts to fashion new identities as art patrons and civic philanthropists, and their rational self-interest in embracing contemporary theories on the relationship between leisure and productivity. In Russia, a theater on an industrial estate had overtones of the aristocratic culture of the eighteenth and early nineteenth centuries, when nobles built lavish theaters for spectacles acted out by serf-actors, educated and costumed by their masters.[80] When one wealthy Moscow manufacturer invited his workers and employees to dine at his home and watch a performance, he was simultaneously performing a traditional ritual in which the employer distributes symbolic gifts to his workers, acting out a newer social role as a cultural philanthropist, and imitating the behavior of a landed aristocrat on his estate.[81] In a story published by Chekhov in 1896 about a doctor's visit to a textile factory near Moscow, over dinner a smug governess points to the winter theater as proof of the owner's generosity toward her workers.[82]

Besides its symbolic role for factory owners, theater was also appealing because of the civilizing and disciplinary functions that were ascribed to it. P. E. Lukovskii, a Moscow industrialist, argued that theater was a "precious school" capable of saving "drunkards and dissolute persons" by giving them "a good means of instruction and self-education." He urged other factory owners who were interested in "raising the mental and moral level of their workers, in luring them from the taverns and debauchery," to join together to create a permanent theater in an industrial center. It was in their own self-interest to do so, for theater would lead to "greater order in factory life and even increased productivity."[83]

The influential economist A. I. Chuprov echoed these arguments in a report on educational programs and organized entertainments for workers, issued in 1898 by the Permanent Commission on Technical Education of the Moscow branch of the Imperial Russian Technical Society. Referring to the recent legislation limiting the length of workdays to eleven and a half hours and guaranteeing Sunday and holiday rest, Chuprov pointed out that employers could no longer raise productivity by making workers work longer but would have to increase the quality of the work accomplished. This could be achieved by giving workers access to education and recreational opportunities, which would lower their consumption of alcohol and thereby increase the skill and intensity of their labor. "Thus economic motives supplement and reinforce what is dictated by moral and sanitary considerations," he concluded.[84]

Did providing factory workers with "rational recreations" like theater performances actually lower the incidence of holiday drunkenness, as factory owners hoped it would? While some were convinced enough to keep subsidizing factory theaters for years, others were not so certain. One industrialist complained to a factory inspector that he had spent thousands on a theater, library, and tea house to create an environment in which drinking was discouraged, but without any results.[85] From the workers' point of view, going once a week to a *narodnoe gulian'e* might have been entertaining, but it was hardly a substitute for passing after-work hours with friends in the tavern. Nor were theater and tavern mutually exclusive. According to Shcheglov, some visitors to the Nevskii Society's park left early in order to make it to the tavern before closing time.[86] The theaters, dances, and other recreations organized by factory owners did offer workers an alternative model of holiday behavior, however, one that at least some of them embraced. In the words of a St. Petersburg joiner, who responded to one of the Nevskii Society's questionnaires in the language of self-improvement: "When a person is in the park, he is bound by propriety, and in enjoying the plays, he temporarily forgets his bad instincts. If he likes the play, he gives himself over to it entirely, tries to imitate the refinement, and tries to interpret what he can't understand. The benefit is that he utters fewer crude oaths. And this saves his material situation: outside of the park he knows no better recreation than the taverns and womanizing." He nevertheless complained that there were too many drunks in the area around the open-air stage.[87]

TEMPERANCE THEATERS

The supposed linkage between "rational recreations" and sobriety had become a commonplace in discussions of the alcohol problem by the time

Figure 9. An engraving of the Guardianship of Popular Temperance's summer theater at the Tauride Gardens. St. Petersburg, 1898. *Niva,* no. 35 (29 August 1898): 693.

the St. Petersburg Guardianship of Popular Temperance was founded in 1898, and it immediately began organizing a wide variety of low-priced entertainments in the city's working-class districts. The *narodnye gulian'ia* held during the summer in the Tauride Gardens and year-round at Ekateringof featured plays, variety shows, music, dancing, and other entertainments for an admission fee of five to ten kopeks. In 1899 another *gulian'e* opened in Petrovskii Park, along with a theater at the Old Glass Works. The guardianship also organized holiday *gulian'ia* and shows at the Mikhailovskii Manège from 1898 to 1901, at the Poliustrovskii Garden in 1898 and 1899, at the Iunkerskii Manège in 1898, and at the Semenovskii Parade Ground in 1900 and 1901.

The pride of the St. Petersburg Temperance Guardianship was the Nicholas II People's House. Looming above the Aleksandrovskii Park in the city's Petersburg district, scarcely more than a stone's throw from the Peter and Paul Fortress, the People's House was by far the largest cultural and entertainment facility in the Russian empire. Constructed of iron and concrete in the Art Nouveau style, it had originally housed the Arts Pavilion at

Figure 10. The Emperor Nicholas II People's House (left) and its opera house (right). St. Petersburg, 1910s. Courtesy of the Central State Archive of Documentary Films and Photographs, St. Petersburg.

the 1896 All-Russian Exposition in Nizhnii Novgorod. After the exposition concluded, the structure was taken apart and its skeleton transported to St. Petersburg, where it was reassembled and converted by the guardianship into a recreational complex with a dining hall, tearoom, lending library, reading rooms, and a theater with 1,500 seats and standing room for another 1,500 persons. In 1911 a separate theater for opera was added. During the summer months, the guardianship organized *narodnye gulian'ia* in the adjoining Aleksandrovskii Park, which on holidays drew tens of thousands to enjoy the shows, concerts, and rides.[88] Other temperance guardianships, as well as local governments, educational societies, and consumers' cooperatives, soon followed St. Petersburg's example, and by 1913 at least 222 people's houses were operating throughout the empire, 124 of them under the auspices of the temperance guardianships.[89]

Of course, Russia was not alone in constructing people's houses and theaters as a means of promoting sober, "rational" recreations among the common people.[90] In Britain, temperance societies had been sponsoring dry recreations since the 1840s, and in London a people's palace was constructed in the 1860s, another in the 1880s. British temperance advocates established didactic music halls in London, Glasgow, and other cities beginning in the 1870s.[91] A group of socialist intellectuals inaugurated Berlin's Freie Volks-bühne in 1890, a members-only theater for Social-Democratic workers, which cultivated a naturalistic and socially conscious repertoire. Conflicts over whether art or politics should guide the theater's repertoire led in 1895 to the creation of a second theater, the Neue Freie Volksbühne. Together the two theaters boasted a total membership of 68,000 by 1912.[92] In France a great deal was written about bringing theater to the people, most notably by Romain Rolland, but the sole people's theater that enjoyed any lasting suc-cess was Maurice Pottecher's Théâtre du peuple, in the rural Alsatian village of Busang.[93] The Russian people's houses may have borne some influence of contemporary European ideas about "people's palaces" and *"maisons de peuple,"* but the Russian people's theaters were essentially an indigenous development, and only in Russia were people's theaters established on such a wide scale and with such financial support from the state.

While theater was an important part of the recreational programs of the temperance guardianships throughout the empire, none of them devoted so much energy to organizing theater performances as the ones in St. Peters-burg and Moscow, where enormous sums were expended on staging operas, plays, and even ballets for popular audiences.[94] Nowhere else did people's theaters operate on this vast scale, attract huge audiences on a regular basis, or entrench themselves so firmly in cultural life as in these two cities. In St. Petersburg, for example, the guardianship put on 9,630 performances for some 74 million people at its theaters and *gulian'ia* from 1898 to 1914.[95] The St. Petersburg guardianship's other cultural and educational projects paled in comparison to theater. Whereas it sponsored some 5,482 religious lec-tures on temperance during the same time period, only 1,718,474 persons attended them, while only 373,511 books were checked out from its fifteen lending libraries. Lectures on medicine and hygiene were even less popular, except during epidemics of cholera and other diseases. Even the guardian-ship's network of eating houses and tearooms, which aimed to attract work-ing people away from the taverns by offering hot meals at low prices, fell far behind the theaters in terms of total attendance, though they were visited by over 21 million people from 1898 to 1914.[96]

If the temperance theaters dominated the St. Petersburg popular theater scene, the theater at liberal philanthropist Countess Sofiia Panina's Ligovskii People's House was also a prominent landmark. Run by the actor Pavel Gaideburov and his wife Nadezhda Skarskaia, from 1903 until the outbreak of World War I it staged classics and contemporary works that earned them recognition throughout the Russian theater world. The only private philanthropical venture into people's theater in St. Petersburg, the Ligovskii People's House was regarded by many critics as an exemplary theater due to the quality of its performances and repertoire. Its audiences were relatively small, however, when compared to the crowds that flocked to the theaters run by the Guardianship of Popular Temperance. With only 800 seats, the Ligovskii theater drew 143,969 people to its performances during the ten seasons ending in 1913, an average annual attendance of 14,400, less than 1 percent of the annual attendance at the Nicholas II People's House, which averaged 1,856,126 over the thirteen years from 1900 through 1913.[97]

After the Skomorokh Theater closed in 1898, the only Moscow theaters for popular audiences were those run by factory owners, the holiday *balagany*, a handful of cheap pleasure gardens that operated sporadically, and the performances the Society for Popular Entertainments held at Sokolniki Park.[98] Then, in 1901, the Guardianship of Popular Temperance started holding summer outdoor performances at its Gruzinskii People's House in the Presnia district and gradually developed a network of people's theaters that were very successful with the city's working-class audiences.[99] The Moscow city duma also joined in the people's theater movement. In 1904, after years of futile discussion of various projects, the duma opened a municipal people's theater on Vvedenskaia Square in Lefortovo, a factory district on the eastern outskirts of the city. Managed by the millionaire industrialist and theater patron Aleksei Bakhrushin, the Moscow Municipal People's Theater developed into a first-rate operation, despite its low budget and cast of provincial actors and recent acting school graduates, and often received very favorable reviews in the press.[100] Even so, in Moscow, as in St. Petersburg, the temperance theaters outshone all rivals at the box office.

THE END OF THE 'BALAGAN' SHOWS

The guardianships viewed their theatrical endeavors as a civilized alternative to the fairground *balagany* as well as a sober alternative to the tavern. Reporting in 1908 that in ten years its theaters had staged 533 plays in 4,856 performances, the St. Petersburg guardianship boasted that works from the "classical and artistic repertoire" were featured at 40 percent of the performances and exultantly claimed to have at last vanquished the fairground *balagan* theaters:

> This, more than anything else, proves that the guardianship has managed to fight the uncultivated masses' aspiration for spectacles of a baser sort and arouse in them a love for classical art. . . . It is enough to remember

that with the establishment of the guardianship the low-quality *balagan* entertainments, organized in past years on the Field of Mars and Semenovskii Parade Ground, passed into oblivion. They were replaced by more cultivated entertainments that were better organized and better adapted to the needs and comprehension of the common people.[101]

The temperance theaters did replace the traditional holiday fairground shows, but police intervention played a part in their victory in St. Petersburg. In late 1896, St. Petersburg Governor-General N. V. Kleigels informed the *balagan* showmen that the holiday *narodnye gulian'ia* normally held on the Field of Mars were to be moved to Semenovskii Parade Ground. The showmen's protests that Semenovskii Parade Ground was an unattractive setting and too far from the city center fell on deaf ears, and in 1898 the *narodnye gulian'ia* were forced to quit the Field of Mars. Alekseev-Iakovlev claimed years later that Leifert, Malafeev, and the other leading *balagan* entrepreneurs were unable to attract enough audiences to make ends meet in the new location and vanished from the scene after Easter 1898, but *Theater and Art* reported the following year that the fairground theaters at Semenovskii Parade Ground were as well attended as ever and raking in money at Easter.[102] There is no further mention in the press of the traditional *balagany* after 1899, however, and the last of the old *narodnye gulian'ia* were sponsored by the temperance guardianship in 1900 and 1901.

The demise of St. Petersburg's traditional *narodnye gulian'ia* remains somewhat of a mystery, and there appears to be no single cause behind their disappearance from the urban holiday scene. Certainly, their removal from their former home disrupted normal business for a time, but Semenovskii Parade Ground was hardly on the outskirts of the city at the end of the nineteenth century, and it was quite near to districts with large working-class populations. The entertainments that the temperance guardianship began holding in the spring of 1899 at the Tauride Gardens, even more distant from the heart of St. Petersburg, were apparently sparsely attended by the working classes at first. A journalist for *Theater and Art* blamed this on the dull quality of the entertainments, historical *tableaux vivants* presented with explanations read aloud from the stage that were impossible to hear beyond the front rows, which was why many people preferred the shows at the *balagan* theaters on the muddy Semenovskii Parade Ground.[103] Within a few weeks, however, the temperance theaters had won a following by offering sumptuous adaptations of Pushkin's fairy tales, together with light comedies and plays by Griboedov, Ostrovsky, Leo Tolstoy, and Molière, and were now packing thousands of spectators into their pleasure gardens.[104] Alekseev-Iakovlev himself took charge of the entertainments, putting his two decades of experience in *balagan* showmanship at the service of the temperance theaters and pleasure gardens, which also possessed the advantage of operating all summer or year-round and so had time to cultivate an audience. Popular audiences had become, by the turn of the century, more accustomed to adaptations or even full-length plays at the fairground theaters, so shifts in taste must have played a part in the decline of the *balagany*. Perhaps by 1900 the operators of the fairground theaters had given up in the face of competition from the now entrenched temperance theaters. That year the Shrovetide carnival, in the hands of the temperance guardianship, was well attended, according to the press.[105] The end of the traditional *narodnye gulian'ia* and their *balagan* theaters can perhaps best be explained by a combination of police efforts to remove them from the city center, competition from the temperance guardianship's entertainments, and changes in popular taste.

Kleigels gave the showmen no explanation for the decision to move the site of the fairground from the Field of Mars, but his allusion to the fact that the *gulian'ia* usually drew crowds of up to 30,000 to the heart of the administrative center of the capital led one of the showmen, Alekseev-Iakovlev, to speculate that the government was concerned about the potential for revolutionary unrest at the carnivals. Alekseev-Iakovlev also believed that Kleigels wanted to clear the way for the St. Petersburg temperance guardianship, which was established in the very same year that the *gulian'ia* were forced to move to Semenovskii Parade Ground. Although there is no concrete evidence of the authorities' motives in transferring the holiday fairgrounds away from the city center, it seems likely that they sought to tame the disorder of the *gulian'e* and prevent concentrations of lower-class people from pouring into the administrative and aristocratic districts that surrounded the Field of Mars, located only a few minutes' walk from the Winter Palace.

At stake was control over urban space. During holidays, the poorer populace left the outskirts of the city and brought their revelries to its very core, visibly dominating the foreground of urban life in areas where they were normally confined to the background. At the celebrations held all over the empire to mark the coronation of Nicholas II in Moscow in 1896, rowdy working-class crowds gathered to watch the parade on St. Petersburg's Nevskii Prospekt, while hundreds of people were trampled to death on Moscow's Khodynka Field during the festivities. Nikolai Mikhailovskii cited the problem of crowds congregating in urban centers as a reason to support efforts by organizations like the Nevskii Society to bring recreations to working-class districts.[106] The decision to remove the *narodnye gulian'ia* and their crowds to a less threatening space on Semenovskii Parade Ground also coincided with a growing perception among "respectable" Petersburgers that the city was being taken over by hooligans and prostitutes, a perception borne out to some extent by crime statistics.[107]

A local journalist applauded the move in an article entitled "Holiday Sobriety," predicting that it would have a major impact on restoring sobriety and decorum to the central streets of St. Petersburg during holidays. In the past, he argued, the educated public went to the fairgrounds, and thus it made sense to allot them a space on the Field of Mars, but since in recent years they were attended only by the working classes, there was no reason that these people should be "artificially herded from the outlying districts to the center of the city and then sent back to their distant places of residence." The 1898 Shrovetide, with the *gulian'ia* safely removed to Semenovskii Parade Ground, was a great improvement on the previous disorderly scene around the Field of Mars, claimed the journalist. Where formerly the central thoroughfares leading to the fairgrounds had been blocked with working people and cabs, now all was clear and quiet.[108]

By putting the business of popular entertainment in the hands of the temperance guardianship, while simultaneously banishing from the heart of the capital the carnivals, which since the 1860s had been under intermittent attack for the dubious quality of their entertainments, the authorities probably hoped both to sanitize popular recreations and to distance them from the center of official St. Petersburg. Although the guardianship organized holiday carnivals between 1898 and 1901 at the Mikhailovskii Manège (between Nevskii Prospekt and the Engineering Institute), most of its theaters and entertainment parks were established in working-class districts on the periphery of the city. The Nicholas II People's House, while located quite near the city center, was nonetheless separated from the Winter Palace by the Peter and Paul Fortress and the broad expanse of the Neva River.

In Moscow, by contrast, where the traditional *gulian'ia* and temperance theaters coexisted without police interference for ten years, the regular and lavish spectacles sponsored by the guardianship did a great deal to undermine the popularity of the *balagan* theaters. The Moscow Guardianship began organizing its drama performances in the summer of 1901, yet the Shrovetide carnival on Deviche Field in February 1902 remained well attended by lower-class Muscovites, according to Ivan Shcheglov, who claimed that Moscow popular audiences, unlike those of St. Petersburg, were not yet spoiled by the temperance theaters.[109] By 1911, however, when the city government abolished the *gulian'ia* on Deviche Field in response to neighboring residents' complaints about the noise and filth they produced, the fairground theaters had lost their former glory.[110] A Moscow boulevard newspaper attributed the decline of the *balagan* to changes in popular tastes:

> Once the *balagany*, decorated with the most unbelievable pictures, offering the most unbelievable spectacles, stretched in a long line one after the other, entertaining the audiences of Deviche Field. Now this has vanished into eternity. The *balagan* owners have gone broke, and even on such popular days as Shrovetide the showbooths stand empty. And the common folk could care less about that, preferring rides on the roller coasters and carousels to the most touching and shocking showbooth dramas. The impoverishment is a vivid sign that the undemanding tastes of the crowd have changed, that the crowd has matured in its tastes.

The paper laid the blame for the loss of the fairground shows' appeal at the door of the Moscow Guardianship of Popular Temperance, arguing that temperance theaters had "accustomed the crowd to spectacles of a different type and appearance than the *balagan* hodgepodge. Tastes have developed, demands have gotten higher, and the *balagany* honorably die a natural death."[111] In addition to competition from the rapidly growing theatrical activities of the temperance organization, the proliferation of cinemas after the turn of the century was probably another factor in the decline of the *balagany*. For about forty kopeks one could see a show anytime at the *kinemo*. The first Russian movie, *Stenka Razin* (1908), took its Cossack rebel hero from the folk dramas and *balagan* shows and put him on the silver screen.

It was only when the fairground shows had either vanished or were in their death throes that they were rediscovered and nostalgically idealized by Russian intellectuals. Where for decades the *balagan* had been almost ritually excoriated in the papers at Shrovetide and Easter for its untrammeled vulgarity, at the beginning of the twentieth century popular carnival culture became fashionable in artistic circles, where it was reworked and stylized as high culture. Aleksandr Blok's tragic farce, *The Showbooth*, brought Harlequin and Columbine to the stage of the celebrated actress Vera Komissarzhevskaia's theater in 1906 under the direction of Vsevolod Meyerhold, enlisting the stylistic devices of the *balagan* to parody symbolism and mysticism. Diaghilev astonished Parisian audiences in 1911 with Igor Stravinsky's ballet *Petrushka*, set in a St. Petersburg fairground theater at Shrovetide 1830.[112] After the October Revolution, there was even an attempt to recreate the traditional fairground amusements by the Old Petersburg Society, which organized an old-style *gulian'e* in 1923, but nothing ever came of the project.[113] While the carnivals and *balagany* lived on for a time in the provinces, they gave way in the capitals to the new people's theaters and cinemas, which offered a much greater variety of entertainment to an increasingly sophisticated popular audience.

A SYNTHESIS OF HIGH AND LOW CULTURES

The people's theaters run by the guardianships were intended to reform the holiday behavior of the common people by introducing them to a new cultural aesthetic, yet the contrast between the old fairground theaters and the new people's theaters was not so stark as was often claimed. In 1914, reviewing more than a decade of theatrical activity, the St. Petersburg Guardianship proudly explained its didactic and aesthetic approach to entertainment:

> Every theatre serves a double purpose: on one side it is a pulpit from which resound the words of the preacher instructing the people, secondly it has an aesthetical influence on the masses: it elevates the spectator in purifying his soul, so to say, the same as does every branch of Art.
>
> It is necessary to have in view these two elements of dramatic poetry, in examining the problems of the popular repertoire, which has for its object the widening of the spectators' horizon, in awakening sentiments of humanity and in general to serve in the education of the people. In choosing subjects for the repertoire the Committee has tried to combine these two elements, because the harmony of these elements is the true safeguard of the success of theatrical work. Thus, to teach by amusement is the aim of the theatre according to the Committee.[114]

In practice, however, the temperance theaters did as much to continue the traditions of the fairground shows as to replace them. This is most apparent in the history of the St. Petersburg Guardianship's activities. In order to reform the people, the guardianship first had to attract them to its theaters. To do this, it turned to Aleksei Alekseev-Iakovlev, whose career as a fairground showman had come to an end in 1898, with the removal of the *balagany* from the Field of Mars. He was immediately approached by the head of the guardianship, Prince Alexander Oldenburg, who hired him to take charge of directing performances at the Tauride Gardens and, on its completion in 1900, at the vast Nicholas II People's House.[115]

In approaching his new responsibilities, Alekseev-Iakovlev drew extensively on his experience working in the fairground theaters. He believed that popular theatrical entertainments should consist of a wide variety of genres presented in a festive atmosphere: "After two or three seasons, the garden of the People's House had acquired its characteristic appearance, thanks to the simultaneous functioning of the most diverse spectacles and attractions, concentrated on a relatively small territory. On the [open] stage there were variety shows with some kind of allegorical scene for an apotheosis, on another stage, partially enclosed by a shell, one-act comedies were performed, which, as I became convinced, the public always liked, or symphony concerts." Together with the stage shows, a multitude of attractions and rides were scattered throughout the garden: an observatory with telescopes, a labyrinth with mirrors to render the illusion of infinite space, a miniature railway and train for children, a Ferris wheel, "flying airplane" rides (including one with a "death loop"), and an electric rollercoaster from the crest of which all St. Petersburg was visible. At the end of each evening, the entire garden was illuminated with Bengal lights and fireworks. The combination of shows, rides, and crowds of up to 40,000 on Sundays and holidays, all in a relatively confined space, made the garden of the People's House extremely noisy.[116]

Alekseev-Iakovlev's idea was to attract crowds with exciting shows and attractions, gradually expanding the repertoire as "new tastes and demands" developed among the audiences. For the first few years after the opening of the People's House, the repertoire was similar to that of the larger *balagany* of the Field of Mars, although there was an effort to include "purely enlightening" and "literary" plays. A Sunday, for example, might begin with a dramatized folk tale for children, such as *Kashchei the Deathless*, at eleven o'clock in the morning, followed at one in the afternoon by a spectacular play with many adventures and special effects, often based on one of Jules Verne's novels. After a second afternoon performance, usually of one of Ostrovsky's works, the day's entertainment would conclude at eight o'clock with an opera by a Russian composer, such as *Prince Igor* or *The Snowmaiden*. When audiences had become more accustomed to highbrow theatrical offerings the proportion of serious dramas and operas was increased, yet light comedies, melodramas, and grandiose spectaculars remained an important element of the repertoire.[117]

In its repertoire, interior design, and advertising style, the People's House initially had much in common with the fairground theaters. Operas and classics shared the stage with heart-rending melodramas and eye-catching spectaculars. Dramatizations of episodes from historical and contemporary Russian military engagements occupied a large place in the repertoire, featuring reenactments of the War of 1812, the siege of Sevastopol, and the campaigns of Peter the Great and General Suvorov. *The Heroes of Chemulpo*, staged by Alekseev-Iakovlev in 1904, depicted a recent naval engagement between Russian and Japanese forces in Korea. Fantasy extravaganzas on themes from science fiction as well as Russian folklore were especially popular. In Jules Verne's *Twenty-thousand Leagues Under the Sea*, performed at the People's House in 1910, a cinema projector was employed to create the illusion that the action was taking place underwater. A magical version of *Don Quixote*, originally conceived by Alekseev-Iakovlev for the *balagan* theaters of the Field of Mars, was staged over three hundred times at the People's House.[118]

Like the fairground theaters, the People's House contained a large upper gallery with standing places, for which tickets sold for a *grivennik*, or ten kopeks, and like the gallery audiences of the Field of Mars, the young workers and students who frequented the standing places were referred to as *grivenniki*. The *grivenniki* had the deciding voice as to the success or failure of the shows, which were advertised with gaudy posters that depicted scenes from the performance. Simultaneously with the performances held in the theater auditorium, variety shows, circus acts, balalaika players, and Russian folk chorus and dances offered nonstop entertainment in the adjoining "Iron Hall," where there were no seats and audiences were free to mill about the central stage.[119]

The entertainments at Petrovskii Park also closely resembled those of the traditional St. Petersburg holiday carnivals. Carousels, water slides, peep shows with views of exotic locales like Paris, "where the mademoiselles will drive you mad," shooting ranges, folk dancers, and acrobats all competed for attention with comedies, vaudevilles, short farces, classics, and variety shows performed on open stages.[120] Alekseev-Iakovlev's lavish spectaculars were not only a hit with popular audiences but were remembered by "all Petersburg," according to *Theater and Art*.[121] In 1912 and 1913 *The Taking of Azov* and *Ermak Timofeevich*, longtime favorites from the *balagany* of the Field of Mars and Admiralty Square, were staged at Petrovskii Park as open-air spectaculars before tens of thousands of spectators. At the production of *Azov*, the audience lined one bank of a large pond to watch a grandiose performance that included an artillery duel between floating mock-ups of eighteenth-century warships, culminating in the burning of the Turkish fleet. For *Ermak*, Alekseev-Iakovlev devised underwater machinery to churn the waters of the pond for the final scene in which the hero drowns in the Irtysh River, provoking a universal sigh among the viewers that echoed through the park.[122]

Despite the avowed culturist aims of the Guardianships of Popular Temperance, the theaters they created were never able to avoid reckoning with popular tastes. Although they did stage many of the classics and literary plays that were believed to have a civilizing influence on the people, the theaters had to attract audiences if they were to draw the people out of the

Figure 11. Scenes from Alekseev-Iakovlev's spectacular outdoor production of *The Taking of Azov* in Petrovskii Park. St. Petersburg, 1912. *Teatr i iskusstvo*, no. 34 (26 August 1912): 663.

taverns, and that meant serving up some entertainments from the fairgrounds and commercial pleasure gardens. The Nicholas II People's House had its own directors and a troupe of professional actors, but amateur companies also performed at people's theaters in St. Petersburg and Moscow, choosing plays according to their preferences and abilities. Sometimes the business of organizing entertainments was contracted out to entrepreneurs, who were more concerned with filling the theaters and recouping their

Figure 12. Fedor Shaliapin performing in an opera at the Emperor Nicholas II People's House. St. Petersburg, 1910s. Courtesy of the Bakhrushin Central State Theater Museum.

investment, and "must often yield to the tastes of the crowd, even though those tastes are crude."[123] The people's theaters' troupes were seldom strong, composed of older actors ending their careers and young actors making their debuts, but leading artists from the imperial stages and legitimate commercial theaters also made occasional guest appearances. Fedor Shaliapin, for example, sometimes performed at the Nicholas II People's House, giving a free concert for workers in 1915.[124] The resulting product was an eclectic mixture that continually transgressed the frontiers between "high" and "low," cultural enlightenment and pure entertainment.

MOSCOW TEMPERANCE THEATERS

The theatrical activities of the Moscow Guardianship of Popular Temperance were of much the same character as those sponsored by its St.

Petersburg counterpart, although on a smaller scale. At the park adjoining the Gruzinskii People's House, which opened in 1901 in the working-class Presnia district, the guardianship held summer *narodnye gulian'ia* with a military orchestra, various singing and dancing acts, mandolin and balalaika players, jugglers, acrobats, magic shows, and clown acts.[125] According to the guardianship's report for 1902, audiences especially liked the Russian folk songs and dances, "and, unfortunately, the clowns." In response to "the insistent requests of visitors to the park," the guardianship installed a dance floor, with space for up to 300 dancers, which was so popular that it usually drew more than twice that number. Admission to the park was ten kopeks, entry to the dance floor cost another ten kopeks. In 1902, the summer *gulian'ia* drew over 210,000 people.[126]

From 1902 until 1904, the guardianship also hired the impresario Mikhail Lentovskii to organize winter holiday carnivals at the city Manège. They featured plays and exhibits about Russian history with a strongly patriotic flavor. *Great Russia—Powerful Russia* was a series of *tableaux vivants* based on paintings by V. M. Vasnetsov and V. D. Polenov, summarizing Russian history from Christianization to the 1877–78 Russian-Turkish War. *The Muzhik from Archangel—Mikhail Lomonosov* depicted the role that ordinary people could play in helping Russia advance, recounting the rags-to-riches story of the low-born fisherman's son who by dint of his intelligence and hard work became Russia's leading scientist in the eighteenth century. In 1904, shortly after the outbreak of the Russo-Japanese War, a performance of P. Sukhotin's *A Russian Wedding at the End of the Sixteenth Century* was followed by a series of musical scenes entitled *Glory to All for the Faith, the Tsar, and the Fatherland*. In the center of the Manège a large map of Japan and Korea illustrated the course of the war, while at the end of each evening telegrams with the latest news of Russian troop actions were distributed. Although the Manège *gulian'ia* were well attended, they had to be canceled after 1904 due to the excessive expense of renting the premises from the city.[127]

The Moscow Guardianship initially staged few performances at the Gruzinskii People's House, preferring instead to rent private theaters where it subsidized low-priced concerts, operas, and a handful of plays. These were predominantly attended by workers and artisans, who, interestingly, were much more attracted by opera than by drama. Unable to draw audiences to the plays and concerts, the guardianship decided in 1902 to focus its efforts on opera. Soon it put together its own opera troupe and began holding outdoor summer performances at the park of the Gruzinskii People's House. When the Sergeevskii People's House opened in late 1904, operas were staged in its indoor theaters throughout the winter months. The theaters and parks run by the Moscow Guardianship were more modest and offered less elaborate entertainments than those in St. Petersburg, and they drew relatively smaller crowds. Still, on Sundays and holidays, 10,000–12,000 people usually attended the summer *gulian'ia* at the Gruzinskii People's House. The guardianship did not eschew drama altogether, but operas enjoyed the greatest popularity, attracting such large and socially mixed audiences that ticket scalping became a serious problem.[128]

A NEW SOCIAL SPACE IN THE CITY

The theaters and pleasure gardens of the temperance guardianships, especially those in St. Petersburg, soon began to attract a diverse public from all walks of life, becoming a uniquely democratic public space. A contemporary described the panorama of urban society that attended an opera at the Nicholas II People's House: "Passing through the hall during intermission, you will encounter officers from the navy, the Guards, and the army, lycée and university students, petty officials from every possible bureau, very elegant ladies, and the truly simple folk in correspondingly modest dress."[129] The People's House was so popular among all classes that it competed very successfully with commercial drama and opera theaters, which could not match its low prices.[130] Seating might be hierarchical, determined by the price of the ticket, but everyone had paid his or her money to enter, and all were consumers of the same entertainment.

Some observers welcomed the social mixture of the temperance theaters, hailing it as a harbinger of the democratization of Russian society and culture. Ivan Shcheglov was very critical of many aspects of the guardianships' entertainments, yet he applauded the "mingling of the classes" that he saw at their theaters, where working people had become regular consumers of the same entertainments enjoyed by the middle classes: "It was not long ago that this crowd of common folk in peaked caps that nowadays fills the people's theaters huddled humbly at the tall fences surrounding the various urban theatrical and musical entertainments. And suddenly, as if by magic, what an amazing change of decor: for his ten-kopeks the fellow in the peaked hat has become his own master and is introduced to the common source of cultivated human pleasures!"[131] In an article marking the tenth anniversary of the St. Petersburg Guardianship's activities, Aleksandr Kugel declared that "even the fact that audiences from the lower classes were located in one hall with audiences from the upper classes was very beneficial, as a vivid, living example of the equalization of social groups."[132]

A few critics, claiming that they did not see the common people at the performances, even suggested that the intelligentsia had taken over the people's theaters.[133] They were there, however, only not in the stereotypical working-class garb some observers anticipated, for they had exchanged their workday clothing for more stylish holiday apparel. Confusion over who "the people" were and how they dressed seems to account for some of the conflicting descriptions of popular audiences. In July 1898, for example, a visitor to a *narodnoe gulian'e* at the Tauride Gardens reported that "the audience was the real people; around me was a sea of Russian democracy."[134] Yet only two weeks earlier, another visitor to the same *gulian'e* was disappointed to find not the *narod*, but a crowd in bowlers and top hats "that does everything in its power to distinguish itself from the working-class milieu and to resemble the contemporary respectable public [*chistaia publika*]." The parks run by the temperance guardianships, he complained, had become the arena of these people's attempts to be fashionable, and he added that a physician in one of the city's factory districts had told him that young workers often went without basic necessities in order to appear at the *gulian'ia* in a fashionable dress or hat.[135]

What educated observers often failed to comprehend was that skilled factory workers, artisans, shop assistants, domestic servants, and other relatively urbanized representatives of the lower classes simply did not dress like peasants when they went out on the town. When a certain Dadonov claimed to have seen no workers at performances sponsored by a temperance society in an industrial town and concluded that they were not interested in theater, a Bolshevik worker-activist responded sarcastically: "If Mr. Dadonov did not notice any workers, it is possible that he expected to meet workers at the theater in rolled-up shirtsleeves, as they would be at the factory or when leaving it."[136] At the *gulian'ia* run by the Nevskii Society in the midst of the factory villages along the Shlisselburg Road, far from St. Petersburg's fashionable central districts, workers and domestics in the early 1890s were wearing bowler hats, smart suits, stylish dresses, bustles, and hats with ostrich plumes. In his memoirs of his youth as a metalworker in Moscow and St. Petersburg, Semen Kanatchikov describes the summer holiday outfit of a young, urban, skilled workingman at the turn of the century as comprising "a wide belt, gray trousers, a straw hat, and a pair of fancy shoes." Even migrant working women from the countryside became interested in urban styles after they had been in the city for a while and "adopted the clothing displayed in shop windows and on the pages of the fashion magazines, that is, the garb of the new middle class."[137]

Attire was an important means for workers, especially the young and unmarried, to demonstrate that they had acquired a degree of urban sophistication and to separate themselves from the "gray masses" of recent peasant migrants. Newcomers to the capital were quick to adopt city clothing styles in order to fit into their new surroundings, while among rural peasants, young people often emulated urban fashions.[138] If people in traditional costumes were seldom seen in the theaters of the St. Petersburg Guardianship, this was because urban dress, like theater attendance itself, was a mark of integration into urban life, or at least of the aspiration to appear respectable.[139] Besides, the stages of the guardianship's parks and theaters were not their only attraction. The entertainments often included dances and offered working-class youths a rare opportunity to widen their circle of acquaintances and mix with people of other classes in a unique social space. Naturally, they wore their best clothing. The temperance theaters and pleasure gardens, founded to provide "rational recreations" as an alternative to alcoholic pleasures, had become a part of the emerging urban consumer culture that was capturing the imaginations of Russia's lower classes.

Implicit in middle-class observers' criticisms of working-class attire at the people's theaters and their pleasure gardens is their sense of unease at the profound cultural transformations that were revealed by the lower classes' attempts to fashion new identities in adopting urban fashions and tastes. The *narod*, or at least part of it, was assuming guises that bore little resemblance to the image, so beloved by the Russian intelligentsia, of the morally pure peasant, untainted by urban and foreign influences. A journalist for the liberal paper *Russia* drew a stark contrast between the two kinds of common people that he saw at a St. Petersburg temperance carnival in 1900. On one side of the garden people were engaging in traditional rural round-dancing, while on the other "dandified factory lads with greased-back hair in German [i.e., Western European] outfits and shiny boots" were doing "some indecent dance, picked up from some variety-stage 'actress' . . . , trying to reproduce the cheeky movements of the can-can."[140] The *narod*, it seemed, was acquiring the "wrong" kind of civilization, and the entertainments sponsored by the temperance guardianships were proving to be not the solution, but part of the problem.

POPULAR PROTEST

The crowds that thronged the theaters and pleasure gardens of the temperance guardianships made them ideal forums for expressions of opposition to the autocracy during the upsurge of student and labor unrest that culminated in the 1905 Revolution. In February 1902, nearly five hundred students gathered at the Nicholas II People's House during the evening performance to protest the government ban on certain social activities at the nearby university. Revolutionary leaflets were thrown from the theater gallery during intermission, and during the mêlée that ensued the police detained some sixty-five students.[141] In April 1904 someone dropped copies of a Social Democratic May Day address into the auditorium from the balcony of the People's House. The police quickly confiscated the leaflets, but the perpetrator of the action escaped their detection.[142] A worker who tried the same tactic at the Vasilevskii Island Theater six months later was less fortunate. Arrested and interrogated by the police, he admitted to membership in a radical workers' circle and said that an unknown student had given him the brochures together with money for a theater ticket.[143] The people's houses in Moscow were used for workers' meetings from 1902 until 1905, when the guardianship forbade them after learning that the workers were discussing political issues and criticizing the government.[144]

Workers sometimes also used the temperance theaters for guerrilla protests. F. Bogdanov-Evdokimov, a tobacco worker active in one of Moscow's police-sponsored Zubatov societies during the early 1900s,[145] later described how workers conducted agitation in the garden of a temperance theater: "The people's theater on Gruzinskaia Square often served as a place for large-scale revolutionary agitation. There was a summer garden, . . . which drew up to 10,000 people. At the end of the entertainments a group of tobacco workers would raise an orator up on their shoulders, forming a tight ring to protect him from the tenacious hands of the police."[146]

Bogdanov-Evdokimov's account is confirmed by the records of the tsarist secret police, the Okhrana, which describe an incident at the garden of the Gruzinskii People's House on 3 July 1905, when "a group of workers hoisted up an unknown person who began to shout 'Down with autocracy, down with the government, long live freedom.'" At the same time, persons in the crowd fired two shots and a number of revolutionary proclamations were scattered about. Evidently anticipating trouble, a reinforced police detachment was on hand and succeeded in dispersing the demonstrators, although someone managed to fire a shot at the police at the end of the *gulian'e* as the audience was beginning to leave the park.[147] Of course, spontaneous demonstrations like this were common during 1905, and often much more violent and destructive.[148]

Aside from the relatively minor incidents described by Bogdanov-Evdokimov and the Okhrana, however, it was business-as-usual at the temperance theaters during most of the turmoil of 1905. The Nicholas II People's House was closed for three days following Bloody Sunday on 9

January, as were all of the capital's theaters, but it reopened on 13 January along with the imperial theaters.[149] The October general strike shut the theaters down again. Neither the press nor the Okhrana reported any major demonstrations, riots, or violence at the temperance theaters or their pleasure gardens, which remained open throughout 1905 except for a brief period during the October general strike in St. Petersburg, when all theaters were closed due to the absence of electrical power.[150] Even during the street battles during Moscow's December uprising, none of the temperance theaters sustained much damage. Despite the political passions and strikes sweeping the cities, people appear to have gone to the popular theaters chiefly in search of entertainment, whether to forget or to celebrate. By contrast, the imperial theaters were the scene of several demonstrations and brawls, while Charles Aumont's luxurious and fashionable pleasure garden, Aquarium, was rented out for revolutionary meetings, one of which ended in a brief exchange of shots between worker's militiamen and soldiers in early December. A few days later, the Aquarium and its two theaters were nearly destroyed in the street fighting.[151]

CIVILIZATION OR CORRUPTION?

The temperance theaters were enormously successful and drew Russians from all walks of life to their performances, including people with the means to attend more prestigious theaters. Yet these theaters were routinely castigated in the press for promoting sensational and superficial entertainments at the expense of art and even for morally corrupting the lower classes. Critics argued that the success of the shows did not indicate that the guardianships were giving the people the theater they ought to have. Rather, the people attended the temperance theaters only because they were cheap and satisfied "the crowd's demand for spectacles." The question was not whether the people liked the performances but "what are these tens of thousands seeing?" The answer, according to the Moscow theater journal *Footlights and Life,* was a mediocre repertoire consisting of a few Russian classics stitched together with patriotic dramas, Sherlock Holmes, melodramas like *Sister Teresa,* and a whole range of bloodthirsty and beastly plays.[152]

Given the confusion that reigned over the issue of the "correct" popular repertoire, it was inevitable that the guardianships' hodgepodge of farces, variety shows, circus acts, classic comedies and dramas, operas, ballets, contemporary literary plays, fantasy extravaganzas, and *balagan*-style spectaculars would arouse indignation among the *Kulturträger* who wanted the people's theater to be a "temple of art." One journalist vented his despair at the *narod's* cultural promiscuity: "Contrary to expectations, the common folk quite entirely refuse aesthetic pleasure of the first order for the time being, unless it is reinforced by clowns, Ukrainian and other choruses (often of questionable merit), orchestras, magicians, etc., graciously presented to them along with theater for one and the same ten-kopek coin." Attacking the St. Petersburg Guardianship for the lack of direction in its repertoire, he demanded that it to do away with all of the sideshows that distracted the audiences' attention from the serious works, as well as the extravaganzas that "arouse the undesirable instincts of the ignorant masses with their glitter, gaudy colors, explicit gestures and costumes."[153]

The sin of the temperance theaters was that they played to the crowd. *The Stock-Exchange News* criticized the Nicholas II People's House for staging "vulgar and stupid buffonades" that failed to "instill a civic spirit in spectators," yet at the same time allowed that these productions seemed to satisfy audiences. Describing a performance of Gogol's *The Government Inspector* at the Old Glass Works Theater in St. Petersburg, a reviewer deplored the way an actor hammed the role of Khlestakov and played it for exaggerated comic effect. The people in the cheap seats of the upper tiers loved this, he noted petulantly, which was exactly what the actor was after.[154] What so outraged all of these critics was that the guardianships' theaters were entertaining rather than edifying the people, pandering to rather than transforming popular tastes, descending to the level of the crowd rather than raising the crowd to the heights of Parnassus. Ivan Shcheglov, a firm believer in a special people's repertoire, accused the St. Petersburg Guardianship of having built its People's House "without a foundation" because, he said, it had not bothered to compile a catalog of plays suitable for the common people. The productions, to this thinking, were too lavish and flashy for the people's taste. He professed incomprehension at "the Guardianship's theatrical direction's irresistible striving for excessive luxury and tawdry magnificence in its decorations, to the detriment of the internal side of the business. Neither the direct aim of the people's theater, nor the primitive state of the majority of the audience justifies this grand scale in the least."[155]

Like Ostrovsky in his note to Alexander III,[156] critics of the temperance theaters usually idealized the popular audience, attributing to it their own cultural tastes and values and claiming that the Russian *narod* was alien to the foreign theatrical tinsel they associated with the abased pleasures of the city. Shcheglov believed that the people were more interested in simplicity and the living word than in external effects, despite decades of *balagan* entertainments indicating that the reverse might also be true. In a xeno-phobic vein, he charged the St. Petersburg temperance society with infect-ing the common people with "rotten foreign goods" and "the morality of a French barber" by staging Russified imported works: "When, thanks to these adaptations, the popular spectator sees before him Russian people and a Russian setting and hears sham Russian speech, spiced with false, parasit-ical morality—his healthy, at times naive world-view is traitorously under-mined, and into his maturing rural level of understanding, muddled to a cer-tain degree by the bustle and tinsel of the capital, is unwittingly introduced a new, destructive confusion." In 1903, Shcheglov went so far as to assert that the *gulian'ia* sponsored by the Petersburg Guardianship "not only fail to distract from debauchery, but precisely the opposite, they enflame the instincts and tear at the nerves, traitorously entice to drink and women."[157]

The theaters and parks run by the St. Petersburg Temperance Guardian-ship were also condemned as breeding grounds for hooliganism and prosti-tution, particularly after the guardianship began selling low-alcohol beer in March 1905, in an effort to discourage visitors from tanking up on vodka before their arrival. A resident of the Petersburg district complained that even before the beer sales the neighborhood had become excessively noisy since the opening of the Nicholas II People's House: "For some time the People's House has been drawing all the restless elements of the street: hooligans, pimps, prostitutes, and so on. Even when it still did not sell beer, a whole row of drinking establishments and hotels 'for visitors' [prostitutes and their clients] rose up around the People's House."[158]

The *St. Petersburg Gazette* described the area around the People's House in April 1905 in lurid terms: "The Aleksandrovskii Park's former reputation as a 'drunk park' has been restored. Workers, artisans, and ordinary hooli-gans carouse everywhere: they shout, wrangle, mock passers-by, and block the paths of ladies."[159] One N. Shebuev pointed out that the problem was not the beer but the people's custom of either imbibing heavily before com-ing to the People's House or bringing small bottles of vodka in their pock-ets to mix with beer for a potent concoction called the *ërsh*. He asserted that the inebriated environment of the People's House was the cause of many a young working girl's "fall" into prostitution: "The life of every St. Petersburg prostitute can be divided into four periods: (1) When I visited the People's House. (2) When I went to the 'Bouffe' [theater]. (3) When I hung about the Zoological Garden. (4) When I ambled up and down Nevskii Prospekt." The People's House was no place for families, he added, but a "school for such ladies," and the introduction of beer sales would only insure that their "studies will go . . . much more successfully" than before.[160]

A right-wing journal, citing a spate of attacks on policemen in the Moscow and St. Petersburg people's houses in the autumn of 1905, lambasted them as "dens of iniquity" filled with thieves and warned country people visiting the city to steer clear of their pernicious influence.[161]

The authorities were equally concerned by what they considered to be the licentious atmosphere of the St. Petersburg temperance theaters. In a 1903 report to municipal Governor-General D. F. Trepov on "measures for the eradication of street disorders in St. Petersburg," State Councilor Kobyletskii faulted the temperance guardianship for failing in its mission to divert the working class from holiday debauchery. He graphically described the vestibule of the People's House: "In the dense mass . . . there is a crush, pockets are picked, vulgar expressions are permitted, prostitutes and the men and adolescents who accompany them accost one another freely and unceremoniously. This state of affairs has a harmful influence on the morals of the younger generation which comes into contact with these depraved people." In its present state, Kobyletskii concluded, the People's House was "a negative factor in the moral and educational development of the people."[162]

The attacks on the guardianships peaked in the years following the 1905 Revolution, which had cast into relief official and middle-class fears of lower-class delinquency, often associated with drunkenness and the contaminating influence of urban civilization.[163] A state councilor proposed in 1906 to abolish the guardianships and give their properties to the municipal dumas and rural zemstvos under the supervision of the Ministry of Internal Affairs, on the grounds that the theaters were having no effect on the population's consumption of alcohol. The All-Russian Congress on the Struggle against Alcoholism, meeting in 1909, also criticized the guardianship's theatrical activities for failing to reduce drinking. The same year in the State Council, Senator Anatolii Koni accused the Moscow Guardianship of idealizing drunkenness by staging variety shows in which entertainers performed "hooligan songs" about a trip to the country where they blew their money in a tavern, singing, "A holiday without vodka is like a cow without a tail." The Holy Synod added its voice to the chorus of critics, arguing that among their many faults the theaters had a detrimental influence on popular morality because they brought unspoiled peasant migrants into contact with hard-drinking factory workers.[164]

Theater and Art came to the defense of the guardianships, arguing that despite their many errors they had succeeded in greatly increasing the theater-going public and giving working people a taste for artistic entertainments. Aleksandr Kugel, although he sympathized with the idea that local governments should be involved in organizing entertainments, warned that with so many of the zemstvos and dumas now dominated by reactionaries, the people's theaters might well perish if handed over to them. Sergei Witte, now a member of the State Council, spoke out in support of the Nicholas II People's House, asking why no one proposed to abolish the state-funded Imperial Mikhailovskii Theater for staging worthless French farces. The Finance Ministry response to the guardianships' critics was to claim that it had worked hard to expand the approved popular repertoire (a barely concealed reproach to the Ministry of Internal Affairs), and that its tearooms, reading rooms, and people's houses had "restrained the popular masses from all kinds of excesses" during the 1905 Revolution. In the end, the criticisms of the guardianships were brushed aside after war broke out in 1914, for the wartime prohibition on hard spirits gave the Finance Ministry's temperance campaign a new importance.[165]

ELITE CULTURE AND THE PEOPLE

Ivan Shcheglov, who recorded his observations of opera audiences at the people's theaters of the Moscow Guardianship while on a fact-finding mission for the Finance Ministry in 1903, questioned the value of presenting opera to the people. Although the operas in the temperance theaters were always performed in Russian, he believed that people were unable to understand them. "The impact of opera on the Muscovite common folk is striking," he wrote, "and it would probably be more striking if three-quarters of what takes place on the stage were not utterly incomprehensible to them."[166] According to Shcheglov, a native of Tula province who had recently come to Moscow to work as a waiter in a "third-rate tavern" told him that he had gone to see *Faust* (which he called "Khvaust"), but found it dull. The music was not bad, said the waiter, but he could not make out what the plot was all about.[167] Shcheglov was dismayed by his observation that the common people were far more interested in the operas' performers and costumes than in their plots. To support his contention that popular audiences neither understood nor appreciated what they were seeing on the stage, Shcheglov described their reaction to several operas. What stands out in his accounts of audience reception of opera is not, however, that the people did not "understand" opera but that they viewed it similarly to the way they viewed the shows in the fairground theaters or the films in the *kinemo*, and were most intrigued by the performances' sensational and melodramatic aspects.

At a performance of *Eugene Onegin*, a bootmaker sorted out the plot for a friend: "You see, that tall fellow [Onegin] took the young lady [Olga] away from 'curly' [Lenskii]. Look there: the tall one is laughing away without a care, but 'curly' is goggle-eyed like a madman. It's turned serious; there'll be a levolver [*sic*] before it's over." The audience found the duel between Onegin and Lenskii especially gripping. The greatest excitement was produced not by Lenskii's famous aria before the duel, which passed unnoticed, but by the actual shooting, which brought forth a roar of applause that continued until the curtain fell on the scene.[168]

Popular reactions to other operas were equally unsatisfactory in Shcheglov's eyes. Watching Dargomyzhskii's *Rusalka* (adapted from the text of Pushkin's unfinished dramatic poem, in which a miller's daughter, jilted by her noble lover, drowns herself and becomes a water sprite), the audience laughed good-naturedly at the behavior of the miller, who goes mad from grief at his daughter's death; they identified him with the wisecracking barker familiar to them from the Shrovetide fairgrounds. As for the chorus of scantily clad water sprites, it not surprisingly evoked off-color remarks. At a performance of Rubinstein's *The Demon* (adapted from the poem by Lermontov), it was the supernatural aspect of the opera that intrigued the public, who especially liked the mysterious demon himself, although the action scenes with fistfights and murder met with the most success.[169]

Shcheglov was disconcerted by popular audiences' apparent lack of aesthetic discrimination. By failing to show the proper critical appreciation for opera, they called into question the very possibility that theater could contribute to the creation of a unified culture by inculcating in the people the tastes and cultural preferences of the intelligentsia. Popular audiences clearly enjoyed opera performances, as Shcheglov himself admitted, but they did not read them in the same way as did audiences more familiar with the genre. Instead, they implicitly challenged the conventional meanings of the works they saw, ignoring the composers' artistic ambitions and reacting to the performances according to the criteria of the *balagan* theaters: style was more important than content, and the excitement and pleasure generated by individual special effects and action scenes overshadowed the plot. It is worth noting that when surveyed about their cultural tastes in the 1920s, the majority of Moscow workers who had been to the theater expressed a preference for opera.[170]

The temperance guardianships had released opera from the confines of the imperial theaters and brought it to the people in the form of an inexpensive entertainment affordable to all, but the people brought to the performances their own expectations of what constituted entertainment. That is why educated observers were so dismayed when, side by side with works

Figure 13. Libretto from an opera at the garden of the Alekseevskii People's House. Moscow, 1914. Author's collection.

from the realm of high culture, the temperance theaters served up variety shows, clown acts, and acrobatic displays that appealed to audiences' love of spectacle. By allowing opera and drama to share the same physical and temporal space in their theaters with pure entertainment, the temperance theaters blurred the distinction between "art" and "entertainment." Rather than raising the people to the level of art, the theaters desacralized art by reducing it to the status of a mere spectacle.

Shcheglov's description of audiences at the Moscow temperance theaters offers striking examples of how the common people creatively adapted their experience of opera by appropriating and recycling aspects of the performances. To assist audiences in comprehending opera, the Moscow Guardianship printed up inexpensive librettos. The librettos contained only laconic descriptions of what was happening onstage and did little to foster any deeper understanding of the performances, but the word *libretto,* feminized into *libretta,* was adopted in popular parlance as a glamorous epithet for a love letter (*liubovnaia libretta*) or even a menu (*s"estnaia libretta*). Opera also had an impact on courting techniques. At the dance pavilion of the Gruzinskii People's House, young men softly repeated to their partners the passionate arias they had learned at the opera performances.[171] The attributes of elite culture were being refashioned and put to new uses, as opera was woven into the fabric of urban popular culture.[172]

· · ·

In organizing theatrical entertainments for the people, both Russian industrialists and the Guardianships of Popular Temperance aimed to civilize the people and instill in them an appreciation for the culture of educated Russia. The theaters doubtlessly contributed to the emergence of a new theatergoing public by exposing the urban lower classes to a rich variety of dramas and operas. Yet despite their immense success in making elite culture accessible to popular audiences, the theaters did not fulfill all of the hopes that the people's theater advocates had invested in them. Rather than becoming outposts of cultural mission work, these theaters inherited many of the characteristics of the *balagan* theaters that had delighted popular audiences for generations with spectacles that sought to entertain, not necessarily to edify. They did transform popular tastes to some extent in cultivating new audiences for serious drama and opera, but they also satisfied less cultivated tastes for pure entertainment. Working-class people enjoyed a variety of genres and entertainments just as much as more elite audiences did, and the repertoires of the factory and temperance theaters included many of the same works that were or had been hits in the legitimate theaters. The temperance theaters, in particular, came to occupy the crossroads of "high" and "low" cultures, where, in an atmosphere not unlike that of the traditional holiday fairground, the masterpieces of Russian and European theater competed for attention with spectacular extravaganzas, melodramas, rides, games, dances, and variety shows.

In their pursuit of a unified culture in which all classes could share, the proponents of a people's theater failed to take into account the preferences of popular audiences, whom they regarded as childlike and incapable of determining what was "good" for them. The endless debates over a "people's repertoire" were indicative of the intelligentsia's reluctance to allow the people to demonstrate their preferences by voting with their pocketbooks. In theory, one had only to expose the people to art and they would immediately discern that it was superior to mere spectacle. But in practice, it proved impossible to impose the canon of elite culture on the people, for they were not the passive and malleable consumers that the intelligentsia thought them to be. Popular audiences gave their own interpretations to the plays and operas they saw and adapted the public spaces of the theaters and pleasure gardens to their own needs.

Intended to acculturate and discipline the common people by "rationalizing" their recreations, the factory and temperance theaters did neither. What they did do was to profoundly transform the recreational landscape of St. Petersburg and Moscow, where for the first time low-priced theatrical entertainments became readily available to mass audiences from all walks of life. The urban people's theaters made leisure a commodity, distinct in time and space from the routine of the working day. Unlike the traditional *narodnye gulian'ia* held at Shrovetide and Easter, which lasted only a few days and were rooted in the pre-Christian agrarian calendar, the new people's theaters and carnivals operated year-round and fit the rhythms of the city—attendance was always highest on Sundays and holidays, when the factories, workshops, and stores were closed. They became a part of the experience of urban life, affording visitors, especially the young, a new setting in which to spend their leisure hours, to mingle with people of other social classes, to wear the stylish clothes for which they scrimped and saved, and to enjoy, if only for a day, the fruits of the independence and freedom from patriarchal constraints that big city life could offer.

5 Workers' Theater, Proletarian Culture, and Respectability

Not content to be entertained at either at the people's theaters or their commercial cousins, some Russian workers attempted to be producers as well as consumers of culture. Beginning at the turn of the century, workers began to form drama circles and stage occasional performances for their fellow workers, usually with advice and coaching from middle-class professional or amateur actors. Although their activities were on a small scale, amateur workers' theaters were an important part of the movement by Russian workers to establish networks of alternative cultural and education institutions during the years between the revolutions of 1905 and February 1917.

The proletarian cultural and educational movement, best known by its Russian abbreviation as Proletkult, is often identified with the early years of Soviet power, but its roots are in the prerevolutionary workers' movement.[1] In seeking to explain the origins of Proletkult, scholars have tended to focus on Aleksandr Bogdanov's theory of proletarian culture as elaborated in the decade prior to 1917. According to Bogdanov and his followers, there could be no social revolution without a corresponding cultural revolution. In order to prepare this cultural revolution, workers would have to develop their own proletarian culture to contest the hegemony of bourgeois culture. Guided by the revolutionary intelligentsia, an elite of worker-intellectuals would lay the foundations of a new, distinctly proletarian culture by creating their own science, philosophy, and art based on their class values.[2]

Such was the idea, which on the eve of World War I provoked heated debates among Social Democratic leaders over whether a genuinely proletarian culture could be created under the conditions of capitalism.[3] But what did "proletarian culture" mean to the rank-and-file workers? What would distinguish it from "bourgeois" culture? What role would the intelligentsia play in the construction of proletarian culture? Although it is always more difficult to interpret the reception of an idea than the idea itself, the history of the prerevolutionary workers' theater movement does suggest some answers. For most workers who engaged in creating theater groups, attended the performances of workers' theaters, or read about them in the workers' press, proletarian culture did not mean creating an entirely new culture from scratch. Instead, it meant appropriating the culture of the intelligentsia and using it for political purposes or simply for self-improvement and pleasure.

For radical workers, theater could be a useful weapon in their social and political struggles. "Workers' theater," wrote a contributor to a Bolshevik mass-circulation daily in 1914, "awakens [class] consciousness more easily [than do lectures] and thereby prepares new cadres of conscious members of workers' organizations."[4] The key issue was not so much the class origins of the plays performed as their ideological significance. After all, true art, the workers had learned from their intelligentsia mentors, was always supposed to be critical of the existing order, to expose social ills and suggest solutions to them. And in Russia there existed an enormous body of socially critical dramatic literature. Many of the classics of Russian literature and drama were interpreted as protests against social injustice, bureaucratic corruption, and the oppression of the weak by the strong, and such interpretations were only reinforced by the fact that so many classics had at some time suffered from prohibition by the censorship. A St. Petersburg workers' drama circle organized in 1912, whose repertoire consisted exclusively of the same classic and contemporary literary plays that could be found on the stages of any theater in Russia, could thus state confidently that the plays it had selected were "absolutely ideological" (*bezuslovno ideinye*) in content.[5] The dearth of proletarian dramatists and the virtual absence of socialist plays— a situation exacerbated by the stringent censorship restrictions on what could be performed in theaters attended by lower-class audiences—forced workers to draft the existing "bourgeois" dramatic corpus into the service of the proletarian cause.

Apart from their potential for raising their audiences' "class consciousness," workers' theaters also had an important symbolic significance. To organize or attend a workers' theater was an assertion of respectability, or *kul'turnost'*, not unlike taking evening classes or reading the "thick" journals of the intelligentsia. Such theaters were proof that working men and women not only aspired to the cultural heritage of the intelligentsia but were no less, or maybe even more, capable of appreciating art than were the upper classes. Reporting on a 1913 performance of Sofiia Belaia's *The Unemployed* by a local group of amateur worker-actors, a Perm worker argued: "In bourgeois circles they say that if workers are admitted every-where they will destroy all culture. No. We will prove that we are already taking under our wing all of the so-called cultural acquisitions that are use-ful to us, since the bourgeoisie no longer has the strength to work in that area, that is, in the realm of art."[6]

But there remained a dilemma: to create their own theaters, workers often found that they still needed the assistance and technical expertise of professional actors and directors. Workers tried to solve this dilemma by putting the accent on the class character of their performances, by defining a workers' theater as one where worker-actors performed a repertoire of their own choosing before worker-audiences.

RESPECTABILITY AND SELF-IMPROVEMENT

Workers' drama circles were usually made up of people whom contempo-raries often called "worker-intellectuals (*rabochie-intelligenty*): the young, skilled, better-paid, literate workers who also dominated the legal trade unions and educational societies that developed after the 1905 Revolution. Most members of St. Petersburg workers' clubs, for example, were single, aged between eighteen and twenty-five, and earned forty to fifty rubles per month, according to a 1914 survey of working-class life in the city.[7] These workers often cultivated an interest in literature and art and took pride in the respectability that their cultural choices signified. Would-be worker-intellectuals commonly referred to themselves as "conscious," in order to emphasize the distance that separated them from the unskilled and semi-skilled, or "gray" masses, whom they viewed as backward, uncouth, and "unconscious" (*nesoznatel'nye*). Striving to distinguish themselves by their respectable choices in clothing, reading material, and leisure pursuits, worker-intellectuals often embraced the middle-class standard of "rational recreation" advocated by socialists as well as industrialists.[8]

Of course, the worker-intellectual was to a great extent an abstraction, an ideal type constructed as much by the revolutionary intelligentsia as by the workers who embraced the ideal. There was more than a little wishful think-ing and a good dash of romanticism in the conventional stereotype of the skilled worker—independent, proficient, and industrious—who spent his evenings attending lectures on political economy or reciting the verses of Nekrasov, preferred *Kapital* to *Kopeika*, eschewed Petrushka for Chekhov, did not curse or drink to excess, dressed neatly, and tried to raise the con-sciousness of his less "advanced" fellow workers. It was primarily a male identity; the female worker was customarily regarded as "a creature of a lower order" by male workers.[9] Not every worker calling himself "conscious" corresponded fully to the ideal, but it was nevertheless a powerful vision of an alternative culture in which skilled, educated workers could distinguish themselves from the backward mass of workers without renouncing their own working-class identity. The cultural milieu of the "conscious" workers was an "alternative culture" in the sense that it offered these workers an alternative to the culture of everyday life of the semi-peasant mass of unskilled workers that surrounded them. It was also an alternative to the easy pleasures of urban life, for it defined leisure primarily as an opportunity for self-improvement rather than as merely a time to have fun.

Workers who aspired to the status of intellectuals within the working-class cultural hierarchy asserted their identity through a code of behavior that was calculated to demonstrate their respectability and set them off from other workers. As Semen Kanatchikov, a village-born worker who strove to fashion for himself a new identity as a skilled and cultivated Moscow pattern-maker, explained in his memoirs, "It usually happened that no sooner did a worker become conscious than he ceased being satisfied with his social environment; he would begin to feel burdened by it and would then try to socialize only with persons like himself and to spend his free time in more rational and cultural ways."[10] For some workers, including Kanatchikov, these yearnings led to participation in Marxist study groups and contacts with radical students and members of the revolutionary underground. To assert one's "consciousness" did not necessarily entail political commitments, however.[11] Worker-intellectuals also expressed their identity by taking evening courses, reading the "thick" journals, visiting museums, attending public lectures, going to the theater, or participating in a literary-dramatic circle. All of these activities—political, educational, or cultural—brought workers into contact with representatives of the intelligentsia, with whom they had an ambivalent relationship. Even though the worker-intellectuals looked to the intelligentsia as role models and sources of knowledge and organizational skills, they also resented their subordination to their tutors.[12]

The workers' theater movement, as it emerged and developed during the two decades prior to the February 1917 Revolution, was shaped by the aspirations and behavioral codes of those workers who sought both to better themselves individually and to forge a new working-class culture, one in which skilled, educated workers could demonstrate their respectability and *samodeiatel'nost'* (independent initiative). Workers' amateur theaters became symbols of the worker-intellectuals' efforts at self-cultivation, their organizational initiative, and their rejection of the paternalistic efforts of the privileged classes to bring culture to them. At the same time, the workers' theaters offered a means for spreading enlightenment to the gray, "unconscious" masses and bringing them into the ranks of the conscious.

In some respects, the workers' theaters shared the goals of the people's theaters. Like the factory owners, temperance advocates, and liberal *Kulturträger*, the organizers of the workers' theaters hoped to "improve" the way workers spent their leisure time, and they often adopted the discourse of "rational recreations," with its emphasis on edification and respectability. Yet there was a key difference. Whereas the people's theaters were envisioned primarily as a means of handing down to the common people the cultural and moral values of educated society, the workers' theaters were a grass-roots effort that aimed at self-improvement, asserted the proletariat's cultural independence, and sometimes promoted class solidarity.

WORKERS' THEATER BEFORE 1905

Because of the severe restrictions that the government imposed on organizational activity of any kind, only a handful of workers' dramatic circles existed before the 1905 Revolution. Workers did, however, make occasional attempts to stage plays and conduct literary readings for factory audiences. Amateur affairs, they seldom attracted attention from the press and left few traces of their existence other than brief mentions in the memoirs of workers who participated in them.

Workers at St. Petersburg's Obukhov armaments factory established two drama circles at the turn of the century, headed by the lathe operators Nikolai Georgievich Gromov and Ivan Alekseevich Lvov-Belozerskii. Both men belonged to the "aristocracy" of highly skilled, well-paid, worker-intellectuals. Konstantin Skorobogatov, a teenage worker active in one of the troupes, later described Gromov as a fastidious dresser who "even came to work at the [factory's] mine-shop in patent leather shoes." Skorobogatov was also educated and skilled; at the time of his participation in the drama circle he was working in the factory laboratory doing analyses of steel. Although the workers had no professional help, Lvov-Belozerskii had previously done some acting while working at a factory in Nizhnii Novgorod.[13] The Obukhov troupes "mainly staged the great classics," including Ostrovsky's *The Forest, A Lucrative Position, The Heart Is Not a Stone,* Chekhov's *Ivanov,* and Gorky's *Philistines* and *The Lower Depths.*[14] Tickets cost between ten kopeks and one ruble, but even so the receipts did not always cover the cost of lighting and decorations, and the actors were often forced to make up the difference out of their own pockets. One troupe was kicked off the factory premises after it staged *The Lower Depths*, which the censors prohibited for performance before popular audiences until 1905, and its leaders were eventually arrested.[15]

Skorobogatov went on to build a career as a semi-professional actor in various theater companies, touring around St. Petersburg and the provinces while continuing to work off and on at the Obukhov factory. After the October Revolution, he became famous as one of the first actors to play Lenin on stage. His career, while unusual, illustrates the possibility amateur acting offered some workers to transcend their proletarian origins and even to forge new social identities.

Workers occasionally performed at the factory theaters sponsored by paternalistic industrialists. In Moscow, workers at the Prokhorov cotton mill staged several plays during the 1890s, as did workers at the Einem candy factory in 1902–03.[16] At St. Petersburg's Nevskii Society for the Organization of Popular Recreations a workers' acting troupe was formed under the guidance of Evtikhii Karpov in the mid-1890s.[17] Lack of financial support and artistic guidance, together with police harassment, made it difficult for most independent workers' theatrical groups to survive for very long, however. In 1903 the members of a St. Petersburg typographers' mutual aid society formed a Music and Drama Circle, but it soon evolved into a social club due to legal restrictions and the high cost of organizing entertainments.[18]

One workers' drama circle, at Stanislavsky's ribbon factory, was able to flourish due to the director's support. In 1902 Stanislavsky helped a group of young workers to form their own troupe to perform at his factory's theater and sent actors from the Moscow Art Theater to assist them, even providing the workers with free passes to the Moscow Art Theater.[19] The troupe invited workers from all over the district to their performances. One member of the circle later claimed that the young worker-actors led a strike at the factory in 1905.[20] The troupe enjoyed unusual longevity due to Stanislavsky's patronage and was still active after the October Revolution, staging performances in factories, Red Army units, and orphanages.[21]

THEATER AND THE WORKERS' MOVEMENT AFTER 1905

Independent workers' theaters began to proliferate only in the decade following the 1905 Revolution, and their growth paralleled that of the legal trade-union movement during these years.[22] Trade unions were legalized on 4 March 1906, together with workers' cultural-educational societies, which could organize lectures, excursions, drama circles, and other forms of self-improvement. Membership in the unions and cultural-educational societies, particularly in St. Petersburg and Moscow, was predominately drawn from the ranks of the labor intelligentsia—skilled, literate, urbanized male workers with above-average wages—and only a small percentage of the industrial working class was active in such organizations.[23]

Union membership declined precipitously following Prime Minister Stolypin's "coup d'état" of 3 June 1907, which ushered in an era of repressive policy toward the labor movement. Hundreds of unions were closed or refused registration, and union membership dwindled.[24] By June 1909 the ten largest Moscow unions had a combined total of only 1,231 dues-paying members, down from a high of 10,000 just two years earlier.[25] In the new political climate, less vulnerable forms of organization such as clubs, consumers' cooperatives, cultural-educational societies, and literary-dramatic circles came to play a vital role in keeping the labor movement alive. As the Bolshevik trade union activist Semen Kanatchikov observed, "The difficult conditions force the trade unions to limit themselves almost exclusively to cultural-educational work, and in that sphere they have displayed great energy."[26] With assistance from sympathetic intellectuals, unions organized lectures, evening courses, concerts, and excursions.[27]

Workers' drama circles also became a significant, if relatively small, component of the legal labor movement during the period of repression that set in after 1907. Some circles were formed as independent groups with their own charters, but most functioned under the auspices of a workers' club. The clubs sponsored a variety of cultural and educational events but often had trouble attracting large audiences, for many workers were loath to spend their precious leisure hours listening to lectures. Deploring this "indifferent attitude toward clubs," a metalworkers' journal noted that workers seemed to find dances, musical evenings, and declamation and singing circles more attractive ways of spending their free time than school or lecture attendance.[28] Such complaints about workers' apparent lack of educational and cultural aspirations were common. Discussing the lack of interest in lectures on the part of workers in St. Petersburg's Vyborg district, the metalworker's journal accused them of having no desire "to acquaint themselves with contemporary scientific thought, to dispel their intellectual darkness with [science's] life-giving rays, and in general to break out of a condition of nearly primitive savagery."[29]

One way to boost workers' interest was by combining enlightenment with entertainment. Where lectures often drew only thirty or forty people, theater performances usually attracted several hundred.[30] The members of a St. Petersburg drama circle explained the problem as a lack of "rational recreations": "Our oppressed masses are so downtrodden that they find lessons too boring, and are loath to attend them. The masses must first be made interested somehow, and for this reason rational recreations should be organized so as to arouse their interest in knowledge."[31]

Clubs like Source of Light and Knowledge and Enlightenment therefore founded drama circles to complement their lecture programs.[32] The circles were usually made up of younger workers, and they were among the few workers organizations where women could participate on an equal footing with men, since talented actresses were always needed. The repertoires of the circles were well within the bounds of the classical literary canon, including works by Ostrovsky, Chekhov, Pushkin, and Leo Tolstoy, as well as foreign authors such as Schiller, Shakespeare, and Ibsen.

In preparing their performances, most circles relied on the assistance of sympathetic actors and directors from the intelligentsia. A circle that functioned with no outside help instead might model its performances on productions that members had seen in professional theaters. Vladimir Voronov, a young worker who was active in St. Petersburg's Porokhovskii Literary-Dramatic Circle, recounted in his memoirs how in 1908 the group chose to stage one of Ostrovsky's plays that was then running at the Imperial Aleksandrinskii Theater. Finding it difficult to decide how to perform their roles, they solved the problem by copying professional actors:

> We had no director and, to tell the truth, we didn't think one was necessary. After long agonizing, searching, and arguing, we decided to go as a group to the Aleksandrinskii Theater. We wanted to see how famous artists played our roles, to learn from them and to memorize the stage settings so that we could repeat them at home. The visit helped us. Our rehearsals became more assured, and we all tried to help one another by remembering how the Aleksandrinskii actors performed.[33]

Many of the circles were linked to a faction of the Russian Social Democratic Workers' Party, and some pursued political aims. Bolsheviks in particular tended to view cultural organizations as adjuncts to the political struggle and often endeavored to use them for fund-raising and propaganda purposes. Some drama circles donated their earnings to the revolutionary underground, while others used rehearsals as a cover for holding discussions of political and social issues.[34] The circles were also a place to meet other workers and socialize; Voronov attended his first illegal political gathering as a result of the contacts he had made in the Porokhovskii circle.[35] These activities did not go unnoticed by the police, who monitored the circles carefully and were usually present at performances.

Drama circles were a vital part of a distinctive working-class subculture that began developing in the repressive political climate that set in after June 1907. Together with clubs, cultural-educational societies, and consumers' cooperatives, amateur theater groups offered workers an opportunity to show that they belonged to the labor intelligentsia and to take pleasure from their collective efforts at self-improvement. And the workers' theater movement, like the cultural-educational movement of which it was a part, was very much about self-improvement. In these workers' attempts to appropriate the heritage of the dominant culture there was an element of *embourgeoisement,* which reflected the desire of skilled, educated workers to overcome the barriers that separated them from the privileged classes. Some workers active in the drama circles, like Konstantin Skorobogatov and Vladimir Voronov, eventually succeeded in becoming recognized professional actors. Yet to join a club or organize a workers' theater was not only an assertion of *kul'turnost',* for it could also be a political act. These organizations often combined cultural and political activities, which could result in clashes with the authorities.[36] Moreover, in forming their own cultural institutions workers saw themselves as assuming responsibility for their intellectual and cultural improvement and thereby overcoming their longstanding dependence on the good will of intelligentsia *Kulturträger.*

Letters and articles in the workers' press of the period attest to a growing desire to do without the help of the intelligentsia, as illustrated in the following remarks by a contributor to the Menshevik journal *Hope* in 1908: "Workers have shown an aspiration for learning. They have understood that the need for education, like all the other fundamental necessities of the working class, can be fully satisfied only when the workers *themselves* take matters into their own hands and create *their own* workers' enlightenment institutions, which can provide them with unfalsified [i.e., genuine] spiritual nourishment."[37]

Given their reliance on the intellectuals who gave lectures, conducted excursions to museums, and provided advice on staging plays, however, it remained difficult for workers "to take matters into their own hands" entirely. Many clubs were forced to halt their activities during the summer months, "when the entire intelligentsia leaves for their dachas."[38] As Victoria Bonnell observes in her study of labor organizations in St. Petersburg and Moscow during this period, "The tension between workers' aspirations for autonomy and their continuing reliance on intellectuals created a frustrating dilemma for workers and a situation of incipient conflict with their intelligentsia mentors."[39]

This conflict became increasingly pronounced following the massacre in April 1912 of a peaceful assembly of miners at the Lena gold mines in

Siberia, an event that provoked a massive wave of strikes and demonstrations on a scale reminiscent of the 1905 Revolution. The post-1912 surge in union and strike activity was accompanied by an increasing interest in workers' theaters, which attracted regular coverage in *Pravda*, the workers' newspaper with by far the largest circulation.[40] In June 1912 *Pravda* observed that whereas previously "the idea of creating a workers' theater expressed itself only in the organization of sporadic workers' drama circles, which ended their existence after staging two or three plays," the effort was now proceeding on "more solid ground."[41] A few months later the newspaper hailed the recent creation of several workers' drama circles in St. Petersburg and their success on the stages of the industrial districts on the city's outskirts as a sign that "workers' aspiration to independent activity [*samodeiatel'nost'*] is growing ever wider and embracing ever newer spheres." In the city's Bolshaia Okhta district, for example, a workers' troupe organized several performances of one-act comedies and vaudevilles in 1912 and 1913.[42] *Uncle Vanya* and *Philistines* were staged in 1912 by workers belonging to the Stasiulevich cultural-educational society; after the society was shut down by the authorities in October of that year the troupe continued meeting, and in December they presented Ostrovsky's *Poverty Is No Vice*. A group of St. Petersburg cultural-educational and professional organizations created a literary-artistic center in 1912 in order to "systematically" stage performances by workers.[43]

The increasing interest in workers' theaters was not confined to St. Petersburg. In Moscow, reported *Pravda* in 1912, "there exist several different drama circles among workers at present. They independently learn and stage various plays."[44] One such circle, formed by textile workers in the Danilov district, grew out of a literary-musical evening held by members of the workers' cooperative society Solidarity in February 1912. The workers decided to organize entertainments on a more regular basis, and in March some fifteen of the "most conscious" workers met to hear a report by a worker on the need for a workers' theater to stage serious plays at affordable prices. They chose a play about working-class life (Sofiia Belaia's *The Unemployed*), collected money to purchase a copy of it, and assigned roles.[45]

Unacquainted with stage techniques, the workers were able to get advice from a peasant cooperative theater in the village of Golitsyno (Moscow province), which had been organized in 1908 by some local members of the intelligentsia. Another problem was women's reluctance to take part in the circle's activities; the fallen actress was a well-known figure in popular literature. Some women believed that the workingmen merely wanted an excuse to flirt with them, while others were forbidden to go on stage by their parents. At last a complete cast was assembled, and the troupe began holding evening rehearsals. The first performance was held on a Sunday afternoon in late May in a rented hall on the south side of Moscow; tickets were priced at twenty-five kopeks and up. The Danilov workers staged the play three times, and their success attracted new members, making a total of twenty-two men and eight women. Significantly, their next step was to hire an actor from one of the imperial theaters to direct their performances. Over the next few months they staged several more plays, including Gorky's *The Lower Depths*, with the goal of acquainting audiences with life in different segments of Russian society. At each performance programs were given out describing the content of the play and evaluating it from both an artistic and an ideological point of view.[46]

PROLETARIAN CULTURE?

The proliferating workers' theaters were not without their detractors, who criticized them for their low artistic level and for distracting workers from more important tasks. A contributor to a Bolshevik paper argued in early 1914 that, although it was necessary to counter the harmful influence of the cheap popular theaters, amateur workers' theaters were not the answer. Lacking acting experience and unable to afford the necessary technical equipment, the worker-actors, like all inexperienced amateurs, could produce only "anti-artistic images." If some of the workers did turn out to be gifted actors, they would leave the factory and become professionals. Moreover, the amateur circles would only sap the strength of the labor movement by diverting the energies of "the most cultivated, advanced workers" from organizational work. Instead of trying to create workers' theaters "of doubtful worth," cultural-educational societies should enter into agreements with the existing "good" theaters in order to obtain a supply of discounted tickets for their members, encourage these theaters to offer special matinee performances for workers, and try to exercise an influence on the choice of repertoire.[47]

These same criticisms were taken up a few months later by Ivan Kubikov, writing in the Menshevik *Our Workers' Newspaper*. He supported the effort to democratize art, which he defined as "raising the cultural level of the masses" and rejecting the "vulgar theatrical tinsel" of the theaters of the temperance societies, along with the cheap boulevard press and "heartrending novels."[48] But the repertoires of the workers' theaters lacked "consistency," for together with the works of Gorky and Chekhov they often staged "unartistic rubbish." Instead of performing the "best" of Ostrovsky's plays, Kubikov observed, workers' troupes invariably chose the same works that had been "worn out by all Russian amateurs"—*Poverty Is No Vice* and *A Much Frequented Spot.* The problem was not the censorship but a lack of "independence" in the workers' choice of repertoire. The acting of the worker-amateurs, moreover, showed no distinction in Kubikov's view; even after the typographical workers wrested control of their drama circle from the managers and foremen, the quality of the performances did not improve, nor did the selection of plays. In short, the worker's theater groups differed little from middle-class amateurs.[49]

Kubikov called for the establishment of a permanent workers' theater in which professional actors would perform under the direction of workers' organizations, as was the case in Western Europe. He pointed out that St. Petersburg already had a theater "which heeds the voice of the workers' press and tries to take into account all advice and instruction as to repertoire"—Pavel Gaideburov's theater at the Ligovskii People's House. There was no point in wasting six weeks in preparing a good production of *A Much Frequented Spot* when workers could see the play at Gaideburov's theater or even at the theaters of the temperance guardianships. The workers' time would be better spent learning about science and literature.[50]

Defenders of amateur workers' theaters countered with the claim that these theaters were embryonic manifestations of a distinctly proletarian culture. The awakening proletariat needed its own theater, contended Bolshevik Dmitrii Lentsov, because it required "spiritual support on the path of its class aspirations," something that could not be found in the "bourgeois" theaters. Art always reflected the class outlook of its creators, and from a Marxist point of view it was simply "unacceptable" to suggest that workers should "make use of the achievements of bourgeois art." Avoiding the question of where the workers were to find a dramatic repertoire that was not "bourgeois" in its origins, Lentsov instead expressed the hope that "the worker-artist will appear to embody the images of the future worker-dramatist."[51]

Lentsov also dismissed the argument that the amateur performances drew workers away from more urgent tasks. He pointed out that, like the bourgeoisie, "the working class is not alien to diversity in its aspirations," and it would be useless to try and force all "conscious" workers into one mold, for that would only result in "more bad agitators, orators, and organizers." The real problem was the censorship, which kept plays dealing with the class struggle off the stage. Although a true workers' theater was still impossible to achieve, in the meantime it was necessary to "welcome and facilitate all of the creative beginnings of self-taught workers," which carried in them the seeds of the proletarian culture of the future.[52]

Lentsov's views were seconded by "A. K.," a contributor to the Bolshevik daily *The Worker*, who claimed that "true defenders of democracy" should not oppose the workers' theaters; instead, they should "welcome these new aspirations of the cultivated workers' milieu." Like the industrialists, bureaucrats, temperance activists, and other proponents of people's theaters, "A. K." was confident in the power of theater to transform the so-called dark masses; the only difference was that he sought to awaken their class consciousness rather than to civilize them. By successfully staging "proletarian plays with vivid proletarian types," workers' theater could

> draw into its milieu those who, under other circumstances, would perish in the prosaic swamp of philistinism [*meshchanstvo*] and unconsciousness. The unconscious masses don't like to attend lectures because they find them boring and often difficult to understand, but they go with pleasure to the theater, where the performance doesn't require any special intellectual effort on the part of the spectator. The workers' theater is an easier way to awaken the consciousness and thus prepare new cadres of conscious members of workers' organizations.[53]

He was convinced that the workers' theaters were evidence of a nascent proletarian culture. "The working class," he proclaimed, "is now already strong enough to oppose the philistine morality and lachrymose homilies of the bourgeois theater with its own proletarian ideals—of this there can be no doubt."[54] The struggle for a proletarian culture thus came to be seen as an extension of the political and economic struggle, at least in the pages of *Pravda* and other socialist dailies.

THE REPERTOIRE OF WORKERS' THEATERS

Despite the radical rhetoric about a new proletarian culture, the repertoires of the workers' theaters were generally quite conservative. They mainly staged classics or contemporary plays by writers with established reputations. The works by Ostrovsky, Pushkin, Leo Tolstoy, Gogol, Chekhov, Gorky, and Hauptmann that the workers' theaters favored were staple fare in all Russian theaters in the decade before the revolution; they constituted the backbone of the conventional Russian stage repertoire. Although some workers and their mentors paid lip service to the idea that a purely proletarian culture with its own dramatic literature was in the making, most workers appear to have been for more concerned with taking the established high culture into their own hands and making it theirs.

When a St. Petersburg drama circle chose a repertoire for its first season in 1912, it claimed to have been guided by the principle that "plays should be absolutely ideological, lifelike, and close to the understanding of the workers; theater should facilitate the cultural self-determination of the working masses."[55] Although most of the plays selected dealt with the plight of the oppressed, the corruption of the powerful, or generational conflict, the repertoire was still quite conventional: Chekhov's *Uncle Vanya*, Viktor Ryshkov's *The First Swallow*, Gorky's *The Lower Depths* and *Philistines*, Sergei Naidenov's *Vaniushin's Children*, Gogol's *The Government Inspector*, and Ostrovsky's *Poverty Is No Vice*, *The Forest*, and *Diary of a Scoundrel*. These plays were typical of the repertoires of most workers' theaters, yet they were also commonly performed in imperial and commercial theaters in St. Petersburg, Moscow, and the provinces.

In what sense, then, could such plays be considered "ideological"? Worker-actors could of course ad-lib, making slight alterations in the text in order to draw attention to elements of class conflict in a play. For example, in a 1907 production of *Poverty Is No Vice* by a group of Obukhov workers, Konstantin Skorobogatov played Liubim Tortsov, the good-hearted drunkard whose intercession saves his niece from his brother's attempt to marry her to a rich suitor, freeing her to marry her true love, a poor clerk. The workers performed the play before a working-class audience at the summer theater of the Nevskii Society, known popularly as the Vienna because it was located on land rented from the Vienna Brewery. Skorobogatov later recalled how when he spoke the lines, "I'm not a factory owner, I haven't robbed the poor," the audience responded noisily and someone shouted out—"That's right, beat the rascals!"[56] The actual lines are, "I'm not Korshunov [the rich merchant about to marry Liubim Tortsov's niece], I haven't robbed the poor."[57] It is impossible to know whether Skorobogatov actually substituted "factory owner" for "Korshunov" in his performance or has simply embellished the story in his memoir; in either version, the lines retain their power as a denunciation of the rich, powerful, and corrupt.

Poverty Is No Vice and *The Forest* were famous for their satirical portraits of wealthy people who abuse the poor; they contain rich material for interpretations emphasizing social conflict. In the 1890s, a number of workers surveyed in St. Petersburg and Riazan in the 1890s who had seen Ostrovsky's work at theaters sponsored by factory owners and temperance societies said that they particularly liked the plays for similar reasons.[58] *The First Swallow*, written by the prolific and now forgotten Viktor Ryshkov, whose plays on topical issues were popular in the early twentieth century, examines the pernicious effects of the penetration of capitalism into rural Russia.[59] *Uncle Vanya*, of course, depicts the various conflicts among members of an intelligentsia family in the 1890s; it may have been chosen for presentation as a commentary on the bleakness of the years of reaction and the helplessness of the intelligentsia. Reviewing a performance of *Uncle Vanya* by the Stasiulevich Society workers, a worker explained: "In this play, as in a mirror, is reflected the life of people in the 1880s and 1890s, when everything living was crushed. In the play we see not a single positive character who would struggle with this spiritual stagnation."[60]

The Lower Depths, which premiered at the Moscow Art Theater, became an overnight sensation due to its somber, naturalistic depiction of life in a Moscow flophouse; it was widely regarded as both an indictment of social injustice and a paean to man's capacity for self-liberation.[61] The play's revolutionary cachet was only enhanced by the fact that until 1905 it had been prohibited for performance before popular audiences. Gorky's *Philistines*, first performed in 1902, is an outright attack on the depravity of the bourgeoisie. The bourgeoisie is represented by the family Bessemenov (the name means "family-less" or "seed-less"), to which is contrasted the new worker-hero represented in the character of their adopted son Nil, who is committed to the class struggle and, incidentally, is in a workers' drama circle. In Nil, Gorky created Russian literature's most enduring image of the prerevolutionary worker-intellectual, who is also the only truly positive character in the play. A young worker who read *Philistines* a year or two after its premiere later recalled that Nil became a hero for him and other "conscious workers of the time."[62] *Vaniushin's Children*, written by a member of Gorky's *Znanie* group, is a "progressive" play about generational conflict within the contemporary merchant class; it was widely performed throughout Russia in the early twentieth century. *The Government Inspector* and *Diary of a Scoundrel* are Russia's most famous and scathing satires of official corruption and remain topical even today. True, these plays offered workers a wealth of material for attacking both the existing order and the "powers that be," yet they were also very much a part of contemporary mainstream culture.

WORKERS' THEATER AS AN ALTERNATIVE CULTURE

Workers' theaters were, if effect, the embodiment of the aspirations of the self-styled labor intelligentsia for an alternative culture, one that would uphold the old nineteenth-century canon of socially critical, realistic art (a canon that had been coming under increasing attack from the modernist camp since the turn of the century). Of course, the precarious legal status of working-class organizations in imperial Russia and the extremely low levels of participation in them prevented the emergence of the sort of well-developed network of cultural institutions that characterized the German Social Democratic labor movement.[63] Yet there was clearly a strong desire within the ranks of the minority of skilled, educated, urbanized workers to create for themselves such an alternative culture, and these worker-intellectuals perceived the workers' theaters as an important step toward the realization of this goal.

Discussing a St. Petersburg workers' theater's production of Aleksei Pisemsky's *A Bitter Fate*, a mid-nineteenth-century drama about serfdom, the reviewer exultantly hailed the performance as a sign that workers were beginning to achieve an independence in the cultural sphere that was commensurate with their independence in politics and trade unions:

> Soon there will be the [worker's] own theater, and many of their own worker-artists and singers, who are now successfully being cultivated in several societies. There will be musicians, worker-dramatists, worker-decorators, and painters. Soon there will be workers' drama, comedy, and even opera, however difficult the latter undertaking may be. Then the workers will have no reason to be drawn to the bourgeois theater, where only rarely can they find wholesome artistic pleasure from which they might also derive a beneficial lesson.[64]

Workers' theater was envisioned as an alternative to the commercial amusement parks, cinemas, and state-sponsored temperance theaters that attracted the ostensibly backward masses of "unconscious" workers with their melodramas, spectaculars, operettas, and can-cans. It was also an alternative to the symbolist and modernist tendencies of the upscale theaters. In 1913, using language that, apart from its class terminology, strikingly resembles the fulminations of generations of intelligentsia critics of the pernicious influence of Petrushka and the *balagany* on the people, a worker explained the importance of an alternative workers' theater:

> The grave and extremely harmful influence of cheap theater and cinema on the proletariat's psyche cannot be denied. Through them the vulgarity [*poshlost'*] that the bourgeoisie strews over the outskirts [of the city] under the guise of "art" enters into workers' lives.
> Organized workers face the problem of how to resist this vulgarity. Clearly we cannot limit ourselves to angry talk about the harm of bourgeois influences. Convincing though that talk may be, it cannot quench the workers' thirst for spectacles and theater. We must quench that thirst for aesthetic sensations without resort to the sort of theaters and cinemas one now finds on the [city's] outskirts; we must found our own workers' theater.[65]

In other words, workers' theater was to be a bulwark against the contaminating influence of the commercial popular culture that labor activists feared would divert the working class from the path of self-improvement.

Antipathy to the ostensibly baneful impact of popular culture was rife in the Russian labor movement. The worker-poet and *Pravda* correspondent Leontii Kotomka, for example, bemoaned the cinema's attraction for workers and castigated it as "the incarnation of bourgeois vulgarity."[66] The enormously popular Pinkerton novels were similarly attacked in trade union publications for their corrupting influence on workers' hearts and minds. In 1910 the journal of the St. Petersburg metalworkers union poignantly confessed that tales of the Pinkerton detectives' adventures had acquired "a thousand times more readers than our workers' journals and brochures."[67] Another article in the same journal partially blamed what it claimed to be a decline in working-class morality on the fact that "serious economic literature has disappeared from our desks, replaced by all kinds of trashy Pinkerton works."[68] The metalworkers' journal also castigated the phonograph for seducing workers away from union activities; it even published a poem satirizing a worker who drops out of the union and buys a phonograph to occupy his free time instead. The verses conclude with an ironic reference to the incompatibility of being "conscious" and enjoying records: "I'm a conscious worker, I'll throw out all the books, and let the phonograph play until late at night."[69] Deploring the popularity of boulevard newspapers among factory workers, the trade-union journal *The Metalworker* cautioned that "the consumption of this literary trash can lead to the development among us of the psychology of the French [!] workers, who assume an indifferent attitude toward all public issues."[70]

The workers' theaters were also an alternative to the theaters and other entertainments organized for them by factory owners and temperance societies. "Just as the recreations formerly organized by the bourgeoisie in cooperation with the bureaucracy were crude and reckoned on the bad taste and absence of aesthetics among the workers," wrote the Bolshevik worker Dmitrii Rodnov, "so now is the artistic recreation of the workers, organized by themselves, both artistic and attractive."[71] Like detective novels, phonographs, movies, the boulevard press, and other manifestations of commercial popular culture (usually referred to as "bourgeois culture") that were proving so attractive to workers in the prewar years, the factory and temperance theaters were seen as a danger to the labor movement, threatening to undermine the morals of the working class with their supposedly trashy spectacles.

St. Petersburg's Nicholas II People's House was a favorite target for outbursts of indignation by the workers' intelligentsia. In a letter to a Bolshevik daily, a young worker describing one of the theaters at the People's House: "The acrobats, gymnasts, clowns, etc. give no pleasure to the worker's soul, but on the contrary, develop coarse instincts in him. The music thunders, vulgar jokes are heard, the air in the enormous hall grows stale because of insufficient ventilation—these are all the amusements available to the people. It is not surprising that the backward [*nerazvitoi*] worker hurries to the tavern to wash away his inadequacies with alcohol."[72]

The solution, the young worker concluded, was for workers to join unions and educational societies and to organize their own performances in order to "find rest and receive an answer to their aspirations for light."[73] Another worker condemned the People's House for playing "polkas, marches, and utterly worn-out waltzes that can be heard on the phonograph in any tearoom or pub." The theater's atmosphere and repertoire, he contended, "not only don't ennoble audiences, they vulgarize and corrupt them."[74]

Reviews of performances by workers' drama circles often drew attention to the sense of solidarity they fostered thanks to the bonds of class linking actors and audiences. In its account of a performance of *A Bitter Fate* by Moscow workers in 1916, the journal of the printers' union described it as "a closed circle of workers, united by their love for art and brought together by Pisemsky's drama."[75] The reviewer added that it was impossible to separate the stage from the hall, for the performance was a communion of actors and spectators.

Seldom did the partisans of workers' theater attempt to argue that the performances were of high quality. Instead, they emphasized the sympathy of audiences for their fellow workers. Responding to the suggestion that inexperienced actors would only arouse smiles at the most tragic moments, one worker countered that "a spectator who has a conscious attitude toward the performance of the worker-actor will forgive him his blunders and fill in the gaps with his own imagination."[76] But not all workers were so tolerant of poor acting, regardless of its class origins. Describing a performance of Gogol's *Marriage* by members of the Khamovniki Consumers' Society, a Moscow worker complained that the actors barely knew their lines, used improper diction, and displayed their indifference to art.[77]

Many performances were no doubt painfully amateurish. Even sympathetic reviewers often admitted that workers had trouble portraying characters from other social groups. Still, it was not the skill displayed in the performances but the fact that they were created by and for workers that seems to have mattered most. The amateur theatrical, a common pastime of the Russian middle classes, was now appropriated by workers as an affirmation of their identity as cultivated people who appreciated drama.[78]

Nevertheless, there were tensions between the proponents of a political theater and those who saw workers' theaters primarily as a means of acquainting the working masses with a culture hitherto reserved for the privileged classes. One St. Petersburg troupe even split over this issue. In 1913 a group of workers on Vasilevskii Island founded the Workers' Theater and invited Pavel Sazonov, an actor from the Gaideburov theater, to direct performances. During the 1913–14 season the troupe staged performances of works by Gorky, Hauptmann, Ostrovsky, Leo Tolstoy, Pisemsky, and others, earning favorable reviews in the labor press. In the spring of 1914, however, a conflict broke out within the troupe over its ideological orientation. One group, led by Sazonov, pledged itself to uphold the standard of "pure, nontendentious, classless, sacred art," while a minority saw in art "the manifestation of real life [and] the influence of class domination."[79] In a declaration of secession, the minority faction argued that the troupe had demonstrated "an unconscious attitude" and had failed to understand the purpose of a workers' theater, "having set itself on the path of merely entertaining workers."[80]

The immediate cause of the split was a disagreement not over repertoire but over the troupe's decision to invite liberal literary critics to give pre-performance lectures on Hauptmann and Saltykov-Shchedrin. In the view of the minority, the critics had failed to present their subjects from a class point of view; for instance, the lecture on Hauptmann had made no reference to the radical social content of the German playwright's work. Some of the disgruntled workers decided to form a separate troupe that would use the stage to "illuminate the class position of the working masses and show the way out of that position."[81] The breakaway Workers' Theater was soon shut down by the Okhrana, and some of its members were sentenced to administrative exile, but the troupe nonetheless continued staging performances around St. Petersburg.[82] One of its members, Aleksei Mashirov, later played a key role in the creation of Proletkult in 1917 and, under the pseudonym "Samobytnik," became a well-known "proletarian poet" in the 1920s.[83]

TENSIONS BETWEEN WORKERS AND INTELLIGENTSIA

Another source of potential discord was the frequent reliance of the workers' troupes on the assistance of the intelligentsia for advice and assistance in putting together their productions. Some workers were anxious to avoid appearing dependent on the intelligentsia. For example, the author of a 1913 article calling for the St. Petersburg cultural-educational societies to form a

Figure 14. The actors of Anna Brenko's "Workers' Theater," the day after their performance of Ostrovsky's *The Marriage of Balzaminov, or You Get What You Look For* to raise money for the Prechistenskie Workers' Courses. Moscow, 1915. *Vechernie izvestiia,* 23 November 1915.

united workers' theater, while admitting that "to form a workers' troupe of actors . . . is not an easy business and demands at the beginning the help of experienced persons [i.e. professional actors from the intelligentsia]," cautioned that "the ideological leadership, which is primarily expressed in the choice of repertoire, should be in the hands of the workers' organizations."[84]

Yet few workers' theaters were able to function without outside assistance. In Moscow, actors from the Moscow Art Theater (among them the young Evgenii Vakhtangov) gave acting lessons at the Prechistenskie Worker's Courses and organized a troupe of about twenty workers who met twice a week to rehearse adaptations of stories by Chekhov, Turgenev, Korolenko, and Gorky, as well as vaudevilles and light comic skits.[85] The actress Anna Brenko later supervised the troupe and opened a free drama school for some twenty-five workers. The workers staged several plays by Ostrovsky and in August 1915 opened their own Workers' Theater with a performance of Ostrovsky's *The Storm*, which was praised by one theater journal as reminiscent of "the graduation show of a 'real' drama studio."[86] During the Civil War the theater performed before units of the Red Army, and a number of Brenko's students went on to become professional actors.[87]

Workers also got valuable assistance from the Section for Assisting the Organization of Factory and Village Theaters, which began working under the auspices of the Moscow branch of the Imperial Russian Technical

Society in 1911. The Section was composed of various theater figures, writers, artists, and other liberal intellectuals active in the movement to bring theater to the people. Among its members were the artists V. D. Polenov, I. A. Repin, V. M. Vasnetsov, P. A. Briullov, the director A. A. Sanin, the opera singer Fedor Shaliapin, and the actor N. V. Skorodumov. It provided factory and village theaters with plays, scenery, costumes, and artistic guidance at a low cost, organized exhibits and lectures, and conducted drama courses. Many workers' troupes in Moscow benefited from the Section's services, including the aforementioned Danilov workers. A group of workers who attended the Section's courses formed an amateur troupe under the direction of Moscow Art Theater actor Dmitrii Tolbuzin that performed in factories in Moscow and neighboring provinces.[88]

In 1912 the Section reorganized itself and became a division of the Moscow Society of People's Universities. Although most trade unions, cultural-educational societies, and socialist newspapers were suppressed at the outbreak of World War I in 1914, the Section, as well as many workers' theater groups, continued to function as before. In 1915 the Section opened a new headquarters, called the Polenov House in honor of the Section's president, artist and set designer Vasilii Polenov. The castle-like building housed a theater and a large stock of theatrical costumes, scenery, and sets for various plays.[89] Together with the Imperial Russian Theatrical Society, the Section initiated an All-Russian Congress of People's Theater Activists to discuss ways to further the establishment of theaters for lower-class audiences. Some 365 activists took part in the congress, which opened in Moscow in late 1915, including many people who had long been involved in the organization of people's theaters (Evtikhii Karpov, Nikolai Popov, Larissa Bunakova, Anatolii Kremlev, and Nikolai Timkovskii), as well as representatives of worker and peasant theater groups.

The congress brought to a head the tensions between workers and their intelligentsia mentors. The main dispute centered around the definition of people's theaters. Liberal intellectuals conceived of people's theaters as primarily cultural institutions, while the workers wanted to emphasize the theaters' class character and political significance. The intelligentsia activists took a traditional liberal *Kulturträger* view of the people's theater and held that it should be chiefly a means to democratize art by making it accessible to the common people. In the resolutions presented by the Committee on Repertoire, people's theater was initially defined as "a democratized theater, having art as its foundation."[90] The "democratic workers' group" rejected this formulation, arguing that this definition stood for "art for art's sake" and neglected the social and ideological functions of theater. After a long and sometimes stormy debate, the workers succeeded in substituting a resolution stating that people's theater, possessing a "self-sufficient artistic-aesthetic value," was at the same time a means of influencing the masses' "ideological outlook, independence, and organization."[91]

The workers' group also objected to any emphasis on a play's "artistic value" as the fundamental criterion for determining repertoire, claiming that a play's ideological content was of equal importance.[92] Significantly, the workers wanted the congress to recognize that the choice of repertoire should be in the hands of "local democratic organizations," meaning trade unions, cooperatives, and cultural-educational societies composed of workers or peasants rather than intellectuals. This proposal, which challenged the intelligentsia's claim to cultural leadership (and foreshadowed subsequent struggles in postrevolutionary Russia over who would control cultural organizations like Proletkult) failed to win approval due to heated objections from other delegates, one of whom accused the workers' group of attempting to "oppress the intelligentsia."[93]

· · ·

The prerevolutionary workers' theater movement reflected the diverse and sometimes conflicting aspirations of workers who sought to create their own cultural institutions and networks. For some, workers' theater was first and foremost a weapon of propaganda and political struggle, while others saw it as a means of acquainting workers with elite culture. Viewed in the context of the workers' theaters, "proletarian culture" meant different things to different people. In its most basic sense, it was simply the opportunity for workers to organize and stage theater performances independently. The performances might aim to raise social and political awareness and promote proletarian solidarity, but the heart of the matter was that workers enjoyed staging plays because theater was an important part of the elite culture they hoped to make their own. At the grass-roots level, proletarian culture sometimes had a radical political and social significance, but its form was culturally conservative, for the workers' theaters tended to accept mainstream cultural standards even as they challenged the exclusion of the working class from the mainstream of Russian cultural life. What the worker-intellectuals, similar to middle-class art patrons, wanted from consuming the right cultural products was self-improvement and respectability. After the October Revolution this cultural conservatism, together with a strong desire for organizational autonomy, would often bring workers into conflict with Proletkult activists who tried to impose their more utopian vision of proletarian culture as a complete break with the past.[94]

Although the workers' theaters attempted to emulate rather than do away with the established high culture, this does not necessarily mean that in staging ("bourgeois") plays from the conventional repertoires of theaters attended by the privileged classes workers were subjecting themselves to the "hegemony" of the dominant culture that produced the texts. In the theater, texts acquire meaning in performance, and it is the use to which a text is put that determines its significance and value for performers and audiences. The consumption of cultural products is itself a creative process that produces meanings, and many of the plays that were so popular among workers' theater groups offered them a readily accessible source of meanings that could be used to oppose the social order that subordinated them.[95] Indeed, much of Russian artistic culture was highly critical of the sociopolitical structure of autocracy, and art had long been viewed as a powerful weapon in the struggle against it. In staging classic and contemporary plays about social issues, workers "made do" with what was available to them, and there was a good deal.[96]

The prerevolutionary workers' theater produced neither a corpus of proletarian dramatic literature nor a distinctively proletarian aesthetic of performance.[97] Not even its most fervent exponents made such a claim. Instead, they argued that the workers' theaters were preparing the soil for the proletarian culture that would someday flower under socialism. From this perspective, amateur performances by workers were a sign of their aspirations for art and their power to create it for themselves. There may have been no proletarian drama, but there were proletarian theaters, for theater is an art of performance—in making theater, workers could lay a claim to artistic creation. As Kleinbort pointed out in his 1913 article "The Workers' Intelligentsia and Art," theater was the most accessible of all art forms to workers with no formal preparation:

> It is self-evident that of the various spheres of art, painting, and music lend themselves with greatest difficulty to the callused hands of the factory worker. There are self-taught painters and musicians, but with homemade means it is generally not easy to achieve results. And we will hardly be mistaken in saying that what is characteristic here is not worker-talent, but a hint of the talent that may eventually appear. But the exact opposite is true with theater, which is at all events accessible and democratic. Find a barn where you can build even a small stage, put up the boards and a calico curtain—and it's ready. Ability comes of its own accord, so long as there is sincerity and freshness of feeling.
> This is why the path to workers' theater is the most trodden: it is the

"fortress" of workers' art, in which, evidently, the self-taught worker is most persistent in his artistic quest, most enterprising in finding the means to apply his artistic abilities.[98]

Finally, in performing and attending performances in their own theaters, workers implicitly rejected the passive role assigned to them by the proponents of "rational recreations" meant to "civilize" the common people from above. The labor press may have at times employed the discourse of "rational recreations," yet it was still the workers' troupes that selected the plays they staged, whether they chose them for their ideological, their political, or simply their entertainment value. And if they got help and advice from the intelligentsia, it was still the worker amateurs who performed on the stage. Though never completely autonomous, workers' theater was above all *samodeiatel'nost'*—doing it for yourself.

6   The People at the Theater: Audience Reception

The people's theaters aimed to transform audiences, but what in fact was their impact on the common people who attended their performances? What place did the theaters have in the lives of the urban working classes? Did they, as the *Kulturträger* hoped they would, civilize audiences and "soften" popular morality, or at least integrate the common people into a universal Russian national culture? Were they agents of bourgeois cultural hegemony, promoting consent to the sociopolitical status quo? Did melodramas and patriotic spectaculars foster a "culture of consolation" and undermine class consciousness? Or did they become part of a new repertoire of lower-class cultural practices, replete with symbolic meanings, providing new opportunities for working people to transgress established class boundaries, experiment with new forms of sociability and self-identity, and encounter unfamiliar ways of life?

The significance of theatrical entertainments for the audiences who saw them is not easy to assess, but some inferences and conclusions can be drawn from the observations of contemporaries and from audience surveys conducted by the theaters' sponsors. The audience surveys are particularly interesting, for they contain the firsthand comments of the workers themselves and reflect their immediate impression of what was for many their first exposure to theater. At the same time, the survey responses are hardly representative of the "silent majority," for they were written only by workers who were literate enough to set down their thoughts on paper and who took the theater performances seriously enough to bother with answering the often detailed questionnaires. There are almost no responses from women workers, for example, due not to a lack of women in the audiences, for contemporary observers often noted that large numbers of women attended the performances, but more probably due to their relatively low levels of literacy. In 1897 only 21.3 percent of the female industrial workers in European Russia were literate, as opposed to 53.5 percent of the males.[1]

Audience surveys must also be handled with caution due to the tendency of any questionnaire to prompt certain kinds of answers. One survey asked about the moral significance of the plays, implying that this is important in evaluating drama and should be highlighted in the response. Another asked workers how they spent their free time before the theater opened, suggesting a before and after dichotomy, whereby viewing performances represented an improvement for those who attended, and inviting responses that previously there was little to do but drink, fight, or gamble. The workers most able and willing to answer the questionnaires were likely to be those who shared the enlighteners' view of theater as a moral educational institution for self-improvement and would probably have been prone to respond in kind.

Evidence from firsthand descriptions of audience behavior and reactions, though valuable, is equally problematic. Contemporary observers were almost invariably educated Russians who were either committed to the idea of a didactic people's theater or shared many of the culturist assumptions of the people's theater activists. Their accounts of performances and audience reactions are often patronizing in tone, foregrounding evidence that confirms their convictions about the civilizing power of art and the people's receptivity to it. As Liubov Gurevich, the liberal editor and publisher of *The Northern Herald* and a prominent cultural critic, stated in 1896, "The crowd goes to see the high jinks of the fairground barkers, but it would also go to see serious works of art if they were made accessible."[2] The appetite of the *narod* for melodramas, farces, spectaculars, and variety shows was usually blamed on the organizers of the shows, who were condemned for pandering to rather than lifting the tastes of the crowd.

Workers' accounts, while representing the view from below, also have their biases. The workers who wrote memoirs or articles in the press were seldom representative of the rank and file, but belonged to the highly literate, skilled, and relatively well-paid upper stratum of the working class. They used theater attendance and interest in serious drama as a confirmation of their respectability and the ability of workers to transcend the cultural stereotypes that relegated them to the lower echelons of Russian society. Their memoirs, often written long after the Bolshevik Revolution had given them opportunities for upward social mobility and assigned lowbrow entertainments to the dustbin, usually emphasize the desire of workers for the classics or naturalistic dramas about working-class life and social conflict that their socialist mentors deemed they should like.

Yet all of these sources on the audience and its response to theater can be extremely useful if read critically. By comparing the various descriptions of audience reactions, placing them into the context of what we know about contemporary urban life, and reading between the lines of the descriptions with an awareness of the authors' points of view, it is possible to open a window on popular audiences' encounters with theater in an urban setting. Theater is a collective experience, and the evidence, however flawed, of audience responses to performances at least permits the investigation of textual reception; readers' responses, by contrast, are much more difficult to assess, since the reading process is individual and not observable; nor were mass surveys of readers conducted. Naturally, there was no single response to any performance or text. Audiences were differentiated by their levels of literacy, degree of assimilation into urban culture, familiarity with theater, and expectations of the performances. What popular audiences saw and heard on the stage was partly shaped by their life experiences, and by examining theater performances in relation to urban working-class life we can make some tentative conclusions about tastes, reception, and the impact of theater on audiences.

Theories of reception are thought-provoking and of some assistance when examining the experiences of audiences at the people's theaters. Wolfgang Iser has argued in his work on the reading process that the comprehension of a text is "inseparable from the reader's expectations"; Iser's idea of a dynamic and interactive relationship between the text and the reader can be readily applied to people's theaters and their publics by positing a likely range of audience expectations based on our knowledge of urban working-class life and culture. Iser's concept of the "implied reader," which locates the range of reader responses in the structure of the author's text, is not applicable to people's theater, however, since almost all of the plays and operas performed were originally written for aristocratic or middle-class audiences with a range of prior cultural knowledge and expectations very different from those of the common people. Hans Robert Jauss calls our attention to the changing horizons of audience expectations in time, while Stanley Fish argues that readers' experiences are socially constructed, lying outside of authorial intention and uncontrolled by the text itself. Although reader-response criticism, with its constructions of theoretical audiences, is more suited to the concerns of literary criticism than to an historical analysis examining real and observable audiences, its emphasis on the role of audiences in producing meaning is a useful approach when considering urban popular audiences' experiences in the social and cultural setting of people's theaters.[3]

THE NATURE OF THE AUDIENCE

The audiences surveyed at the Nevskii and Riazan societies, though predominately made up of local factory workers, were far from homogeneous. Shcheglov described the public of one of the Nevskii Society's *gulian'ia* in the early 1890s: "unskilled factory workers [*zavodskie chernorabochie*], working women from the neighboring textile factories, skilled workers [*masterovye*] with their wives and children, soldiers with their city girlfriends." His description of the wide variety of dress to be seen on the dance floor, ranging from peasant garb to more citified jackets, bustles, and hats, affords an idea of the motley composition of the popular audience.[4] Differing greatly in their levels of education and their degree of assimilation into urban life, workers naturally had varying attitudes toward theater performances, which are reflected in their responses to the surveys. In Riazan, for example, the opinions of railway workers and those of factory workers were often quite different; judging from their comments, the latter group was more skilled and had a higher level of literacy.

According to contemporary accounts of performances in factory theaters, many workers initially had trouble mastering theatrical conventions. At the Ivanovskaia textile factory, for example, audiences often failed to realize when one play had ended and another play had begun, so signs indicating the name of each play were hung on the curtain prior to each performance. Other viewers had the opposite problem and thought each act a separate play. Moreover, many mistook the actors' curtain calls for a continuation of the action. After one performance of Ostrovsky's *Poverty Is No Vice*, the appearance of the actors onstage to take their bows provoked the audience to conclude that Korshunov had married Liubushka after all, since they came out holding hands.[5]

Workers sometimes reacted to theater in ways that middle-class observers found disconcerting. At the end of a performance at the Tsindel cotton mill of Ostrovsky's *Even a Cat Has Lean Times*, in which a rich suitor arrives at the beginning of the final act with a wedding gift, only to be rebuffed and leave in anger, workers remarked, "They're all so smart, they chased off the old man and kept the gift for themselves," thereby focusing on a detail that had escaped both the playwright and the director. Sergei Popov, the director of the Ivanovskaia textile factory, found that audiences were much more interested in the intrigues of opera than in the music. Konstantin Skorobogatov, who as a young skilled worker at St. Petersburg's Obukhov factory was taken to a performance of *Tristan and*

Figure 15. Open-air summer stage in the park of the Vasilevskii Island Theater for Workers. St. Petersburg, 1898. *Niva*, no. 35 (29 August 1898): 693.

Isolde at the Imperial Mariinskii Theater by a friendly engineer, found that the music made it difficult for him to follow the lyrics.[6]

Nikolai Popov admitted his surprise in finding that worker and intelligentsia audiences could react to one and the same performance in very different ways. In 1891, attending a performance at a Yaroslavl factory of *Parasha the Siberian Girl*, Nikolai Polevoi's melodrama about a girl who goes to St. Petersburg to right the wrongs her father has suffered, he found that the worker audience was far more interested in the special effects and new sets than in the play's content. They found the snowflakes that fell throughout the action especially engrossing.[7] This preoccupation with special effects was not uncommon, particularly among less-educated workers; 80 percent of the railway workers who responded to the Riazan Society's survey indicated that they were more interested in the performance itself than in the play's content. At the same time, 71 percent of the factory workers, whose responses indicate that they were better educated than the railway workers, emphasized content as the factor that determined whether or not they liked the plays.[8] The experience of theater was very much dependent on the consumer's particular sociocultural profile.

Audiences at the people's theaters run by the temperance guardianships were even more diverse, since they attracted people from all walks of urban life. Factory workers, domestic servants, seamstresses, shop clerks, waiters, day laborers, and soldiers occupied the cheaper seats and standing room in the balconies, while the better seats were the province of middle-class theatergoers whose more expensive tickets partially subsidized the less fortunate. The balconies, known for their boisterous response to performances, were quick to demonstrate their approval or disapproval. At open-air stages like the one in the Tauride Gardens, audiences were less segregated. The Ligovskii People's House drew a more working-class public to its performances, many of whom also attended the People's House's evening courses. Audiences at all of the people's theaters were heterogeneous, and no one "popular mentality" can be ascribed to them. A variety of attitudes to theater and responses to performances characterize the audiences who spent their kopeks on a day's or an evening's entertainment, and each viewer went with his or her own individual expectations.

VOICES FROM THE AUDIENCE

During the late 1890s and early 1900s, there were a few attempts to gauge the attitudes of working-class audiences by handing out written surveys. There are three main sources on urban workers' firsthand reactions to theater, coming respectively from St. Petersburg, Kiev, and Riazan, a medium-sized industrial city southeast of Moscow. In 1895 St. Petersburg's Nevskii Society conducted an audience survey, after which a selection of the responses was published in the populist journal *Russian Wealth* by Nikolai Mikhailovskii, who used them to demonstrate the moral and educational potential of people's theater. Workers were asked whether they were satisfied with the entertainments offered at the *narodnye gulian'ia*, what moral and material significance the entertainments had for them, and whether they found the plays comprehensible. In Kiev, a certain Bulgakova collected workers' views on the meaning of theater in order to determine what repertoire was most appropriate for them, and some of the comments were published in *Theater and Art*.[9]

In 1898 the Riazan Society for Popular Entertainments, which organized recreations much like those of the Nevskii Society in a factory district outside of Riazan, attempted a much more detailed survey. The Riazan survey asked respondents to state their profession, how often they attended the *gulian'ia* and theater performances, how they spent their leisure time prior to the existence of the organized recreations, what kinds of plays they liked and which plays they would like to see staged in the future, whether they liked the variety shows and, if not, what should replace them. The survey also asked them to propose changes or improvements in the entertainment program. The survey got a lukewarm response, however, perhaps due to its novelty. For most of the workers attending the *gulian'ia* and theater performances, this may well have been the first time they had ever been asked to express their opinions in writing. During the summer of 1898 some 3,000 printed questionnaires were distributed, but by the end of the summer only 156 had been returned, and of these nearly a third were incomplete or contained nonsensical or indecent answers that could not be used. One member of the society, theater historian Baron N. V. Drizen, speculated that the paucity of responses might well be due to a "striving to throw off the tutelage of the educated classes" on the part of the common people. Indeed, some factory workers' responses to the survey indicate that they resented what they felt to be a patronizing attitude on the part of the performances' organizers.[10]

Workers' comments on the plays they saw indicate that theater had a multiplicity of significances for them. There was no ideal type of spectator from the people, for each brought his or her own expectations, life experiences, and cultural background to the performances. For many workers, seeing a play was a novel form of entertainment that afforded an opportunity to forget, if briefly, the cares and drudgery of everyday life. A Kiev worker, writing with labored syntax, said he liked theater "because when I have a depression in me there is nowhere I can get rid of it like the theater" (*ia teatr liubliu v tom, chto kogda v menia* [sic] *kakaia toska, to ia inache nigde ne mogu ee razveiat', krome teatra*), adding that in the theater he forgot "my whole life, whether it's good or bad," and felt "happy, as if in an earthly paradise."[11] For him, theater was a form of escape into another world. His enchantment with theater was shared by a worker at St. Petersburg's Obukhov factory, who wrote awkwardly of his gratitude to the members of the Nevskii Society:

> The Lord Himself taught the Nevskii Society to organize entertainments for the people, for which many poor people give great thanks to the society. I don't have the heart to write about morality [*u menia dukhu ne khvataet vylozhit' na bumagu nravstvennost'*], but I will say that my heart is never so glad as when I watch the open-air stage. I can't say anything about whether the plays are understandable or interesting, but there wasn't a play I didn't like.[12]

His tone is deferential toward his social betters, a tone commonly used by workers in addressing their employers. Interestingly, both the Kiev and the Petersburg workers expressed their delight in the aesthetic aspect of theater in religious terms, possibly associating it with the beauty of the Orthodox service. Neither can explain how he interpreted the plays. They may have been too inarticulate to explain what they liked about the plays, or perhaps they were simply too self-conscious or embarrassed to try, but what comes through clearly is the excitement of their encounter with drama.

Other workers, evidently better educated, responded using more secular terms of critical evaluation, yet also underlined the pleasure they received from attending the performances. A woman worker from St. Petersburg's Pal factory, whose detailed comments were the most thoughtful and complex of all those cited by Mikhailovskii, emphasized the theater's hypnotic effect:

> The worker forgets his condition for a time; he is entirely absorbed in what he sees and hears in the theater. Theater is rest for the people, but not the kind of rest we know at home. You come to the theater and attentively watch and listen to what is happening on the stage. You listen so hard that you see nothing around you except the stage. You escape into what you see and hear, and feel as though you were a character in the play [*kak budto chuvstvuesh' deistvuiushchim litsom*].[13]

For her, attending theater was more than an escape, it was a means to assume other identities and vicariously take part in another kind of life.

For a worker from the Nevskii machine works, the Nevskii Society's pleasure garden and entertainments were a sort of alternative model of existence, which he contrasted favorably to everyday life: "In your park I encountered neither heavy drinking nor drunks; I did not encounter groups of men carnivorously examining the women passing by; I did not encounter any effort to cheat the poor at the snack bar; I did not encounter dirty scenes at the park's exit. But for the first time I encountered something to make the worker's heart beat joyfully and his life seem more cheerful."[14] A joiner from the railway car workshops even wrote a poem to express his satisfaction, calling the park a "Nevskii Oasis" where his mind found "a wonderful world, intoxicating in its beauty," in comparison to the surrounding world, where "depravity goes arm in arm with drunkenness." Another worker, from the Thornton woolens factory, likened the entertainments to "a spring of fresh water flowing into a bog," in which the fish, "stifled by the putrid bog water," are "refreshed."[15] Such comments suggest that for some workers theater held out the promise of an alternative world of respectable pleasures where they could find solace from the hardships of their usual environment.

Not all workers expressed their gratitude in such flattering terms. Notes of class resentment also found their way onto the pages of the completed questionnaires, and a few respondents challenged their benefactors' paternalistic ethos. At the end of his questionnaire a Riazan worker added, with unconcealed sarcasm, "Of course I haven't expressed my thanks to the initiators of the *narodnye gulian'ia*, when in our gray and colorless life there are no other enjoyments, and for that reason it is impossible not to say thank you for those crumbs which fall to, as you say, your 'younger brother,' from your table of plenty."[16] The term "younger brother" (*mladshii brat*) was commonly used by intelligentsia philanthropists to refer to the objects of their good intentions, the *narod*, and was often associated with Russian populism. By employing it here the man clearly expresses his resentment at patronizing "do-gooders" from the educated classes as well as at their privileged lives, mockingly mimicking the ingratiating tone used by peasants addressing the gentry, or by "backward" workers addressing their bosses.

Other workers wanted to see more cheerful plays and expressed dissatisfaction with moralizing plays about vice and suffering. "It is very hard to watch plays like *The Storm* on some wonderful summer evening, when a person is in such a happy mood," complained a worker from the Obukhov factory, "and on the whole such a repertoire, which leaves a gloomy impression, should be avoided."[17] His sentiments were echoed by the joiner-poet who, criticizing the Nevskii Society for presuming to instruct workers from the stage, called for more escapist fare:

> Many of the plays were unsatisfactory and even brought on vexing impressions. Last summer plays from factory life were performed several times, and a few from peasant life, but those plays were so tedious that it would seem the director could see from the unrest of the audience whether they liked them or not. Immoral factory debauch was depicted on the stage, true, with great originality, but why would a factory worker want to watch this prosaic action on the stage when it is offensive to him in real life? How can you blame a man who has practically gone out of his mind after protracted labor? Look at how they come out of the factory in the evening—like madmen let out onto God's earth. In such a life a person doesn't have time to think about guarding his morals. Except for Nekrasov, no playwright-benefactor has been found to write a play not about the factory yard, but about what goes on behind the impenetrable walls of the factory—isn't that where the main culprits responsible for female immorality are concealed? A person comes to the park to give his body a rest, but instead they tear his soul apart. You may say that I don't like to see my image in the mirror. To the contrary, not everyone here is like Steshka, but it hurts to see people represented that way. Even if it is a people's stage, I ask you not to give us what we are sick and tired of, but what we don't know in life.[18]

The joiner-poets' tone is defensive, excusing immorality by citing the harsh conditions of factory labor, but he also objects that not all (male) workers resemble Steshka, a villainous character in Evtikhii Karpov's naturalistic melodrama *The Free and Easy Life* who seduces a married peasant girl who has come to the city to find work. By "the main culprits responsible for female immorality," the joiner is apparently referring to factory foremen, who often subjected women workers to abuse and even sexual molestation; in this way he is distancing workers like himself from this behavior, although male workers were also known to treat women that way. Working women frequently complained about sexual harassment by men, both supervisors and workers, on the factory floor. Hence the joiner's objection to the play's exposure of sexual impropriety may reflect a male viewpoint not shared by those working-class women in the audiences, who perhaps felt vindicated when they saw the injustices they suffered at men's hands condemned on the stage.[19]

A number of responses to the surveys neglected the entertainment factor entirely, emphasizing instead theater's importance as a source of moral instruction. "Theater is the most instructive thing in life," wrote a Kiev worker, "it shows people's lives and their situation and their good and bad sides and their thoughts."[20] Such workers, whose often rather sophisticated comments suggest that they were more skilled and educated than most of their fellows, expressed a functional attitude toward theater similar to that of peasants toward literature. Prerevolutionary and early Soviet studies of peasants' reading habits demonstrated that peasants sought moral instruction in their reading matter—saints' lives were among the most popular books because they provided moral guidance and models for living. Although Jeffrey Brooks has argued that workers "were not as apt to demand didacticism of literature, and they did not require as clear a message as did the peasants," the survey responses suggest that highly literate and articulate workers were equally attracted to clear-cut moral lessons and sometimes regarded the plays they saw as secular versions of the saints' lives. As Mark Steinberg has shown, worker-intellectuals who took up the pen to write autobiographies often constructed "self-identities as striving individuals, as heroes and outsiders," in which there are "echoes of the lives of saints (often the first literature that workers encountered), with their inspiring accounts of exceptional individuals suffering in the pursuit and in the service of truth."[21] In their reception of plays dealing with moral dilemmas and conflicts, some workers could strongly identify with characters who resembled their own self-image as people who struggled and suffered for justice and dignity.

This attitude is particularly apparent in the comments of a Riazan worker who explained that he liked Ostrovsky's plays *The Forest* and *Poverty Is No Vice* because they offered examples of moral, virtuous struggle:

> In them are very vividly portrayed people with pure and elevated souls who struggle with petty, dirty people who are sometimes powerful, but corrupt. Suffering, they do not give up their ideals, which heaven has indicated to them. Looking at them, you yourself prefer to be a Neschastlivtsev or a Liubim than a fat cat. If possible, it wouldn't be a bad idea to put on some Shakespeare sometime. These brilliant works cannot but please. There's no need to be embarrassed by weak amateurs: it is enough if they are read from the stage by different persons, and what is great in them will be understood. There is a boundless striving toward ideas.[22]

Even though this worker's reference to Shakespeare and the facility with which he expressed his thoughts make it reasonable to assume that he belonged to the "workers' intelligentsia," the writer nonetheless describes Ostrovsky's characters in distinctly saintly terms and demands that theater offer a clear moral message.

Many of the factory workers whose responses and attitudes indicate that they had attained a relatively high level of education displayed a similar preference for edifying plays, confirming the hopes the *Kulturträger* had invested in the people's theater. As mentioned earlier, 71 percent of the Riazan factory workers who responded to the survey said they judged plays on the basis of their content more than on the quality of the performance. Some even rejected entertainments if they lacked any educational message. "What I didn't like were works where there was only vulgarity and a cleverly woven love intrigue, because this is immoral and provides no food for the mind," wrote one worker in Riazan. Unlike the St. Petersburg joiner, he favored plays about the unattractive sides of daily life "because they are instructive: people become accustomed to understanding baseness in all its forms and will be on their guard whenever they come into contact with it in the future."[23]

The woman from St. Petersburg's Pal factory who found theater so engrossing explained why it was also so instructive: "On the stage we see our shortcomings as if in a mirror. Theater corrects people's shortcomings. A person can't see a fault in himself, but in the theater, attentively following the play they're performing, you see the good and bad sides of the characters and afterward you apply all that to yourself, and if you see some kind of fault in yourself, then you try to correct it, because you see how stupid and silly it is."[24] Theater, she confessed, had taught her that it was "shameful and stupid" to talk about her friends behind their backs. A skilled St. Petersburg worker expressed the same sentiments: "You can see what is required in life and that stinginess, pride and deceit can ruin a life; having seen all of this, you vividly remember it forever, and as soon as you want to deceive someone you remember the performance where deceit led to worse things, and you leave that bad vice alone."[25]

Theater, like literature, could be seen as a practical lesson in morality and an aid to self-improvement and was appreciated as such by workers searching for models of self-improvement. What seems clear, however, is that theater did not create the desire for self-improvement but rather confirmed prior expectations that literature and art would offer moral guidance. These expectations colored or even determined the responses to the performances.

Some workers explicitly compared theater to literature, stating that they found attending performances far more instructive than reading. A Kiev worker felt that "theater is nothing less than a temple of learning; in reading books a person can't get what he gets from theater." Another wrote that he initially went to the theater just to have a good laugh, but the plays he saw had made him realize that "theater is nothing less than a reflection of life according to time and customs, and it depicts character types which you don't grasp so accurately in books you read, no matter with how much talent the author portrays them. Theater teaches [us] to understand what is good and shun what is bad."[26]

Theater could also be a window on the lives and comportment of the privileged classes, a guide to respectable behavior and good manners. Writing with evident difficulty, a worker from St. Petersburg's Spasskii textile mill explained, "Theater performances acquaint [us] with the life and ways of the people we have to serve, [help us] to correct ourselves and to please their tastes."[27] The woman at the Pal factory also noted that "theater acquaints us with a different, higher class of people. We see their life, their views on life and their attitude toward the lower classes."[28] Another textile worker identified morality with education:

> The significance of these entertainments is that they can benefit a person, since in comedy and drama two sorts of people are represented. To the first sort belong people who are crude and uneducated, and they are also ignorant, wily and pushy, and inclined to drunkenness, depravity, gluttony, exploitation and even the most vile treachery toward innocent people. To the second sort belong people who are educated and kind, who do good deeds and try to share their knowledge and resources, if they have any, and don't even spare themselves in doing what would benefit humanity.[29]

At first glance, comments like these appear self-abasing and to indicate an acceptance of the superiority of the educated and an acknowledgment of the workers' ignorance, lack of cultivation, and inferiority. But they can also be read as testimonies to theater's ability to reveal the hierarchy of cultural values and offer workers an opportunity for cultural empowerment through emulation of the values of positive characters seen onstage. Bourdieu has highlighted the ways in which adopting the dominant language can be liberating for subordinate social groups.[30] By appropriating the discourse of the educated elite, as in the above responses to the questionnaires, and by imbibing new codes of behavior, working people could assert their right to be regarded as dignified human beings worthy of respect. The demand for respectful treatment was an important issue for the Russian labor movement from the end of the nineteenth century and a prominent feature in the 1905 and 1917 revolutions, particularly among workers who identified themselves as "conscious." The seeming acceptance of elite moral values expressed by some workers in describing their views of the performances can be understood as an expression of their desire to acquire the means to elevate their social status and so to contest their subordinate position.[31]

In contrast to these workers, however, other survey respondents favorably regarded plays that portrayed social conflict and confirmed their sense of injustice. A Riazan worker, for example, claimed that workers preferred plays about daily life "in which the contemporary life of our people is observed, as well as the attitude of the strong toward the weak and the rich toward the poor and the arbitrary way they treat them."[32] Another Riazan worker expressed a similar opinion: "We like Russian plays because we are familiar with the lives and models of the characters, with their incorrigibility and despotism and the strivings of others to escape from that position."[33] Such attitudes may well account for the popularity of Ostrovsky, whose critical portrayals of rich, despotic merchants and their oppressed families and employees were often mentioned by workers as their favorite plays.

A number of responses indicate that many workers had trouble interpreting the plays and would have appreciated more guidance. A worker at the Thornton factory claimed that few people were able to understand the performances at the Nevskii Society and suggested that someone should explain beforehand the moral of the play and indicate who were the evil characters and what had made them that way. Indeed, exposure to theater seems to have made this worker painfully aware of his ignorance, for he concluded his comments with an expression of thanks to "the toiling members of the [Society] and well-wishers of the benighted people." Another factory hand said that he could say nothing about which plays were comprehensible and interesting, but recommended that the society post written explanations of "how to understand the plays."[34] Although literacy is not a reliable indicator of intelligence and overall intellectual development, it is nonetheless reasonable to assume that if some literate workers had difficulty grasping the meaning of plays, then the illiterate or semi-literate "silent majority" encountered similar problems.

The Riazan survey asked respondents to comment on the quality of the performances they had seen, and many of the responses suggest that workers were unhappy with the careless attitude often displayed by the troupes who performed in factory theaters. Several criticized amateur actors for their inadequate knowledge of their roles and insufficient rehearsal. They found such negligence offensive and suggested that it showed a lack of respect for the critical faculties of the common people. "It's not good that people appear on the stage who think that they can get away with anything before a worker audience," complained one worker, adding, "There's no need to name these persons, they are already the talk of the town among the workers."[35]

Some resented the notion that they were receiving a kind of charity from the organizers of the entertainments. Expressing his dissatisfaction with the quality of the variety shows sponsored by the Riazan Society, a worker wrote:

> The kind of gentlemen who perform [in the shows] come onto the stage and lounge in an armchair, just as though they were in their study, thus giving you to understand that they are saying, "Be grateful that I am condescending to you." Then they start reading some dry little things [*sukhie veshchitsy*], and what's more have the gall [*derzost'*] to call them humorous. The gentlemen performers are mistaken in thinking that if it's a *narodnoe gulian'e* then critical evaluation is out of the question.[36]

A factory storeman, objecting specifically to the characterization of the entertainments as "popular" (*narodnoe*), disliked even the term *narodnoe gulian'e*, and proposed that it be removed from advertising posters. "Is there really such a thing as a promenade of cattle [*gulian'e skotov*]?," he asked ironically. "If some [i.e., the intelligentsia] don't want to be called people [*narod*], then let them remain cattle."[37] Other evidence indicates that these workers were not alone in viewing cultural charity as an affront to their dignity. In 1915 Fedor Shaliapin, Russia's most famous opera singer, gave a free performance at the Nicholas II People's House, but workers from several factories refused to accept the tickets. As workers from the Lessner factory explained, they earned enough to pay for the tickets and found the idea of a free performance offensive and condescending.[38]

About a third of the Riazan factory workers who responded to the survey wanted to take a more active role in the entertainments and proposed the creation of an orchestra and acting troupe made up of workers. "It would be a very useful thing if you gave the ordinary worker a chance to try out his abilities and thus be not a spectator but a performer, which of course would really interest the workers," argued one, who said that he had seen workers perform in other cities.[39] Suggested another, who had read favorable newspaper reviews of performances by workers in Moscow, St. Petersburg, and Kharkov, perhaps including the workers' troupe at the Nevskii Society, "Try a rehearsal and you will see that we make no worse an effort than your 'amateurs' of theatrical art. Your intelligentsia act the fool, but workers, so to speak, act from life." One worker, citing articles in some "thick journals" in support of his arguments, wrote:

> It is necessary and good to organize performances, and entertainments in general, where the worker would not be a passive spectator but a participant. There's no need to fear that we would act poorly; in any case there are some among us who are no worse than amateurs from the intelligentsia. An orchestra could also be put together; it won't be necessary to look for participants, just put up a notice and right away worker amateurs will show up. Plays from the lives of workers could be staged, for example, *The Workers' Settlement*, *On His Own Two Feet*, the plays of Potekhin in general, Hauptmann's *The Weavers*, and so on.[40]

All three plays cited deal with some form of social injustice or oppression and offered workers an opportunity to act out onstage the conflicts which they experienced in daily life, taking on the roles of the oppressors as well as the "insulted and injured." In Karpov's naturalistic melodrama *The Workers' Settlement* a worker loses his wife to the attentions of his boss due to his heavy drinking. *On His Own Two Feet* is a comedy about generational conflict by Aleksei Potekhin, a playwright known for his populist sympathies. It depicts a stubborn and lecherous noble landlord who quarrels with his children and forces his daughter to renounce her beloved because of his inferior social standing, prompting his son to leave in protest. Gerhardt Hauptmann's well-known drama describes an uprising of Silesian weavers in response to their employer's harsh and unfair treatment. It was banned in Russia from print or performance but circulated in socialist and workers' circles in the form of illegal translations.[41] In his autobiography Kanatchikov mentions the disturbing effect it had on him when he read a surreptitiously obtained copy, "stirring up my animosity toward the rich and my pity for the oppressed," but adds that the play was unsatisfying because it could provide none of the guidance he was seeking as to "how I should live and what I should do."[42] For Kanatchikov, who at this time was a young peasant migrant trying to fashion a new identity as a "conscious" skilled worker in a Moscow factory, *The Weavers* offered a degree of emotional catharsis but not instruction in how to act and so failed to meet the expectations he brought to it.

The urge to take entertainment into their own hands appears to have been limited to those workers to whom contemporaries referred as "conscious," "advanced," or "worker-intellectuals." Many of the forty-seven factory workers who responded to the Riazan survey clearly belonged to this group, and their attitudes differed sufficiently from those of the railway workers to cause the society to separate them in its report on the survey results. According to the authors of the report, the factory workers "were distinguished by their seriousness, thoroughness, and the practicality of their remarks," whereas most of the railway workers simply indicated that they were satisfied with the entertainments and could offer no suggestions for improving them.[43] In their responses to the survey, the factory workers displayed a sense of their collective identity and distinct interests as workers, sometimes mixed with resentment at being the objects of charity from above; they also displayed a breadth of reading not apparent in statements by other workers.

Unlike the railway workers, the factory workers most often evaluated performances according to the content of the play, rather than according to the skill and style with which it was presented. In addition to approving of plays by Ostrovsky and Gogol, which virtually all the workers in the various surveys knew and liked, the Riazan factory workers expressed a desire to see more plays from Russian life and historical plays. Significantly, Karpov's *The Workers' Settlement* was the play they most frequently mentioned as one they would like to see staged.[44] Written especially for popular audiences, it was one of the few existing plays in 1899 that focused on the lives of Russian factory workers; Semen Kanatchikov remembered that it made a great impression on educated workers in St. Petersburg at the turn of the century.[45]

Not all workers relished seeing grim factory life depicted on the stage, however. It was precisely Karpov's factory melodramas that the St. Petersburg joiner found so tedious and offensive, and none of the railway workers mentioned either Karpov or his plays. What made *The Workers' Settlement* so attractive to so many other workers from the intellectual elite? Taking into account the preference they showed for edifying plays about everyday life, the desire they expressed to create a workers' amateur troupe, and one worker's comment that "workers act from life," a plausible answer is that Karpov's play offered them the possibility of playing roles familiar to them from their own life experience. The general dissatisfaction with the quality of performances by intelligentsia amateurs, coupled with a longing to demonstrate their abilities and show that workers were "no worse than amateurs from the intelligentsia," indicate that at least some workers wished to assert themselves as "cultured" persons in no way inferior to members of the more privileged classes. For them theater was not merely entertainment but a symbol of the knowledge and culture they sought to assimilate.

It would be an exaggeration to suggest that these attitudes were typical of the workers who attended performances at people's theaters. The carefully thought out comments of the articulate workers contrast sharply with the indifference that most displayed toward the Riazan Society's attempt to solicit their views. Over 20,000 persons attended the *narodnye gulian'ia* in Riazan in 1899, yet only 47 factory workers responded to the survey, along with 39 railway workers.[46] In St. Petersburg, nearly 100,000 attended the Nevskii Society's entertainments every summer in the mid-1890s.[47] The handful of comments cited by Mikhailovskii or contained in the Riazan survey report hardly constitute a representative sample of their attitudes toward the theater performances. Only the literate could answer the questionnaires, although some of the returns seem to have been authored collectively. Still, the surveys do offer insights into the responses to theater of some of those on whom it seems to have had the most impact.

STRANGE LAUGHTER

Middle-class observers of popular audiences' reactions to performances were often puzzled by their tendency to laugh at inappropriate moments. Audiences were sometimes aroused to laughter by murder and death scenes, declarations of love, or passionate kisses, a response that particularly upset the sensibilities of intelligentsia amateur performers. Observers tried to explain the untoward laughter in various ways, arguing that it was evoked by audiences' nervousness and excitement, that it indicated approval of actors' skill in carrying off their roles so naturally, or that it expressed skepticism at exaggerated pathos. While such explanations often reveal more about the observers' views of their subject and were used to emphasize the "otherness" of the *narod* and its distance from the intelligentsia, accounts of this "strange laughter" and what may have provoked it can offer insights into popular psychology and expectations at performances.[48]

The journalist Sergei Sutugin claimed that people who were newcomers to theater were most likely to laugh at the wrong time, out of nervousness. Having come to the theater expecting to find amusement, they were waiting for a chance to laugh; any clever turn of phrase or sudden gesture gave them that chance. The spectacle itself transfixed and hypnotized them, according to Sutugin, citing a couple he saw at St. Petersburg's Petrovskii Park who stood for hours before the stage, too far away to hear a word.[49] Much of Sutugin's discussion of popular audiences is based on abstract or literary images of the *narod*, but nervous laughter is a common phenomenon, and other sources bear testimony to the mesmerizing effect of performances on unaccustomed spectators.[50] Laughter was also one of the ways *balagan* audiences expressed their approval, according to the fairground showman Alekseev-Iakovlev, and it is likely that newcomers to the people's theaters did the same.[51] For audiences more familiar with the fairground theaters and Petrushka shows than the conventions of literary theater, laughter was what it was all about; drinking added to the merriment, and violence and misogyny were funny.[52] These audiences were prepared to have a laugh, and they did.

Other laughter was more problematic. An actor who had performed the role of the peasant Nikita in *The Power of Darkness* before popular audiences dozens of times recounted that the drama was well liked and aroused empathy. Yet he was puzzled that spectators invariably laughed when Nikita, who has murdered his illegitimate child under his mother's pressure, asks her for more light to dig a hole to conceal the corpse. A stagehand explained that when Nikita asks for more light, after having earlier told his mother to dig the hole herself, he reveals himself to be less than a man in submitting to be ordered about by women: "He's a woman, not a muzhik. How can you not laugh?"[53] Audiences read Nikita's behavior as inappropriate to his gender—he is a "mama's boy," albeit a murderous one. Transgression of gender roles is a stock device in humor, regardless of social class or cultivation, and many popular viewers responded with what for them was an appropriate reaction to Nikita's weakness. Patriarchal cultural norms, prevalent among lower-class Russians, could color audience's reception of an otherwise moving tragedy.

At the people's theater in Saratov, a large commercial and industrial city on the Volga, working-class audiences burst into laughter at a death scene in Hermann Sudermann's *Heimat* (*Homeland,* known in English as *Magda*) and at an old man's pronouncement of a curse on his son in Averkiev's *The Old Days of Kashirsk*. The observer of these reactions, a journalist sitting in the upper balconies, thought that this kind of response was due to the actors' bad technique. Overplaying dramatic scenes, sticking to their character types whatever the role, using exaggerated gestures for effect, the actors made the scenes funny to audiences who did not know what to expect, being unfamiliar with either the text or the conventions of theater. In a series of articles on popular audiences published in *Theater and Art* in 1901, P. Kazantsev underlined the common spectators' propensity to laughter, which he considered to be both a normal reaction to overwrought acting and a reflection of their love of the comic. He observed that audiences would forgive an actor almost anything if he made them laugh, to the point where even the entrance of an actor regarded as a comic elicited laughter. Depictions of romantic feelings and adventures also commonly provoked laughter and cynical comments, presumably among male spectators, but women may not have found sexual peccadilloes so amusing. Kazantsev relates a conversation with a woman at a performance of Ostrovsky's *Easy Money*, in which an avaricious wife enters into a liaison with a suitor who tricks her into believing he can afford to keep her in luxury: "They should show how old women grow old. We've already seen all this: how wives deceive their husbands, how husbands run around on the wives. I've been there myself."[54]

MATCHMAKING AND MARRIAGE

Working-class audiences were fond of Ostrovsky's matchmaking comedies and Gogol's classic *Marriage*, according to Shcheglov's accounts, and often identified with the characters and situations. Audiences may well have found these plays relevant to their experiences in the city. Gender relations among the working classes of St. Petersburg and Moscow were influenced by the fluidity of the cities' migrant populations, the small number of nuclear family households, and the large ratio of men to women. Waves of young job-seeking peasants, mostly single men and women, poured into Russia's cities in the half century following the Emancipation, almost tripling their populations by 1914. Men who found work in the city often returned to the country to marry, left their wives in the village, and went back to the city for a few years. With so many men having marriage ties in the village or committed to remaining single, the chances of finding a spouse in the city were slim for migrant women workers, while the opportunities for taking a lover and bearing children out of wedlock were far greater than in rural Russia. Although the proportion of men living with their wives and families in the city began rising after the turn of the century and women increasingly were able to translate courtship into marriage, single women in the city, with little of the protection and restraint that patriarchal family ties provided in the countryside, remained easy prey to sexual exploitation, a situation attested to by the high rates of illegitimate birth.[55] As Barbara Engel points out, "Village patterns of early and universal marriage encouraged women migrants to nurture unrealistic expectations about whether and when they would wed, . . . [which] contributed to illegitimate births by making women more vulnerable to seductive promises of marriage, and/or more willing to settle for a consensual union."[56] Popular ditties, or *chastushki*, testify to the perils working-class women faced in negotiating the hazards of sexual relations in the hope of obtaining the security offered by legal marriage.

At a Nevskii Society performance of Ostrovsky's *An Old Friend Is Better Than Two New Ones*, the public freely discussed the characters and their behavior and appreciated the play's portrayal of domestic life, especially the matchmaking scenes. Factory girls were particularly interested by Vasiutin's vacillation in declaring his love to Olenka, finding her situation near to their own hearts. "He's a fake, that's for sure," remarked one to her girlfriend, who responded, "You'll see, she'll marry him yet! He's got just the same character as Petka." Everyone liked Vasiutin's explanation of why he had a bit to drink before setting off to court his beloved—not to be drunk, but to have some "fantasies" in his head; it would be a different story, he observed, if he had read books. Not surprisingly, the factory girls were very pleased when Olenka got the young man at the end of the play.[57]

Gogol's *Marriage* was almost invariably a big hit with working-class audiences, and Shcheglov gives a fairly detailed account of an 1898 performance at St. Petersburg's Ligovskii Park. One of the best-known comedies of the Russian stage, the play is about how Ivan Podkolesin, a bachelor, is brought by the matchmaker Kochkarev to meet a prospective bride. At her home he encounters several other suitors and becomes so terrified by the thought of marriage that he jumps out the window to escape. The men in the Ligovskii audience sympathized with Ivan's waverings, nicknaming him "Vanka," and were not at all surprised by his decision to take flight. They especially appreciated his comment that poorly made boots would not produce a good impression in proper society, and they laughed heartily at the matchmaker's statement at the end that he would convince Ivan to return, one worker suggesting that he might as well "search for the wind in the field." For male workers who aspired to personal development or who lacked the financial resources to support a wife and family and regarded marriage as burden, Vanka Podkolesin was a character with whom they could easily identify.[58]

THE APPEAL OF MELODRAMA

Melodrama was the subject of seemingly endless discussion among people's theater advocates, whose only point of agreement was that the common people had a boundless appetite for its improbable plots and heartrending scenes. The unparalleled antipathy to melodramatic effects among critics, especially in debates over the correct repertoire for the *narod*, owed much to the tenacity of psychological realism's hold on Russian literary culture since the mid-nineteenth century. Ivan Shcheglov, one of the few defenders of melodrama's place in the popular repertoire, argued that it answered the common people's desire to see good and evil sharply differentiated, the heroic triumph of morality, and characters and situations that were out of the ordinary. Others took the view that true respect for audiences lay not in accommodating to their tastes but in elevating them to an appreciation of realism in drama. *Theater and Art*, in a review of one of Shcheglov's volumes on popular theater, allowed that melodrama could be appropriate only temporarily, as a means of giving the people a taste for drama before introducing them to "truly artistic works," as children first acquired a taste for reading through fairy tales. The Section for Assisting the Organization of Factory and Village Theaters came to a similar conclusion in 1916, deciding to include melodrama in its recommended repertoire for people's theaters as a transitional stage in the cultural development of the popular audience.[59]

Whatever the prejudices of the *Kulturträger*, all available evidence points to melodrama's popularity. Shcheglov's view about the appropriateness of melodrama for popular audiences may have been shared by few of his contemporaries, but other observers despairingly confirmed that it was a perennial favorite. Nikolai Popov, who took over management of the Vasilevskii Island Theater in 1902 and attempted to win audiences over to serious drama with productions in the style of the Moscow Art Theater, found that "no innovations, even in the guise of artistic ensemble, interested the public, who were captivated only by melodramatic acting in heartrending plays." Popov tried to meet audience tastes halfway by staging some literary plays with sharp dramatic effects, like the Dutch writer Herman Heijermans's drama about the tragic death of poor sailors on an unseaworthy ship due to the greed of a ship owner, *The Good Hope*, but receipts continued to be low and he was forced to give up the enterprise after a few months. Imported melodramas such as Dennery's *The Grace of God* (translated by Nekrasov) and *The Two Orphans*, Victor Ducange's *Thirty Years, or The Life of a Gambler*, Brisbarre and Nus's *The Poor of*

Paris, Decourcelle's *Two Youngsters*, and Camoletti's *Sister Teresa or Elizabeth Soarez* reigned on the stages of the people's theaters until the October Revolution, and afterward in Proletkult and other Soviet amateur theaters.[60]

Why was melodrama so appealing to popular audiences in the big cities? Melodrama is of course one of the most durable and universal genres in theater (and cinema), and its longevity can be explained by the diverting entertainment provided by its action-packed plots and sensational revelations. Part of melodrama's appeal may be due to its "essential democratic" nature, as Peter Brooks has argued, for melodrama suggests that "a poor persecuted girl can confront her powerful oppressor with the truth about their moral condition."[61] There is little firsthand evidence on the reception of melodrama by working-class audiences, apart from laconic remarks in reviews about how one or another play was enthusiastically received with applause and curtain calls. Ivan Shcheglov, however, left fairly detailed descriptions of performances of melodrama at the Vasilevskii Island Theater in 1892 and at the St. Petersburg commercial pleasure garden "America" in 1901. Although a champion of melodrama's moral value for the common people, Shcheglov does make his prejudices clear, and his observations shed some light on the meaning of melodrama for lower-class audiences in a specific time and setting.

In the 1890s and early 1900s, the audiences at the Vasilevskii Island Theater were famous for their love of melodrama. The audience was very heterogeneous on weekdays, but on Sundays and holidays the "democratic" element predominated: skilled and unskilled workers, day laborers, shopkeepers, soldiers, lackeys, seamstresses, cooks, maids, and women in peasant garb. *The Two Orphans*, a renowned French tearjerker about the perils of two young girls confronting the seductive pleasures of the big city and ultimately becoming ladies, one through marriage and the other by discovering her real parents, was one of the theater's biggest hits. When one performance had to be canceled in the middle due to flood warnings, viewers refused to leave until reassured that they could see what happened to the two orphans another day at no charge. Shcheglov attributed the appeal of *The Two Orphans* to the common folk's need to see an ideal world where evil is punished and virtue rewarded by the hand of Providence. The tale also presented an imaginary world where instant social mobility was possible.[62]

At the America garden, young workers stood in the rain to watch *The Grace of God* from behind the barrier separating them from the seated public. The sentimental tale of the young peasant Maria's journey from an impoverished village to find work in Paris struck a chord with the workers, many of whom had also left their own native villages to seek their fortunes in St. Petersburg. According to Shcheglov, the workers especially identified with the touching scene of her mother's blessing on Maria's departure, her explanation of the poverty that drove her to Paris, and her determination to retain her virtue in the face of sexual temptation. He describes, probably with some literary license, a young prostitute's tears when the mother admonishes Maria to work hard, pray, and remember her family, two seam- stresses' relief when Maria refuses to give into the seductive pleas of an aris- tocratic suitor, and their expressions of empathy when she is stricken by the news of his marriage to another. In the end the suitor turns out to be unwed and marries Maria. Clearly these stories of the trials faced by single women alone in the big city were close to the experiences of many women in the audience, who may have wished that the hand of Providence had come to their aid when they were faced with difficult choices as to whether to remain alone or to enter into consensual unions, and perhaps bear children out of wedlock; such women may well have dreamt of finding a marquis. Many men and women could certainly identify with the pains of separation from their families and hope for an equally happy conclusion to their expe- riences in St. Petersburg.[63]

The appeal of melodrama may have lain in its ability to offer audiences the chance to imagine a just social order and to collectively identify with poor but virtuous characters who are morally superior to the privileged vil- lains they confront. Melodrama offered both the fantasy of social reconcil- iation and the images with which to contest the social order. In his work on popular literature, Michael Denning suggests that reading sensationalist stories of working girls becoming ladies is more than mere escapism, for it allows readers to affirm their lives as working girls and simultaneously examine the differences between the wealthy and the poor. The French melodramas staged before Russian working-class audiences, like American dime novels, can be understood as representations of "social cleavage, as attempts to find metaphors and stories adequate to these divisions (worker as 'honest mechanic,' 'knight of labor,' as 'working-girl') and to contest the received and enforced metaphors of the dominant order (worker as 'tramp' or 'outlaw')."[64] In Russian labor studies the urge to challenge the subordi- nate position of workers in the dominant ideology has usually been associ- ated with the "vanguard" worker-intellectuals who left written records of their psychological quests, but many other less gifted workers may have also experienced the longing to transcend their class position, if only for an evening, and melodrama could provide food for their imaginations.[65]

PATRIOTISM AND POLITICS

Patriotic plays and extravaganzas were a regular feature of the temperance theaters, particularly at the Emperor Nicholas II People's House, which specialized in grandiose scenic effects. Glinka's opera *A Life for the Tsar*, associated after 1905 with the nationalist right-wing movement,[66] often opened the winter season, and the spectacular dramatizations of historical and contemporary battles usually drew large crowds. Reviews of performances tell only that patriotic spectaculars, with their special effects and action-packed plots, were received with enthusiasm, but were audiences applauding the patriotic message or the entertaining presentation? In the throes of the ill-starred Russo-Japanese War, a reviewer noted that Viktor Krylov's *1812* did little to inspire the audience with its depiction of Russians' heroic resistance to Napoleon: "It is impossible not to remark the attitude of the public to the scenes on the stage. The French bayonet the Russians or a Russian with a club bangs the head of a Frenchman from around the corner of a peasant hut, and there is no excitement in the auditorium. You feel the tense, thoughtful attention, and parallels with the present inadvertently arise; a consciousness of the horror, the uselessness of all that, then as now, reigns over everyone."[67] Writing in the weekly *Herald of the Temperance Guardianships* in the autumn of 1904, Sergei Solomin made a shrewd assessment of the relationship between patriotic feeling and theater. "Patriotism is never aroused by the stage," he wrote. "On the contrary, at moments of patriotic enthusiasm theater responds to the general mood with patriotic melodramas."[68]

At the Nicholas II People's House, the most pathetic scenes in patriotic plays could sometimes produce guffaws. A scene in which a bridegroom goes off to war and his bride, falling to the ground in tears, cries, "Kill me or let me go with him!," was greeted with laughter and lewd comments. In another scene, the enemy is at the city gates, cannon shots are heard, and the crowd onstage doff their hats, piously intoning, "Let us pray for the salvation of Russia"—to the snickers of the audience.[69] Sutugin attributed the laughter to the common people's sensitivity to exaggerated sentimentality and bombastic posing, implying that they were more natural and quicker to discern falsity than were educated people, but these reactions can also be explained without romanticizing the *narod*. Although departure for military service was usually considered to be a family tragedy, marked by tears and lamentations, soldiers' wives had little respect in popular culture; they were often raped by their fathers-in-law and were widely believed to be promiscuous in their husbands' absence. The laughter at the bride's pitiful cries could be understood, from a male point of view, as a mocking reaction to her sentiments in terms of both her possible fate and the sexual opportunities that her separation would open up.[70] Lofty expressions of patriotic feeling, when people are about to face the enemy, are easily laughed at, especially by the people who would be likely to suffer most and might well be more disposed to pray for themselves in a similar situation. The laughter might also reflect that what popular patriotism did exist was focused more on the figure of the tsar, the Orthodox faith, the home, and a sense of otherness from non-Orthodox foreigners, than on abstract entities like the Russian nation.[71]

Despite the popularity of the patriotic spectaculars, it would be simplistic to argue that the people's theaters simply taught acquiescence to the political status quo. The people's theaters, even those sponsored by the state, did not force-feed a relentless diet of patriotism, even during wartime. They also frequently staged, especially after 1905, naturalistic dramas about the sufferings of the working class such as those by Karpov and Belaia; they even performed "oppositional" works by Gorky and Naidenov, associated in the minds of Russian audiences with political dissent. Gorky's *Lower Depths* became a favorite in the people's theaters after the censors ended its prohibition in 1905. The play offered scenes that challenged a social order that condemned its characters to life in a flophouse, as well as some characters who rose above their surroundings to demand treatment as human beings.[72] It was extremely popular among workers, who often staged it in their amateur theaters.

There is no direct correlation between political consciousness and tastes in cultural products. For example, a Menshevik newspaper reported with dismay in 1913 that St. Petersburg workers vigorously applauded at a popular performance of a notoriously anti-Semitic play, *The Sons of Israel*. Many of these workers, however, had recently struck to protest the tsarist regime's anti-Semitic propaganda in the Beilis case, in which a Jewish man was wrongly accused of the ritual murder of a Christian youth. The play had provoked massive student demonstrations when it premiered at the Suvorin Theater in 1900 under the title *The Smugglers*, resulting in the refusal of a number of actors to perform in it. The paper recounted how "the working-class youths and proletarian girls applauded all the vileness that was poured on the Jews from the stage" and asked how it was possible to reconcile the workers' sympathy for the plight of the Jews as expressed during the political strike with their positive response to a play in which Jews were painted as born criminals. When the Menshevik journalist asked some of the workers about their attitude to the play, they explained that the play's anti-Semitic message had "gone over their heads" and that they simply liked the way it was performed.[73] It is impossible to determine whether the workers' response to the socialist intellectual was disingenuous, but it is worth noting that anti-Semitism was common within the Russian working class.[74] The workers had supported a political strike against the autocracy's anti-Semitic policies, yet they were also undisturbed by the play's unsavory depiction of Jewish characters, which may have confirmed their personal prejudices.

• • •

The evidence on audience reception, albeit limited, does point to some conclusions about the significance of theatrical entertainments for popular audiences. To a degree, theater offered an escape from the monotony of life and work. Even if some people had trouble understanding the plays, they were able to appreciate the visual qualities and special effects of the spectacle itself. Some of the workers who responded to the surveys took a utilitarian view of theater, seeing it as a source of moral instruction. Their comments on the power of theater to portray the consequences of good and bad actions tend to support Ivan Shcheglov's observation that popular audiences liked to see good and evil sharply differentiated, the former rewarded and the latter punished.[75] Similarly, L. M. Kleinbort, in his study of prerevolutionary worker audiences, emphasized their practical outlook on theater, which he attributed to their "immature tastes."[76] It is apparent, however, that such an attitude was present even among the most literate workers. If, as Jeffrey Brooks has suggested, peasants "transposed the habits of reading associated with religious materials to secular texts,"[77] many educated workers also brought these habits to the theater, possibly, in some cases, reinforced by their experiences in evening classes or socialist study groups. Seeing characters from the privileged classes in plays also heightened workers' consciousness of the gulf that separated them from the world of the privileged. Some responded with expressions of a desire to improve themselves by emulating the behavior of the characters they saw; for others, plays depicting the lives of the upper classes increased their resentment of the social hierarchy and their subordinate place in it.

Audiences sometimes reacted to plays in ways that surprised and confounded educated observers, for the messages contained in the texts of the plays were filtered through the expectations audiences brought to their encounter with the theater. Matchmaking comedies, for example, were not entirely comic for audiences to whom matchmaking was a familiar institution. Expectations and cultural background were the determining factors in how audiences responded to performances, suggesting that they were not transformed by their encounter with theater but rather used theater to confirm outlooks and beliefs conditioned by the material and psychological experiences of everyday life. The voices of the people's theater audiences tell us that they found—or did not find—what they were looking for in the theaters. Like all audiences, they were not empty vessels to be filled with either education or entertainment but arrived at the theater door with a set of expectations as to what they would get and reacted accordingly.

The melodramas and patriotic spectaculars that the people saw in the theaters certainly did not foster a "culture of consolation" or stymie the development of class consciousness. The factories where workers wept at the plight of the orphans Henrietta and Louisa and rejoiced at their ultimate good fortune were the same factories that were swept with unrest, beginning in the 1890s and culminating in the 1905 and 1917 revolutions. The enjoyment of light entertainment does not preclude the development of a radical political consciousness—it was possible to be a both a Bolshevik and a fan of melodrama. Working conditions, disrespectful treatment, low wages, and, perhaps most importantly, the tsarist regime's failure to allow trade unions to act as legitimate voices for working-class grievances—these were the issues that radicalized Russian workers and led them to confront the autocracy. Stedman Jones makes a roughly similar point in arguing against analyses that examine popular recreations in isolation and portray them as instruments of social control that instill "false consciousness": "The necessity to obtain work, to remain fit for work, and to made ends meet is far more important than any packaged consumerist ideology which succeeds in intruding upon the worker's weekly or nightly period of rest and recuperation."[78] Neither the easy pleasures of melodrama nor the thrilling special effects of *The Taking of Azov* did anything to alleviate the underlying causes of working-class discontent.

Conclusion

The concept of theater for the people was a response to elite anxieties about the cultural gulf between educated Russia and the common people. The idea of a people's theater, that is, of a didactic theater that would bring the culture of the intelligentsia to the masses, was predicated on the belief that theater was capable of transforming audiences. This belief rested on three assumptions shared by virtually all proponents of people's theaters. First, theater, by virtue of its powerful visual impressions, was assumed to be accessible and comprehensible to all. Second, its combination of entertainment and edification supposedly made theater an ideal means of communicating ideas. Third, the common people were assumed to be malleable, impressionable, even childlike, and thus easily influenced by what they saw and heard on the stage.

By creating special theaters for the urban lower classes, educated Russians were engaging in a form of cultural populism. They sought to enlighten the "simple folk" by offering them the intellectual heritage of the intelligentsia. Convinced as they were of the universal validity of their culture, the founders of the people's theaters were, for the most part, determined to convert the masses into consumers of that culture. Ostensibly, one needed only to expose the common folk to the timeless works of Pushkin, Gogol, Ostrovsky, and other venerated representatives of Russian and European letters and they would be won over to an appreciation of "serious" theater. The people would then reject the trashy melodramas and sensational adventure plays with which the unscrupulous fairground showmen were bent on corrupting them and would become enthusiastic, if unsophisticated, admirers of "art." Once the common people had embraced the culture of the intelligentsia, all Russians would be united in a national culture of consensus.

Yet, despite their shared faith in the transforming power of theater, the proponents of people's theater held quite diverse views as its ultimate purpose. Some felt that the people's theater should primarily serve to democratize art, others equated it with school and saw it as a means of educating the common people, while still others viewed the people's theater foremost as a "rational recreation" that would supplant the tavern as the focus of working-class leisure.

At the same time, supporters of the people's theater often disagreed as to whom it was to serve. Although everyone concurred that the people's theater was meant to civilize the common people, or *narod*, there was no such accord on what civilizing the *narod* entailed, or how the *narod* should be defined. Was the civilizing process meant to produce a people who appreciated art? Who behaved more respectably? Or who simply consumed less alcohol in their leisure hours? Were "the people" peasants? Or were factory workers, artisans, clerks, and domestic servants also part of the *narod*? The very concept of a "people's theater" was rooted in a dualistic conception of Russian society and culture as divided, albeit temporarily, into the "intelligentsia" and the "*narod*," a notion that had its origins in the pre-Emancipation servile order and was proving increasingly inapplicable to the diverse populations of turn-of-the-century Moscow and St. Petersburg.[1] The sharp line that had once delineated the intelligentsia and the *narod* was becoming blurred, as urban migrants from the countryside began to acquire more education and shed their peasant costumes in favor of citified attire, but the terminology used to describe the people remained the same, thus exacerbating the confusion over who was to benefit from the cultural tutelage that the people's theaters were to provide.

These divergent views of the goals of the people's theater and its intended audience led to endless debates over what repertoire was most appropriate for the people. What stands out in the discussions of the "correct" repertoire is the Russian intelligentsia's extreme reluctance to allow market forces to determine the content of what the people saw onstage, to allow entertainment to take priority over edification and enlightenment. This hostility toward the marketization of cultural products was especially apparent in the negative attitudes of educated observers toward the fairground shows. Rather than catering to the tastes of their audiences, the people's theaters were supposed to elevate those tastes, and the intelligentsia was on the whole quite censorious when it came to determining the sort of cultural fare that was appropriate for popular consumption. In this respect my findings confirm those of Jeffrey Brooks, who has argued that "both revolutionary and nonrevolutionary Russians who participated in cultural life often shared a conviction that cultural choices could be curtailed in the name of high ideals."[2]

Although the Finance Ministry lent its support to temperance theaters, on the whole the authorities regarded popular theater with varying degrees of apprehension, fearing that they might acquaint the people with dangerous ideas that could have unpredictable consequences. In an effort to control the content of what the people saw and heard, the government subjected all theaters patronized by popular audiences to more severe restrictions than those applying to other theaters. Censorship policy was based on the reasoning that due to the "backwardness" and "impressionability" of the common people, they had to be protected from exposure to many works deemed harmless for educated audiences. To be sure, in the wake of the 1905 Revolution censorship did become relatively more lenient, but on the whole there was a fundamental continuity in the goals of censorship policy up to 1917. The government was especially concerned to keep the people from seeing works that satirized the authorities or the Church, depicted social antagonisms, or presented immoral behavior in an insufficiently negative light. Despite the regime's professed interest in promoting historical awareness among the masses, historical plays long familiar to audiences in the legitimate theaters were often prohibited for performance before popular audiences, particularly when they treated issues like regicide, rebellion, and the Time of Troubles.

The double standard in censorship policy was galling to the supporters of the people's theater, who sometimes even felt that the government was prohibiting the wrong plays, thwarting their attempts to acquaint the masses with the classics of Russian and European drama but approving operettas and farces of dubious artistic merit. But if the censorship did indeed inhibit efforts to bring some classic and literary plays to popular audiences, popular theaters were nonetheless allowed to present a wide range of Russian and European classics, melodramas, farces, comedies, and contemporary dramas. In any event, the authorities were not always successful in regulating performances. Because they focused on the play's written text rather than on the performances of that text, the censors were unable to cope with important elements of theater such as gesture, intonation, makeup, and audience response. More importantly, the censors were simply unable to monitor the people's theaters and other popular stages carefully enough to make sure that they adhered to the special restrictions that applied to them. Regulations were so profuse and complex that local authorities often erred and allowed performances of banned works, while the lack of newspaper coverage of the people's theaters made it difficult for the censors to uncover violations.

By the early 1900s numerous people's theaters were offering low-priced or free performances to the working people of Moscow and St. Petersburg. Most of these performances were organized by industrialists or state-subsidized temperance societies, in an attempt to promote theater as a "rational recreation" that would supplant the tavern as the center of working-class leisure. Beginning in the 1880s, the owners of many St. Petersburg and Moscow factories began building theaters and organizing holiday performances in an effort to transform the way their workforce spent its free time by replacing traditional recreations, such as pub crawling, gambling, and fistfights, with more orderly and "respectable" entertainments. By inculcating in their workers a taste for sober, moral recreations, industrialists hoped to reduce holiday drunkenness and the attendant absenteeism and thereby increase labor discipline and productivity.

The factory theaters were well attended, yet their impact on alcohol consumption and labor productivity is doubtful. Workers could always have a few drinks before or after the performance, or simply pocket a bottle and bring it with them. The real significance of the factory theaters is that they offered many workers, especially those who had recently migrated from the countryside and had little education or exposure to urban cultural institutions, a first glimpse into the cultural world of educated Russia. Theater was a window on the lifestyles of other classes, providing working-class audiences with new images of comportment that they could appropriate for themselves, but also heightening their awareness of the distance that separated them from privileged society.

In Moscow and St. Petersburg, the officially sponsored Guardianships of Popular Temperance, operating under the aegis of the Finance Ministry, proved to be the most ardent and effective promoters of the people's theater. Embracing with enthusiasm the idea that theater could wean the masses away from excessive alcohol consumption by providing them with a more "rational" way of spending their leisure hours, the Moscow and St. Petersburg guardianships spent huge sums on theaters and outdoor stages where drama, opera, and even ballet were performed before millions of spectators. By exposing the urban lower classes to the "civilizing influence" of art, in a setting more decorous than that of the traditional holiday fairground theaters, the guardianships hoped to transform the people's behavior, morals, and tastes. As the St. Petersburg Temperance Guardianship explained, its goal was "to teach by amusement."[3]

In practice, however, the temperance theaters soon came to resemble the fairground theaters that they initially sought to supplant. Classics shared the billing with farces and variety shows, while prostitution, drunkenness, and "hooliganism" appear to have been no less common at the temperance theaters than on the holiday fairgrounds. Critics, perhaps unfairly, contended that the temperance theaters did not elevate the people by exposing them to art but rather degraded art by reducing it to entertainment. Still, the temperance theaters exposed the people to many of the works of Ostrovsky, Chekhov, Gorky, Fonvizin, Pushkin, Pisemsky, Glinka, and other masters of Russian drama and opera, and in so doing contributed to the development of a mass audience for what had previously been the culture of the educated elite. It is worth remembering, too, that operetta and farce were as much a part of the culture of the privileged classes as were Ostrovsky and Fonvizin, just as heavy drinking was not confined to the lower classes.

The leading role that industrialists and the Finance Ministry played in the development of people's theaters is striking for two reasons. First, people's theaters were initially conceived as a means for educated society to serve and enlighten the common people and at the same time to contest the autocratic state's monopoly on public activity, but industrialists and government officials were much more successful than was the liberal intelligentsia in actually establishing theaters in Russia's two largest cities. For all their talk and projects, the *Kulturträger* proved unable to muster the energy and resources to establish the people's theaters of their dreams. To be sure, the theaters run by Countess Panina and the Moscow duma were exceptions, as were the activities of the Moscow Section for Assisting the Organization of Factory and Village Theaters, but their activities paled beside those of the factory and temperance theaters. Second, despite the opportunities that theater offered to reach a mass audience, neither the industrialists nor the government's temperance theaters were imaginative or confident enough to even attempt to use theater to promote a coherent ideology. Unlike their American counterparts, who used theater performances to promote an explicitly patriotic and capitalist ideology in the industrial drama movement of the 1910s and 1920s, Russian industrialists did not commission plays for their factory theaters that espoused the benefits of hard work, temperance, and thrift.[4] They merely used plays from the established repertoire and hoped that exposure to them would "civilize" the workforce. The autocratic state was similarly unimaginative, even though it encouraged explicitly patriotic works in its temperance theaters. As a journalist commented during the Russo-Japanese War, the patriotic plays were either outdated or followed the same tired formula inherited from the *balagan* theaters and their *tableaux vivants* of scenes from the Russo-Turkish

War: "The Turks fall about chock-a-block, and our soldier stands like a fine fellow and smokes his pipe."[5] The military spectaculars may have been immensely entertaining, but they did little to foster a sense of national patriotism or to explain why the Russian nation might be worth fighting and dying for.

In the years following the 1905 Revolution, the idea of a people's theater was appropriated by workers seeking to create a new form of proletarian culture, the workers' theater. The worker's theater movement reflected workers' conflicting attitudes toward culture and its place in their lives. Some workers viewed theater largely as a weapon in their political struggle and a means of raising class consciousness and fostering proletarian solidarity. Others were more interested in using theater to make elite culture accessible to workers and thus demonstrate the workers' respectability and capacity to appreciate the cultural heritage of educated Russia. For many workers, however, amateur theatricals were simply a way to have a good time, an outlook that became pronounced after the fall of the autocracy eliminated the barriers to popular initiative.

Although the goals of the workers' theater movement in some ways resembled those of the people's theaters that were promoted by educated society, the workers' theaters aimed not to further the emergence of a culture that would unite all Russians but to demonstrate the proletariat's cultural independence from the tutelage of the intelligentsia. In practice, however, there were tensions between workers' aspirations for cultural autonomy and their need for assistance from sympathetic intellectuals in organizing performances. While few workers' troupes were able to do without the advice and technical expertise of the intelligentsia, they laid claim to the creation of a genuinely proletarian culture by emphasizing the class character of performances and by defining a workers' theater as one where workers selected and performed plays before an audience of workers.

Despite the talk of building a "proletarian culture," however, the repertoires of the workers' theaters were quite conventional, consisting largely of the same plays that were performed in theaters all over Russia. Workers active in theater both embraced the values of the "hegemonic" dominant culture and adapted its cultural products to their own purposes. Indeed, the extensive body of socially critical Russian dramatic literature afforded workers many opportunities to criticize the corruption of the powerful, lament the sufferings of the weak at the hands of the strong, and relate these themes to the plight of workers and their oppression by capital.

The prerevolutionary people's theater movement was a product of the

Russian intelligentsia's faith in the power of culture to shape society and its longing for a unitary culture that would embrace Russians of all classes. The people's theater idea reflected the intelligentsia's desire to serve the people and improve their lot by means of "small deeds" such as cultural and educational work. Yet, as I have tried to show, the people's theaters were also an exercise in cultural power, an attempt to impose the cultural values of educated Russia upon the people. The proponents of a people's theater spoke in terms of democratizing culture by bringing it to the people, but they also sought to use theater to reform and discipline the comportment of the people, to impose on them a standard of "good art." As the St. Petersburg Literacy Committee put it, the goal of the people's theater was "the substitution of crude and immoral pleasures with rational recreations that further, as far as possible, the general and moral education of the people."[6] I would agree with students of Russian peasant culture that the intention of the liberal and socialist intelligentsias' efforts at cultural enlightenment was a form of "colonization,"[7] although members of the intelligentsia certainly did not see it this way, believing that they were serving the common people by introducing them to a more rational, progressive way of life.

But intentions are not the same as their consequences. The people often proved not to be the passive consumers of culture that the intelligentsia thought them to be. While the discourse surrounding the people's theater emphasized edification over entertainment, popular audiences sometimes responded to performances in ways that bewildered and dismayed educated observers, and their responses did not necessarily coincide with the hopes the intelligentsia had invested in art as an agent of moral and social transformation. The people's theaters exposed the common people to art, but audiences transformed "high culture" into a form of popular culture by interpreting it after their own fashion, thereby challenging the intelligentsia's assumptions about theater's potential to foster a unified culture that would close the gap between educated Russia and the people.

In evaluating the significance of the theaters in the lives of the people who made up their audiences, it is therefore crucial to raise the issue of reception. Studies of popular culture that draw conclusions about popular attitudes based on an analysis of texts do not sufficiently take into account the problems inherent in evaluating the manner and context in which these texts were consumed.[8] This is, of course, understandable, for reading is usually an individual activity, done in private, and it is difficult, if not impossible, to reconstruct readers' impressions of what they read with any precision. Theater performances, by contrast, are consumed in public by an audience whose reactions can be, and often are, described by observers. By focusing not on dramatic texts but on accounts of particular performances, descriptions of audiences, and responses to audience surveys, I have sought, within the limits of the available source material, to emphasize the diversity of the people's reactions to what they saw and heard on the stage. After all, the essence of theater lies not in the text performed but the meanings that the text acquires in the context of its performance.

Because audiences differed greatly in their level of education and degree of prior exposure to art, their attitudes toward performances at the people's theaters were quite varied, as contemporary observers often remarked. Since some of the sponsors of factory theaters distributed questionnaires soliciting workers' opinions of the plays they had seen, we do have some evidence as to how some workers regarded the performances. Responses to the questionnaires fell roughly into two categories. For most workers, the performances were a novel form of entertainment and a welcome distraction from the cares of everyday life. They were less interested in the content of the plays they saw than in the visual impression of the performance and had little to say about how the factory theaters could be improved. A small group of workers who, judging by the sophistication of their responses, belonged to the minority of skilled, moderately educated workers, took a more critical attitude toward the factory theatricals. These workers expressed a functional attitude toward theater and sought enlightenment and instruction in the plays they saw. In their evaluations of the plays, the more educated workers emphasized content over performance. Many were unhappy with the careless attitude often displayed by the amateur troupes that came to perform before worker audiences and found such negligence offensive. Not all workers were content to remain spectators, sober consumers of the entertainments offered to them by paternalistic employers and intelligentsia amateur actors. A small but significant number articulated a clear desire to take an active part in the performances and demonstrate that they were capable of creating art themselves.

The people's theaters may have failed to make the recreations of the common people more "rational," but they nonetheless had a profound impact on the recreational landscapes of Moscow and St. Petersburg. They gave the urban lower classes, for the first time, access to low-priced entertainment on a regular basis and as such were part of an emerging consumer culture in which entertainment was a commodity. By exposing the common people to middle-class entertainment culture and allowing them to consume it, the urban people's theaters may have made the lower classes more sensitive to the tremendous barriers that still lay between them and the privileged classes and perhaps contributed to the polarization of Russian society.[9] At the same time, people's theaters and pleasure gardens offered the people an opportunity to demonstrate their aspiration to be a part of urban life. They were settings where working people could relax, socialize, wear their best clothing, and become acquainted with new forms of culture. In the case of the temperance theaters, Russians of all social classes were brought together in a uniquely democratic public space, which, unlike the holiday fairgrounds, existed year-round and was a regular part of urban life. Like the penny press and the expanding corpus of popular literature, people's and workers' theaters contributed to the process of defining a new urban popular culture oriented to personal choice and distinct both from traditional peasant culture and the elite culture that the intelligentsia so cherished.

Epilogue

The February Revolution of 1917 inspired new hope for the democratization of culture, hope mixed with the apprehension that the people might well destroy Russia's artistic heritage unless they were taught to appreciate it. The end of the autocracy's control over the popular theaters brought many changes, some of them surprising to contemporaries. The abolition of censorship, contrary to expectations, did not result in an outpouring of new plays reflecting the new freedom of expression.[1] Many of the people's theaters were taken over by municipal governments or district soviets, but they either functioned largely as before or were used for political meetings and occasional lowbrow entertainments. At the same time, a multitude of new cultural-educational departments, sections, and societies sprang up with the goal of introducing the people to the various branches of the arts, particularly theater. New professional theaters were organized by workers' organizations, while the number of amateur workers' theaters mushroomed. Yet although the people gained unprecedented freedom in their choice of entertainments, their choices seldom lived up to the hopes of those educated Russians who believed that the autocracy was the main impediment to the development of didactic popular theater and that the people would choose edifying entertainment if only they were offered it.

Efforts to democratize theater after February took two forms. First, the democratization of the existing theatrical culture through free performances, special subscriptions for soldiers' and workers' committees, and the establishment of new theaters dedicated expressly to serving the lower classes. This was essentially a continuation of the old people's theater idea. In April, actors from the Moscow Art Theater set up a "people's art theater" in barracks on Deviche Field, the home of the fairground theaters in bygone days. One factory's enlightenment commission rented the Vasilevskii Island

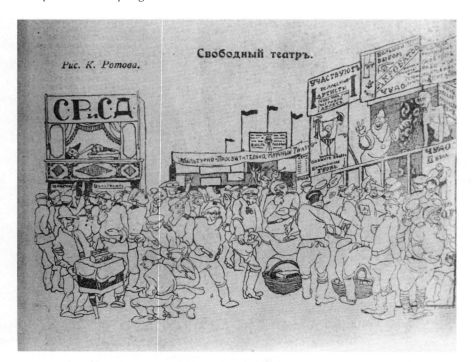

Figure 16. Cartoon entitled "Free Theater," satirizing the lowbrow entertainments that characterized many of the popular theaters that sprang up after the February Revolution in 1917. It unfairly likens the theater of the Moscow Soviet of Workers' and Soldiers' Deputies to a fairground puppet show. *Binoculars,* no. 1 (1917).

Theater to stage topical plays that highlighted the class struggle, such as V. Evdokimov's *Children of Sin,* in which an unscrupulous factory owner preys on a young woman worker and pays with his life when her boyfriend learns what he has done. A reserve battalion organized a "soldiers' theater" in Krestovskii Park, staging plays that included Belaia's *The Unemployed,* Gorky's *The Lower Depths,* and Ostrovsky's *A Much Frequented Spot.* The cultural-educational section of the Moscow Soviet of Soldiers' Deputies was especially active in organizing performances for soldiers from the Moscow garrison and also sent troupes of mobilized actors on tours of the front. The cultural-educational section of the Petrograd duma, headed by the Bolshevik Anatoly Lunacharsky, took over the theaters of the city's temperance guardianship and assigned one-time Moscow Art Theater actress Mariia Andreeva to introduce a more "artistic" repertoire. The former imperial theaters distributed discounted or free tickets to factories and regiments, as did the Moscow Art Theater. Plans were even considered to convert the Mikhailovskii and Malyi theaters into people's theaters. The Moscow Soviet of Workers' Deputies rented a theater and hired the entire troupe to perform operas for workers, while the soldiers' soviet opened its own theater devoted to drama. Interestingly, the "soviet" theaters adopted a traditional *Kulturträger* line with regard to repertoire, which was to be purely "artistic," without regard to politics. On the evening of 25 October, the day the Bolsheviks and their supporters seized power in Petrograd, Moscow's Soldier's Theater opened with a performance of that old favorite by Ostrovsky, *Poverty Is No Vice*.[2]

A new audience now filled the upmarket theaters, rubbing shoulders with the old theatergoing public in the stalls and occupying the boxes of grand dukes in the former imperial theaters. It was often an undisciplined audience, unused to the conventions of behavior in the theater. People smoked, talked, and chewed seeds during performances. On one occasion a group of soldiers demanded seats at gunpoint, while audiences sometimes intervened to stop performances that offended their political sensibilities. In May, for example, soldiers protested against variety shows that satirized Lenin, and in October a sailor fired shots at an actor for singing "Christ Is Risen" at a charity concert for the families of sailors killed in battle.[3]

By the end of 1917, many liberal intellectuals had become disenchanted with the prospects for bringing culture to the masses, but the hope that culture could still be a force for civilizing the *narod* did not die out. A theater critic, discussing the recently opened Soldier's Theater in the wake of the October Revolution, during which the Bolshoi Theater was shelled and the Malyi Theater looted, remarked that whereas only a year before such a theater would have been welcomed by the entire intelligentsia, "for many of us our personal romance with the *narod* is over for good." But even if illusions about the *narod* had been shattered, he added, it was still necessary to think about how to "turn an ignorant and cruel mass of barbarians into people of culture."[4]

The second form of theatrical "democratization" occurred not from the top down but from the bottom up. This was the establishment by workers of amateur "proletarian," "socialist," and "workers' " theaters. By the summer of 1917, a new term appeared to describe such attempts to create working-class cultural institutions – "culture building" (*kul'turnoe stroitel'stvo*). These efforts ostensibly aimed not merely to introduce the working class to the culture of old, "bourgeois" Russia but to lay the groundwork for a new, socialist workers' culture. In practice, however, the workers' theaters, like

their prerevolutionary counterparts, bore little resemblance to the proletarian "culture building" Bogdanov and the Proletkult theorists had envisioned. Left to their own devices, workers tended to embrace the very "bourgeois" culture they were supposed to be challenging.

Like other workers' organizations, theaters of this type proliferated in
1917, particularly in Petrograd. They appeared spontaneously at factories
and in working-class neighborhoods and usually had no clear political orientation. In fact, there was a marked lack of agreement among workers and
their socialist mentors as to the purpose of a workers' theater. Petrograd's
"First Proletarian Literary-Dramatic Society" aimed to unite working-class
lovers of the arts and give them the opportunity to spend their free time
"rationally and beneficially." In contrast, the organizational committee of the
"First Petrograd Workers'-Socialist Theater," which included Lunacharsky
and other Bolshevik proponents of "socialist" theater, called for its members
to propagandize among workers the idea of an artistic and ideological proletarian theater that would be a weapon in the struggle for socialism.[5]

The activities of most workers' theaters did not so much further the construction of a socialist alternative culture as reflect the variety of popular
tastes. A literary-musical evening held at the Putilov factory's theater in
honor of a former Social Revolutionary terrorist, for example, featured
erotic dances by actresses from Petrograd's Lin cabaret. Two workers wrote
to Gorky's newspaper *New Life* to protest the "vulgarity" of the show, in
which the dancers "aroused man's basest instincts, . . . putting their hands
on their hips, jerking their shoulders, and grimacing."[6]

The district soviet closed the Moscow municipal people's theater on
Vvendenskaia Square and dismissed the troupe that Bakhrushin had assembled over the years, using the auditorium for political meetings and sometimes organizing entertainments like *The Naughty Girl*, a farce staged by a
local cabaret director. A journalist lamented the passing of the people's theater, expressing the sense of shock and disbelief that much of the Russian
intelligentsia experienced as 1917 waned: "On the stage where model performances of Chekhov or Ostrovsky were held, the new bosses stage
farces. . . . The masses, for whom a model theater was built, have destroyed
it to trade in pornography on its ruins."[7] For educated Russians who had
dreamed of bringing art to a people who were thought to be thirsty for it,
the world seemed to have turned upside down.

Larisa Reisner, a Bolshevik journalist who visited a number of the
Petrograd workers' theaters during the summer of 1917, found that they
tended to adapt their programs to the tastes of their "uncultivated spectators," staging the same plays that ran in the middle-brow "bourgeois" the-

aters. After visiting a *tantsul'ka* (also known as a *balka*, this was an evening of theater following by dancing), Reisner noted with disappointment that these affairs resembled nothing so much as "bourgeois" balls and worried about the danger that the proletariat was acquiring only "superficial, external culture."[8] She described a performance of the melodrama *Fatal Love* at an amateur workers' theater in the city's Vyborg district, a hotbed of support for the Bolsheviks in 1917. The actors had rented costumes from Leifert, the city's premiere supplier of costumes:

> She's wearing orange gauze with green sequins. He has on a white suit, gloves, and a garish tie. Of course, the play is no play, but a long and vulgar story of God knows what authorship. They perform it in their own fashion: curses alternate with heartrending hysterics, some of the servant's body motions are unrepeatable, and the overall tone is blatantly vulgar.
>
> But that's not the point. The audience and the performers themselves see the awkwardness of the whole act, and the worthlessness of the characters. The most tragic clashes evoke universal laugher.

Reisner clearly had some sympathy for the amateur theater's efforts. She noted that everyone enjoyed the play despite the production's shortcomings and each scene concluded to thunderous applause, but she also expressed the hope that the art and taste of the proletariat would improve with time. The danger was that efforts by professionals to improve proletarian art would take the initiative in the creative process away from the amateurs.[9]

These accounts of spontaneously organized entertainment in 1917 suggest that worker-intellectuals and other champions of "proletarian culture" were very much a minority when Russia emerged from under the heavy hand of tsarist regulation of public life. Many workers appear to have been far more interested in joining in the pleasures of the "bourgeoisie" than in "culture building," for the revolution's promises seem to have included, judging by the tremendous upsurge in amateur theatricals that began in 1917, the chance to have some bourgeois fun. The socialist cultural-educational organizations attempted to raise the quality of artistic production by offering professional guidance, but worker-amateurs often rejected assistance out of fear that the professionals would drive them from the stage. Eventually, efforts to institute centralized control over the theaters and other proletarian cultural organizations led to a Petrograd conference of factory committees, cultural-educational societies, clubs, and people's theaters, organized by a commission of radical and liberal intellectuals that included Evtikhii Karpov, Maxim Gorky, and Anatoly Lunacharsky. The conference met in October and founded a "Central Bureau of Proletarian Cultural-Educational Societies," the embryo of Proletkult.[10]

After the October Revolution, the Bolsheviks enlisted theater and cinema in their efforts to acquaint the population with the meaning of socialism, but at the same time they, like the prerevolutionary *Kulturträger*, saw theater as a tool for civilizing the masses. Itinerant troupes performed before workers at the front, peasants were encouraged to form amateur theater groups, Proletkult put its energies into building a proletarian culture, and Lunacharsky's People's Commissariat of Enlightenment (Narkompros) tried valiantly to foster an appreciation for the classics of Russian literature and drama through its Theatrical Department (TEO Narkompros). In 1919, the Emperor Nicholas II People's House, renamed after the German socialist martyr Karl Liebknecht, hosted the Red Army Studio's production of *The Overthrow of Autocracy*. Other people's theaters and houses were given to workers' clubs or, like the Moscow Municipal People's Theater, became palaces of culture. The former director of the Nicholas II People's House, Alekseev-Iakovlev, put his experience in creating *balagan* shows and mass spectacles at the service of the new regime; he organized a political carnival for May Day in 1918, where his contribution was a float with tsarist policemen singing ditties from behind bars, and helped to stage *The Third International* on the steps of the People's House in 1919. He also worked on Red extravaganzas like *The Blockade of Russia*, adapting the techniques and special effects of the patriotic *Taking of Azov* (1912) to create a naval battle in which revolutionary workers break the Allied blockade.[11]

The Bolshevik leaders, for the most part intellectuals, shared the much of the prerevolutionary intelligentsia's sense of duty to the common people and embraced their civilizing mission with enthusiasm. "Rational recreations," including theater and reading as well as sports, mass parades, and street festivals, were a not entirely new way to enlighten and discipline proletarian minds and bodies. Sounding much like an Old Regime factory owner, Trotsky argued for cinema to be enlisted in the war against alcohol in order to raise productivity.[12] The Bolsheviks made widespread use of both theater and cinema to propagandize the illegitimacy of the autocracy and the Provisional Government and to inculcate socialist values in the people.

To be sure, the Bolsheviks were divided in their approach to theater. Lenin and most of the Bolshevik leaders agreed with Lunacharsky's view that the old classical dramatic canon had to be preserved and brought to the people, while Nikolai Bukharin and Proletkult leaders like Platon Kerzhentsev argued for a new proletarian theater with a revolutionary repertoire. Lunacharsky himself wrote a few plays, including the historical melodrama *Oliver Cromwell*, and defended heroic melodrama as a genre of revolutionary theater accessible to the people; Bukharin attacked him as an artistic reactionary.[13] The people, however, were rather lukewarm in their reception of the classics and often rejected the revolutionary repertoire. Lunacharsky saw the multiplication of workers' and peasant drama circles after the revolution as an indication of "the instinctive upsurge of the masses toward art and especially toward theater,"[14] but Viktor Shklovsky, working at the theater section of Narkompros, remembered the upsurge differently: "No one knows what to do with the circles; they multiply like infusoria. Neither the absence of fuel and good, nor the Entente, nothing can stop their development. . . . 'And if you close us down,' they tell us, 'we'll put on the vaudevilles in secret.' And Russia acts and acts, some kind of elemental process is taking place, by which living tissue is transformed into theatrical fabric."[15]

There was certainly a lot of theatrical activity, but the workers' circles and Proletkult amateur theaters mostly staged old melodramas, comedies, and vaudevilles that didn't fit well with the culturalist aspirations of the new order. The revolutions of 1917 seemed to have unleashed mass culture rather than proletarian culture. As a Russian historian of the postrevolutionary amateur theater has pointed out, political-enlightenment organizations often hired professional and amateur actors, and they brought with them the repertoire they had known under the Old Regime, sowing the seeds of mass entertainment throughout Russia. Demobilized soldiers also spread an entertainment-oriented repertoire to villages, along with cabaret artist Aleksandr Vertinskii's songs and urban dance fashions like the "American two-step."[16] Red Army theaters and drama circles usually held to the Proletkult platform but had to battle against audience preferences for old-fashioned entertainment.[17]

According to the futurist poet Vladislav Khodasevich, working in the Petrograd theatrical department of Narkompros in 1918: "We put together repertoires for theaters that did not want to know us. We tried to slip in a classical repertoire: Molière, Shakespeare, Gogol, Ostrovsky. The Communists tried to replace it with a revolutionary repertoire that did not exist. Sometimes 'local delegates' came to us and, to the shame of Kameneva [the head of the department], announced that the proletariat does not want to see either Shakespeare or revolution, and demands vaudevilles."[18]

The poet Aleksandr Blok, visiting Petrograd's newly renamed Karl Liebknecht People's House in the summer of 1918, found that it was still delighting popular audiences with melodramas, vaudevilles, and other low-brow fare. "The diverse public," he observed, "which includes not only the petty bourgeoisie but the genuine proletariat, considers this place its own and is accustomed to flood the spacious grounds of the park; the stage of the People's House satisfies the tastes of the majority." Blok, who at the time was chairman of the repertoire section of Narkompros's Theatrical Department, argued that Narkompros should not simply exclude plays beloved by audiences but unsuitable or even harmful from the official point of view; it should compete with them by promoting better plays that would slowly transform popular taste and drive the melodramas from the stage. He even praised the festive atmosphere of the People's House and its ability to "turn dramatic water into theatrical wine," but his relatively pluralistic view of popular theater was hardly representative of Bolshevik cultural policy.[19]

The battle between proletarian cultural ideology and the *Kulturträger* principles of Narkompros was resolved with the former's defeat in the 1920, but the problem of how to transform popular tastes would continue to vex the Bolsheviks for years to come.[20] As for the old Emperor Nicholas II People's House, it survived the civil war and another world war to be refurbished in the mid-1980s as part of Gorbachev's temperance campaign, which among other measures attempted to offer the population more of what had once been called "rational recreations." It reopened in 1988 as a "Miuzik-holl" and at present is also home to a casino.

Appendix of Titles

Easy Money	Beshenye den'gi
Ermak Timofeevich, Conqueror of Siberia	Ermak Timofeevich, Pokoritel' Sibiri
Ermak Timofeevich, or the Conquest of Siberia	Ermak Timofeevich, ili Pokorenie Sibiri
Ermak Timofeevich, or Volga and Siberia	Ermak Timofeevich, ili Volga i Sibir'
Eugene Onegin	Evgenii Onegin
Even a Cat Has Lean Times	Ne vse kotu maslenitsa
Fatal Love	Rokovaia liubov'
The Fatal Step	Rokovoi shag
Fighting the Indians, or Around the World in Eighty Days	Bor'ba s indeitsami, ili Poezdka vokrug sveta v 80 dnei
The First Distiller	Pervyi vinokur
The First Swallow	Pervaia lastochka
The Forest	Les
The Free and Easy Life	Zhit'e privol'noe
Generalissimo Suvorov	Generalissimus Suvorov
The George Mine	Shakhta "Georgii"
Godfather Ivan	Kum Ivan
The Government Inspector	Revizor
The Grandfather of the Russian Fleet	Dedushka russkogo flota
The Great Day	Velikii den'
Great Russia—Powerful Russia	Velikaia Rus'—Rus' moguchaia
The Groom from the Cutlery Department	Zhenikh iz nozhevoi linii
The Hand of the Almighty Has Saved the Fatherland	Ruka vsevyshnego otechestvo spasla
A Happy Day	Schastlivyi den'
A Hard Lot	Tiazhkaia dolia
The Hare	Zaiats
The Heart Is Not a Stone	Serdtse ne kamen'
The Heroes of Chemulpo	Geroi Chemul'po
The Heroic Feats of the White General, or the Liberation of the Slavs	Geroicheskie podvigi belogo generala, ili Osvobozhdenie slavian
How the Frenchman Took Moscow	Kak frantsuz Moskvu bral
The Indian Princess's Bridegroom	Zhenikh indiiskoi printsessy
Ivan the Simpleton and the Power of the Enchanted Pike, or The Volga Bandits	Ivanushka-Durachok i vlast' zakoldovannoi shchuki, ili Volzhskie razboiniki
Japan's War with Russia	Voina Iaponii s Rossiei
Jubilee	Iubilei
Kashchei the Deathless	Kashchei bessmertnyi
The Keys to Happiness	Kliuchi schast'ia

The Kidnapped Bride	Pokhishchennaia nevesta
Krechinskii's Wedding	Svad'ba Krechinskogo
Life and Death, or Hard Labor and Homecoming	Zhizn' i smert', ili Katorga i vozvrashchenie
A Life for the Tsar	Zhizn' za tsaria
Life Is Going By	Zhizn' ukhodit
Love and the Motherland	Liubov' i rodina
The Lower Depths	Na dne
A Lucrative Position	Dokhodnoe mesto
Marriage	Zhenit'ba
The Master	Barin
Matrena the General's Wife	General'sha Matrena
The Merchant Kalashnikov	Kupets Kalashnikov
Miller, Sorcerer, Cheat, and Matchmaker	Mel'nik, koldun, obmanshchik i svat
The Minor	Nedorosl'
A Much Frequented Spot	Na boikom meste
The Muzhik from Archangel— Mikhail Lomonosov	Muzhik iz Arkhangel'ska—Mikhail Lomonosov
The Naughty Girl	Shal'naia devochka
Night Watch	Nochnoe
The Old Days of Kashirsk	Kashirskaia starina
An Old Friend Is Better Than Two New Ones	Staryi drug luchshe novykh dvukh
On His Own Two Feet	Otrezannyi lomot'
On Maneuvers	Na manevrakh
The Overthrow of Autocracy	Sverzhenie samoderzhaviia
Parasha the Siberian Girl	Parasha sibiriachka
The Partition	Razdel
Peter the Great	Petr Velikii
Peter the Great at the Battle of Poltava	Petr Velikii na bitve pod Poltavoi
Philistines	Meshchane
The Poor Bride	Bednaia nevesta
Port Arthur	Port-Artur
Poverty Is No Vice	Bednost' ne porok
The Power of Darkness	Vlast' t'my
Prince Igor	Kniaz' Igor'
Prince Serebrianyi	Kniaz' Serebrianyi
The Proposal	Predlozhenie
Rebirth	Vozrozhdenie
Russian Heroes at Sevastopol	Russkie geroi v Sevastopole
A Russian Wedding at the End of the Sixteenth Century	Russkaia svad'ba v iskhode 16 veka
Russians across the Balkans in 1878	Russkie za Balkanami v 1878

Sevastopol	Sevastopol'
The Shame of Germany	Pozor Germanii
The Showbooth	Balaganchik
The Simple Girl and the Refined Girl	Prostushka i vospitannaia
Sit in Your Own Sled	Ne v svoi sani ne sadis'
The Smallholder	Odnodvorets
The Smugglers	Kontrabandisty
The Snowmaiden	Snegoruchka
The Sons of Israel	Syny Izrailia
The Sponger	Nakhlebnik
Stenka Razin, the Volga Bandit	Sten'ka Razin—razboinik volzhskii
The Storm	Groza
The Taking of Azov	Vziatie Azova
The Taking of the Fortress Geok-Tepe	Vziatie kreposti Geok-Tepe
Tarelkin's Death	Smert' Tarelkina
Tornado	Smerch
To the Far East	K dal'nemu vostoku
Tsar Maximilian	Tsar' Maksimilian
Tsar Nebuchadnezzar	Tsar' Navukhodonosor
The Tsar's Grace Is the Joy of the People	Tsarskaia milost'—radost' naroda
Uncle Vanya	Diadia Vania
Under His Highness's Wing	Pod krylom ego svetlosti
The Unemployed	Bezrabotnye
The Uniform	Vitsmundir
Vaniushin's Children	Deti Vaniushina
Vanka the Steward	Van'ka kliuchnik
Vasilisa Melenteva	Vasilisa Melent'eva
The Village Widow	Mirskaia vdova
War and Peace	Voina i mir
A Ward of the Mistress	Vospitanitsa
A Wealthy Man	Bogatyi chelovek
The Wedding	Svad'ba
Welcome News	Zhelannaia vestochka
The White General	Belyi general
Woe from Wit	Gore ot uma
The Workers' Settlement	Rabochaia slobodka
The World Is Not Without Good People	Svet ne bez dobrykh liudei
The Would-be Master	Mnimyi barin
You Can't Live as You Please	Ne tak zhivi, kak khochetsia

NON-RUSSIAN TITLES

Around the World in Eighty Days	Poezdka vokrug sveta v 80 dnei
Belisarius	Velizar

The Blue Bird	Siniaia ptitsa
The Bourgeois Gentleman	Meshchanin v dvorianstve
Civil Death [La morte civile]	Sem'ia prestupnika
Don Juan	Don Zhuan
An Enemy of the People	Doktor Shtokman
Faust	Faust
Fuenteovejuna	Orechii istochnik
The Good Hope	Gibel' nadezhdy
The Grace of God [La grâce de Dieu]	Materinskoe blagoslovenie
Love and Intrigue	Kovarstvo i liubov'
Magda [Heimat]	Rodina
The Marriage of Figaro	Bezumnyi den', ili Zhenit'ba Figaro
Mary Stuart	Mariia Stiuart
The Miser	Skupoi
La muette de Portici	Fenella
The Poor of Paris	Parizhskie nishchie
The Robbers	Razboiniki
Sister Teresa or Elizabeth Soarez	Za monastyrskoi stenoi
The Sorceress	Koldun'ia
The Sunken Bell	Potonuvshii kolokol
Thirty Years, or The Life of a Gambler	Tridtsat' let, ili zhizn' igroka
Tsar and Carpenter	Tsar'-plotnik
The Two Orphans	Dve sirotki
Two Youngsters [Les deux gosses]	Dva podrostka
Virgins in Name Only [Les demivierges]	Polu-devstvennitsy
William Tell	Vil'gel'm Tell
The Winter's Tale	Zimniaia skazka

Notes

INTRODUCTION

1. The meeting with Trepov is described in Vladimir Nemirovitch-Dantchenko, *My Life in the Russian Theatre*, trans. John Cournos (New York, 1968), 181–82. Here Nemirovich remarks that the meeting was on the eve of the premiere of Chekhov's *Seagull* (18 December 1898); actually, it was on 16 January 1899. See L. M. Freidkina, *Dni i gody Vl. I. Nemirovicha-Danchenko. Letopis' zhizni i tvorchestva* (Moscow, 1962), 152–53.

2. K. S. Stanislavskii, *Stat'i. Rechi. Besedy. Pis'ma* (Moscow, 1953), 101; Vl. I. Nemirovich-Danchenko, *Stat'i. Rechi. Besedy. Pis'ma* (Moscow, 1952), 63.

3. See, for example, John Russell Stephens, *The Censorship of English Drama, 1824–1901* (Cambridge, 1980).

4. Aleksandr Kugel', lead article, *Teatr i iskusstvo*, no. 2 (13 January 1908): 25.

5. Jeffrey Brooks, *When Russia Learned To Read: Literacy and Popular Culture, 1861–1917* (Princeton, 1985), 319.

6. Lars Kleberg, "'People's Theater' and the Revolution: On the History of a Concept Before and After 1917," in *Art Society, Revolution: Russia, 1917–1921*, ed. N. A. Nilsson, Stockholm Studies in Russian Literature, no. 11 (Stockholm, 1979), 179–97; Robert Russell, "People's Theater and the October Revolution," *Irish Slavonic Studies*, no. 7 (1986): 65–84. Kleberg's focus on the theories of well-known intellectuals leads him to claim that "the first man in Russia to speak of 'the people's theater' was the playwright Aleksandr Ostrovskij," in 1882, and that "the breakthrough of the concept of the people's theater in Russia, which occurred in the years after 1905, had less to do with the rapid spread of the existing popular stages than with Symbolism and the intelligentsia's self-criticism after the abortive revolution" (180–81). In fact, the concept of the people's theater had been discussed in the press since the emancipation of the serfs in 1861, and many had been established before 1905.

7. Romain Rolland, *Le théâtre du peuple* (Paris, 1903); David James Fisher, "Romain Rolland and the French People's Theatre," *The Drama Review* (March

1977): 75–90; idem, *Romain Rolland and the Politics of Cultural Engagement* (Berkeley, 1988); Viacheslav Ivanov, *Po zvezdam* (St. Petersburg, 1909); Bernice Glatzer Rosenthal, "Theatre as Church: The Vision of the Mystical Anarchists," *Russian History / Histoire russe* 4, no. 2 (1977): 122–41.

8.   James von Geldern, *Bolshevik Festivals, 1917–1920* (Berkeley, 1993).

9. Michel Foucault, *Discipline and Punish: The Birth of the Prison*, trans. Alan Sheridan (New York, 1977). On the applicability of Foucault's concepts to Russia, see Laura Engelstein, "Combined Underdevelopment: Discipline and the Law in Imperial and Soviet Russia," *American Historical Review* 98, no. 2 (1993): 338–53.

10. Tony Bennett, *The Birth of the Museum: History, Theory, Politics* (London, 1995).

11. Brooks, *When Russia Learned To Read*.

12. Ben Eklof, *Russian Peasant Schools: Officialdom, Village Culture, and Popular Pedagogy, 1861–1914* (Berkeley, 1986), 482.

13. Gary Thurston, "The Impact of Russian Popular Theatre, 1886–1915," *Journal of Modern History* 55 (June 1983): 267; idem, "Theatre and Acculturation in Russia from Peasant Emancipation to the First World War," *Journal of Popular Culture* 18, no. 2 (Fall 1984): 3–16.

14. Gary Thurston, *The Popular Theatre Movement in Russia, 1862–1919* (Evanston, 1998), 288–89.

15. My understanding of discourse is of course derived from the work of Michel Foucault, especially his *Discipline and Punish* and *The History of Sexuality*, vol. 1, *An Introduction*, trans. Robert Hurley (New York, 1978).

16. John Fiske, *Reading the Popular* (Boston, 1989), 3.

17. Peter Bailey, *Leisure and Class in Victorian Britain: Rational Recreations and the Contest for Control, 1830–1885* (London, 1978).

CHAPTER ONE

1. Vladimir Propp, *Russkie agrarnye prazdniki* (Leningrad, 1963); Elizabeth A. Warner, *The Russian Folk Theatre* (The Hague, 1977), 1–38, 43–66.

2. Russell Zguta, *Russian Minstrels: A History of the Skomorokhi* (Philadelphia, 1978).

3. Ibid., 13, 47–48, 50–63.

4. The best-known example of Russian ecclesiastical drama is the "furnace show" (*peshchnoe deistvo*), introduced in the early sixteenth century, which recounted the story from the Book of Daniel of the three Israelite youths who were cast into a fiery furnace as punishment for refusing to worship pagan idols. Echoes of this theme can perhaps be found in the oral folk drama *Tsar Maximilian*, which appeared in the late eighteenth century and continued to be performed well into the Soviet period. In it the tsar's son, Adolf, is punished and eventually executed for his unwillingness to worship pagan gods. Simon Karlinsky, *Russian Drama from Its Beginnings to the Age of Pushkin* (Berkeley, 1985); Warner, *Russian Folk Theatre*, 155–209. For an informative but hostile

account of the Russian Orthodox church's attitude to theater, see M. I. Gudnovtsev, *Tserkov' i teatr* (Moscow, 1970).

5. Karlinsky, *Russian Drama*, 37–43.

6. A. A. Kizevetter, *Pervyi obshchedostupnyi teatr v Rossii* (Petrograd, 1917), 6–10; S. S. Danilov, *Ocherki po istorii russkogo dramaticheskogo teatra* (Leningrad, 1948), 71–77.

7. Karlinsky, *Russian Drama*, 24–32.

8. N. S. Tikhonravov, *Russkie dramaticheskie proizvedeniia 1672–1725 godov*, vol. 1 (St. Petersburg, 1874), 41.

9. Danilov, *Ocherki*, 74–75.

10. Kizevetter, *Pervyi obshchedostupnyi teatr*, 10–11.

11. Danilov, *Ocherki*, 76–77; Kizevetter, *Pervyi obshchedostupnyi teatr*, 18; Karlinsky, *Russian Drama*, 46–48.

12. L. Starikova, *Teatral'naia zhizn' starinnoi Moskvy: Epokha. Byt. Nravy* (Moscow, 1988), 94–96; idem, *Teatr v Rossii XVIII veka* (Moscow, 1997), 12–19; Karlinsky, *Russian Drama*, 47–49.

13. L. N. Semenova, "Obshchestvennye razvlecheniia v Peterburge v pervoi polovine XVIII v.," in *Staryi Peterburg: Istoriko-etnograficheskie issledovaniia* (Leningrad, 1982), 160–62; Starikova, *Teatral'naia zhizn'*, 18–22.

14. Semenova, "Obshchestvennye razvlecheniia," 151.

15. Ibid., 151–52; Starikova, *Teatral'naia zhizn'*, 113–14.

16. Semenova, "Obshchestvennye razvlecheniia," 148–49. In Moscow, according to one historian, even the gentry continued to take part in public fist combats on holidays as late as the reign of Catherine the Great. M. I. Pyliaev, *Staraia Moskva* (St. Petersburg, 1891), 8.

17. Ivan Zabelin, "Iz khroniki obshchestvennoi zhizni v Moskve v XVIII stoletii," in *Sbornik obshchestva liubitelei rossiiskoi slovesnosti na 1891 god* (Moscow, 1891), 557–61.

18. E. M. Kuznetsov, comp., *Russkie narodnye gulian'ia po rasskazam A. Ia. Alekseev-Iakovleva v zapisi i obrabotke Evg. Kuznetsova* (Leningrad, 1948), 9–10; I. G. Georgi, *Opisanie rossiisko-imperatorskogo stolichnogo goroda Sanktpeterburga i dostoprimechatel'nostei v ego okrestnostiakh* (St. Petersburg, 1794), 655–56; Starikova, *Teatral'naia zhizn'*, 186–87; idem, *Teatr v Rossii*, 51–78; V. D. Kuz'mina, *Russkii demokraticheskii teatr XVIII veka* (Moscow, 1958).

19. A. A. Iartsev, "Pervye fabrichnye teatry v Rossii," *Istoricheskii vestnik* (May 1900): 648; Danilov, *Ocherki*, 84; Karlinsky, *Russian Drama*, 63–64.

20. Pyliaev, *Staraia Moskva*, 18–22; Richard Wortman, *Scenarios of Power: Myth and Ceremony in Russian Monarchy*, vol. 1 (Princeton, 1995), 119–20.

21. Wortman, *Scenarios of Power*, vol. 1, 56–58.

22. Cited in S. Zhislina, "Iz istorii narodnogo teatra," *Narodnoe tvorchestvo*, no. 12 (1938): 55–56.

23. Ibid.; Zabelin, "Iz khroniki," 576–79; Kuz'mina, *Russkii demokraticheskii teatr*, 164–65; M. V. Kachalov, "Narodnyi teatr v Moskve na Devich'em pole: Materialy k istorii teatra v XVIII veke," *Istoricheskaia biblioteka*, no. 5

(May 1878): 1–10. Zhislina claims that the Moscow theater closed because it failed to attract audiences, but Zabelin makes a more convincing case in arguing that it was the plague epidemic of 1771 that led to the theater's closure.

24. Nicholas A. Hans, *History of Russian Educational Policy (1701–1917)* (New York, 1964), 18, 26–27.

25. Modest Kittary, the Moscow professor who was instrumental in getting imperial permission to establish a people's theater as part of the 1872 Polytechnic Exposition held on the bicentennial of the tsar's birth, pointed out in his petition that Peter himself had been a supporter of people's theater, as evidenced by his *komediinaia khramina*. RGIA, f. 1282, op. 2, d. 1901, l. 26.

26. On the organization and political significance of the imperial theaters, see Murray Frame, *The St. Petersburg Imperial Theaters: Stage and State in Revolutionary Russia, 1900–1920* (Jefferson, N.C., 2000), 8–10, 19–35; idem, "Censorship and Control in the Russian Imperial Theatre During the 1905 Revolution and Its Aftermath," *Revolutionary Russia* 7, no. 2 (December 1994), 165–76. On the place of the imperial theaters in Russian cultural life, see Arkady Ostrovsky, "Imperial and Private Theatres, 1882–1905," in *A History of Russian Theater*, ed. Robert Leach and Viktor Borovsky (Cambridge, 1999), 218–53.

27. *Istoriia russkogo dramaticheskogo teatra v semi tomakh*, ed. E. G. Kholodov et al., vol. 2 (Moscow, 1977), 449–542; vol. 3 (Moscow, 1978), 218–338; vol. 4 (Moscow, 1979), 285–418; vol. 5 (Moscow, 1980), 412–537; vol. 6 (Moscow, 1982), 440–509; vol. 7 (Moscow, 1987), 445–503; Iu. Dmitriev, *Tsirk v Rossii* (Moscow, 1977), 101–4; Catherine A. Schuler, *Women in Russian Theatre: The Actress in the Silver Age* (London, 1996), 23–25; I. F. Petrovskaia, *Teatr i zritel' rossiiskikh stolits, 1895–1917* (Leningrad, 1990), 62–64, 113–14.

28. V. A. Teliakovskii, *Vospominaniia* (Leningrad, 1965), 77; Ivan Shcheglov, *Narod i teatr. Ocherki i issledovaniia sovremennogo narodnogo teatra* (St. Petersburg, [1911]), 39; V. I. Voronov, *Put' k stsene* (Moscow, 1958), 61–62; K. Skorobogatov, "Ot rabochei zastavy. Vospominaniia artista," part 1, *Zvezda*, no. 1 (January 1967): 148; idem, *Zhizn' i stsena* (Leningrad, 1970), 79–80; *Vestnik trezvosti*, no. 226 (October 1913): 17; A. Frolov, *Probuzhdenie. Vospominaniia riadovogo rabochego*, part 1 (Kiev, 1923), 27–28; N. A. Sakharov, "Iz proshlogo," in *Fabrika knigi Krasnyi Proletarii. Istoriia tipografii "T-va I. N. Kushnerev i Ko."* (Moscow, 1932), 217.

29. A. M. Konechnyi, "Peterburgskie narodnye gulian'ia na maslenoi i paskhal'noi nedeliakh," in N. V. Iukhneva, ed., *Peterburg i guberniia: Istoriko-etnograficheskie issledovaniia* (Leningrad, 1989), 24. The word *balagan*, which is of Persian origin, originally referred to any temporary wooden structure that could be easily assembled and disassembled. By the second quarter of the nineteenth century, it had come to designate the temporary wooden theaters erected at fairgrounds.

30. A. F. Nekrylova, *Russkie narodnye gorodskie prazdniki, uveseleniia i zrelishcha* (Leningrad, 1988), 177–80.

31. Ibid., 194; Konechnyi, "Peterburgskie narodnye gulian'ia," 37; I. Iu.

Polenov, "Park trudiashchikhsia imeni A. M. Gor'kogo," in *Sady i parky Leningrada* (Leningrad, 1981), 48–49; *Doklad No. 81 Moskovskoi gorodskoi upravy ob uprazdnenii narodnykh gulianii na Devich'em pole i u Presnenskoi zastavy i ob otkrytii takovykh na gorodskoi zemle za Presnenskoi zastavoi, szadi fabriki br. Mamontovykh. 28 fevralia 1911 g.* (Moscow, 1911), 2–3.

32. Kuznetsov, *Russkie narodnye gulian'ia*, 64, 67. For a good discussion of the cycle of urban holidays and the celebrations, see Nekrylova, *Russkie narodnye gorodskie prazdniki*. According to Nekrylova, over thirty *gulian'ia* were held each year in Moscow, other than at Shrovetide and Easter, some of which featured *balagan* shows among their entertainments, but they attracted virtually no attention from the press and little is known about the content of the shows. Puppet shows featuring Petrushka were most certainly present, but more technically complex theatrical spectacles were not.

33. Cited in A. G. Levinson, "Razvitie fol'klornykh traditsii russkogo iskusstva na gulianiiakh" (kandidatskaia dissertatsiia, Vsesoiuznyi nauchno-issledovatel'skii institut iskusstvoznaniia, Moscow, 1980), 82.

34. Kuznetsov, *Russkie narodnye gulian'ia*, 12.

35. Levinson, "Razvitie fol'klornykh traditsii," 83–87; M. I. Pyliaev, *Staryi Peterburg* (St. Petersburg, 1903), 434; Edward Jerrman, *St. Petersburg: Its People, Their Character and Institutions*, trans. Frederick Hardman (New York, 1855), 78–79.

36. Kuznetsov, *Russkie narodnye gulian'ia*, 13–14 n.14.

37. On the puppet theaters, see Catriona Kelly, *Petrushka: The Russian Carnival Puppet Theatre* (Cambridge, 1990).

38. Cited in Nekrylova, *Russkie narodnye gorodskie prazdniki*, 180.

39. A. V. Leifert, *Balagany* (Petrograd, 1922), 42; Kuznetsov, *Russkie narodnye gulian'ia*, 112.

40. Kuznetsov, *Russkie narodnye gulian'ia*, 68–71. Alexandre Benois describes a typical harlequinade of the 1870s in his introduction to Leifert, *Balagany*, 10–12.

41. Konechnyi, "Peterburgskie narodnye gulian'ia," 32–33.

42. Kuznetsov, *Russkie narodnye gulian'ia*, 54, 102–4; Leifert, *Balagany*, 13–14.

43. *Peterburgskii listok*, 31 January 1870. Several different versions of *Dmitrii the Pretender* and *Ermak* premiered in the imperial theaters in the nineteenth century (*Istoriia russkogo dramaticheskogo teatra*, vol. 2, 472, 474; vol. 3, 250; vol. 5, 443). The story of Dmitrii the Pretender, one of the pretenders to the Russian throne during the Time of Troubles in the late sixteenth and early seventeenth centuries, was the subject of plays by Aleksandr Sumarokov (*Dmitrii the Pretender*, premiered between 1771 and 1782) and Alexander Ostrovsky (*Dmitrii the Pretender and Vasilii Shuiskii*, premiered 1867), among others. The two best-known versions of the story of Ermak are Petr Plavilshchikov's *Ermak Timofeevich, the Conqueror of Siberia* (premiered 1804) and Nikolai Polevoi's *Ermak Timofeevich, or Volga and Siberia* (premiered

1829). The *balagan* play mentioned above was probably an adaptation of the former.

44. Brooks, *When Russia Learned To Read*, 79, 183.

45. Kuznetsov, *Russkie narodnye gulian'ia*, 52–54.

46. RGALI, f. 659, op. 4, d. 123, l. 303 (poster advertising *Russkie za Balkanami v 1878 g.* at Easter 1879). Leifert, *Balagany*, 49–59, contains a list of St. Petersburg *balagan* shows from 1880 through 1898.

47. See Michael Booth, *Victorian Spectacular Theatre* (London, 1981).

48. *Peterburgskii listok*, 4 and 5 February 1890.

49. Kuznetsov, *Russkie narodnye gulian'ia*, 90–94; Leifert, *Balagany*, 34–38.

50. Leifert, *Balagany*, 32, 43–44, 49; the titles are taken from 1879 posters in RGALI, f. 659, op. 4, d. 123, ll. 300, 304.

51. Leifert, *Balagany*, 38. My emphasis.

52. Kuznetsov, *Russkie narodnye gulian'ia*, 82–84. For his production of *You Can't Live As You Please*, Alekseev-Iakovlev adapted the libretto from Aleksandr Serov's operatic version of the play, *The Power of Evil* (Vrazh'ia sila).

53. Ibid.

54. "Balagany i narodnyi teatr," *Peterburgskii listok*, 4 February 1890.

55. A. Ia. Alekseev-Iakovlev, "Vospominaniia," unpublished manuscript, OR RNB, f. 1130, d. 317, l. 31; "Stolichnaia i provintsial'naia khronika," *Syn otechestva*, no. 7 (17 February 1857): 153; no. 36 (10 February 1862): 281; no. 38 (13 February 1862); Lev Ivanov, "Balagany (Iz vospominanii)," *Stolitsa i usad'ba*, no. 48 (15 December 1915): 4; *Peterburgskii listok*, 25 February 1891.

56. Ivanov, "Balagany," 4; Leifert, *Balagany*, 31–32, 48; Kuznetsov, *Russkie narodnye gulian'ia*, 48–50.

57. I. A. Belousov, *Ushedshaia Moskva* (Moscow, 1929), 353; Ivanov, "Balagany," 6; Leifert, *Balagany*, 60.

58. Kelly, *Petrushka*, especially 59–139, 217–225; Nekrylova, *Russkie narodnye gorodskie prazdniki*, 76–93; A. Alferov, "Petrushka i ego predki," in *Desiat' chtenii po literature* (Moscow, 1895), 175–205.

59. Konechnyi, "Peterburgskie narodnye gulian'ia," 43.

60. Jerrman, *St. Petersburg*, 78.

61. Leifert, *Balagany*, 72. Although I am not suggesting that the fairgrounds were thronged with drunks, evidence of the importance of alcohol in holiday celebrations is so frequently found in contemporary accounts that it is hard to believe that only a handful of the tens of thousands of fairgoers became intoxicated during the course of a day spent at the *gulian'e*. Note that the word *gulian'e* is the noun form of the verb *guliat'*, which means (1) to walk, (2) to skip work or play hooky, and (3) to carouse, and in last meaning almost invariably involves putting away a few drinks.

62. A. F. Nekrylova, "Ocherki-shestidesiatniki," in *Russkaia literatura i fol'klor (Vtoraia polovina XIX v.)* (Leningrad, 1982), 131–77.

63. G. Uspenskii, "Narodnoe gulian'e v Vsesviatskom," *Zritel'*, no. 21 (1 June 1863): 661.

64. V. A. Sleptsov, "Balagany na Sviatoi," in *Polnoe sobranie sochinenii*, 3rd ed., rev. (St. Petersburg, 1903), 368–69.

65. Idem, "Igry i zrelishcha," in *Vasilii Sleptsov. Neizvestnye stranitsy. Literaturnoe nasledstvo*, vol. 71 (Moscow, 1969), 361–67.

66. K. I. Chukovskii, "Literaturnaia sud'ba V. A. Sleptsova," in *Vasilii Sleptsov*, 9–10.

67. V. K. Arkhangel'skaia, "Pisateli-demokraty o narodnom teatre," in *Nasledie revoliutsionnykh demokratov i russkaia literatura* (Saratov, 1981), 226–44. The charge of corrupting the public in the interests of profit was also leveled in the 1900s against the early Russian film industry. See N. M. Zorkaia, *Na rubezhe stoletii. U istokov massovogo iskusstva v Rossii 1900–1910 godov* (Moscow, 1976), 89–91.

68. D. Danchin, "Nechto o nashikh balaganakh," *Peterburgskii listok*, 6 April 1868.

69. *Balaganshchiki: Ocherki zhizni i nravov artistov i antrepenerov* [sic] *uveselitel'nykh zavedenii i prazdnichnykh balaganov* (St. Petersburg, 1868); *Peterburgskii listok*, 31 January 1870.

70. S. T. Semenov, "Soldatka," in *V rodnom derevne* (Moscow, 1962), 69.

71. "Balagany i narodnye teatr," *Peterburgskii listok*, 4 February 1890; Kuznetsov, *Russkie narodnye gulian'ia*, 86–87.

72. Constantin Stanislavski, *My Life in Art*, trans. J. J. Robbins (New York, 1956), 324.

73. V. I. Lenin, *Polnoe sobranie sochinenii*, 5th ed., vol. 6 (Moscow 1959), 131.

74. Leifert, *Balagany*, 33, 37, 39; Alekseev-Iakovlev, "Vospominaniia," ll. 25, 27; Kuznetsov, *Russkie narodnye gulian'ia*, 90.

75. A similar process of appropriation is evident in folk theater and early cinema. See A. F. Nekrylova and N. I. Savushkina, eds., *Fol'klornyi teatr* (Moscow, 1988), 78–79; Zorkaia, *Na rubezhe stoletii*, 99–111.

76. Vladimir Mikhnevich, *Peterburgskoe leto* (St. Petersburg, 1887), 55–73; A. Pleshcheev, "Ostrova," *Stolitsa i usad'ba*, nos. 19–20 (10 October 1914): 8–10; A. Z. Serpoletti, "Moskovskie uveselitel'nye sady. Ocherk s 1867 g.," unpublished manuscript, 1928, GTSTM, f. 533, d. 33–34; Al'bin Konechnyi, "Shows for the People," in *Cultures in Flux: Lower-Class Values, Practices, and Resistance in Late Imperial Russia*, ed. Stephen P. Frank and Mark D. Steinberg (Princeton, 1994), 121–30.

77. Serpoletti, "Moskovskie uveselitel'nye sady," l. 5; Kuznetsov, *Russkie narodnye gulian'ia*, 36–44; Konechnyi, "Shows for the People," 125–26; Nekrylova, *Russkie narodnye gorodskie prazdniki*, 193; *"Arkadiia." Desiatiletie so dnia ee osnovaniia, 1881–1891* (St. Petersburg, 1891), 14, 22; Iu. A. Dmitriev, *Mikhail Lentovskii* (Moscow, 1978), 223–43.

78. Mikhnevich, *Peterburgskoe leto*, 55–62; Kuznetsov, *Russkie narodnye gulian'ia*, 37; Konechnyi, "Shows for the People," 127–28; Serpoletti, "Moskovskie uveselitel'nye sady," ll. 8–15, 31–34.

79. Dmitriev, *Tsirk v Rossii*, 153–69.

80. Steve Smith and Catriona Kelly, "Commercial Culture and Consumerism," in *Constructing Russian Culture in the Age of Revolution, 1881–1940*, ed. Catriona Kelly and David Shepherd (Oxford, 1998), 116–17; Shcheglov, *Narod i teatr*, 210–15; Hubertus Jahn, *Patriotic Culture in Russia during World War I* (Ithaca, 1995), 85–124.

81. Schuler, *Women in Russian Theatre*, 113–27. Brenko was granted official permission to stage only scenes from plays but in fact produced works in their entirety.

82. *Kratkii ocherk deiatel'nosti russkogo dramaticheskogo teatra Korsha v Moskve* (Moscow, 1892); V. P-skii, "Moskovskie pis'ma," *Teatr i iskusstvo*, no. 5 (2 February 1897): 92–93; *Istoriia russkogo dramaticheskogo teatra*, vol. 6, 241–54, 262–83; Ostrovsky, "Imperial and Private Theatres," 219–21, 246–50.

83. Iu. Orlov, *Moskovskii khudozhestvennyi teatr. Legendy i fakty (opyt khoziastvovaniia) 1898–1917 gg.* (Moscow, 1994), esp. 79–84. There are many works on the Moscow Art Theater. A good introduction is Jean Benedetti, "Stanislavsky and the Moscow Art Theatre," in *A History of Russian Theatre*, 254–77.

84. *Bor'ba*, 6 December 1905.

85. Shcheglov, *Narod i teatr*, 341–43; "Itogi letnego sezona," *Novosti sezona*, no. 703 (30 August–2 September 1900): 2.

86. V. Iu. Krupianskaia, "Narodnaia drama *Lodka*, ee genezis i literaturnaia istoriia," in *Kratkie soobshcheniia instituta etnografii Akademii nauk SSSR*, no. 3 (Moscow, 1947), 71.

87. Nekrylova and Savushkina, *Fol'klornyi teatr*, 78–79.

88. N. E. Onchukov, "Narodnaia drama na Severe," in *Izvestiia otdeleniia russkogo iazyka i slovesnosti imperatorskoi Akademii nauk*, vol. 14, book 4 (St. Petersburg, 1909), 218.

89. Nekrylova and Savushkina, *Fol'klornyi teatr*, 78–79.

90. For a good discussion of the origins and development of these and other Russian folk plays, see Warner, *Russian Folk Theatre*, 127–83; and B. Varneke, "Chto igraet narod," *Ezhegodnik imperatorskikh teatrov, 1913*, part 4 (St. Petersburg, 1913), 1–39.

91. N. I. Savushkina, *Russkaia narodnaia drama* (Moscow, 1988), 63–64.

92. P. N. Berkov, *Russkaia narodnaia drama XVII–XX vekov* (Moscow, 1953), 27–29, 165–70; Warner, *Russian Folk Theatre*, 148–53.

93. N. A. Popov, "Zriteli i teatr," unpublished manuscript (n.d.), RGALI, f. 837, op. 2, d. 120, kn. 1, ll. 46–52.

94. Ninety-one percent of the workers at the Tsindel mill possessed a land allotment. P. M. Shestakov, *Rabochie na manufakture T-va "Emil' Tsindel' " v Moskve* (Moscow, 1900), 75. On the basis of Shestakov's data, one historian concludes that most of these workers had important economic ties with the countryside (Robert Johnson, *Peasant and Proletarian: The Working Class of Moscow in the Late Nineteenth Century* [New Brunswick, N.J., 1979], 41–42).

95. Warner, *Russian Folk Theatre*, 155.

96. Savushkina lists over seventy recorded versions of the play (*Russkaia narodnaia drama*, 214–19).

97. Popov, "Zriteli i teatr," d. 120, kn. 1, l. 49.

98. See Chapter 3 for a discussion of censorship restrictions on plays destined for the popular stage.

99. Popov, "Zriteli i teatr," l. 47.

100. Warner, *Russian Folk Theatre*, 74–78. According to a study in the 1920s, the overwhelming majority of the workers surveyed indicated that they attended church before the revolution. E. A. Kabo, *Ocherki rabochego byta: Opyt monograficheskogo issledovaniia domashnego rabochego byta*, vol. 1 (Moscow, 1928), 132.

101. According to Moshe Lewin, "the wretchedness of the *pop* [parish priest] was proverbial and their drunkenness notorious" among the peasantry ("Popular Religion in Twentieth-Century Russia," in Moshe Lewin, *The Making of the Soviet System* [New York, 1985], 62). While Gregory Freeze claims that the Russian peasants were less anticlerical than their Western European counterparts, he also notes that disrespect for parish priests was common (*The Parish Clergy in Nineteenth-Century Russia: Crisis, Reform, Counter-Reform* [Princeton, 1983], xxix, 61). See also Kimberly Page Herrlinger, "Class, Piety, and Politics: Workers, Orthodoxy and the Problem of Religious Identity in Russia" (Ph.D. dissertation, University of California, Berkeley, 1996); and S. L. Firsov, "Rabochie i pravoslavnaia tserkov' v Rossii v nachale XX v.," in *Rabochie i intelligentsiia v epokhu reform i revoliutsii 1861– fevral' 1917 g.*, ed. S. I. Potolov et al. (St. Petersburg, 1997), 327–39.

102. S. I. Kanatchikov, *A Radical Worker in Tsarist Russia: The Autobiography of Semen Ivanovich Kanatchikov*, ed. and trans. Reginald E. Zelnik (Stanford, 1986), 29.

103. Cited in A. M. Konechnyi, "Obshchestvennye razvlecheniia i gorodskie zrelishcha v Tsarskom Sele (XVIII–nachalo XX v.), in *Etnografiia Peterburga-Leningrada. Materialy ezhegodnykh nauchnykh chtenii*, no. 2, ed. N. V. Iukhneva (Leningrad, 1988), 18.

104. TsIAgM, f. 483, op. 3, d. 1585, ll. 383, 385, 398, 402.

105. I. Orlovskaia, "K voprosu 'O bor'be s al'kogolizmom,' " RGIA, f. 1288, op. 14, 1915, d. 153, l. 67.

106. Shestakov, *Rabochie na manufakture T-va "Emil' Tsindel',"* 72–73. Shestakov mentions neither the folk dramas nor the performances of literary plays that the factory administration began sponsoring in 1894. See *Teatral*, no. 4 (January 1895): 98; Popov, "Zriteli i teatr," d. 120, kn. 1, ll. 41–42, 46.

107. Leifert, *Balagany*, 53.

108. Savushkina, *Russkaia narodnaia drama*, 34.

109. Katerina Clark also discusses Russian intellectual's antipathy to commercial theater in *Petersburg, Crucible of Cultural Revolution* (Cambridge, Mass., 1995), 84–86.

110. A. N. Ostrovskii, "Zapiska o polozhenii dramaticheskogo iskusstva v

Rossii v nastoiashchee vremia," in *Sobranie sochinenii v desiati tomakh*, vol. 10 (Moscow, 1960), 184.

CHAPTER TWO

1. On the Great Reform period, see W. Bruce Lincoln, *The Great Reforms: Autocracy, Bureaucracy, and the Politics of Change in Imperial Russia* (DeKalb, Ill., 1990).

2. Joseph Black, *Citizens for the Fatherland* (Boulder, 1979); Isabel de Madariaga, "The Foundation of the Russian Educational System by Catherine II," *Slavonic and East European Review* 57, no. 3 (July 1979): 369–95; Eklof, *Russian Peasant Schools*, ch. 1.

3. See the discussion in the Introduction; N. A. Rubakin, *Etiudy o russkoi chitaiushchei publike* (St. Petersburg, 1895); L. M. Kleinbort, "Rabochaia intelligentsiia i iskusstvo," *Vestnik Evropy*, no. 8 (April 1913): 215–26; idem, *Ocherki rabochei intelligentsii*, vol. 1 (Petrograd, 1923); idem, "Khronika vnutrennei zhizni," *Russkoe bogatstvo*, no. 8 (August 1913): sec. 2: 338–44.

4. Brooks, *When Russia Learned To Read*, 318.

5. Reginald E. Zelnik, *Labor and Society in Tsarist Russia: The Factory Workers of St. Petersburg, 1855–1870* (Stanford, 1971), 173–99; idem, "The Sunday School Movement in Russia, 1859–1862," *The Journal of Modern History* 27, no. 2 (June 1965): 151–70.

6. D. D. Protopopov, *Istoriia Peterburgskogo komiteta gramotnosti (1861–1895 gg.)* (St. Petersburg, 1898). On attempts by educated society to compete with commercial popular literature, see Brooks, *When Russia Learned To Read*, 333–46.

7. *Istoriia rabochikh Leningrada*, ed. V. S. Diakin et al., vol. 1 (Leningrad, 1972), 97.

8. A. G. Rashin, *Formirovanie rabochego klassa Rossii: Istoriko-ekonomicheskii ocherk* (Moscow, 1958), 149. Levels of literacy were influenced by a variety of factors, including urban residence, skilled employment, gender, and age, and were highest among young males engaged in skilled labor in cities. Statistics on literacy, however, indicate only that those persons classified as literate could read something, as a very minimal standard; they reveal nothing about what kinds of texts could be read, understood, and absorbed.

9. In 1874, the first year for which data are available, 21.4 percent of Russia's military recruits were classified as literate; by 1913 this figure had risen to 67.8 percent. Rashin, *Formirovanie*, 582; Jeffrey Brooks, "The Zemstvos and the Education of the People," in *The Zemstvo in Russia: An Experiment in Local Self-government*, ed. Terence Emmons and Wayne S. Vucinich (Cambridge, 1982), 243–78.

10. *Sankt-Peterburgskie vedomosti*, 31 May 1868.

11. *Otechestvennye zapiski*, no. 6 (June 1868): 255.

12. Ostrovskii, "Zapiska," 168–86.

13. Kh. D. Alchevskaia, *Dramaticheskie proizvedeniia: Ostrovskii v prime-*

nenii k chteniiu v narode (St. Petersburg, 1887). Alchevskaia's work and views are discussed in Thurston, *The Popular Theatre Movement*, 101–15.

14. Zelnik, *Labor and Society*, 224; James H. Bater, *St. Petersburg: Industrialization and Change* (London, 1976), 158–72. The 1863 figures are less reliable than those of 1869, which were based on a genuine citywide census.

15. Rashin, *Formirovanie*, 353–54. As in the case of St. Petersburg, the figures for the later date are based on a citywide census and more reliable than those for 1863.

16. Bater, *St. Petersburg*, 201–7; Zelnik, *Labor and Society*, 247–51.

17. Moral degeneration resulting from urbanization was a common theme in studies of lower-class life. See N. Flerovskii (V. V. Bervi), *Polozhenie rabochego klassa v Rossii* (St. Petersburg, 1869).

18. M. R., "V Peterburge," *Syn otechestva*, no. 217 (10 September 1862): 1709.

19. See Iartsev, "Pervye fabrichnye teatry," 650–52; D. Medvedev, "Narodnyi teatr na Moskovskoi politekhnicheskoi vystavke," *Istoricheskii vestnik* (September 1905): 742–44; S. A. Iur'ev, "Derevenskii teatr," *Artist*, no. 3 (1889): 46–50. Iur'ev's performances are discussed at length in Thurston, "Theater and Acculturation in Russia," 4–7; idem, *The Popular Theatre Movement*, 71–74; and G. A. Khaichenko, *Russkii narodnyi teatr kontsa XIX–nachala XX veka* (Moscow, 1975), 15–20.

20. S. S. Danilov, "Materialy po istorii russkogo zakonodatel'stva o teatre," in *O teatre. Sbornik statei*, ed. S. S. Danilov and S. S. Mokul'skii (Leningrad, 1940), 177–83; I. F. Petrovskaia and V. Somina, *Teatral'nyi Peterburg. Nachalo XVIII veka—oktiabr' 1917 goda* (St. Petersburg, 1994), 162–66.

21. A well-known example is Ivan Turgenev's *A Sportsman's Sketches* (Zapiski okhotnika, 1852), an extremely humane and sympathetic literary treatment of peasants and their plight. The censors forbade a second edition of the book.

22. RGIA, f. 472, op. 60, d. 1942, l. 13. Adlerberg is citing his own 1858 report to Alexander II on the subject.

23. I. Ivanov, "O sovremennoi nevrastenii i starom geroisme," *Teatr i iskusstvo*, no. 50 (12 December 1899): 900–901.

24. Petrovskaia and Somina, *Teatral'nyi Peterburg*, 147.

25. On Dobroliubov's literary criticism, see Rufus W. Mathewson, Jr., *The Positive Hero in Russian Literature*, 2nd ed. (Stanford, 1975), 54–62; Andrzej Walicki, *A History of Russian Thought from the Enlightenment to Marxism*, trans. Hilda Andrews-Rusiecka (Stanford, 1979), 208–9.

26. RGIA, f. 472, op. 60, d. 1942, ll. 13–14.

27. Ibid., ll. 12–13.

28. On the evocation of a *pugachevshchina* (a massive peasant uprising like the one led by Emilian Pugachev in 1773–74) during the preparations for emancipating the serfs, see P. Péchoux, "L'ombre de Pugacev," in *Le statut des paysans libérés du servage, 1861–1961*, ed. R. Portal (Paris, 1962), 128–52.

29. RGIA, f. 472, op. 60, d. 1942, l. 14.

30. R. F. Mikhailova, "K voprosu o sozdanii narodnogo teatra v Rossii v

kontse 60-kh—nachale 70-kh godov XIX veka," in *Vestnik Leningradskogo gosudarstvennogo universiteta*, no. 8, vypusk 2 (Leningrad, 1961), 68; Medvedev, "Narodnyi teatr," 744.

31. *Otechestvennye zapiski*, no. 6 (June 1868): 255.

32. Zelnik, *Labor and Society*, 255–59.

33. Cited in ibid., 255.

34. *Golos*, 1 September 1868.

35. RGIA, f. 472, op. 60, d. 1942, l. 3.

36. Ibid., ll. 3–4. In discussing the police chief's project, R. F. Mikhailova claims that Trepov was really seeking to "distract the common people from the oppositional movement," using the campaign against drunkenness merely to camouflage his real intentions ("K voprosu o sozdanii narodnogo teatra," 70). There is no evidence to support her assertion in any of the official correspondence on the subject, however, even though much of it is marked "Top Secret" and could therefore be presumed to refer to any concealed motives the authorities might have had. Some state officials, such as Minister of Court Adlerberg, were *against* the creation of people's theaters because they feared that such theaters would give the oppositional movement a podium from which to extend their influence to the masses, but no one suggested at this time that the government could use theater to combat the influence of the oppositional movement among the masses.

37. Alfred J. Rieber, "Interest-Group Politics in the Era of the Great Reforms," in *Russia's Great Reforms, 1855–1861*, ed. Ben Eklof, John Bushnell, and Larissa Zakharova (Bloomington, 1994), 75–78.

38. RGIA, f. 1282, op. 2, d. 1902, ll. 9–10.

39. Sollogub's best-known work is the short novel *Tarantas*, published in 1840.

40. RGIA, f. 1282, op. 2, d. 1901, l. 11.

41. Ibid., l. 14.

42. RGIA, f. 472, op. 60, d. 1942, l. 25.

43. Ibid., ll. 12–22.

44. RGIA, f. 1282, op. 2, d. 1902, ll. 17–23.

45. Peterburgskii komitet gramotnosti. Komissiia po voprosu o narodnykh teatrakh, *Doklad komissii po voprosu o narodnykh teatrakh* (St. Petersburg, 1870).

46. "N. G.," "Pervyi narodnyi teatr v Odesse," in *Narodnyi teatr. Sbornik*, ed. E. V. Lavrova and N. A. Popov (Moscow, 1896), 151–54.

47. RGIA, f. 1282, op. 2, d. 1902, l. 41.

48. A. F. Fedotov, foreword to *Nedorosl'* (Moscow, 1886), cited in Lavrova and Popov, *Narodnyi teatr*, 9–10; Medvedev, "Narodnyi teatr," 744–46.

49. I. G. [I. Gorodetskii], "A. F. Fedotov i pervaia popytka osnovaniia narodnogo teatra," *Severnyi vestnik*, no. 5 (May 1895), sec. 2: 93–95.

50. Cited in A. P. Klinchin, "Narodnyi teatr na Politekhnicheskoi vystavke," in *Teatral'noe nasledstvo. Soobshcheniia. Publikatsii.* (Moscow, 1956), 353–54.

51. RGIA, f. 776, op. 25, d. 186, ll. 3–4, 9–10. On Kittary's role in obtaining

the government's approval for the venture, see Medvedev, "Narodnyi teatr," 744–60.

52. M. Kublitskii, "Otkrytie narodnogo teatra," *Vestnik Moskovskoi Politekhnicheskoi vystavki* (5 June 1872). For more detailed accounts of the history of the People's Theater, see Klinchin, "Narodnyi teatr," 347–53; Medvedev, "Narodnyi teatr," 754–61; Khaichenko, *Russkii narodnyi teatr*, 28–37.

53. I. N. Zakhar'in (Iakunin), *Vstrechi i vospominaniia* (St. Petersburg, 1903), 307; N. V. Drizen, *Dramaticheskaia tsenzura dvukh epokh, 1825–1881* (Petrograd, 1917), 285–87. For a complete list of works approved for the theater, see RGIA, f. 776, op. 25, d. 340, ll. 40–45, 52. For the works actually performed, see "Otchet o Narodnom teatre komissii po ustroistvu otdela popecheniia o rabochikh na Politekhnicheskoi vystavke 1872 goda," cited in Klinchin, "Narodnyi teatr," 362–63.

54. W., "Narodnyi teatr v Moskve," *Beseda*, no. 7 (July 1872): 42–43.

55. Fedotov, foreword to *Nedorosl'*, 12.

56. Kh. Z., "Teatral'nye zametki," *Russkie vedomosti*, 3 August 1872.

57. Kh-z, "Otkrytie Narodnogo teatra," *Russkie vedomosti*, 7 June 1872; D. Averkiev, "Narodnyi teatr v Moskve," *Moskovskie vedomosti*, morning edition, 12 June 1872; W., "Narodnyi teatr v Moskve," *Beseda*, no. 7 (July 1872): 39; V. P., "Pervye predstavleniia v Narodnom teatre," *Sovremennye izvestiia*, 6 June 1872; M. Kublitskii, "Otkrytie narodnogo teatra"; idem, "Narodnyi teatr," *Vestnik Moskovskoi Politekhnicheskoi vystavki*, 10 June 1872.

58. RGIA, f. 776, op. 25, d. 186, l. 68. The initiative for this order probably belonged to Timashev rather than Alexander II. Timashev makes no reference to the tsar in his letter to Dolgorukii and states that it is his own recommendation that performances of the play be discontinued. The tsar, whose arrival during the first act and departure in the middle of the second elicited enthusiastic applause and cheers, commented favorably to Kittary on the performance of *The Government Inspector*, which he had personally requested for his visit to the theater (Medvedev, "Narodnyi teatr," 755–57).

59. RGIA, f. 776, op. 25, d. 186, ll. 78–82.

60. Kh. Z., "Moskovskie zrelishcha i uveseleniia," *Russkie vedomosti*, 29 June 1873; *Istoriia russkogo dramaticheskogo teatra*, vol. 5, 252.

61. RGIA, f. 1282, op. 2, d. 1902, ll. 46–52; Lavrova and Popov, *Narodnyi teatr*, 7–8.

62. I. G., "A. F. Fedotov," 96–98; Lavrova and Popov, *Narodnyi teatr*, 7–8; *Moskovskie vedomosti*, obituary (15 February 1895); Stanislavski, *My Life in Art*, 148–204, 210.

63. Fedotov, foreword to *Nedorosl'*, 13.

64. "Smes'. 1. Narodnye teatry," *Russkii vestnik* 99 (May 1872): 425.

65. R. V., "Teatral'nye zametki. Zakrytie Narodnogo teatra," *Russkie vedomosti*, 6 October 1872; Kublitskii, "Narodnyi teatr;" V. S-v, "Po povodu narodnogo teatra," *Vestnik Moskovskoi Politekhnicheskoi vystavki*, 19 July 1872.

66. Schuler, *Women in Russian Theatre*, 127–28; *Istoriia russkogo dramaticheskogo teatra*, vol. 5, 232–38.

67. Ostrovskii, "Zapiska," 179–80. In his "Zapiska," Ostrovsky sometimes uses the terms *natsional'nyi teatr* and *narodnyi teatr* interchangeably to refer to his vision of a theater that would belong to the entire nation. On the various meanings of the term *narodnyi teatr,* see the note on terminology in the Introduction.

68. Ibid., 180–81, 183.

69. Ibid., 182.

70. Ibid., 184

71. Cited in Shcheglov, *Narod i teatr,* 78.

72. Cited in S. Vasiukov, "Vospominaniia o M. V. Lentovskom," *Istoricheskii vestnik* (April 1907): 110.

73. *Russkie vedomosti,* 5 November 1882.

74. Dmitriev, *Mikhail Lentovskii,* 155–57.

75. Ibid., 156.

76. Ibid., 159–60. Installments of *The Bandit Churkin,* by Nikolai Pastukhov, appeared in *Moskovskii listok* in the years 1882–85. See Brooks, *When Russia Learned To Read,* 123–25, 177–83.

77. A. P. Chekhov, *Polnoe sobranie sochinenii i pisem v tridtsati tomakh. Sochineniia,* ed. N. F. Belchikov et al., vol. 16 (Moscow, 1979), 24–25. *The Death of Liapunov,* by Stepan Gedeonov, is a patriotic drama set during the "Time of Troubles" at the beginning of the seventeenth century. The title character perishes in the struggle to liberate Russia from the Poles. It premiered in the Imperial Aleksandrinskii Theater in 1846, and was widely performed throughout Russia in subsequent decades.

78. Vasiukov, "Vospominaniia o M. V. Lentovskom," 117.

79. Ibid.

80. *Moskovskii dnevnik zrelishch i ob"iavlenii,* no. 18 (22 January 1884).

81. Dmitriev, *Mikhail Lentovskii,* 223–43. The Skomorokh closed for the last time in 1898.

82. "Teatr 'Skomorokh,' " *Artist,* no. 26 (January 1893): 168–70; V. P., "Teatr 'Skomorokh,' " *Artist,* no. 24 (March 1892): 131–33; A. V. Amfiteatrov [Old Gentleman, pseud.], "'Vlast' t'my' pered narodom," *Novoe vremia,* 10 December 1895; E. Ber-t., "'Vlast' t'my' na stsene teatra 'Skomorokh' (Beseda s A. A. Cherepanovym)," *Rampa,* no. 2 (31 August 1908): 31–32.

83. "Teatr 'Skomorokh,'" *Artist,* no. 25 (December 1892): 173–75; "Teatr 'Skomorokh,' " *Artist,* no. 26 (January 1893): 168–70; *Moskovskie vedomosti,* 16 February 1895; "Teatr (O narodnom teatre)," *Severnyi vestnik* (April 1895), sec. 2: 54–63.

84. V. P., "Teatr 'Skomorokh,'" *Artist,* no. 19 (January 1892): 172.

85. Nikolai Popov, "'Skomorokh'—kak obshchedostupnyi teatr," *Teatral,* no. 41 (October 1895): 110–11.

86. *Moskovskie vedomosti,* 16 February 1895.

87. Shcheglov, *Narod i teatr,* 47–71 (the citation is on p. 71).

88. On Panina's theater, see the discussion on p. 73 below; S. Panina and P.

Gaideburov, "Iskusstvo v narodnoi auditorii," *Russkaia shkola,* nos. 5–6 (1914): 150–73; Thurston, *The Popular Theatre Movement,* 203–9.

89. *Izvestiia S.-Peterburgskoi gorodskoi dumy,* no. 46 (November 1886): 1069; ibid., no. 8 (March 1893): 922–27; ibid., no. 11 (June 1896): 49–91; Anatolii Kremlev, "Munitsipal'naia bezprintsipnost'," " *Teatr i iskusstvo,* no. 34 (23 August 1915): 624–25; Moskovskaia gorodskaia uprava, *Doklad No. 55 Komissii po narodnym razvlecheniiam i o pol'zakh i nuzhdakh obshchestven-nykh* (Moscow, 1901); *Izvestiia Moskovskoi gorodskoi dumy,* no. 15 (August 1905): 25–35; Vl. I. Nemirovich-Danchenko, *Stat'i. Rechi. Besedy. Pis'ma* (Moscow, 1952), 63; *Zhurnaly Moskovskoi gorodskoi dumy za 1908 g.* (Moscow, 1909), meeting of 18 March, no. 6: 39; A. G. Mikhailovskii, "Deiatel'nost' Moskovskogo gorodskogo upraveleniia v 1913–1916 gg.," *Izvestiia Moskov-skogo gorodskogo dumy. Otdel obshchii* 40, no. 9 (September 1916), 32–33.

90. See Robert W. Thurston, *Liberal City, Conservative State: Moscow and Russia's Urban Crisis, 1906–1914* (New York, 1987), esp. 133–38; Adele Lindenmeyer, *Poverty Is Not a Vice: Charity, Society, and the State in Imperial Russia* (Princeton, 1996), 48–73.

91. Aleksandr Kugel' [Homo Novus, pseud.], "Teatral'noe narodnichestvo," *Peterburgskaia gazeta,* 5 July 1898.

92. Eklof, *Russian Peasant Schools,* 103.

93. On the various movements to enlighten and discipline migrants to the city, see Daniel R. Brower, *The Russian City Between Tradition and Modernity, 1850–1900* (Berkeley, 1990), 140–87; Mary Stuart, "The Ennobling Illusion: The Public Library Movement in Late Imperial Russia," *The Slavonic and East European Review* 76, no. 3 (July 1998): 401–40.

94. Patricia Herlihy, "Strategies of Sobriety: Temperance Movements in Russia, 1880–1914," Occasional Paper No. 238, Kennan Institute for Advanced Russian Studies (Washington, D.C., 1990); Arthur W. McKee, "Taming the Green Serpent: Alcoholism, Autocracy, and Russian Society, 1890–1917" (Ph.D. dissertation, University of California, Berkeley, 1997).

95. Lavrova and Popov, *Narodnyi teatr,* x–xiii; E. N. Medynskii, *Vnesh-kol'noe obrazovanie, ego znachenie, organizatsiia i tekhnika,* 2nd ed. (Moscow, 1916), 288.

96. V. E. Meierkhol'd, *Stat'i, pis'ma, rechi, besedy,* part 1 (Moscow, 1968), 310; Edward Braun, *The Theatre of Meyerhold: Revolution on the Modern Stage* (London, 1979), 20.

97. RGIA, f. 575 (Glavnoe upravlenie neokladnykh sborov i kazennoi pro-dazhi pitei Ministerstva finansov), op. 3, d. 4303, ll. 863–75. These figures do not include performances held at the *narodnye gulian'ia* sponsored by the temper-ance guardianships.

98. I. Inozemstev, "Voprosy narodnogo teatra," part 1, *Teatr i iskusstvo,* no. 2 (10 January 1899): 26.

99. *Trudy Pervogo Vserossiiskogo s"ezda stsenicheskikh deiatelei* (hereafter cited as *TPVSSD*), part 1 (St. Petersburg, 1898): 214–19.

100. Chekhov, *Polnoe sobranie sochinenii i pisem. Pis'ma*, vol. 6 (Moscow, 1978), 214–19, 292, 599; I. N. Vinogradskaia, *Zhizn' i tvorchestvo K. S. Stanislavskogo. Letopis' v chetyrekh tomakh*, vol. 1 (Moscow, 1971), 203.

101. See T. A. Prozorova, "A. M. Gor'kii v bor'be za narodnyi teatr (1892–1904)" (Kandidatskaia dissertatsiia, Gosudarstvennyi institut teatral'nogo iskusstva imeni A. V. Lunacharskogo, Leningrad, 1967).

102. Khaichenko, *Russkii narodnyi teatr*, 236; *Trudy sozvannogo Khar'kovskim obshchestvom gramotnosti 7–12 iiunia 1915 g. v g. Khar'kove s"ezda po voprosam organizatsii razumnykh razvlechenii dlia naseleniia Khar'kovskoi gubernii* (Kharkov, 1915).

103. See *Trudy Pervogo Vserossiiskogo s"ezda deiatelei narodnogo teatra v Moskve, 27 dekabria 1915—5 ianvaria 1916* (Petrograd, 1919) (hereafter cited as *TPVSDNT*).

104. Among the more important and influential works were Ivan Shcheglov, *O narodnom teatre* (Moscow, 1895), which was reissued in several expanded editions under various titles, the last being *Narod i teatr. Ocherki i issledovaniia sovremennogo narodnogo teatra* (St. Petersburg, [1911]); Lavrova and Popov, *Narodnyi teatr*; N. A. Popov, "Ob organizatsii razvlechenii dlia rabochikh. Doklad, prochitannyi na vtorom s"ezde russkikh deiatelei po tekhnicheskomu obrazovaniiu v Moskve, 31 dekabria 1895 g.," *Teatral*, no. 65 (April 1896): 23–37; E. P. Karpov and N. N. Okulov, *Organizatsiia narodnogo teatra i poleznykh razvlechenii dlia naroda* (St. Petersburg, 1899); N. V. Skorodumov, *Novyi metod uproshchennykh postanovok (Ustroistvo stseny i dekoratsii)* (Moscow, 1914); Sektsiia sodeistviia ustroistvu derevenskikh i fabrichnykh teatrov pri M[oskovskom] O[bshchestve] N[arodnykh] U[niversitetov], *Sbornik retsenzii p'es dlia narodnogo teatra*, vol. 1 (Moscow, 1914).

105. A. Izmailov, "Tragediia toskuiushchego iumorista," in Shcheglov, *Narod i teatr*, pp. iii–xxii. Unless otherwise indicated, information on the people's theater activists is drawn from *Teatral'naia entsiklopediia*, 5 vols. and supplement (Moscow, 1961–67). See also the Bibliography under individual authors.

106. Popov, "Zriteli i teatr," d. 119, kn. 1, ll. 74–75.

107. Ibid., d.120, kn. 1, l. 115.

108. E. Karpov, "Vospominaniia i moia zhizn'," unpublished manuscript, n.d., OR RNB, f. 106, d. 163; idem, "Iz avtobiografii E. P. Karpova," *Teatr i iskusstvo*, no. 3 (20 January 1908): 58–59; Aleksandr Kugel' [Homo Novus, pseud.], "Dramaturg-narodnik," *Teatr i iskusstvo*, no. 3 (20 January 1908): 56–57; idem, *Desiatiletie narodnykh gulianii za Nevskoiu zastavoiu. Ocherk deiatel'nosti Nevskogo Obshchestva ustroistva narodnykh razvlechenii* (St. Petersburg, 1895); idem and N. N. Okulov, *Organizatsiia narodnogo teatra i poleznykh razvlechenii dlia naroda* (St. Petersburg, 1899).

109. On the performances that Bunakov and his wife organized for peasants, see L. Bunakova, "Istoriia Petinskogo Narodnogo Doma," in *TPVSDNT*, 153–62; Thurston, "The Impact of Russian Popular Theatre," 249–53; idem, "Theatre in

the Village School: The Bunakovs' Discovery," in *School and Society in Tsarist and Soviet Russia,* ed. Ben Eklof (New York, 1993), 70–94; idem, *The Popular Theatre Movement,* 86–101; and Khaichenko, *Russkii narodnyi teatr,* 44–51.

110. A. N. Kremlev, "S.-peterburgskii obshchestvennyi teatr. Proekt," *Izvestiia S.-Peterburgskoi gorodskoi dumy,* no. 11 (June 1896): 49–91; idem, "Mneniia mezhdunarodnykh kongressov o gorodskikh i narodnykh teatrakh," *Teatr i iskusstvo,* no. 46 (13 November 1911): 881–83; idem, "O S.-Peterburgskom gorodskom teatre," parts 1 and 2, *Teatr i iskusstvo,* no. 44 (30 October 1911): 832–35; no. 45 (6 November 1911): 856–58.

111. S. Zel'tser, *A. A. Briantsev* (Moscow, 1962).

112. S. V. Panina, "Na peterburgskoi okraine," part 1, *Novyi zhurnal,* no. 48 (1957): 163–96; N. F. Skarskaia and P. P. Gaideburov, *Na stsene i v zhizni* (Moscow, 1959); P. P. Gaideburov, *Literaturnoe nasledie. Vospominaniia. Stat'i. Rezhisserskie eksplikatsii. Vystupleniia,* ed. Simen Dreiden (Moscow, 1977), 209–21.

113. Quidam, "Neudachnaia zashchita," *Moskovskie vedomosti,* 28 May 1898; "Narodnye razvlecheniia," *Moskovskie vedomosti,* 28 July 1899.

114. *Moskovskie vedomosti,* 11 December 1902.

115. A. Astaf'ev, "Nechto o spektakliakh dlia naroda," *Moskovskie vedomosti,* 26 March 1902.

116. See, for example, [A. Shevelev], *K voprosu o narodnom teatre (K predstoiashchemu s"ezdu russkikh stsenicheskikh deiatelei)* (Moscow, 1897), 1.

117. "Teatr i narod," *Russkii vestnik* (January 1896): 341–44.

118. "Igra v iskusstve," *Moskovskie vedomosti,* 10 May 1898.

119. For a detailed, albeit tendentious, discussion of church attitudes toward the theaters, see Chudnovtsev, *Tserkov' i teatr.* A. Shevelev, *Tserkov' i zrelishcha. Vzgliad na otnosheniia sv. pravoslavnoi tserkvi k teatral'nym zrelishcham i uveseleniiam* (Moscow, 1892), is an interesting contemporary view of the subject by an opponent of theater. See especially pp. 38–40.

120. E. A. [Episkop Mozhaiskii Aleksandr], "Po voprosu ob ustroistve dlia naroda teatrov," *Moskovskie tserkovnye vedomosti,* no. 6 (5 February 1889): 83–84.

121. Local priests participated in the organization of popular performances in Siberia in 1916. V. S., "Narodnyi teatr v Sibirskikh 'uglakh,' " *Teatr i iskusstvo,* no. 17 (24 April 1916): 351–52.

122. *Teatr i iskusstvo,* no. 33 (14 August 1905): 520; *Obrazovanie,* no. 2 (February 1899): 18–19; *Kostromskie eparkhial'nye vedomosti,* no. 1 (1903): 10–16, cited in Chudnovtsev, *Tserkov' i teatr,* 95; S., "'Soblazniteli narodnye,' " *Rampa i zhizn',* no. 39 (27 September 1915): 2–3.

123. K. Medvedskii, "Literaturnye zametki. O narodnom teatre," *Moskovskie vedomosti,* 13 February 1898.

124. Vasilii Belinskii, "Publichnye uveseleniia dlia naroda," *Russkii trud,* no. 40 (10 October 1899): 8–9.

125. N. Bunakov, "Razmyshleniia po povodu vystavki narodnogo teatra

ustroennoi v Moskve v 1895 g.," in Lavrova and Popov, *Narodnyi teatr*, 72; Ivan Inozemtsev, "Voprosy narodnogo teatra," part 1, *Teatr i iskusstvo*, no. 2 (10 January 1899): 26–27.

126. I. Shcheglov, "Vragi i druz'ia narodnogo teatra," *Novoe vremia*, 22 May 1898. Shcheglov himself was quite moderate in his political views and felt that the people's theater could be a safety valve against the spread of socialist ideas. See idem, "Narodnyi teatr i smeshenie iazykov," *Novoe vremia*, 21 June 1898.

127. V. Stepanov, "Vzgliad na ideal'nyi narodnyi teatr i ego zadachi v nashe vremia," in Lavrova and Popov, *Narodnyi teatr*, 223–25; *TPVSSD*, part 2 (Moscow, 1898), 19. On theater as an educational institution, see also V. Danilevskii's 1898 report to the Kharkov Literacy Society in his *Narodnyi dom, ego zadachi i obshchestvennoe znachenie*, 2nd ed. (Kharkov, 1915), 16–17.

128. Bunakov, "Razmyshleniia," 174; Popov, "O repertuare narodnogo teatra (Zametki)," in *Narodnyi teatr*, p. 244; Inozemtsev, "Voprosy narodnogo teatra," part 2, *Teatr i iskusstvo*, no. 3 (17 January 1899): 50; Iurii Beliaev, "Teatr budushchego," *Rossiia*, no. 4 (1 May 1899); D. L. Tal'nikov, "Narodnyi teatr," *Vestnik Evropy*, no. 2 (February 1916): 298–99.

129. Astra, "Narodniki i teatr," *Birzhevye vedomosti*, 6 August 1898.

130. V. Avseenko, "Dlia naroda," *Peterburgskaia gazeta*, 2 July 1898.

131. "Obshchedostupnye i narodnye teatry," *Birzhevye vedomosti*, 8 June 1898.

132. M. Ivanov, "Muzykal'nye nabroski," *Novoe vremia*, 17 March 1903; Shcheglov, "O detskikh i soldatskikh spektakliakh" (1896), in *Narod i teatr*, 107.

133. Inozemtsev, "Voprosy narodnogo teatra," part 4, *Teatr i iskusstvo*, no. 5 (31 January 1899): 99–100; In. [Ivan Inozemtsev], "Trezvost' osobogo roda," *Birzhevye vedomosti*, 9 July 1899.

134. Shcheglov, "Peterburgskie zametki" (1892), in *Narod i teatr*, 28.

135. See, for example, Kh. D. Alchevskaia, *Chto chitat' narodu*, 3 vols. (St. Petersburg, 1884–1906); A. S. Prugavin, *Zaprosy naroda i obiazannosti intelligentsii v oblasti prosveshcheniia i vospitaniia*, 2nd ed. (St. Petersburg, 1895). Studies of popular reading tastes and attempts to promote inexpensive editions of belles lettres among the common people are discussed in Brooks, *When Russia Learned To Read*, 30–31, 317–52.

136. Peterburgskii komitet gramotnosti, *Doklad*, 4–5.

137. "Repertuar narodnogo teatra," in ibid., 8–12. The list included works by authors such as Ostrovsky, Pushkin, Alexei Tolstoy, Pisemsky, Kukol'nik, Polevoi, Averkiev, Pogoskii, Potekhin, Serov, and Kavos. One of the report's authors, Aleksandr Pogoskii, wrote a few moralistic "people's" books and plays, in addition to working to make "good literature" available to the common people. See Brooks, *When Russia Learned To Read*, 334–36.

138. Viktor Ostrogorskii, "Dobryi pochin. K voprosu o narodnom teatre," *Obrazovanie*, no. 3 (March 1892), sec. 2: 71–73.

139. Iurii Ozarovskii, "Repertuar narodnogo teatra," *Obrazovanie*, nos. 5–6 (May–June 1894), sec. 2: 286–93.

140. Lavrova and Popov, *Narodnyi teatr*, xiv–xxiv.

141. Kremlev, "Proekt," 73–77.

142. RGIA, f. 575, op. 3, d. 4062; Shcheglov, *Narod i teatr*, 388–92.

143. Shcheglov, *Narod i teatr*, 375–85.

144. Chekhov, *Polnoe sobranie sochinenii i pisem. Pis'ma*, vol. 11 (Moscow, 1982), 294.

145. N. Timkovskii, "Vopros ob obshchedostupnom teatre na pervom vserossiiskom s"ezde stsenicheskikh deiatelei," *Russkoe bogatstvo*, no. 5 (May 1897), sec. 2: 28–31.

146. Cited in Inozemtsev, "Voprosy narodnogo teatra," part 3, *Teatr i iskusstvo*, no. 4 (24 January 1899): 76.

147. Cited in Shcheglov, *Narod i teatr*, 23.

148. Stepanov, "Vzgliad," 223–30.

149. N. Bunakov, "Opyt narodnogo teatra," *Russkii nachal'nyi uchitel'*, no. 1 (January 1892): 26.

150. Bunakov, "Razmyshleniia," 169.

151. Kremlev, "Proekt," 66–69. Three-quarters (sixty-five) of the eighty-eight Russian works he recommended were by Pushkin, Gogol, Ostrovsky, and Turgenev. Shakespeare, Byron, Goethe, Schiller, Lope de Vega, and Calderón dominated the repertoire of sixty-seven foreign works.

152. Popov, "Zriteli i teatr," d. 119, kn. 1, l. 78.

153. Popov, "Ob organizatsii razvlechenii," 28–29. My emphasis.

154. Ibid., 35.

155. Kugel', "Teatral'noe narodnichestvo."

156. Kugel', editorial, *Teatr i iskusstvo*, no. 10 (9 March 1897): 182.

157. Shcheglov, "Peterburgskie zametki" (1892), in *Narod i teatr*, 31.

158. Shcheglov, "V zashchitu narodnogo teatra," *Novoe vremia*, 13 May 1898.

159. Daniel Pick, *Faces of Degeneration: A European Disorder* (Cambridge, 1989); J. M. Golby and A. W. Purdue, *The Civilization of the Crowd* (New York, 1984); Bailey, *Leisure and Class*; Stephen P. Frank, "Confronting the Domestic Other: Rural Popular Culture and Its Enemies in Fin-de-Siècle Russia," in Frank and Steinberg, *Cultures in Flux*, 74–107; Stephen P. Frank, *Crime, Cultural Conflict, and Justice in Rural Russia, 1856–1914* (Berkeley, 1999).

CHAPTER THREE

1. See Chapter 2.

2. "Delo ob uchrezhdenii osobogo nadzora za narodnymi teatrami," RGIA, f. 776, op. 25, d. 340, l. 8. *The Power of Darkness* was subsequently banned and appeared on Russian stages only in 1895.

3. D. A. Tolstoi, "Vsepodaneishii doklad ob izdanii vremennykh pravil o poriadke razresheniia p'es, prednaznachaemykh k postanovke na stsene narodnykh teatrov," 21 January 1888, RGIA, f. 776, op. 1, d. 24, ll. 1g–1d.

4. Ibid., ll. 1d–1e.

5. Glavnoe upravlenie po delam pechati, "Tsirkuliar No. 751" (14 February

1888), RGIA, f. 776, op. 26, d. 42, l. 15. The new policy went into effect on 1 May 1888.

6. RGIA, f. 776, op. 25, 26. The reports were bound in volumes covering each year. Other volumes contain official correspondence. There was also a register that was supposed to list all the plays submitted for the popular theaters together with the action taken by the censors. Unfortunately there are not always reports for works listed in the register as prohibited, nor are all the works for which reports exist contained in the register. An arbitrary and some-times misleading selection of reports on works for the popular stage examined between 1895 and 1907 has been published, presumably to demonstrate the harshness of the tsarist censorship: V. A. Tsinkovich, "Narodnyi teatr i dra-maticheskaia tsenzura," in *Teatral'noe nasledstvo* (Moscow, 1956), 375–401. For a more detailed discussion that refers to a few plays not mentioned in this chapter, see my "Fighting the Germs of Disorder: The Censorship of Russian Popular Theater, 1888–1917," *Russian History/Histoire russe* 18, no. 1 (Spring 1991): 1–49.

7. Preliminary theatrical censorship was abolished in France in 1906, in Germany in 1918, and in Britain in 1968.

8. On the censorship of foreign-language works in imperial Russia, see Marianna Tax Choldin, *A Fence Around the Empire: Russian Censorship of Western Ideas Under the Tsars* (Durham, N.C., 1985).

9. Daniel Balmuth, *Censorship in Russia, 1865–1905* (Washington, 1979), 43.

10. "Ustav o tsenzure i pechati. Pravila v rukovodstvo tsenzure," *Svod zakonov Rossiiskoi imperii*, part 2, vol. 14 (St. Petersburg, 1904), ch. 1, sec. 8, col. 56, points 97, 99.

11. W. Bruce Lincoln, *Nicholas I: Emperor and Autocrat of All the Russias* (Bloomington, 1978), 179.

12. Brooks, *When Russia Learned To Read*, 64, 299–301.

13. Ibid., 303–5; Balmuth, *Censorship in Russia*, 75.

14. For a brief discussion of the functioning of the Main Administration for Press Affairs, see Iu. A. Nelidov, "Leningradskaia teatral'naia biblioteka im. A. V. Lunacharskogo," in *Teatral'noe nasledie*, vol. 1 (Leningrad, 1934), 21–23.

15. Danilov, "Materialy," 183.

16. "Ustav o tsenzure i pechati. Pravila v rukovodstvo tsensure," *Svod zakonov Rossiiskoi imperii*, part 2, vol. 14, ch. 1, sec. 8, col. 55, points 93, 95, 96, 102. Here and in the discussion that follows I have translated *soslovie*, which technically means "legal estate" (similar to the German *Stand*), as "class," in order to render more accurately the censors' loose usage of the word to refer to social groupings that, strictly speaking, did not fall into estate categories, such as factory workers. Moreover, the words *soslovie* and *klass* were often used inter-changeably.

17. Cited in Drizen, *Dramaticheskaia tsenzura dvukh epokh*, 287–88. *A Bitter Fate*, by Aleksei Pisemsky, was first performed at the Imperial Aleksandrinskii Theater in 1863. It tells the story of a serf who becomes her

master's mistress and has his child in the absence of her husband, who on his return kills the child and is sentenced to hard labor in Siberia. A total of 169 works were approved for performance at the People's Theater in 1872 (RGIA, f. 776, op. 25, d. 340, ll. 40–45, 52). Its decision to stage Nikolai Gogol's *The Government Inspector*, Denis Fonvizin's *The Minor*, and several plays by Alexander Ostrovsky (all included in the censored repertoire) was severely criticized by the conservative press, which apparently considered these works to be even more dangerous than did the censors. See Klinchin, "Narodnyi teatr na Politekhnicheskoi vystavke," 349–50.

18. RGIA, f. 776, op. 25, d. 186, ll. 11–32; "Repertuary narodnykh teatrov," in Lavrova and Popov, *Narodnyi teatr*, xxix.

19. Daniel Field, *Rebels in the Name of the Tsar* (Boston, 1976), 213. On official and elite views of the common people, see Frank, *Crime, Cultural Conflict, and Justice in Rural Russia.*

20. I. F. Petrovskaia, *Istochnikovedenie istorii russkogo dramaticheskogo teatra* (Leningrad, 1971), 29; Stanislavski, *My Life in Art*, 378–79.

21. On political protest at theaters during the 1905 revolution, see Frame, *The St. Petersburg Imperial Theaters*, 121–33; *Pervaia russkaia revoliutsiia i teatr. Stat'i i materialy*, ed. A. Ia. Al'tshuller et al. (Moscow, 1956), esp. 151–55, 202–9, 227–35, 243, 247–51. Alain Corbin discusses the similar use of theater performances for symbolic political protests in early nineteenth-century France in "L'Agitation dans les théâtres de province sous la Restauration," in *Popular Traditions and Learned Culture in France from the Sixteenth to the Twentieth Century*, ed. Marc Bertrand (Saratoga, Calif., 1985), 106–11.

22. RGIA, f. 776, op. 25, d. 624, ll. 6–7.

23. Glavnoe upravlenie po delam pechati, "Tsirkuliar No. 751" (14 February 1888), RGIA, f. 776, op. 26, d. 42, l. 15; idem, "Tsirkuliar No. 2201" (20 May 1888), RGIA, f. 776, op. 26, d. 42, l. 18.

24. Glavnoe upravlenie po delam pechati, "Tsirkuliar No. 4512" (27 September 1893), RGIA, f. 776, op. 26, d. 42, l. 28; idem, "Tsirkuliar No. 1566" (28 February 1898), RGIA, f. 776, op. 26, d. 42, l. 37. The first such list to be published was the *Alfavitnyi spisok dramaticheskim sochineniiam na russkikh, finskikh i estonskikh iazykakh dozvolennym k predstavleniiu na stsenakh narodnykh teatrov* (St. Petersburg, 1891). Works in the languages of the empire's non-Russian nationalities were examined by censors familiar with those languages.

25. RGIA, f. 776, op. 25, d. 505, l. 24.

26. Ibid., ll. 22–25.

27. Ibid., op. 26, d. 14, l. 16.

28. Ibid., d. 7, l. 76.

29. Ibid., op. 25, d. 597, ll. 174–75; d. 58, l. 24.

30. According to Jeffrey Brooks, the popular literature of the period tended to depict Peter as "a symbol of the kind of modern and Westernized country in which the popular writers believed, and which their readers were apparently willing to accept" ("A Changing View of the Autocrat and the Empire," *Russian*

History/Histoire russe 14, nos. 1–4 [1987]: 4). Since popular writers probably wrote with the censorship as well as the market in mind, their portrayals of Peter may well have been affected by the censors' (and Nicholas's) preference for works in which the tsar appears as a modernizing monarch.

31. RGIA, f. 776, op. 25, d. 603, ll. 2, 4–5, 8, 14.

32. Ibid., d. 735, l. 1, 3.

33. Ibid., d. 869, ll. 4, 9–14.

34. Richard Wortman, "Moscow and St. Petersburg: The Problem of Political Center in Tsarist Russia, 1881–1914," in *Rites of Power: Symbolism, Ritual and Politics Since the Middle Ages,* ed. Sean Wilentz (Philadelphia, 1985), 264; and idem, "'Invisible Threads': The Historical Imagery of the Romanov Tercentenary," *Russian History/Histoire russe* 16, nos. 2–4 (1989): 389–408.

35. RGIA, f. 776, op. 25, d. 505, l. 25; ibid., d. 1077, ll. 1–2.

36. Ibid., op. 26, d. 33, l. 174.

37. See *Istoriia russkogo dramaticheskogo teatra v semi tomakh,* vol. 7, 447.

38. RGIA, f. 776, op. 26, d. 16, l. 121.

39. Ibid., d. 58, l. 8.

40. Ibid., d. 22, l. 68.

41. I have not been able to locate a report explaining the reason for lifting the prohibition on *Vasilisa Melent'eva,* only an entry in the register of plays submitted for the popular theater indicating that it was approved with excisions in November 1905 (ibid., d. 57, l. 109). Stage depictions of Ivan remained a highly sensitive issue for the censors. In 1907, for example, Alexei Tolstoy's classic treatment of the tsar in *The Death of Ivan the Terrible* was judged unfit for performance before popular audiences (ibid., l. 128).

42. Petrovskaia and Somina, *Teatral'nyi Peterburg,* 255–56; "Repertuary narodnykh teatrov," lviii.

43. RGIA, f. 776, op. 25, d. 720, ll. 1–14.

44. Ibid., op. 26, d. 25, l. 118.

45. Ibid., d. 24, l. 101; *Teatr i iskusstvo,* no. 4 (25 January 1909): 70.

46. RGIA, f. 776, op. 26, d. 23, l. 57.

47. Ibid., op. 25, d. 505, ll. 27–33; Jahn, *Patriotic Culture,* 131–32, 158–59, 165–66.

48. Both works were approved with excisions in 1890. RGIA, f. 776, op. 26, d. 57, ll. 13, 17.

49. Ibid., d. 12, l. 38.

50. Ibid., d. 7, ll. 187–88. The *balagan* version was probably an adaptation of Ostrovsky's play of the same title.

51. Ibid., l. 283.

52. Aleksandr Kramov, "Eto bylo v Kieve," in *E. A. Lepkovskii. 45 let v teatre. Iubiliarnyi sbornik. Stat'i i vospominaniia* (Leningrad, 1930), 69–71; Petrovskaia, *Teatr i zritel',* 162; A. Ia. Al'tshuller, "Provintsial'nyi teatr v period pervoi russkoi revoliutsii," in *Pervaia russkaia revoliutsiia i teatr,* ed. A. Ia. Al'tshuller, 229–31.

53. RGIA, f. 776, op. 26, d. 24, l. 174; ibid., d. 25, ll. 248, 261.

54. Ibid., d. 7, ll. 191, 257.

55. See Chapter 2.

56. RGIA, f. 776, op. 26, d. 24, l. 216. Lamkert's political reliability gives added weight to his comments as a statement of official policy. He was later chosen by Stolypin to head the government's official news agency (Louise McReynolds, "Autocratic Journalism: The Case of the St. Petersburg Telegraph Agency," *Slavic Review* 49, no. 1 [1990]: 53–54).

57. RGIA, f. 776, op. 26, d. 58, l. 22; ibid., d. 29, l. 160; N. Tamarin [Okulov], "Narodnyi Dom Imperatora Nikolaia II," *Teatr i iskusstvo*, no. 10 (6 March 1911): 207–8.

58. RGIA, f. 776, op. 26, d. 24, ll. 105–6.

59. Ibid., d. 57, l. 29.

60. Ibid., d. 24, l. 227.

61. Ibid., d. 57, l. 29; d. 24, l. 227; d. 23, l. 126; d. 84, l. 149.

62. Ibid., d. 12, l. 105; d. 23, l. 179.

63. "Ustav o tsenzure i pechati. Pravila v rukovodstvo tsenzure," col. 56, points 95, 96.

64. RGIA, f. 776, op. 26, d. 12, ll. 45, 120; ibid., d. 24, l. 228.

65. Ibid., d. 27, l. 38; d. 24, l. 65. The censor appears to have been unaware that *Sinichkin* had already been performed at the Vasilevskii Island Theater for Workers in the early 1890s. See "Repertuary narodnykh teatrov," lvii.

66. RGIA, f. 776, op. 26, d. 21, l. 45; ibid., d. 24, l. 168; d. 27, l. 164.

67. A note in the censors' register indicates that *The Workers' Settlement* was unconditionally approved for popular theaters in 1895 (ibid., d. 57, l. 34).

68. Ibid., d. 29, ll. 201–2.

69. Ibid., d. 27, l. 190.

70. Ibid., d. 12, ll. 20–21, 211.

71. Ibid., d. 7, l. 268. Other examples of plays prohibited for popular theaters because they did not make criminals sufficiently repent and suffer for their wrongdoing are found in d. 12, l. 99; d. 16, l. 44; d. 24, l. 140; d. 25, ll. 54, 216; d. 84, l. 76.

72. Ibid., d. 25, l. 54.

73. Ibid., d. 23, l. 140; d. 84, ll. 40, 141, 168.

74. Ibid., d. 25, l. 252.

75. Ibid., d. 84, l. 52.

76. Ibid., d. 25, l. 23; d. 27, l. 85.

77. K. S. Stanislavskii, *Sobranie sochinenii v vos'mi tomakh*, ed. M. N. Kedrov et al., vol. 5 (Moscow, 1958), 280.

78. *TPVSSD*, part 1, 216–17; "Nuzhdy russkogo teatra (Zapiska stsenicheskikh deiatelei)," *Teatr i iskusstvo*, no. 7 (13 February 1905): 98–99; *Teatr i iskusstvo*, no. 42 (15 October 1906): 637.

79. *TPVSDNT*, 190; V. Tikhonovich, "Voprosy narodnogo teatra," *Uchitel' i shkola*, nos. 15–16 (August 1915): 28–29.

80. RGIA, f. 776, op. 25, d. 775, ll. 11–36.

81. *Teatr i iskusstvo*, no. 47 (20 November 1905): 723; RGIA, f. 776, op. 25, d. 783, ll. 30, 33–34.

82. TsIAgM, f. 16, op. 24, d. 1, t. IV, ll. 29–32; RGIA, f. 776, op. 25, d. 1060, l. 19; ibid., d. 624, l. 74.

83. RGIA, f. 776, op. 25, d. 624, ll. 157–58; *Protokoly Osobogo soveshchaniia, uchrezdennogo pod predsedatel'stvom D. F. Kobeko, dlia sostavleniia novogo ustava o pechati (10 fevralia—4 dekabria 1905 g.)* (St. Petersburg, 1913).

84. A recent study emphasizes the limited effectiveness of tsarism's policing efforts. See Fredric S. Zuckerman, *The Tsarist Secret Police in Russian Society, 1880–1917* (New York, 1996).

85. The files of the press administration contain numerous reports on popular theaters that failed to adhere to the restrictions on their repertoires. RGIA, f. 776, op. 25, d. 859; ibid., d. 899.

86. Ibid., op. 26, d. 42, ll. 19, 24, 33, 39, 51, 57, 58, 62, 64, 68, 77, 97.

87. Ibid., op. 25, d. 633, ll. 12–13.

88. Ibid., d. 1179, ll. 17–18.

89. Ibid., d. 624, l. 4.

90. Glavnoe upravlenie po delam pechati, "Tsirkuliar No. 758" (25 January 1906), RGIA, f. 776, op. 25, d. 858, l. 1; B. Glagolin, "Akterskaia otsebiatina," *Teatr i iskusstvo*, no. 27 (2 July 1906): 425–27.

91. RGIA, f. 776, op. 25, d. 911, l. 1; A. A. Briantsev, *Vospominaniia. Stat'i. Vystupleniia. Dnevniki. Pis'ma*, comp. A. N. Gozenpud (Moscow, 1979), 51–52. For example, in Aleksandr Griboedov's *Woe from Wit* the censors deleted the lines referring to the "tsars" of the animal kingdom, "Kto chto ni govori, Khot' i zhivotnye, a vse-taki tsari!" ("Whatever you say, even if they're animals, they're still tsars!"). Had these verses not been crossed out, suggests Briantsev, "no one would have paid any attention to them."

92. A. Chargonin, "Neskol'ko slov o repertuare narodnykh teatrov," *Teatr i iskusstvo*, no. 32 (7 August 1905): 513–15; RGIA, f. 776, op. 26, d. 57, ll. 93–121.

93. RGIA, f. 776, op. 26, d. 24, l. 236.

94. Ibid., d. 22, l. 258.

95. Ibid., d. 25, l. 10.

96. Ibid., op. 25 d. 1181, ll. 2–30; op. 26, dd. 57, 58.

97. See, for example, Ivan Shcheglov, "Narodnye gulian'ia v Peterburge," *Novoe vremia*, 5 May 1898; Karpov and Okulov, *Organizatsiia narodnogo teatra*, 16; and A. Iuzhin-Sumbatov, "Lichnye zametki ob obshchikh voprosakh teatra," part 5, *Teatr i iskusstvo*, no. 40 (29 September 1902): 716.

98. "Repertuary narodnykh teatrov," xliv–xlvii, lv–lviii; *Istoriia russkogo dramaticheskogo teatra*, vol. 6, 537–40.

99. The discussion of repertoire is based on a variety of sources, including theater periodicals such as *Artist, Teatral'naia gazeta, Teatral, Teatr i iskusstvo, Rampa, Rampa i zhizn'*, and *Maski*; the archives of the censors and of the Finance Ministry; Lavrova and Popov, *Narodnyi teatr; Istoriia russkogo dramaticheskogo teatra;* and L. M. Lotman, ed., *Istoriia russkoi dramaturgii (vtoraia*

polovina XIX—nachalo XX veka) (Leningrad, 1987). There is as yet no complete survey or even list of all the Russian plays from the prerevolutionary period.

100. See Chapter 6 for a discussion of popular reception.

101. Vl. Linskii, "Zlobodnevnaia dramaturgiia," parts 1 and 2, *Teatr i iskusstvo*, no. 22 (30 May 1904): 425–27; no. 23 (6 June 1904): 440–42; P. Veinberg, "Patrioticheskie i narodnye p'esy," *Peterburgskaia gazeta*, 14 June 1904.

102. On patriotic theater during the war, see Jahn, *Patriotic Culture*, 124–49.

103. P. Iu. [Petr Iuzhhnii], "Narodnyi dom," *Teatr i iskusstvo*, no. 38 (21 September 1914): 757–58; N. Tamarin [Okulov], "Narodnyi dom," *Teatr i iskusstvo*, no. 49 (7 December 1914): 934.

104. *Teatr i iskusstvo*, no. 36 (7 September 1914); 728; no. 8 (22 February 1915): 128; no. 23 (7 June 1915): 412; no. 25 (21 June 1915): 443; no. 36 (6 September 1915): 664.

105. GTsTM, f. 1, op. 1, d. 5908, l. 1 (newspaper clipping from *Rannee utro*, March 1909).

106. On Russian adaptations of imported farces, see Impressionist (B. I. Bentovich), "Zverinye p'esy," parts 1 and 2, *Teatr i iskusstvo*, no. 3 (19 January 1897): 47–48; no. 9 (2 March 1897): 170–72.

107. Petrovskaia, *Teatr i zritel'*, 196.

108. "Sovremennoe obozrenie. S.-Peterburg. 'Rabochaia slobodka' g. Karpova," *Artist*, no. 19 (1892): 180–82; -f- [N. E. Efros], "Shakhta 'Georgii,' " *Novosti dnia*, 12 May 1902; Skorobogatov, *Zhizn' i stsena*, 77; Kanatchikov, *Radical Worker*, 103.

109. See Chapter 2.

110. "Rabochii teatr," *Pravda*, 30 May 1913; Nik. Kirilov, "Moskovskii Danilovskii Muzykal'no-dramaticheskii Kruzhok pri Obshchestve Pisatelei 'Solidarnost.' Uchreditel'noe sobranie," *Nash put'*, no. 4 (29 August 1913): 3; Kleinbort, *Ocherki rabochei intelligentsii*, vol. 2, 49.

111. M., "Iskusstvo i kul'tura," *Trudovoi Don*, 20 June 1923; A. K-na, "Teatr-Klub," *Komsomol'skaia Pravda*, 14 October 1926. On Belaia, see the entry in Marina Ledkovsky, Charlotte Rosenthal, and Mary Zirin, eds., *Dictionary of Russian Women Writers* (Westport, Conn., 1994), 72–73.

112. *Vestnik teatra*, no. 2 (1919): 4, cited in M. V. Iunisov, "Sel'skii liu-bitel'skii teatr Rossii (1917–1941 gody)" (Kandidatskaia dissertatsiia, Rossiiskii institut iskusstvoznaniia, Moscow, 1993), 56.

113. On the sexual question in Russian literature, see Laura Engelstein, *The Keys to Happiness: Sex and the Search for Modernity in Fin-de-Siècle Russia* (Ithaca, 1992), 359–420. She refers to dramatizations of the literary works on "the popular stage," but the working classes could seldom afford to visit the relatively expensive theaters that were permitted to stage such plays. They could, of course, see the film versions in the cinema.

CHAPTER FOUR

1. Rashin, *Formirovanie*, 354.

2. Victoria E. Bonnell, *Roots of Rebellion: Workers' Politics and Organizations in St. Petersburg and Moscow, 1900–1914* (Berkeley, 1983), 22; *Rabochee dvizhenie v Rossii v XIX veke: Sbornik dokumentov i materialov*, vol. 4, part 1 (1895–1917), ed. L. M. Ivanov (Moscow, 1961), viii; Rashin, *Formirovanie*, 110.

3. Rashin, *Formirovanie*, 593. Rates of literacy varied enormously even among urban workers. In St. Petersburg, for example, 73 percent of metalworkers were literate in 1897, as opposed to only 44 percent of the less skilled textile operatives. In Moscow, almost 70 percent of all male industrial workers had achieved basic literacy by 1902, compared to 19.3 percent of the female workers. Ibid., 591, 597. On the rise of literacy in prerevolutionary Russia and its sociocultural impact, see Brooks, *When Russia Learned To Read*, ch. 1.

4. Shestakov, *Rabochie na manufakture T-va "Emil' Tsindel'*,*"* 72–73.

5. On the place of the tavern in prerevolutionary Russian working-class life, see Laura Phillips, *Bolsheviks and the Bottle: Drink and Worker Culture in St. Petersburg, 1900–1929* (DeKalb, Ill., 2000), 72–84.

6. Kanatchikov, *Radical Worker*, 10.

7. Cited in Zelnik, *Labor and Society*, 292; idem, "'To the Unaccustomed Eye': Religion and Irreligion in the Experience of St. Petersburg Workers in the 1870s," *Russian History/Histoire russe* 16, nos. 2–4 (1989): 307.

8. Iartsev, "Pervye fabrichnye teatry v Rossii," 650–51; Jo Ann Ruckman, *The Moscow Business Elite: A Social and Cultural Portrait of Two Generations, 1840–1905* (DeKalb, Ill., 1984), 92–94; Thomas Owen, *Capitalism and Politics in Russia: A Social History of the Moscow Merchants, 1855–1905* (Cambridge, 1981), 24, 27–28.

9. On the temperance movement in Russia, see Herlihy, "Strategies of Sobriety," and her forthcoming book, *Alcoholic Empire*; McKean, "Taming the Green Serpent"; and Phillips, *Bolsheviks and the Bottle*, 9–19. On Britain and the United States, see Brian Harrison, *Drink and the Victorians: The Temperance Question in England, 1815–1872* (London, 1971); Barbara L. Epstein, *The Politics of Domesticity: Women, Emancipation and Temperance in Nineteenth-century America* (Middletown, Conn., 1986).

10. RGIA, f. 575, op. 11, d. 374, ll. 13–14.

11. *Rukovodiashchie ukazaniia dlia deiatel'nosti Popechitel'stv o narodnoi trezvosti, odobrennye Ministrom Finansov 28 ianvaria 1897 goda* (Chernigov, 1897), 40–41.

12. RGIA, f. 575, op. 3, d. 4303, l. 875. These figures must be used with caution, for there are some variations in the statistics given by the Finance Ministry and the guardianships in their various publications (see, for example, "O narodnom teatre," *Vestnik popechitel'stv o narodnoi trezvosti*, no. 6 [14 February 1904]: 143–45, which gives a figure of 1,342 theater performances for 1899). This may be due to differences in how theater performances were counted—

separately, or as part of the *narodnye gulian'ia*. The figures I have cited are adequate, however, for the purposes of comparison, and to give an idea of the scope of the guardianships' activities.

13. *Sbornik tsirkuliarov, rasporiazhenii i raz"iasnenii po uchrezhdeniiu popechitel'stv o narodnoi trezvosti* (St. Petersburg, 1901), 54–63; L. S. "Teatr i muzyka. Okhlazhdennoe uvlechenie," parts 1–3, *Moskovskie vedomosti*, 26, 27, 28 April 1900; *Novoe vremia*, 12 March 1900; *Vestnik finansov*, no. 12 (1902), cited in *Teatr i iskusstvo*, no. 20 (12 May 1902): 392–94.

14. Other summertime popular entertainments were held at Ligovskii Park, in St. Petersburg's Aleksandr Nevskii district (sponsored by the Zhukov factory in conjunction with the St. Petersburg Temperance Society); Preobrazhenskii Parade Ground (Red Cross Committee); Petrovskii Park (St. Petersburg City Executive Committee). Two moderately priced commercial amusement parks had summer theaters: the Zoological Garden and Kartavova's Park (formerly "Amerika"). See I. Shcheglov, "Narodnye gulian'ia v Peterburge (Zametki i vpechatleniia). Desiat' narodnykh teatrov," parts 1–3, *Novoe vremia*, 5, 13, 22 July 1898.

15. *Narod*, 9 October 1899.

16. *Vsia Moskva. Adresnaia i spravochnaia kniga na 1898 g.* (Moscow, 1898), 841; Joseph Bradley, *Muzhik and Muscovite: Urbanization in Late Imperial Russia* (Berkeley, 1985), 160 n. 15. In St. Petersburg, where the average annual wage of workers was 314 rubles in 1900, tickets in the gods of the imperial theaters ranged from ten to twenty kopeks, in the balconies from forty to ninety kopeks. Gerald D. Surh, *1905 in St. Petersburg: Labor, Society, and Revolution* (Stanford, 1989), 23–25; Frame, "Censorship and Control in the Russian Imperial Theatres," 171.

17. On the rise of cinema in prerevolutionary Russia, see Zorkaia, *Na rubezhe stoletii*; Denise Youngblood, *The Magic Mirror: Moviemaking in Russia, 1908–1918* (Madison, 1999); Yuri Tsivian, *Early Cinema in Russia and Its Cultural Reception*, trans. Alan Bodger (London, 1994). My discussion of cinema is largely drawn from these sources.

18. The novel is discussed in Engelstein, *Keys to Happiness*, 404–14; and in Zorkaia, *Na rubezhe stoletii*, 168–79. On the film, see Youngblood, *Magic Mirror*, 57–60.

19. Youngblood, *Magic Mirror*, 40.

20. On social differentiation at the cinema, see ibid., 41; Tsivian, *Early Cinema*, 26–28, 33–35.

21. Editorial, *Teatr i iskusstvo*, no. 28 (13 July 1914): 594–95.

22. On Russian cabaret, see Lawrence Senelick, "Boris Geyer and Cabaretic Playwrighting," in *Russian Theatre in the Age of Modernism*, ed. Robert Russell and Andrew Barratt (New York, 1990), 33–37; Harold B. Segal, *Turn-of-the-Century Cabaret: Paris, Barcelona, Berlin, Munich, Vienna, Cracow, Moscow, St. Petersburg, Zurich* (New York, 1987), ch. 6; Liudmilla Tikhvinskaia, *Kabare i teatry miniatiur v Rossii, 1908–1917* (Moscow, 1995).

23. The "theaters of the street" are discussed in Tikhvinskaia, *Kabare*, 195–

204. See also Fedor Sollogub, "Nechto vrode teatra," *Teatr i iskusstvo*, no. 41 (7 October 1912): 786–88; P. Solianyi, "Teatry miniatur," *Teatr i iskusstvo*, no. 42 (19 October 1914): 824–26; Boris Geier, "Teatromaniia," *Den'*, 30 December 1914.

24. K. S-v, "Nashestvie teatrov-miniatiur," *Teatr i iskusstvo*, no. 19 (10 May 1915): 324.

25. A *balagannyi ded* was a type of stand-up comedian who recited and improvised humorous verses and couplets, usually from the balcony of a *balagan* theater.

26. E. Karpov, *Desiatiletie narodnykh gulianii za Nevskoi zastavoi: Ocherk deiatel'nosti Nevskogo Obshchestva ustroistva narodnykh razvlechenii* (St. Petersburg, 1895), 3–4.

27. Ibid., 3.

28. Skorobogatov, "Ot rabochei zastavy," part 1: 136–38.

29. Ibid., 138. On organized fist combats as sport and popular entertainment in factory settlements, see Daniel R. Brower, "Labor Violence in Russia in the Late Nineteenth Century," *Slavic Review* 41 (Fall 1982): 425–27. They remain popular in many parts of Russia today.

30. "Narodnye razvlecheniia," *Birzhevye vedomosti*, 19 January 1898; Zelnik, "'To the Unaccustomed Eye,' " 306–8.

31. See Chapter 1.

32. Karpov, *Desiatiletie narodnykh gulianii*, 4, 14; Popov, "Ob organizatsii razvlechenii dlia rabochikh," 29.

33. Shcheglov, *Narod i teatr*, 5–6; Karpov, *Desiatiletie narodnykh gulianii*, 5–6.

34. Cited in Karpov, *Desiatiletie narodnykh gulianii*, 7.

35. Popov, "Ob organizatsii razvlechenii," 31; P. Golubev, "Narodnye doma—dvortsy," *Russkoe bogatstvo*, no. 12, (1901), sec. 2: 5.

36. *Spisok nagrad prisuzhdennykh na Vserossiiskoi Sel'skoi-Khoziastevennoi vystavke v Moskve, 1895 g., po otdelu komiteta gramotnosti* (Moscow, 1895), 12.

37. Karpov, *Desiatiletie narodnykh gulianii*, 8; Lavrova and Popov, *Narodnyi teatr*, xliii.

38. Karpov, "Iz avtobiografii," 58–59.

39. A. A. Brianskii, "Karpov i teatr dlia rabochikh," unpublished manuscript, 1926, OR RNB, f. 106, d. 23, l. 3; Skorobogatov, "Ot rabochei zastavy," part 2: 173–74.

40. Skorobogatov, *Zhizn' i stsena*, 91–92; Briantsev, *Vospominaniia*, 47–49; Zel'tser, *Briantsev*, 53; *Teatr i iskusstvo*, no. 23 (6 June 1899): 425; Nevskoe obshchestvo ustroistva narodnykh razvlechenii, *Otchet komiteta za 1903–1904 god* (St. Petersburg, 1905), 9–12.

41. *Teatr i iskusstvo*, no. 43 (25 October 1898): 767; no. 47 (22 November 1898): 847.

42. Interview with Karpov in Iurii Beliaev, "Teatr budushchego," *Rossiia*, 1 May 1899. Karpov states that this assessment is based on audience surveys. To be sure, it could reflect his own preferences as to what the people should like, or

even the respondents' attempts to give the "right" answers. Still, I would argue that these were probably genuine preferences, for these three plays are still widely considered among the most entertaining products of Russian drama. That does not mean, however, that audiences failed to respond well to the more lowbrow fare that also appeared on the stage.

43. *Teatr i iskusstvo*, no. 29 (19 July 1909): 496

44. Nikolai Mikhailovskii, "Literatura i zhizn'," *Russkoe bogatstvo*, no. 6 (1895), sec. 2: 60; "Teatr i muzyka," *Moskovskie vedomosti*, 28 March 1895; Briantsev, *Vospominaniia*, 47; Skorobogatov, "Ot rabochei zastavy," part 2: 173.

45. Popov, "Ob organizatsii razvlechenii," 34; *Komik*, no. 3 (17 August 1906): 7.

46. Brianskii, "Karpov i teatr dlia rabochikh," l. 6. Excerpts from the survey were published by Nikolai Mikhailovskii in "Literatura i zhizn'," and are discussed in Chapter Six.

47. *Teatr i iskusstvo*, no. 43 (25 October 1898): 767; no. 47 (22 November 1898): 847.

48. Shcheglov, *Narod i teatr*, 7.

49. Ibid., 7–17.

50. Shcheglov, "Narodnye gulian'ia v Peterburge," *Novoe vremia*, 5 July 1898.

51. Shcheglov, *Narod i teatr*, 23.

52. "Narodnyi teatr na Vasil'evskom ostrove," *Syn otechestva*, 10 February 1887. See also "V teatre dlia rabochikh," *Novosti i Birzhevaia gazeta*, 8 February 1887; "Peterburg," *Teatr i zhizn'*, 9 February 1887.

53. Popov, "Ob organizatsii razvlechenii," 26–29; *Teatral*, no. 18 (May 1895): 85; *Novosti i Birzhevaia gazeta*, 19 February, 1902; -skii, "K 25-letiu pervogo narodnogo teatra v Peterburge," *Teatr i iskusstvo*, no. 6 (5 February 1912): 130–31; Petrovskaia and Somina, *Teatral'nyi Peterburg*, 252–59.

54. "K voprosu o repertuare narodnykh teatrov," *Birzhevye vedomosti*, 23 February 1898.

55. Shcheglov, *Narod i teatr*, 27.

56. N. Timkovskii and N. Popov, "Pervaia vystavka narodnogo teatra: Obzor vystavki," in Lavrova and Popov, *Narodnyi teatr*, 28–29.

57. Popov, "Ob organizatsii razvlechenii," 25–26.

58. *Ligovskii sad dlia rabochikh: Otchet za pervyi god (1898)* (St. Petersburg, 1899), 2.

59. Ibid., 3–7; "Doma dlia rabochikh S.-Peterburga," *Novoe vremia*, 19 April 1898. There were five readings on geography, two of literature, one for children, and one lecture on the dangers of drink.

60. *Ligovskii sad*, 9–26; Ivan Shcheglov, "*Zhenit'ba* Gogolia u Rasteriaevoi bashni," *Novoe vremia*, 7 July 1898; *Teatr i iskusstvo*, no. 42 (18 October 1898): 743.

61. *Ligovskii sad*, 27–28. The Zhukov factory intended to open a consumers' society for its employees and made plans to build some apartments for workers

in the area with assistance from the St. Petersburg Temperance Society, but I have not been able to determine whether any of the projects were realized.

62. See Allan K. Wildman, *The Making of a Workers' Revolution: Russian Social Democracy, 1891–1903* (Chicago, 1967), ch. 3; Gerald D. Surh, *1905 in St. Petersburg: Labor, Society, and Revolution* (Stanford, 1989), 51–98.

63. *Teatr i iskusstvo,* no. 49 (6 December 1898): 899–900.

64. Skorobogatov, "Ot rabochei zastavy," part 2: 163.

65. "Narodnyi Dom Nobelia," *Vestnik popechitel'stv o narodnoi trezvosti,* no. 19 (12 May 1905): 406–8.

66. Old Gentleman (A. V. Amfiteatrov), "Moskva. Tipy i kartinki," *Novoe vremia,* 29 April 1895; Popov, "Ob organizatsii razvlechenii," 23–24.

67. Iartsev, "Pervye fabrichnye teatry," 646; *Teatr i iskusstvo,* no. 9 (2 March 1897): 162; "Teatr," *Severnyi vestnik,* no. 6 (June 1895), sec. 2: 64; Karpov and Okulov, *Organizatsiia narodnogo teatra i poleznykh razvlechenii dlia naroda,* 5.

68. *Prokhorovskaia Trekhgornaia manufactura v Moskve. 1799–1899. Istoriko-statisticheskii ocherk* (Moscow, 1900), 64; *Teatral,* no. 7 (February 1895): 107–8; *Teatr i iskusstvo,* no. 51 (19 December 1899): 928–29; *Artist,* no. 37 (May 1894): 235.

69. *Teatral,* no. 4 (January 1895); A. Gorev, "Provintsial'naia pechat'," *Severnyi vestnik,* no. 6 (1896), sec. 2: 304; *Teatral,* no. 17 (May 1895): 53; GARF, f. 7952, op. 3, d. 263, l. 246; ibid., f. 63 (1903), d. 31, ch. 2, l. 79; RGIA, f. 776, op. 25, d. 624, ll. 57, 76, 113.

70. Gorev, "Provintsial'naia pechat'," 304.

71. GTsTM, f. 324, d. 168118; ibid., d. 136928.

72. S. M. Popov, "Narodnye spektakli na Ivanovskoi fabrike (Zvenigorodskogo uezda), 1890–1916," unpublished manuscript, 1927, GTsTM, f. 532, d. 145962.

73. According to a Sunday program from the Moscow-Kursk railway workshops in November 1901, for example, a ticket to the evening's performance of a light comedy entitled the bearer to a discounted admission to the dance floor, which remained open until 3:00 AM. RGIA, f. 776, op. 25, d. 624, l. 55.

74. N. Laman, "Fabrichnyi teatr v Moskve," *Khudozhestvennaia samodeiatel'nost',* no. 1 (1963): 30–33; *Russkie vedomosti,* 25 April 1904; GARF, f. 7952, op. 3, d. 573, ll. 137–40; *Ranee utro,* 12 April 1909; *Rampa i zhizn',* no. 2 (15) (12 April 1909): 242.

75. *Teatr i iskusstvo,* no. 29 (18 April 1899): 504.

76. TsIAgM, f. 483, op. 3, d. 1584, ll. 18, 41, 45, 331, 383, 385, 398, 402; d. 1623, ll. 198, 201, 567, 574, 579, 584–89, 596.

77. RGALI, f. 2097, op. 2, d. 789.

78. *Russkie vedomosti,* 15 February 1905.

79. Edith W. Clowes, "Merchants on Stage and in Life: Theatricality and Public Consciousness," in *Merchant Moscow: Images of Russia's Vanished Bourgeoisie,* ed. James L. West and Iurii A. Petrov (Princeton, 1998), 155. See also Karen Pennar, "Daily Life Among the Morozovs," in *Merchant Moscow,*

79–80, on the aristocratic attributes of the wealthy middle-class lifestyle. The turn-of-the-century rage for amateur theatricals among the Russian middle classes is described in M. V. Iunisov, "'Lishnii' teatr: o liubiteliakh i ikh 'gubiteliakh,'" in *Razvlekatel'naia kul'tura Rossii XVIII–XIX vv. Ocherki istorii i teorii*, ed. E. V. Dukov (St. Petersburg, 2000), 372–93.

80. See Priscilla Roosevelt, "Emerald Thrones and Living Statues: Theater and Theatricality on the Russian Estate," *The Russian Review* 50, no. 1 (1991): 1–13; and Laurence Senelick, "The Erotic Bondage of Serf Theatre," *The Russian Review* 50, no. 1 (1991): 24–34.

81. B. I. Martynov, "V bor'be s guzhonovskoi kul'turoi," unpublished manuscript (n.d.), GARF, f. 7952, op. 3, d. 300, ll. 17–18.

82. A. P. Chekhov, "Sluchai iz praktiki," in *Sobranie sochinenii i pisem. Sochineniia*, vol. 10 (Moscow, 1977), 74.

83. "Teatr dlia fabrichnykh," *Novosti dnia*, 23 April 1896.

84. A. I. Chuprov, "Ob ekonomicheskom znachenii obrazovatel'nykh i vospitatel'nykh uchrezhdenii dlia rabochego klassa," in *Obrazovatel'no-vospitatel'nye uchrezhdeniia dlia rabochikh i organizatsiia obshchedostupnykh razvlechenii v Moskve* (Moscow, 1898), 35. See also Nikolai Timkovskii's report to the Second Congress of Russian Activists in Technical and Professional Education, "Znachenie razvlechenii dlia uchashchikhsia i rabochikh," *Teatral*, no. 64 (April 1896): 26–36; and *Obshcheobrazovatel'no-vospitatel'nye uchrezhdeniia dlia rabochikh i organizatsiia obshchedostupnykh razvlechenii v Moskve* (Moscow, 1898), 35.

85. F. P. Pavlov, "Ten Years of Experience (Excerpts from Reminiscences, Impressions, and Observations of Factory Life)," in *The Russian Worker: Life and Labor Under the Tsarist Regime*, ed. and trans. Victoria E. Bonnell (Berkeley, 1983), 148–49.

86. Shcheglov, *Teatr i narod*, 25.

87. Cited in Mikhailovskii, "Literatura i zhizn'," 58.

88. V. Prokof'ev, "Narodnyi dom Imperatora Nikolaia II," *Novoe vremia*, 13 December 1900; *The Temperance Committee of St. Petersburg, 1899–1914* (St. Petersburg, 1914), 5–9.

89. V. Charnoluskii, "Narodnye doma v Rossii po issledovaniiu za 1913 god (na 1 ianvaria 1914 g.)," in *Narodnyi dom* (Petrograd, 1918), 378. All of the people's houses run by cooperatives were in rural areas. Of the 134 urban people's houses, 101 were operated by the temperance guardianships. These figures are from a survey conducted at the expense of Countess Sofiia Panina in 1913 and include only those people's houses that responded to the survey.

90. For a survey of European movements to construct people's houses and palaces, see Mario Scascighini, *La maison du peuple: le temps d'un édifice de classe* (Lausanne, 1991).

91. Bailey, *Leisure and Class in Victorian Britain*, 57–59, 108, 163; David Bradby and John McCormick, eds., *People's Theatre* (London, 1978), 34–35; E. King, *The People's Palace and Glasgow Green* (Glasgow, 1985).

92. Cecil W. Davies, *Theatre for the People: The Story of the Volksbühne* (Austin, Tex., 1977), 71.

93. Maurice Pottecher, *Le théâtre du peuple: Renaissance et destinée du théatre populaire* (Paris, 1899); Helen Whitman Machan, "The Popular-Theater Movement in France: Romain Rolland and the Revue d'Art Dramatique" (Ph.D. dissertation, University of Illinois, 1950); David J. Fisher, "The Origins of the French Popular Theater," *Journal of Contemporary History* 12, no. 3 (July 1977): 461–97; idem, *Romain Rolland.*

94. From 1899 through 1909, for example, the St. Petersburg Guardianship spent 5,695,029 rubles on theater performances (excluding expenditures on *narodnye gulian'ia*), accounting for 67 percent of the total sum spent on theater by all of the temperance guardianships in the empire. The Moscow Guardianship spent the next largest amount, 798,723 rubles, or just over 9 percent of the total. RGIA, f. 575, op. 3, d. 4303, ll. 867, 869.

95. *The Temperance Committee of St. Petersburg,* 7–8, 29. There is a slight discrepancy in the attendance figures cited by the committee in its report. On p. 8, a figure of 74,597,214 is given, while on p. 29 the figure is 73,972,078.

96. Ibid., 8–11, 14, 30.

97. On the Ligovskii theater, see S. V. Panina, "Na peterburgskoi okraine," part 1, *Novyi zhurnal*, no. 48 (1957): 189–93; *Zapiski Peredvizhnogo-obshche-dostupnogo teatra*, no. 1 (March 1914); Panina and Gaideburov, "Iskusstvo v narodnoi auditorii," 150–73 (the attendance figures I give above are based on a table on p. 170); and Thurston, "The Impact of Russian Popular Theatre," 264–65 (on p. 264, Thurston gives a slightly higher attendance figure of 145,605).

98. Iu. Engel', "Pervye shagi," *Russkie vedomosti*, 8 September 1901.

99. See *Otchety Moskovskogo stolichnogo popechitel'stva o narodnoi trezvosti* (Moscow, 1903–15).

100. I. Ignatov, "Moskovskii gorodskoi narodnyi dom," *Russkie vedomosti*, 12 June 1905; Ivan Shcheglov, "Narodnyi teatr v Moskve," *Slovo*, 3 June 1909; S. M., "V narodnom dome," *Golos Moskvy*, 12 November 1909; *Moskovskii listok*, 12 January 1913; Zavsegdatai, "Iz Moskvy," *Teatr i iskusstvo*, no. 26 (28 June 1915): 463.

101. *Kratkii ocherk deiatel'nosti S.-Peterburgskogo gorodskogo popechitel'stva o narodnoi trezvosti, 1898–1908* (St. Petersburg, 1908), 8, 10.

102. Kuznetsov, *Russkie narodnye gulian'ia*, 99–100; Konechnyi, "Peterburgskie narodnye gulian'ia," 43; *Teatr i iskusstvo*, no. 18 (2 May 1899): 342.

103. *Teatr i iskusstvo*, no. 18 (2 May 1899): 342.

104. Ibid., no. 31 (1 August 1899): 536.

105. "Shirokaia maslenitsa (Progulka po narodnym gulian'iam). Na Semenovskom platsu," *Peterburgskii listok*, 14 February 1900.

106. N. K. Mikhailovskii, *Otkliki*, vol. 1 (St. Petersburg, 1904), 412.

107. On middle-class perceptions of the threat to public order posed by hooliganism at the turn of the century, see Joan Neuberger, *Hooliganism: Crime, Culture, and Power in St. Petersburg, 1900–1914* (Berkeley, 1993).

According to a statistical analysis by Boris Mironov, crime rates were rising in Russia throughout the last third of the nineteenth century, an increase he attributes to rapid urbanization and industrialization. B. N. Mironov, "Prestupnost' v Rossii v XIX–nachale XX veka," *Otechestvennaia istoriia*, no. 1 (January–February 1998): 24–42.

108. V. Avseenko, "Prazdnichnaia trezvost'," *Peterburgskaia gazeta*, 7 April 1898.

109. Ivan Shcheglov, "Narodnye gulian'ia v Moskve," *Torgovo-Promyshlennaia gazeta*, 13 March 1902.

110. "Khronika Moskovskogo gorodskogo upravleniia. Ob uprazdnenii narodnykh gulianii na Devich'em pole," *Izvestiia Moskovskoi gorodskoi dumy*, otdel obshchii, nos. 6–7 (June–July 1911): 40–42

111. *Moskovskii listok*, 25 May 1911.

112. On the carnival's influence on Russian modernism, see J. Douglas Clayton, *Pierrot in Petrograd: The Commedia dell'Arte/Balagan in Twentieth-Century Russian Theatre and Drama* (Montreal, 1993); and Kelly, *Petrushka*, 140–78.

113. *Obshchestvo "Staryi Peterburg." 1921–1923* (Petrograd, 1923).

114. *The Temperance Committee of St. Petersburg*, 6–7.

115. Kuznetsov, *Russkie narodnye gulian'ia*, 146–48.

116. Ibid., 148–49.

117. Ibid., 148, 154.

118. Ibid., 156–57; *Teatr i iskusstvo*, no. 2 (10 January 1910): 42.

119. Kuznetsov, *Russkie narodnye gulian'ia*, 154–55.

120. Ibid., 142–44; Shcheglov, "'Bol'shoi bochenok' ili Son na iavu (Iz zapisnoi knizhki)," *Slovo*, 18 July 1908.

121. *Teatr i iskusstvo*, no. 3 (16 January 1911): 56.

122. *Teatr i iskusstvo*, no. 34 (25 March 1913): 658; Kuznetsov, *Russkie narodnye gulian'ia*, 144–46.

123. G. Fomin, "O narodnykh teatrakh," *Vestnik popechitel'stv o narodnoi trezvosti*, no. 30 (31 July 1904): 671.

124. "Malen'kaia khronika," *Teatr i iskusstvo*, no. 17 (26 April 1915): 295.

125. In 1908 the Gruzinskii People's House was replaced by the Alekseevskii People's House, which was located in the same district on Second Brestskaia Street.

126. *Otchet Moskovskogo stolichnogo popechitel'stva o narodnoi trezvosti za 1902 god* (Moscow, 1903), 5–7.

127. *Otchet Moskovskogo stolichnogo popechitel'stva o narodnoi trezvosti za 1904 god* (Moscow, 1905), 145; newspaper clippings, GTsTM, f. 144, d. 959, ll. 47–56; *Kratkii obzor deiatel'nosti Moskovskogo stolichnogo popechitel'stva o narodnoi trezvosti za 10 let* (Moscow, 1911), 16.

128. *Kratkii obzor deiatel'nosti Moskovskogo stolichnogo popechitel'stva*, 125; *Otchet Moskovskogo stolichnogo popechitel'stva o narodnoi trezvosti za 1905 god* (Moscow, 1906), 188.

129. Az., "Opera narodnogo doma," *Peterburgskii dnevnik teatrala*, 2 May 1904.

130. *Teatr i iskusstvo*, no. 26 (26 June 1911): 501.

131. Ivan Shcheglov, "Zagadki peterburgskogo narodnogo teatra," *Novoe vremia*, 6 March 1903. This article was also published in idem, *Narod i teatr*, 195–209.

132. *Teatr i iskusstvo*, no. 2 (13 January 1908): 25.

133. See, for example, G. Fomin, "O razvlecheniiakh, ustraivaemykh dlia naroda," *Vestnik popechitel'stv o narodnoi trezvosti*, no. 29 (24 July 1904): 651–52.

134. Spiridon Bol'shakov, "O narodnom teatre Tavricheskogo sada," *Russkii trud*, 18 July 1898.

135. Staryi, "V zabotakh o men'shem brate," *Peterburgskaia gazeta*, 4 July 1898.

136. Rabochii za rabochikh (I. V. Babushkin), "V zashchitu ivanovo-voznesenskikh rabochikh," Supplement to *Iskra*, no. 9 (October 1901), cited in Khaichenko, *Russkii narodnyi teatr*, 91.

137. Shcheglov, "Narodnye gulian'ia v Peterburge (Zametki i vpechatleniia)," *Novoe vremia*, 5 July 1898; idem, *Narod i teatr*, 16; Kanatchikov, *Radical Worker*, 71; Barbara Engel, *Between the Fields and the City: Women, Work, and Family in Russia, 1861–1914* (Cambridge, 1994), 155

138. See, for example, Engel, 153–55; Kanatchikov, *Radical Worker*, 20–21, 59; D. Zasosov and V. Pyzin, "Vospominaniia. Peshkom po staromu Peterburgu. Kakaia smes' odezhd i lits!," *Neva*, no. 5 (May 1987): 190–92. On the spread of new clothing fashions to villages at the turn of the century, see *The Village of Viriatino: An Ethnographic Study of a Russian Village from Before the Revolution to the Present* , ed. and trans. Sula Benet (New York, 1970), 83–88.

139. See Christine Ruane, "Clothes Shopping in Imperial Russia: The Development of a Consumer Culture," *Journal of Social History* 28, no. 4 (1995): 765–82.

140. T. Ardov, "Narod razvlekaetsia," *Rossiia*, 27 September 1900.

141. Hoover Institution on War, Revolution, and Peace, Okhrana Archive, index XIIIc (2), folder 9, "Svedeniia o brozhenii sredi studentov vysshikh uchebnykh zavedenii imperii za vremia s 6 po 13 fevralia 1902 g."

142. Ibid., folder 6B, Weekly Intelligence Report no. 82 (22 April 1904), item 17. Less than three weeks later, a worker was arrested for whistling his disapproval of autocracy while the tsarist anthem was being played before and after a performance at the St. Petersburg People's House. Ibid., folder 4A, Weekly Intelligence Report no. 85 (13 May 1904), item 9.

143. Ibid., folder 4B, Weekly Intelligence Report no. 107 (14 October 1904), item 19.

144. RGIA, f. 575, op. 575, d. 4196, l. 63.

145. The Zubatov societies were legal workers' organizations set up in 1901 by the Moscow Okhrana chief, Sergei Zubatov, in an effort to divert the labor movement away from political issues by allowing workers to discuss their eco-

nomic grievances. They operated until 1905 and in some cases were infiltrated by Social Democratic organizers. Bogdanov-Evdokimov founded the Moscow union of tobacco workers in 1905 and joined the Social Democratic party, serving as a delegate to the fourth party congress in 1906. See Jeremiah Schneiderman, *Sergei Zubatov and Revolutionary Marxism: The Struggle for the Working Class in Tsarist Russia* (Ithaca, 1976). On F. Bogdanov-Evdokimov, see Bonnell, *Roots of Rebellion*, 128 n. 89.

146. F. Bogdanov-Evdokimov, "Zubatovshchina v Moskve (Vospominaniia rabochego uchastnika)," GARF, f. 6889, op. 1, d. 602, l. 13. This memoir was published under the same title in *Vestnik truda*, no. 9 (November 1923).

147. Hoover Institution on War, Revolution and Peace, Okhrana Archive, index XIIIc (2), folder 6B, Weekly Intelligence Report no. 147 (21 July 1905), item 21.

148. On outbreaks of violence by crowds during 1905, see Laura Engelstein, *Moscow, 1905: Working-Class Organization and Political Conflict* (Stanford, 1982), 123–49, 197–221; Neuberger, *Hooliganism*, ch. 2.

149. *Teatr i iskusstvo*, no. 3 (16 January 1905): 42.

150. *Teatr i iskusstvo*, nos. 42–43 (23 October 1905): 651; "Khronika narodnykh razvlechenii," *Vestnik popechitel'stv o narodnoi trezvosti*, no. 35 (3 September 1905): 623–24.

151. Frame, *The St. Petersburg Imperial Theaters*, 121–28; Engelstein, *Moscow, 1905*, 197–98; E. A. Sartseva, "Kafeshantan Sharlia Omona," in Dukov, *Razvlekatel'naia kul'tura Rossii*, 366–69; Serpoletti, "Moskovskie uveselitel'nye sady," ll. 45–48, 65–66; Shcheglov, *Narod i teatr*, 357. The Aquarium's popularity as a meeting place was probably due to its central location, near the corner of Tver'skaia Street and the Sadovoe ring boulevard, approximately halfway between the working-class Presnia district and the Kremlin.

152. Skromnyi, "K vremenam," *Teatr i iskusstvo*, no. 4 (22 January 1905): 52–54; A. Ardov, "O narodnom teatre," *Rampa i zhizn'*, no. 26 (1909): 641.

153. D. Boretskii, "Po povodu spektaklei teatrov popechitel'stva narodnoi trezvosti," *Novoe vremia*, 29 July 1899.

154. "Okolo teatra," *Birzhevye vedomosti*, eve. ed., 23 May 1905; *Teatr i iskusstvo*, no. 15 (11 April 1899): 295.

155. Shcheglov, "Zagadki."

156. See Chapter 2.

157. "Po povodu spektaklei popechitel'stva," *Novoe vremia*, 28 June 1899; Peterburgskii flaner, "'Amury i zefiry' popechitel'stva o narodnoi trezvosti," *Rossiia*, 4 February 1900; S. Smirnova, "V zashchitu zefirov i amurov (Pis'mo v redaktsiiu)," *Rossiia*, 8 February 1900; Shcheglov, "Zagadki"; idem, "Otchet o letnei poezdke v 1903 godu dlia obozreniia provintsial'nykh narodnykh teatrov," in *Narod i teatr*, 362.

158. *Rus'*, 21 March 1905.

159. "Bliz narodnogo doma," *S.-Peterburgskie vedomosti*, 14 April 1905.

160. *Rus'*, 8 May 1905. On prostitution at the People's House and its garden, see also Neizvestnyi, "Miniatury," *Moskovskie vedomosti*, 19 June 1915.

161. Den', "Opiat' narodnye doma," *Deiatel'* (Kazan), no. 19 (October 1905): 448.

162. "O meropriiatiiakh k iskoreneniiu ulichnykh besporiadkov v S.-Peterburge," TsGIA SPb, f. 569, op. 17, d. 1662, l. 5. I am indebted to Gerald D. Surh for sharing this report with me.

163. See Neuberger, *Hooliganism*, ch. 2; Engelstein, *The Keys to Happiness*, ch. 7.

164. *Birzhevye vedomosti*, 8 November 1906; RGIA, f. 575, op. 3, d. 4162, l. 184; D. N. Borodin, "Popechitel'stva o narodnoi trezvosti," in *Vserossiiskii s"ezd po bor'be s pianstvom*, vol. 2 (St. Petersburg, 1909), 905; A. F. Koni, "Popechenie o narodnoi trezvosti," *Vestnik Evropy*, no. 6 (1908): 773–95; RGIA, f. 575, op. 3, d. 4286, l. 132; ibid., d. 4111, l. 215; op. 3, d. 4303, ll. 774–75; "Sv. sinod o narodnom teatre," *Teatr i iskusstvo*, no. 21 (26 May 1913): 447–48.

165. *Teatr i iskusstvo*, no. 21 (27 May 1907): 339; no. 50 (16 December 1907): 832 ; no. 2 (13 January 1908): 25; no. 21 (26 May 1913): 447; RGIA, f. 575, op. 11, d. 194, ll. 1–10.

166. Shcheglov, "Otchet o letnei poezdke," in *Narod i teatr*, 348.

167. Ibid., 347.

168. Ibid., 349–50. The citation is on p. 349. The bootmaker was mispronouncing the word "revolver" (*revol'ver*).

169. Ibid., 350.

170. E. Kabo, "Rabochaia kul'tura i rabochii byt," *Prizyv*, no. 3 (March 1925): 60. The surveys give some indication of prerevolutionary tastes, for many of the workers questioned had not been to the theater since the revolution.

171. Shcheglov, "Otchet o letnei poezdke," 349, 354.

172. The Ligovskii People's House staged its first opera, *Boris Godunov*, in 1908, and operas were performed at the Putilov factory during World War I. *Teatr i iskusstvo*, no. 7 (17 February 1908): 128; no. 41 (9 September 1915): 822. The expense involved was prohibitive, however, for most people's theaters.

CHAPTER FIVE

1. On the ideological origins of Proletkult, see Zenovia Sochor, *Revolution and Culture: The Bogdanov-Lenin Controversy* (Ithaca, 1988), 3–77. Lynn Mally briefly discusses the influence of the workers' cultural and educational movement on the origins of Proletkult in *Culture of the Future: The Proletkult Movement in Revolutionary Russia* (Berkeley, 1990), 14–17.

2. John Biggart, "Anti-Leninist Bolshevism: The Forward Group of the RSDRP," *Canadian Slavonic Papers* 23 (June 1981): 146–50.

3. See, for example, the Menshevik A. Potresov's critique of efforts to develop a proletarian culture under capitalism, "O literature bez zhizni i o zhizni bez literatury: Tragediia proletarskoi literatury," *Nasha zaria*, no. 6 (1913): 65–75, which provoked an extensive debate in 1913 and 1914. Potresov's arguments

and the responses they elicited in Social Democratic circles are discussed in V. L. L'vov-Rogachevskii, *Ocherki proletarskoi literatury* (Moscow, 1927), 47–51.

4. A. K., "O rabochem teatre," *Rabochii*, 23 June 1914.

5. A. P-v., "Rabochii teatr v Peterburge," *Pravda*, 24 June 1912. The repertoire announced for the theater's first season included Chekhov's *Uncle Vanya*, Gorky's *The Lower Depths* and *Philistines*, Gogol's *The Government Inspector*, and four works by Ostrovsky. The Russian adjective *ideinyi* and its noun form *ideinost'*, which are derived from word "idea" (*ideia*), are difficult to render in English. At the turn of the century, literary critics sometimes referred to the later plays of Henrik Ibsen as *ideinye p'esy*, or plays about ideas. In Social Democratic circles, however, the words *ideinye* and *ideinost'* were commonly used to characterize something as having an ideological perspective—thus, *ne khvataet ideinosti* meant that an (implicitly correct) ideological coloration was lacking. In this context, to describe plays as *ideinye* was to make a statement about the value of their ideological content.

6. "Rabochii teatr," *Pravda*, 30 May 1913.

7. L. Kurprianova, "Rabochii Peterburg," in *S. Peterburg i ego zhizn'* (St. Petersburg, 1914), 214.

8. The socialist press deplored holiday drunkenness as much as the industrialists did, but for very different reasons. *Pravda*, for example, claimed in 1912 that workers who drank excessively on holidays were more likely to work for low wages, to tolerate abuse from their bosses, and to engage in strikebreaking. A. P., "Alkogolizm i rabochii klass," *Pravda*, 5 May 1912.

9. Kanatchikov, *Radical Worker*, 93. Kanatchikov also notes his "surprise and admiration" upon meeting women workers "who argued logically and debated just like the rest of us." The attitudes of male workers in the labor movement toward female workers are discussed in Rose L. Glickman, *Russian Factory Women: Workplace and Society, 1880–1914* (Berkeley, 1984), 198–208, 215–18.

10. Kanatchikov, *Radical Worker*, 102.

11. Although the term "conscious worker" was often used, especially within the trade union and Social Democratic movements, to imply adherence to radical or socialist political views, it was also used in a broader sense to refer simply to "worker-intellectuals," who might well be more moderate in their politics.

12. Reginald E. Zelnik, "Russian Bebels: An Introduction to the Memoirs of Semen Kanatchikov and Matvei Fisher," part 2, *The Russian Review* 35, no. 4 (October 1976): 422–43; Wildman, *The Making of a Workers' Revolution*, 89–103, 127–28, 194–95; Tim McDaniel, *Autocracy, Capitalism, and Revolution in Russia* (Berkeley, 1988), 208–12.

13. Skorobogatov, *Zhizn' i stsena*, 50.

14. It is somewhat curious that Skorobogatov includes recent works by Chekhov and Gorky under the rubric of "great classics." This may be because he is writing some sixty years after the fact, when these plays (with the possible exception of *Philistines*) had indeed become established as "classics" in the

Soviet canon. Perhaps he is simply underlining the fact that the workers were staging not just any contemporary plays but plays by the two writers who at the time were widely considered to be Russia's foremost dramatists.

15. Skorobogatov, *Zhizn' i stsena*, 50–54.

16. *Artist*, no. 37 (May 1894): 235; *Teatr i iskusstvo*, no. 51 (December 19, 1899): 928–29; RGIA, f. 776, op. 25, d. 624, l. 76.

17. Karpov, "Iz avtobiografii," 59.

18. Mark D. Steinberg, *Moral Communities: The Culture of Class Relations in the Russian Printing Industry, 1867–1907* (Berkeley, 1992), 100.

19. N. Laman, "Fabrichnyi teatr v Moskve," *Khudozhestvennaia samodeiatel'nost'*, no. 1 (1963): 30–33; GARF, f. 7952, op. 3, d. 573, ll. 137–40.

20. GARF, f. 7952, op. 3, d. 573, ll. 140, 144.

21. Laman, "Fabrichnyi teatr," 33.

22. On workers' organizations before 1905, see Bonnell, *Roots of Rebellion*, 73–103.

23. Ibid., 210–21; Robert B. McKean, *St. Petersburg Between the Revolutions: Workers and Revolutionaries, June 1907–February 1917* (New Haven, 1990), 78–79; I. V. Levin, "Rabochie kluby v Peterburge (1907–1914 gg.)," part 1, in *Materialy po istorii professional'nogo dvizheniia v Rossii*, vol. 3 (Moscow, 1925), 99–107.

24. I. M. Pushkareva, *Rabochee dvizhenie v Rossii v period reaktsii, 1907–1910 gg.* (Moscow, 1989), 90.

25. Bonnell, *Roots of Rebellion*, 324.

26. S. I. Kanatchikov, "Kul'turno-prosvetitel'naia deiatel'nost'," *Vozrozhdenie*, nos. 5–6 (April 1909): 51.

27. Ibid., 51–52; Bonnell, *Roots of Rebellion*, 261–62.

28. M. Leont'ev, "Obshchestva samoobrazovaniia v 1910 g.," *Nash put'*, no. 12 (14 January 1911): 10–11.

29. Batrak, "Uchen'e-svet," *Nash put'*, no. 9 (7 November 1910): 8.

30. Levin, "Rabochie kluby," part 2, in *Materialy po istorii professional'nogo dvizheniia*, vol. 4 (Moscow, 1925): 217.

31. "Zaiavlenie Porokhovskogo Literaturno-Dramaticheskogo Kruzhka," *TPVSDNT*, 133. The report is referring to the circle's conclusions based on seven years of experience organizing theater performances since 1908.

32. Levin, "Rabochie kluby," part 2, 217.

33. Voronov, *Put' k stsene*, 61–62.

34. Ibid., 108; A. M. Filippov, "Revoliutsionnoe gnezdo," *Sud idet*, no. 4(68) (February 1927): 193–94; Boris Roslavlev, "Rabochii teatr: Iz vospominanii o zhizni rabochikh teatral'n. kruzhkov do revoliutsii," *Rabochii teatr*, no. 25 (23 June 1925): 4.

35. Voronov, *Put' k stsene*, 69.

36. T. Sapronov, *Iz istorii rabochego dvizheniia (po lichnym vospominaniiam)* (Moscow, 1925), 13–14, 16, 19–24, 50–51, 59; G. A. Arutiunov, *Rabochee dvizhenie v Rossii v period novogo revoliutsionnogo pod"ema, 1910–1914 gg.* (Moscow, 1975), 102–5.

37. V. L., "O kul'turno-prosvetitel'noi deiatel'nosti," *Nadezhda*, no. 1 (31 July 1908): 2. Cited in Bonnell, *Roots of Rebellion*, 333.

38. Kanatchikov, "Kul'turno-prosvetitel'naia deiatel'nost'," 55.

39. Bonnell, *Roots of Rebellion*, 333–34.

40. *Pravda* and its successors were published from April 1912 until July 1914. A Menshevik daily, *Luch*, was published under various titles from September 1912 to January 1914. Both papers focused on practical issues of general interest and succeeded in attracting a relatively large working-class readership that was not limited to members of the two fractions. *Pravda* had a circulation of 30,000–60,000; the *Luch* circulation fluctuated between 5,000 and 17,000. (McKean, *St. Petersburg*, 149–50). However, as McKean has convincingly argued (p. 152), "the bedrock for the socialist press was furnished by the 'worker-intellectual'—the small stratum of skilled male operatives in both factory and artisanal establishments who sought to widen their mental horizons beyond the level of minimum literacy and popular fiction." This is the same stratum that was most active in the workers' theater movement.

41. A. P-v., "Rabochii teatr v Peterburge."

42. "Teatr," *Pravda*, 13 November 1912; "Spektakl' rabochikh," *Pravda*, 3 April 1913.

43. Rabochii B. I-v., "Rabochii spektakl'," *Pravda*, 21 September 1912; Kleinbort, "Rabochaia intelligentsiia i iskusstvo," 222–23; Khaichenko, *Russkii narodnyi teatr*, 212.

44. N. Sh., "Dramaticheskie kruzhki rabochikh," *Pravda*, 28 October 1912.

45. Kleinbort, *Ocherki rabochei intelligentsii*, 48–49.

46. Ibid., 49–50; N. Sh., "Dramaticheskie kruzhki rabochikh"; "Rabochie spektakli," *Pravda*, 19 January 1913. The Golitsyno theater group is discussed in Khaichenko, *Russkii narodnyi teatr*, 223–26; and in Thurston, *Popular Theater*, 222–25.

47. A. T., "O rabochem teatre: Rabochie i iskusstvo," *Proletarskaia pravda*, 12 January 1914.

48. Ivan Kubikov, "Rabochii teatr," part 1, *Nasha rabochaia gazeta*, 9 May 1914.

49. Ibid., part 2, *Nasha rabochaia gazeta*, 10 May 1914.

50. Ibid., part 3, *Nasha rabochaia gazeta*, 22 May 1914.

51. D. Lentsov, "Rabochii teatr," *Put' pravdy*, 20 April 1914.

52. Ibid.

53. A. K., "O rabochem teatre."

54. Ibid.

55. A. P-v., "Rabochii teatr v Peterburge"; Kleinbort, "Rabochaia intelligentsiia i iskusstvo," 222–23.

56. Skorobogatov, *Zhizn' i stsena*, 81.

57. A. N. Ostrovskii, *P'esy* (Moscow, 1973), 156 (Act 3, scene 12).

58. These surveys and the responses to them are discussed in Chapter Six.

59. The play was performed at the Imperial Malyi Theater in Moscow in 1904–5, and at St. Petersburg's Suvorin Theater in 1905.

60. Rabochii B. I-v., "Rabochii spektakl'," *Pravda*, 21 September 1912.

61. On the reception of *The Lower Depths* by contemporary audiences, see Petrovskaia, *Teatr i zritel'*, 144–45.

62. S. Markov, cited in E. N. Gugushvili and A. Z. Iufit, *Bol'shevistskaia pechat' i teatr* (Leningrad, 1961), 45 n. 3.

63. See Vernon Lidtke, *The Alternative Culture: Socialist Labor in Imperial Germany* (New York, 1985).

64. Obodriaiushchii, "*Gor'kaia sud'bina* Pisemskogo v 'Rabochem teatre,' " *Rabochii*, 25 May 1914.

65. Iv. Petrovich, "O rabochem teatre," *Za pravdu*, 3 November 1913.

66. Leontii Kotomka, "Kinematograf i rabochie," *Put' pravdy*, 30 March 1914.

67. *Nash put'*, no. 3 (25 June 1910): 3–7.

68. Ibid., no. 11 (20 December 1910): 7.

69. Sinebluznik, "Gramofon i soiuz," *Nash put'*, no. 6 (30 August 1910): 3.

70. *Metallist*, no. 15 (1 June 1912): 8. The popularity among workers of the "kopek" newspapers and trade union journalists' hostility toward them are discussed in Brooks, *When Russia Learned To Read*, 137, 330, 331–32.

71. Dmitrii Rodnov, "Razvlecheniia rabochikh," *Pravda*, 25 May 1912.

72. Molodoi rabochii, "Razvlecheniia dlia naroda: Narodnyi dom," *Za pravdu*, 3 November 1913.

73. Ibid.

74. V. Slob, "Chem vospityvat' narod: Pis'mo k redaktsiiu," *Pravda*, 25 January 1913.

75. Goriun, "Teatr rabochikh," *Naborshchik i pechatnyi mir*, no. 201 (September 1916): 2052.

76. Lentsov, "Rabochii teatr." The writer signs himself "*rabochii* D. Lentsov."

77. Dorogomilovskii rabochii, "Spektakl' rabochikh," *Ob"edinenie*, no. 3 (24 February 1915): 15.

78. On middle-class amateur theater, see Iunisov, "'Lishnii' teatr."

79. "O raskole v 'Rabochem teatre,' " part 2, *Put' pravdy*, 27 April 1914.

80. Ibid., part 1, *Put' Pravdy*, 18 April 1914.

81. Ibid., part 2, *Put' Pravdy*, 27 April 1914.

82. A. I. Mashirov-Samobytnik, "Kak my nachinali: Vospominaniia," in *Zabytym byt' ne mozhet* (Moscow, 1963), 113.

83. On Mashirov's role in the founding of Proletkult, see Mally, *Culture of the Future*, 100–101.

84. Petrovich, "O rabochem teatre."

85. A. D. Dikii, "Narodnye talanty," in *Prechistenskie rabochie kursy: Pervyi rabochii universitet v Moskve* (Moscow, 1948), 187. These evening courses, established by the Moscow branch of the Imperial Russian Technical Society in 1897, offered workers instruction in a wide variety of subjects.

86. A. M., "A. A. Brenko i 'Rabochii teatr,' " *Rampa i zhizn'*, no. 37 (13 September 1915): 11.

87. Khaichenko, *Russkii narodnyi teatr*, 233.

88. On the section's many activities, see Otdel sodeistviia ustroistvu fabrichnykh i derevenskikh teatrov pri Moskovskom otdelenii Imperatorskogo Russkogo tekhnicheskogo obshchestva, *Otchet deiatel'nosti Otdela za vremia ot 11 maia 1911 g. po 11 maia 1912 g.* (Moscow, 1912).

89. "Otkrytie doma imeni V. D. Polenova," *Utro Rossii*, 30 December 1915.

90. *TPVSDNT*, 345.

91. Ibid., 347–54.

92. Ibid., 354–57.

93. Ibid., 375–76. Similar arguments about the class nature of art and the role of intellectuals in proletarian cultural organizations dominated the worker-peasant theater conference held in November 1919. See Lynn Mally, *Revolutionary Acts: Amateur Theater and the Soviet State, 1917–1938* (Ithaca, 2000), 21–22.

94. Mally, *Culture of the Future.*

95. On consumption as a creative process in which culture consumers negotiate the uses and meanings of cultural products, see John Fiske, *Understanding Popular Culture* (Boston, 1989), and Paul Willis, *Common Culture: Symbolic Work at Play in the Everyday Life of the Young* (Milton Keynes, England, 1990).

96. The concept of "making do," that is, the adaptation and manipulation of imposed cultural systems by subordinate groups, is borrowed from Michel de Certeau, *Arts de Faire* (Paris, 1980), esp. 75–94. Although Certeau's work deals with the culture of everyday life, the concept is equally applicable to artistic culture.

97. A handful of plays were written by working-class authors, according to L. M. Kleinbort, but they were staged in workers' theaters only rarely, if at all. Kleinbort mentions only one such performance, in Moscow, but does not indicate whether it was by a workers' troupe. L. M. Kleinbort, *Ocherki narodnoi literatury (1880–1925 gg.)* (Leningrad, 1924), 287. Censorship restrictions may have been responsible for keeping these plays off the stage.

98. Kleinbort, "Rabochaia intelligentsia i iskusstvo," 222.

CHAPTER SIX

1. Rashin, *Formirovanie*, 593.

2. L. Gorev (L. I. Gurevich), "Provintsial'naia pechat'," *Severnyi vestnik*, no. 6 (1896), part 2: 306.

3. Wolfgang Iser, "The Reading Process," in *New Directions in Literary History*, ed. Ralph Cohen (London, 1974), 283–84; idem, *The Implied Reader: Patterns of Communication in Prose Fiction from Bunyan to Beckett* (Baltimore, 1974); Hans Robert Jauss, "Literary History as a Challenge to Literary Theory," *New Literary History*, no. 2 (1967), 11–19; Stanley Fish, *Is There a Text in This Class? The Authority of Interpretive Communities* (Cambridge, Mass., 1980).

4. Shcheglov, *Narod i teatr*, 7, 16.

5. S. M. Popov, "Narodnye spektakli na Ivanovskoi fabrike"; idem, "Zametki o fabrichno-narodnom teatre," *Russkii nachal'nyi uchitel'*, no. 10 (October 1895): 490; N. A. Popov, "Zriteli i teatr," d. 119, kn. 1, ll. 82–83.

6. Nikolai Popov, "O repertuare narodnogo teatra (Zametki)," in *Narodnyi teatr*, 255; S. M. Popov, "Narodnye spektakli na Ivanovskoi fabrike," l. 8; Skorobogatov, "Ot rabochei zastavy," part 1, 148.

7. N. A. Popov, "Zriteli i teatr," d. 119, kn.. 1, ll. 16–17.

8. "Doklad ob otvetakh posetitelei gulianii i teatra Riazanskogo obshchestva narodnykh razvlechenii," unpublished manuscript, 1899, RGB, f. 358, karton 11, d. 4, l. 10.

9. Mikhailovskii, "Literatura i zhizn'," 42–61. Some of the responses cited by Mikhailovskii also appear in Thurston, "Theatre and Acculturation"; and idem, *The Popular Theatre Movement*, 136–39. I have been unable to locate the originals of the survey in RGIA, RGALI, GTsTM, or GARF. They could be in the St. Petersburg regional archive (TsGIA SPb), which was closed during my research. Bulgakova published the results of her survey in a Kiev newspaper, cited extensively in N. Nikolaev, "Po povodu odnoi ankety," *Teatr i iskusstvo*, no. 4 (25 January 1904): 87–89.

10. "Doklad," l. 4; N. V. Drizen, *Materialy k istorii russkogo teatra* (Moscow, 1905), 254–55.

11. Cited in Mikhailovskii, "Literatura i zhizn'," 55.

12. Nikolaev, "Po povodu odnoi ankety," 88.

13. Mikhailovskii, "Literatura i zhizn'," 56.

14. Ibid., 57.

15. Ibid., 59.

16. "Doklad," ll. 27–28.

17. Mikhailovskii, "Literatura i zhizn'," 54.

18. Ibid., 59. The allusion to Nekrasov's drama is unclear. It may refer to Nikolai Nekrasov, a populist writer famous for his socially critical civic poetry.

19. Glickman, *Russian Factory Women*, 141–43; S. A. Smith, "Workers Against Foremen in St. Petersburg, 1905–1917," in *Making Workers Soviet: Power, Class, and Identity*, ed. Lewis H. Siegelbaum and Ronald Grigor Suny (Ithaca, 1994), 120–21; Engel, *Between the Fields and the City*, 137–39.

20. Nikolaev, "Po povodu odnoi ankety," 88.

21. Brooks, *When Russia Learned To Read*, 30–33; Eklof, *Russian Peasant Schools*, 273–77; Mark D. Steinberg, "Worker-Authors and the Cult of the Person," in *Cultures in Flux*, 182.

22. "Doklad," ll. 12–13. In Ostrovsky's *The Forest*, Neschastlivtsev (meaning "the unhappy one") is a provincial actor who saves an oppressed servant girl from suicide. Liubim Tortsov is a noble and sensitive drunkard in Ostrovsky's *Poverty Is No Vice*, who prevents his brother from marrying his daughter to a rich but corrupt old merchant.

23. Ibid., l. 12.

24. Mikhailovskii, "Literatura i zhizn'," 56.

25. Ibid., 57.

26. Nikolaev, "Po povodu odnoi ankety," 88–89.

27. Mikhailovskii, "Literatura i zhizn'," 57.

28. Ibid., 56.

29. Ibid., 55.

30. Pierre Bourdieu, *Distinction: A Social Critique of the Judgment of Taste*, trans. Richard Nice (Cambridge, Mass., 1984).

31. See Zelnik, "Russian Bebels," part 1, 272–77; Bonnell, *Roots of Rebellion*, 43–72; Mark D. Steinberg, "Vanguard Workers and the Morality of Class," in Siegelbaum and Suny, *Making Workers Soviet*, 66–84.

32. "Doklad," l. 12.

33. Ibid., l. 11.

34. Cited in Mikhailovskii, "Literatura i zhizn'," 55.

35. "Doklad," ll. 14–15.

36. Ibid., l. 15.

37. Ibid. The reader will recall that the literal meaning of *narodnoe gulian'e* is "promenade of the people." *Narodnoe* is the adjectival form of the collective noun *narod* (people) and is similar to the French *populaire*. The noun and adjectival forms were (and still are) often used by educated Russians to refer to the uneducated, although they may also denote all the people, as in *russkii narod* (the Russian people) or *narodnoe khoziaistvo* (national economy).

38. "Malen'kaia khronika," *Teatr i iskusstvo*, no. 17 (26 April 1915): 295.

39. "Doklad," l. 20.

40. Ibid., ll. 21–22.

41. On workers' attitudes toward *The Weavers*, see Reginald E. Zelnik, "*Weber* into *Tkachi*: On a Russian Reading of Gerhard Hauptmann's Play *The Weavers*," in *Self and Story in Russian History*, ed. Laura Engelstein and Stephanie Sandler (Ithaca, 2000), 218–19, 240.

42. Kanatchikov, *Radical Worker*, 33–34, 401–2 n. 13.

43. "Doklad," ll. 4–5. Unfortunately, the report gives no indication of the precise occupation or level of skill of the railway workers, a broad category ranging from unskilled track-layers to highly skilled metalworkers. It seems likely, however, that the railway workers cited in the survey were unskilled workers.

44. Ibid., l. 10.

45. Kanatchikov, *Radical Worker*, 105.

46. *Otchet Riazanskogo obshchestva ustroistva narodnykh razvlechenii s 25 fevralia 1900 g. po 25 fevralia 1901 g.* (Riazan, 1901), 17–18; "Doklad," ll. 4–5.

47. Karpov, *Desiatiletie narodnykh gulianii*, 12–13.

48. "O smekhe," *Novoe vremia*, 15 September 1896; N. A. Popov, "Narodnye spektakli," ll. 4–5; idem, "Zriteli i teatr," d. 119, kn. 1, l. 95; P. Kazantsev, "S verkhov narodnogo teatra," parts 1 and 2, *Teatr i iskusstvo*, no. 36 (2 September 1901): 636–37, no. 37 (9 September 1901): 653–55; Sergei Sutugin, "Narod i narodnyi teatr," part 1, *Teatr i iskusstvo*, no. 31 (28 July 1902): 567–69; N. Negorev, "Mysli o narodnom teatre," parts 1–2, *Teatr i iskusstvo*, no. 33 (16 August 1915):

605–8, no. 34 (23 August 1915): 627–29 (large sections of this article were plagiarized from Sutugin, "Narod i narodnyi teatr").

49. Sutugin, "Narod i narodnyi teatr," part 1, 567.

50. See, for example, N. A. Popov, "Zriteli i teatr," d. 119, kn. 1, ll. 16–17.

51. Kuznetsov, *Russkie narodnye gulian'ia*, 112.

52. On carnival humor, see Kelly, *Petrushka*, 81–93; and idem, "A Stick with Two Ends, or, Misogyny in Popular Culture: A Case Study of the Puppet Text 'Petrushka,'" in *Sexuality and the Body in Russian Culture*, ed. Jane T. Costlow, Stephanie Sandler, and Judith Vowles (Stanford, 1993), 73–96.

53. T. N. Selivanov, "O narodnom teatre," cited in Kazantsev, "S verkhov narodnogo teatra," part 1, 637.

54. Kazantsev, "S verkhov narodnogo teatra," part 2, 653–55.

55. Kanatchikov, *Radical Worker*, 52–53; Engel, *Between the Fields and the City*, 126–65; Bradley, *Muzhik and Muscovite*, 215–29. James H. Bater, "Between Old and New: St. Petersburg in the Late Imperial Era," in *The City in Late Imperial Russia*, ed. Michael F. Hamm (Bloomington, 1986), 51–55.

56. Engel, *Between the Fields and the City*, 137.

57. Shcheglov, *Narod i teatr*, 19–20.

58. Ibid., 171–76; *Ligovskii sad*, 22.

59. Shcheglov, *Narod i teatr*, 28–29, 33–38; [A. Kugel'], editorial, *Teatr i iskusstvo*, no. 4 (25 January 1898): 74; Sergei Iablonovskii, "Melodrama i narod," *Teatr i iskusstvo*, no. 33 (14 August 1916): 662–66.

60. N. A. Popov, *Zriteli i teatr*, d. 120, kn. 1, l. 111; S. Sutugin, "Vasileostrovskii teatr," *Teatr i iskusstvo*, no. 43 (20 October 1902): 779, no. 47 (17 November 1902): 880–81; I. K., "Teatral'nyi kur'er, " *Peterburgskaia gazeta*, 25 November 1904; P. V., "Tavricheskii teatr," *Teatr i iskusstvo*, no. 25 (15 June 1903): 485, no. 27 (29 June 1903); Lo., "V Tavricheskom teatre," *Teatr i iskusstvo*, no. 32 (12 August 1907): 517; N. N., "Narodnyi dom," *Teatr i iskusstvo*, no. 39 (30 September 1907): 630; N. Tamarin, "Narodnyi Dom Imperatora Nikolaia II," *Teatr i iskusstvo*, no. 9 (26 February 1912): 192; Lynn Mally, *Revolutionary Acts: Amateur Theater and the Soviet State, 1917–1938* (Ithaca, 2000), 36.

61. Peter Brooks, *The Melodramatic Imagination: Balzac, Henry James, Melodrama, and the Mode of Excess* (New Haven, 1976), 44.

62. Shcheglov, *Narod i teatr*, 27, 36–37, 181.

63. Ibid., 210–15; Engel, *Between the Fields and the City*, 159–65.

64. Michael Denning, "Cheap Stories: Notes on Popular Fiction and Working-Class Culture in Nineteenth-Century America," *History Workshop Journal*, no. 22 (Autumn 1986): 6–7, 14–15.

65. Zelnik, "Russian Bebels"; Steinberg, "Vanguard Workers."

66. Heinz-Dietrich Löwe, "Political Symbols and Rituals, 1900–1914," *Slavonic and East European Review* 76, no. 3 (July 1998): 453–54, 461–62.

67. "Narodnye doma," *Vestnik popechitel'stv o narodnoi trezvosti*, no. 38 (25 September 1904): 833.

68. Sergei Solomin, "Narodnaia drama," *Vestnik popechitel'stv o narodnoi trezvosti*, no. 32 (14 August 1904): 704.

69. Sutugin, "Narod i narodnyi teatr," part 1, 567. The plays are not identified.

70. Engel, *Between the Fields and the City*, 138–39.

71. David Moon, "Peasants Into Russian Citizens? A Comparative Perspective," *Revolutionary Russia* 9 (June 1996): 43–81; Steve Smith, "Citizenship and the Russian Nation during World War I: A Comment," *Slavic Review* 59, no. 2 (Summer 2000): 318–20, passim; Löwe, "Political Symbols and Rituals," 465–66.

72. Skorobogatov, *Zhizn' i stsena*, 201–2.

73. "Rabochie i teatr," *Novaia rabochaia gazeta*, 24 October 1913.

74. On working-class anti-Semitism, see Charters Wynn, *Workers, Strikes, and Pogroms: The Donbass-Dnepr Bend in Late Imperial Russia, 1870–1905* (Princeton, 1992).

75. Shcheglov, *Narod i teatr*, 37.

76. Kleinbort, *Ocherki rabochei intelligentsii*, 2: 12.

77. Brooks, *When Russia Learned To Read*, 32.

78. Gareth Stedman Jones, "Class Expression versus Social Control? A Critique of Recent Trends in the Social History of Leisure," in *Languages of Class: Studies in English Working Class History, 1832–1982* (Cambridge, 1983), 87.

CONCLUSION

1. For an excellent discussion of the complexity of social identities in Russia's migrant cities, see James von Geldern, "Life in Between: Migration and Popular Culture in Late Imperial Russia," *The Russian Review* 55, no. 3 (July 1996): 365–83.

2. Brooks, *When Russia Learned To Read*, 356.

3. *The Temperance Committee of St. Petersburg*, 6–7.

4. Hiroko Tsuchiya, "'Let Them Be Amused': The Industrial Drama Movement, 1910–1929," in *Theatre for Working-Class Audiences in the United States, 1830–1980*, ed. Bruce A. McConachie and Daniel Friedman, Contributions in Drama and Theatre Studies, no. 14 (Westport, Conn., 1985), 97–110.

5. Vl. Linskii, "Zlobodnevnaia dramaturgiia," part 3, *Teatr i Iskusstvo*, no. 24 (13 June 1904): 458.

6. Peterburgskii komitet gramotnosti, *Doklad*, 3.

7. Frank, "Confronting the Domestic Other," 107. See also idem, *Crime, Cultural Conflict, and Justice*.

8. See, for example, Brooks, *When Russia Learned To Read*; Louise McReynolds, *The News Under Russia's Old Regime: The Development of a Mass-Circulation Press* (Princeton, 1991); Daniel R. Brower, "The Penny-Press and Its Readers," in Frank and Steinberg, *Cultures in Flux*, 147–67.

9. The seminal work on social polarization in prerevolutionary Russia is

Leopold H. Haimson, "The Problem of Social Stability in Urban Russia, 1905–1917," parts 1 and 2, *Slavic Review* 23, no. 4 (December 1964): 619–42; 24, no. 1 (March 1965): 1–22.

EPILOGUE

1. See Anthony Swift, "Kul'turnoe stroitel'stvo ili kul'turnaia razrukha? Nekotorye aspekty teatral'noi zhizni Moskvy i Petrograda v 1917 g.," in *Anatomiia revoliutsii: 1917 god v Rossii. Massy, partii, vlast'*, ed. V. Iu. Chernaev et al. (Moscow, 1994), 401–4.

2. *Utro Rossii*, 12 April 1917; ibid., 23 April 1917; "Teatr na Vasilevskom ostrove," *Novaia zhizn'*, 10 June 1917; G. G. "Soldatskii teatr," *Novaia zhizn'*, 26 May 1917; *Put' osvobozhedeniia*, no. 3 (20 August 1917): 20–22; V. L. Lapshin, *Khudozhestvennaia zhizn' Moskvy i Petrograda v 1917 godu* (Moscow, 1983), 411.

3. "Khronika," *Pravda*, 16 May 1917; "Voennaia zhizn': Pis'mo soldata," *Pravda*, 6 June 1917; *Teatr i iskusstvo*, no. 18 (30 April 1917): 296–97; *Teatr i iskusstvo*, no. 49 (3 December 1917): 823.

4. I. Dzhonson, "Moskovskie pis'ma," *Teatr i iskusstvo*, no. 52 (24 December 1917): 871.

5. *Pravda*, 22(9) May 1917; *Teatr i iskusstvo*, no. 21 (21 May 1917): 352; "Kul'turnoe stroitel'stvo," *Novaia zhizn'*, 23 July 1917.

6. *Novaia zhizn'*, 2 July 1917.

7. GTsTM, f. 1, d. 5908, l. 49 (newspaper clipping); *Artist i zritel'*, no. 1 (1 October 1917): 11.

8. Larisa Reisner, "Rabochii teatr," *Novaia zhizn'*, 10 August 1917; idem, "Kul'turnoe stroitel'stvo. V rabochikh kvartalakh," *Novaia zhizn'*, 22 October 1917.

9. Larisa Reisner, "Liubitel'skie teatry soldat i rabochikh," *Novaia zhizn'*, 19 September 1917.

10. "Pervaia Petrogradskaia Konferentsiia proletarskikh kul'turno-prosvetitel'nykh organizatsii," *Rabochii i soldat*, 28 October 1917.

11. Von Geldern, *Bolshevik Festivals*, 125–30, 172–74; Kuznetsov, *Russkie narodnye gulian'ia*, 164–66.

12. Leon Trotsky, "Vodka, the Church, and the Cinema," in *Problems of Everyday Life* (New York, 1973). The article was first published in 1923.

13. Sheila Fitzpatrick, *The Commissariat of Enlightenment: Soviet Organization of Education and the Arts Under Lunacharskii, October 1917–1921* (Cambridge, 1970), 139–61.

14. A. V. Lunacharskii, *Teatr i revoliutsiia* (Moscow, 1924), 26.

15. Cited in A. Mazaev, *Prazdnik kak sotsial'no-khudozhestvennoe iavlenie* (Moscow, 1978), 349.

16. M. V. Iunisov, "Sel'skii liubitel'skii teatr," 48–51.

17. *Krasnoarmeiskii teatr* (Petrograd, 1921); *Vestnik teatr*, no. 27 (1920): 6.

18. Vladislav Khodasevich, "Koleblemyi trenozhnik," in *Izbrannoe* (Moscow, 1991), 393.

19. A. A. Blok, "O repertuare kommunal'nykh i gosudarstvennykh teatrov, in *Sobranie sochinenii v vos'mi tomakh,* vol. 6 (Moscow, 1962), 276–80 (citations on 276 and 279).

20. Mally, *Culture of the Future;* idem, *Revolutionary Acts;* Richard Stites, *Russian Popular Culture: Entertainment and Society since 1900* (Cambridge, 1992).

Selected Bibliography

ARCHIVAL MATERIALS

Gosudarstvennyi arkhiv Rossiiskoi Federatsii (GARF)
  Fond 7952, Istoriia fabrik i zavodov g. Moskvy
Gosudarstvennyi tsentral'nyi teatral'nyi muzei im. A. A. Bakhrushina
  (GTsTM)
  Fond 1, A. A. Bakhrushin
  Fond 144, M. V. Lentovskii
  Fond 150, N. I. L'vov
  Fond 324, A. A. Iartsev
  Fond 532, S. M. Popov
  Fond 533, Sobranie vospominanii i dnevnikov
Otdel rukopisei. Rossiiskaia gosudarstvennaia biblioteka (OR RGB)
  Fond 358, N. A. Rubakin
Otdel rukopisei. Rossiiskaia natsional'naia biblioteka (OR RNB)
  Fond 106, A. A. Brianskii
  Fond 1130, E. P. Gershuni
Rossiiskii gosudarstvennyi arkhiv literatury i iskusstva (RGALI)
  Fond 659, Moskovskaia kontora Imperatorskikh teatrov
  Fond 837, N. A. Popov
  Fond 2097, Obshchestvo russkikh dramaticheskikh pisatelei i opernykh kom-
    pozitorov
Rossiiskii gosudarstvennyi istoricheskii arkhiv (RGIA)
  Fond 472, Kantseliariia ministerstva imperatorskogo dvora
  Fond 575, Glavnoe upravlenie neokladnykh sborov i kazennoi prodazhi pitei,
    Ministerstvo finansov
  Fond 776, Glavnoe upravlenie po delam pechati, Ministerstvo vnutrennikh del
  Fond 1282, Kantseliariia Ministra vnutrennikh del
Tsentral'nyi gosudarstvennyi istoricheskii arkhiv Sankt-Peterburga (TsGIA
  SPb)
  Fond 569, Kantseliariia Peterburgskogo gradonachal'nika

Tsentral'nyi istoricheskii arkhiv goroda Moskva (TsIAgM)
  Fond 16, Kantseliariia general-gubernatora
  Fond 483, Moskovskoe uezdnoe politseiskoe upravlenie
Hoover Institution on War, Revolution and Peace
  Okhrana Archive

NEWSPAPERS AND PERIODICALS

Artist
Birzhevye vedomosti
Bor'ba
Deiatel'
Ezhegodnik imperatorskikh teatrov
Gazeta kopeika
Istoricheskii vestnik
Izvestiia Moskovskoi gorodskoi dumy
Izvestiia S.-Peterburgskoi gorodskoi dumy
Komik
Luch (*Novaia rabochaia gazeta*, *Severnaia rabochaia gazeta*, *Nasha
   rabochaia gazeta*)
Maski
Metallist
Mir bozhii
Moskovskie vedomosti
Moskovskii dnevnik zrelishch i ob"iavlenii
Moskovskii listok
Naborshchik i pechatnyi mir
Narod
Nash put'
Nasha zaria
Niva
Novaia zhizn'
Novoe vremia
Novosti dnia
Obozrenie teatrov
Obrazovanie
Otechestvennye zapiski
Peterburgskaia gazeta
Peterburgskii listok
Pravda (*Rabochaia pravda*, *Pravda truda*, *Za pravdu*, *Proletarskaia pravda*,
   Put' pravdy, *Trudovaia pravda*)
Rabochii
Rampa
Rampa i zhizn'
Rossiia

Rus'
Russkaia mysl'
Russkaia shkola
Russkie vedomosti
Russkii nachal'nyi uchitel'
Russkii trud
Russkii vestnik
Russkoe bogatstvo
S.-Peterburgskie vedomosti
Severnyi vestnik
Slovo
Sovremennik
Studiia
Teatr
Teatr i iskusstvo
Teatr i narod
Teatral'naia gazeta
Teatral'naia Rossiia
Teatral
Uchitel' i shkola
Vestnik Evropy
Vestnik Moskovskoi Politekhnicheskoi vystavki
Vestnik popechitel'stv o narodnoi trezvosti
Zapiski Peredvizhnogo-Obshchedostupnogo Teatra

PRIMARY SOURCES

Alchevskaia, Kh. D. *Chto chitat' narodu.* 3 vols. St. Petersburg, 1884–1906.

———. *Dramaticheskie proizvedeniia: Ostrovskii v primenenii k chteniiu v narode.* St. Petersburg, 1887.

Alekseev-Iakovlev, Aleksei. "Vospominaniia." Unpublished manuscript, 1930. OR RNB, f. 1130, d. 317, ll. 1–31.

Alfavitnyi spisok dramaticheskim sochineniiam na russkikh, finskikh i estonskikh iazykakh dozvolennym k predstavleniiu na stsenakh narodnykh teatrov. St. Petersburg, 1891.

Alferov, A. "Petrushka i ego predki." In *Desiat' chtenii po literature,* 175–205. Moscow, 1895.

Ardov, A. "O narodnom teatre." *Rampa i zhizn',* no. 26 (27 September 1919): 641–42.

"Arkadiia." Desiatiletie so dnia ee osnovaniia, 1881–1891. St. Petersburg, 1891.

Armand, L., and A. Nikitin. *Narodnye doma.* Moscow, 1918.

Baedeker, Karl. *Russia: A Handbook for Travellers.* London, 1914.

Balaganshchiki: Ocherki zhizni i nravov artistov i antrepenerov [sic] uveselitel'nykh zavedenii i prazdnichnykh balaganov. St. Petersburg, 1868.

Belousov, I. A. *Ushedshaia Moskva.* Moscow, 1929.

Ber-t, E. "'Vlast' t'my' na stsene teatra 'Skomorokh.' Beseda s A. A. Cherepan-ovym." *Rampa,* no. 2 (31 August 1898): 31–32.

Briantsev, A. A. *Vospominaniia. Stat'i. Vystupleniia. Dnevniki. Pis'ma.* Comp. A. N. Gozenpud. Moscow, 1979.

Bunakov, N. "Razmyshleniia po povodu vystavki narodnogo teatra, ustroennoi v Moskve v 1895 g." In *Narodnyi teatr. Sbornik,* ed. E. V. Lavrova and N. A. Popov, 168–75. Moscow, 1896.

Bunakova, L. "Zametki o narodnom teatre," *Teatr i iskusstvo,* no. 36 (5 September 1910): 663–66.

Buzinov, Aleksei. *Za nevskoi zastavoi.* Moscow, 1930.

Chargonin, A. "Neskol'ko slov o repertuare narodnykh teatrov." *Teatr i iskusstvo,* no. 32 (7 August 1905): 513–15.

Charnoluskii, V. "Narodnye doma v Rossii po issledovaniiu za 1913 god (na 1 ianvaria 1914 g.). In *Narodnyi dom.* Petrograd, 1918.

Chekhov, A. P. *Polnoe sobranie sochinenii i pisem v tridtsati tomakh.* 30 vols. Ed. N. F. Belchikov et al. Moscow, 1974–83.

Chuprov, A. I. "Ob ekonomicheskom znachenii obrazovatel'nykh i vospitatel'-nykh uchrezhdenii dlia rabochego klassa." In *Obrazovatel'no-vospitatel'-nye uchrezhdeniia dlia rabochikh i organizatsii obshchedostupnykh razvlechenii v Moskve,* 29–35. Moscow, 1898.

Danilevskii, V. *Narodnyi dom, ego zadachi i obshchestvennoe znachenie.* 2nd ed. Kharkov, 1915.

Dikii, A. D. "Narodnye talanty." In *Prechistenskie rabochie kursy. Sbornik statei i vospominanii,* 186–88. Moscow, 1948.

Dobson, G., and F. De Haenen (illustrator). *St. Petersburg.* London, 1910.

Doklad No. 81 Moskovskoi gorodskoi upravy ob uprazdnenii narodnykh gulianii na Devich'em pole i u Presnenskoi zastavy i ob otkrytii takovykh na gorodskoi zemle za Presnenskoi zastavoi, szadi fabriki br. Mamontov-ykh. 28 fevralia 1911 goda. Moscow, 1911.

"Doklad ob otvetakh posetitelei gulianii i teatra Riazanskogo obshchestva nar-odnykh razvlechenii." Unpublished manuscript, 1899. RGB, f. 358, karton 11, d. 4.

Drizen, N. V. *Materialy k istorii russkogo teatra.* Moscow, 1905.

Durov, Anatolii Leonidovich. *Na stsene i na arene.* Moscow, 1984.

Dvadtsatipiatiletie tovarishchestva sitse-nabivnoi manufaktury "Emil' Tsindel' " v Moskve, 1874–1899. Moscow, 1899.

E. A. [Episkop Mozhaiskii Aleksandr]. "Po voprosu ob ustroistve dlia naroda teatrov." *Moskovskie tserkovnye vedomosti,* no. 6 (5 February 1889): 83–84.

Fabrika knigi Krasnyi Proletarii. Istoriia tipografii byv. "T-va I. I. Kushnerev i Ko." Moscow, 1932.

Feoktistov, E. M. *Vospominaniia E. M. Feoktistova: za kulisami literatury i politiki.* Leningrad, 1929.

Frolov, A. *Probuzhdenie. Vospominaniia riadovogo rabochego.* Part 1. Kiev, 1923.

Gaideburov, P. P. *Literaturnoe nasledie. Vospominaniia. Stat'i. Rezhisserskie eksplikatsii. Vystupleniia.* Ed. Simen Dreiden. Moscow, 1977.

Georgi, I. G. *Opisanie rossiisko-imperatorskogo stolichnogo goroda Sanktpeterburga i dostoprimechatel'nostei v ego okrestnostiakh.* St. Petersburg, 1794.

Glagolin, V. "Akterskaia otsebiatina." *Teatr i iskusstvo,* no. 27 (2 July 1906): 425–27.

Gnedich, P. "Starye balagany." *Teatr i iskusstvo,* no. 14 (6 April 1914): 324–27.

Golubev, P. "Narodnye doma-dvortsy." *Russkoe bogatstvo,* no. 12 (1901), sec. 2: 1–40.

Gorin-Goriainov. *Aktery (iz vospominanii).* Leningrad, 1947.

Gosudarstvennyi sovet. *Stenograficheskie otchety.* 13 vols. St. Petersburg, 1906–17.

I. G. [I. Gorodetskii] "A. F. Fedotov i pervaia popytka osnovaniia narodnogo teatra." *Severnyi vestnik,* no. 5 (1895), sec. 2: 93–98.

Iablonovskii, Sergei. "Melodrama i narod." *Teatr i iskusstvo,* no. 33 (14 August 1916): 662–66.

Iartsev, A. A. "Pervye fabrichnye teatry v Rossii." *Istoricheskii vestnik* (May 1900): 644–53.

Impressionist [B. I. Bentovich]. "Zverinye p'esy." Parts 1–4. *Teatr i iskusstvo,* no. 3 (19 January 1897): 47–48; no. 5 (2 February 1897): 87–88; no. 9 (2 March 1897): 170–72; no. 13 (30 March 1897): 263–64.

Inozemtsev, I. "Voprosy narodnogo teatra." Parts 1–4. *Teatr i iskusstvo,* no. 2 (10 January 1899): 26–27; no. 3 (17 January 1899): 50–52; no. 4 (24 January 1899): 74–76; no. 5 (31 January 1899): 99–100.

Iur'ev, Iu. M. *Zapiski.* Leningrad, 1948.

Iuzhin-Sumbatov, A. I. *Zapiski, stat'i, pis'ma.* Ed. V. Filippov. Moscow, 1951.

Ivanov, Lev. "Balagany (Iz vospominanii)." *Stolitsa i usad'ba,* no. 48 (15 December 1915): 3–6.

Ivanov, Viacheslav. *Po zvezdam.* St. Petersburg, 1909.

"Iz istorii teatrov peterburgskogo popechitel'stva o narodnoi trezvosti." *Teatr i iskusstvo,* no. 52 (29 December 1907): 881–83.

Jerrman, Edward. *St. Petersburg: Its People, Their Character and Institutions.* Trans. Frederick Hardman. New York, 1855.

Kanatchikov, S. "Kul'turno-prosvetitel'naia deiatel'nost' v Peterburgskikh professional'nykh soiuzakh." *Vozrozhdenie,* nos. 5–6 (April 1909): 50–56.

———. *A Radical Worker in Tsarist Russia: The Autobiography of Semen Ivanovich Kanatchikov.* Ed. and trans. Reginald E. Zelnik. Stanford, 1986.

Karpov, E. *Desiatiletie narodnykh gulianii za Nevskoi zastavoi. Ocherk deiatel'nosti Nevskogo Obshchestva ustroistva narodnykh razvlechenii.* St. Petersburg, 1895.

———. "Iz avtobiografii E. P. Karpova." *Teatr i iskusstvo,* no. 3 (20 January 1908): 58–59.

———. "Vospominaniia i moia zhizn'." Unpublished manuscript, n.d. OR RNB, f. 106, d. 163.

Karpov, E. P., and N. N. Okulov. *Organizatsiia narodnogo teatra i poleznykh razvlechenii dlia naroda.* St. Petersburg, 1899.

Kazantsev, P. "Teatr, kak sredstvo vneshkol'nogo obrazovaniia." Parts 1–4. *Teatr i iskusstvo,* no. 42 (17 October 1904): 742–45; no. 43 (24 October 1904): 761–63; no. 44 (31 October 1904): 777–78; no. 45 (7 November 1904): 793–95.

Kleinbort, L. M. "'Istoriia rabochego teatra,' kak tema dnia." *Zhizn' iskusstva,* no. 24 (16 April 1925): 8–9.

———. "Khronika vnutrennei zhizni." *Russkoe bogatstvo,* no. 8 (August 1913): sec. 2: 338–44.

———. *Ocherki narodnoi literatury (1880–1925 gg.).* Leningrad, 1924.

———. *Ocherki rabochei intelligentsii.* 2 vols. Petrograd, 1923.

———. "Rabochaia intelligentsiia i iskusstvo." *Vestnik Evropy,* no. 8 (August 1913): 215–26.

Koni, A. F. "Popechenie o narodnoi trezvosti." *Vestnik Evropy,* no. 6 (June 1908): 773–95.

Kratkii obzor deiatel'nosti Moskovskogo stolichnogo popechitel'stva o narodnoi trezvosti za 10 let. Moscow, 1911.

Kratkii ocherk deiatel'nosti Prokhorovskoi Trekhgornoi manufaktury po tekhnicheskomu i obshchemu obrazovaniiu rabochikh, 1816–1899. Moscow, 1899.

Kratkii ocherk deiatel'nosti russkogo dramaticheskogo teatra Korsha v Moskve. Moscow, 1892.

Kratkii ocherk deiatel'nosti S-Peterburgskogo gorodskogo popechitel'stva o narodnoi trezvosti, 1898–1908. St. Petersburg, 1908.

Kratkii ocherk deiatel'nosti S-Peterburgskogo gorodskogo popechitel'stva o narodnoi trezvosti, 1898–1912. St. Petersburg, 1913.

Kremlev, A. N. "Mneniia mezhdunarodnykh kongressov o gorodskikh i narodnykh teatrov." *Teatr i iskusstvo,* no. 46 (13 November 1911): 881–83.

———."O S.-Peterburgskom gorodskom teatre." Parts 1 and 2. *Teatr i iskusstvo,* no. 44 (30 October 1911): 832–35; no. 45 (6 November 1911): 856–58.

———. "S.-Peterburgskii obshchestvennyi teatr. Proekt." *Izvestiia S.-Peterburgskoi gorodskoi dumy,* no. 11 (June 1896): 49–91.

Kubikov, Ivan. "Rabochii teatr." Parts 1–3. *Nasha rabochaia gazeta,* 9, 10, 22 May 1914.

Kublitskii, M. "Otkrytie narodnogo teatra." *Vestnik Moskovskoi Politekhnicheskoi vystavki,* 5 June 1872.

———. "Narodnyi teatr." *Vestnik Moskovskoi Politekhnicheskoi vystavki,* 10 June 1872.

Kugel', Aleksandr [Homo Novus, pseud.]. "Dramaturg-narodnik." *Teatr i iskusstvo,* no. 3 (20 January 1908): 56–57.

———. "Teatral'noe narodnichestvo." *Peterburgskaia gazeta,* 5 July 1898.

Kuprianova, L. "Rabochii Peterburg." In *S. Peterburg i ego zhizn'.* St. Petersburg, 1914.

Kuznetsov, E. M., comp. *Russkie narodnye gulian'ia po rasskazam A. Ia. Alekseev-Iakovleva v zapisi i obrabotke Evg. Kuznetsova*. Leningrad, 1948.
Lavrova, E. "Dobryi pochin. K voprosu o narodnoi teatre." *Obrazovanie*, no. 3 (March 1892), sec. 2: 69–74.
———. "Narodnye spektakli v derevne." *Obrazovanie*, no. 2 (February 1896), sec. 2: 62–76.
Lavrova, E. V., and N. A. Popov, eds. *Narodnyi teatr. Sbornik*. Moscow, 1896.
Leifert, A. V. *Balagany*. Petrograd, 1922.
Ligovskii sad dlia rabochikh: Otchet za pervyi god (1898). St. Petersburg, 1899.
Linskii, Vl. "Zlobodnevnaia dramaturgiia." Parts 1 and 2. *Teatr i iskusstvo*, no. 22 (30 May 1904): 425–27; no. 23 (6 June 1904): 440–42.
Lotman, L. M., ed. *Istoriia russkoi dramaturgii (vtoraia polovina XIX— nachalo XX veka)*. Leningrad, 1987.
M. M. "Chto vidno, i chego ne vidat' (Pis'ma iz Moskvy). *Otechestvennye zapiski*, no.10 (October 1872), sec. 2: 297–307.
Martynov, B. I. "V bor'be s guzhonovskoi kul'turoi." Unpublished manuscript, n.d. GARF, f. 7952, op. 3, d. 300.
Medynskii, E. N. *Vneshkol'noe obrazovanie, ego znachenie, organizatsiia i tekhnika*. 2nd ed. Moscow, 1916.
Mikhailovskii, Nikolai. "Literatura i zhizn'." *Russkoe bogatstvo*, no. 6 (1896), sec. 2: 42–62.
———. *Otkliki*. Vol. 1. St. Petersburg, 1904.
Mikhnevich, Vladimir. "Peterburgskie sady i ikh etnografiia." In *Peterburg-skoe leto*, 52–87. St. Petersburg, 1887.
Monakhov, N. F. *Povest' o zhizni*. Leningrad, 1961.
Moskovskaia gorodskaia uprava. *Doklad No. 55 Kommissii po narodnym razvlecheniiam i o pol'zakh i nuzhdakh obshchestvennykh*. Moscow, 1901.
M-v. "Moskovskoe stolichnoe popechitel'stvo." *Vestnik popechitel'stv o narod-noi trezvosti*, no. 13 (3 April 1904): 343–49.
Narodnyi dom. Petrograd, 1918.
Negorev, N. "Mysli o narodnom teatre." Parts 1 and 2. *Teatr i iskusstvo*, no. 33 (16 August 1915): 605–8; no. 34 (23 August 1915): 627–29.
Nemirovich-Danchenko, V. I. *Retsenzii. Ocherki. Stat'i. Interv'iu. Zametki. 1877–1942*. Moscow, 1980.
———. *Stat'i. Rechi. Besedy. Pis'ma*. Moscow, 1952.
———. *Teatral'noe nasledie*. 2 vols. Moscow, 1952–54.
Nemirovitch-Dantchenko, Vladimir. *My Life in the Russian Theatre*. Trans. John Cournos. New York, 1936. Reprint, New York, 1968.
Nikolaev, N. "Po povodu odnoi ankety." *Teatr i iskusstvo*, no. 4 (25 January 1904): 87–89.
"Nuzhdy russkogo teatra (Zapiska stsenicheskikh deiatelei)." *Teatr i iskusstvo*, no. 7 (13 February 1905): 98–99.
Obshcheobrazovatel'no-vospitatel'nye uchrezhdeniia dlia rabochikh i organi-zatsiia obshchedostupnykh razvlechenii v Moskve. Moscow, 1898.

Obshchestvo "Staryi Peterburg." 1921–1923. Petrograd, 1923.

Onchukov, N. E. "Narodnaia drama na Severe." In *Izvestiia otdeleniia russkogo iazyka i slovesnosti imperatorskoi Akademii nauk*, vol. 14, book 4, 215–39. St. Petersburg, 1909.

O-skii, A. "Opyt narodnogo teatra." *Obrazovanie*, no. 1 (January 1892), sec. 2: 28–31.

Ostrogorskii, Viktor. "Dobryi pochin. K voprosu o narodnom teatre." *Obrazovanie*, no. 3 (March 1892), sec. 2: 69–74.

Ostrovskii, A. N. "Zapiska o polozhenii dramaticheskogo iskusstva v Rossii v nastoiashchee vremia." In *Sobranie sochinenii v desiati tomakh*, 10: 168–86. Moscow, 1960.

Otchet Riazanskogo obshchestva ustroistva narodnykh razvlechenii s 25 fevralia 1900 g. po 25 fevralia 1901 g. Riazan, 1901.

Otchet Riazanskogo obshchestva ustroistva narodnykh razvlechenii za 1901–1902 god. Riazan, 1902.

Otchety Moskovskogo stolichnogo popechitel'stva o narodnoi trezvosti. 13 vols. Moscow, 1903–15.

Ozarovskii, Iurii. "Repertuar narodnogo teatra (Opyt sistematicheskogo kataloga p'es dlia narodnogo teatra)." *Obrazovanie*, nos. 5–6 (May–June 1894), sec. 2: 286–93.

Panina, S., and P. Gaideburov. "Iskusstvo v narodnoi auditorii." *Russkaia shkola*, nos. 5–6 (1914): 150–73.

Panina, S. V. "Na peterburgskoi okraine." Parts 1 and 2. In *Novyi zhurnal*, no. 48 (1957): 163–96; no. 49 (1957): 189–203.

"Pervyi s"ezd stsenicheskikh deiatelei." In *Ezhegodnik imperatorskikh teatrov. Prilozhenie*, book 3: 118–32. St. Petersburg, 1898.

"Peterburgskie balagannye pribautki, zapisannye V. I. Kel'sievym." In *Trudy etnograficheskogo otdela imperatorskogo obshchestva liubitelei estestvoznaniia, antropologii i etnografii*, book 9: 113–18. St. Petersburg, 1889.

Peterburgskii komitet gramotnosti. Komissiia po voprosu o narodnykh teatrakh. *Doklad komissii po voprosu o narodnykh teatrov.* St. Petersburg, 1870.

Popov, N. A. "Narodnaia trezvost' i deshevoe iskusstvo." *Rampa i zhizn'*, no. 30 (26 July 1915): 9–11.

———. "O repertuare narodnykh teatrov. (Zametki)." In *Narodnyi teatr. Sbornik*, ed. E. V. Lavrova and N. A. Popov, 237–56. Moscow, 1896.

———. "Ob organizatsii razvlechenii dlia rabochikh. Doklad, prochitannyi na vtorom s"ezde russkikh deiatelei po tekhnicheskomu obrazovaniiu v Moskve, 31 dekabria 1895 g." *Teatral*, no. 65 (April 1896): 23–37.

———. "'Skomorokh'—kak obshchedostupnyi teatr." *Teatral*, no. 41 (October 1895): 109–19.

———. "Zriteli i teatr." Unpublished manuscript, n.d. RGALI, f. 837, op. 2, dd. 119, 20.

Popov, S. M. "Narodnye spektakli na Ivanovskoi fabrike (Zvenigorodskogo uezda),1890–1916." Unpublished manuscript, 1927. GTsTM, f. 532, d. 145962.

P[opov], S[ergei]. "Zametki o fabrichno-narodnom teatre." *Russkii nachal'nyi uchitel'* (October 1895): 482–91.

Pottecher, Maurice. *Le théâtre du peuple: Renaissance et destinée du théâtre populaire.* Paris, 1899.

Prokhorovskaia Trekhgornaia manufaktura v Moskve. 1799–1899. Istoriko-statisticheskii ocherk. Moscow, 1900.

Protokoly Osobogo soveshchaniia, uchrezhdennogo pod predsedatel'stvom D. F. Kobeko, dlia sostavleniia novogo ustava o pechati (10 fevralia—4 dekabria 1905 g.). St. Petersburg, 1913.

Protopopov, D. D. *Istoriia Peterburgskogo komiteta gramotnosti (1861–1895 gg.).* St Petersburg, 1898.

Prugavin, A. S. *Zaprosy naroda i obiazannosti intelligentsii v oblasti prosveshcheniia i vospitaniia.* 2nd ed. St. Petersburg, 1895.

Redin, E. K. *Narodnyi teatr.* Kharkov, 1898.

"Repertuary narodnykh teatrov." In *Narodnyi teatr. Sbornik,* ed. E. V. Lavrova and N. A. Popov, xxix–lxv. Moscow, 1896.

Roslavlev, Boris. "Rabochii teatr: Iz vospominanii o zhizni rabochikh teatral'n. kruzhkov do revoliutsii." *Rabochii teatr,* no. 25 (23 June 1925): 4–6.

Rubakin, N. A. *Etiudy o russkoi chitaiushchei publike.* St. Petersburg, 1895.

Rukovodiashchie ukazaniia dlia deiatel'nosti Popechitel'stv o narodnoi trezvosti, odobrennye Ministrom finansov 28 ianvaria 1897 goda. Chernigov, 1897.

S. "Soblazniteli narodnye." *Rampa i zhizn',* no. 39 (27 September 1915): 2–3.

S. Peterburg i ego zhizn'. St. Petersburg, 1914.

S-v., K. "Nashestvie teatrov-miniatiur." *Teatr i iskusstvo,* no. 19 (10 May 1915): 324.

S-v., V. "Po povodu narodnogo teatra." *Vestnik politekhnicheskoi vystavki,* 19 July 1872.

Sakharov, N. A. "Iz proshlogo." In *Fabrika knigi Krasnyi Proletarii. Istoriia tipografii "T-va I. N. Kushnerev i Ko."* Moscow, 1932.

Sapronov, T. *Iz istorii rabochego dvizheniia (po lichnym vospominaniiam).* Moscow, 1925.

Sbornik tsirkuliarov, rasporiazhenii i raz"iasnenii po uchrezhdeniiu popechitel'stv o narodnoi trezvosti. St. Petersburg, 1901.

Sektsiia sodeistviia ustroistvu derevenskikh i fabrichnykh teatrov pri Moskovskom Obshchestve Narodnykh Universitetov. *Otchet o deiatel'nosti Sektsii s 1 sentiabria 1913 g. po 1 sentiabria 1914 g.* Moscow, 1915.

———. *Sbornik retsenzii p'es dlia narodnogo teatra.* 2 vols. Moscow, 1914–16.

Semenov, S. T. "Soldatka." In *V rodnom derevne,* 61–90. Moscow, 1962.

Shcheglov, Ivan. *Narod i teatr. Ocherki i issledovaniia sovremennogo narodnogo teatra.* St. Petersburg, [1911].

———. *Narodnyi teatr v ocherkakh i kartinakh.* St. Petersburg, 1898.

———. *O narodnom teatre.* Moscow, 1895.

———. *V zashchitu narodnogo teatra. Zametki i vpechatlenii.* St. Petersburg, 1903.

Shestakov, P. M. *Rabochie na manufakture T-va "Emil' Tsindel' " v Moskve.*
Moscow, 1900.

[Shevelev, A.] *K voprosu o narodnom teatre (K predstoiashchemu s"ezdu russkikh stsenicheskikh deiatelei).* Moscow, 1897.

Shevelev, A. *Tserkov' i zrelishcha. Vzgliad na otnosheniia sv. pravoslavnoi tserkvi k teatral'nym zrelishcham i uveseleniiam.* Moscow, 1892.

Skarskaia, N. F., and P. P. Gaideburov. *Na stsene i v zhizni.* Moscow, 1959.

-skii. "K 25-letiiu pervogo narodnogo teatra v Peterburge." *Teatr i iskusstvo,* no. 6 (5 February 1912): 130–31.

Skorobogatov, K. "Ot rabochei zastavy. Vospominaniia artista." Parts 1 and 2. *Zvezda,* no. 1 (January 1967): 131–49; no. 2 (February 1967): 162–82.

———. *Zhizn' i stsena.* Leningrad, 1970.

Skorodumov, N. V. *Novyi metod uproshchennykh postanovok (Ustroistvo stseny i dekoratsii).* Moscow, 1914.

Sleptsov, V. A. *Polnoe sobranie sochinenii.* 3rd ed., rev. St. Petersburg, 1903.

Solianyi, P. "Teatry miniatur." *Teatr i iskusstvo,* no. 42 (19 October 1914): 824–26.

Solomin, Sergei. "Sluzhat' li narodnye razvlecheniia pomekhoi molitvy?" *Vestnik popechitel'stv o narodnoi trezvosti,* no. 16 (24 April 1904): 402–4.

Stanislavski, Constantin. *My Life in Art.* Trans. J. J. Robbins. New York, 1956.

Stanislavskii, K. S. *Sobranie sochinenii v vos'mi tomakh.* Ed. M. N. Kedrov et al. Moscow, 1954–61.

———. *Stat'i. Rechi. Besedy. Pis'ma.* Moscow, 1953.

Stepanov, V. "Vzgliad na ideal'nyi narodnyi teatr i ego zadachi v nashe vremia." In *Narodnyi teatr. Sbornik,* ed. E. V. Lavrova and N. A. Popov, 222–36. Moscow, 1896.

Sutugin, S. [E. G. Ettinger]. "Narod i narodnyi teatr." Parts 1–6. *Teatr i iskusstvo,* no. 31 (28 July 1902): 567–68; no. 32 (4 August 1902): 582–84; no. 46 (10 November 1902): 846–48; no. 49 (1 December 1902): 922–25; no. 50 (8 December 1902): 950–52; no. 51 (15 December 1902): 975–77.

Svetlov, S. F. *Peterburgskaia zhizn' v kontse XIX stoletiia (v 1892 godu).* Ed. S. A. Kovaleva and A. M. Konechnyi. St. Petersburg, 1998.

Svod zakonov Rossiiskoi imperii. 16 vols. St. Petersburg, 1904–5.

Tal'nikov, D. L. "Narodnyi teatr." *Vestnik Evropy,* no. 2 (February 1916): 298–99.

Tamarin, N. [Okulov]. "Narodnyi Dom Imperatora Nikolaia II." *Teatr i iskusstvo,* no. 10 (6 March 1911): 207–8.

———. "Narodnyi teatr." *Zhizn',* nos. 1–3 (January 1897): 97–117.

"Teatr i narod." *Russkii vestnik* (January 1896): 341–44.

Teliakovskii, V. A. *Vospominaniia.* Leningrad, 1965.

The Temperance Committee of St. Petersburg, 1899–1914. St. Petersburg, 1914.

Tikhonovich, V. [V.] "Narodnyi teatr po soobshcheniiam s mest," *Uchitel' i shkola,* nos. 17–18 (October 1914): 1–20.

———. *Samodeiatel'nyi teatr. Posobie dlia instruktorov po samodeiatel'nomu teatral'nomu prosveshcheniiu.* Vologda, 1922.

———. "Voprosy narodnogo teatra." *Uchitel' i shkola,* nos. 15–16 (August 1915): 16–32.

Timkovskii, N. I. "Narodnye i derevenskie teatry." *Teatral,* no. 50 (December 1895): 56–65.

———. "Obrazovatel'noe znachenie narodnogo teatra." *Obrazovanie* (February 1896): sec. 2: 54–61.

———. "Vopros ob obshchedostupnom teatre na pervom vserossiiskom s"ezde stsenicheskikh deiatelei." *Russkoe bogatstvo,* no. 5 (May 1897): sec. 2: 24–34.

———. "Znachenie razvlechenii dlia uchashchikhsia i rabochikh." *Teatral,* no. 64 (April 1896): 24–38.

Timkovskii, N. [I.], and N. [A.] Popov. "Pervaia vystavka narodnogo teatra. Obzor vystavki." In *Narodnyi teatr. Sbornik,* ed. E. V. Lavrova and N. A. Popov, 1–47. Moscow, 1896.

Trudy Pervogo Vserossiiskogo s"ezda deiatelei narodnogo teatra v Moskve, 27 dekabria 1915–5 ianvaria 1916. Petrograd, 1919. Cited as *TPVSDNT.*

Trudy Pervogo Vserossiiskogo s"ezda stsenicheskikh deiatelei. Part 1. St. Petersburg, 1898. Cited as *TPVSSD.*

Trudy sozvannogo Khar'kovskim obshchestvom gramotnosti 7–12 iiunia 1915 g. v g. Khar'kove s"ezda po voprosam organizatsii razumnykh razvlechenii dlia naseleniia Khar'kovskoi gubernii. Kharkov, 1915.

Uspenskii, G. "Narodnoe gulian'e v Vsesviatskom." *Zritel',* no. 21 (1 June 1863): 661.

V. V. "N. F. Bunakov i narodnyi teatr." *Vestnik popechitel'stv o narodnoi trezvosti,* no. 3 (22 January 1905): 55–56.

Varneke, B. "Chto igraet narod." In *Ezhegodnik imperatorskikh teatrov, 1913,* part 4, 1–39. St. Petersburg, 1913.

Vasilii Sleptsov. Neizvestnye stranitsy. Literaturnoe nasledstvo, vol. 71. Moscow, 1969.

Vasiukov, S. "Vospominaniia o M. V. Lentovskom." *Istoricheskii vestnik* (April 1907): 102–22.

Ves' Peterburg. St. Petersburg, 1894–1914.

Ves' Petrograd. Petrograd, 1915–17.

Voronov, V. I. *Put' k stsene.* Moscow, 1958.

Vsia Moskva. Adresnaia i spravochnaia kniga. Moscow, 1896–1917.

W. "Narodnyi teatr v Moskve." *Beseda,* no. 7 (July 1872): 37–43.

Zabelin, Ivan E. *Moskva v ee proshlom i nastoiashchem.* 12 vols. Moscow, 1910–12.

Zakhar'in (Iakunin), I. N. *Vstrechi i vospominaniia.* St. Petersburg, 1903.

SECONDARY SOURCES

Al'tshuller, A. Ia., et al., eds. *Pervaia russkaia revoliutsiia i teatr. Stat'i i materialy.* Moscow, 1956.

———. "Provintsial'nyi teatr v period pervoi russkoi revoliutsii." In *Pervaia russkaia revoliutsiia i teatr. Stat'i i materialy,* ed. A. Ia. Al'tshuller et al, 218–65. Moscow, 1956.

Arkhangel'skaia, V. K. "Pisateli-demokraty o narodnom teatre." In *Nasledie revoliutsionnykh demokratov i russkaia literatura,* 226–44. Saratov, 1981.

Aseev, B. N., and A. G. Obraztsovaia, eds. *Russkii dramaticheskii teatr.* Moscow, 1976.

Bailey, Peter. *Leisure and Class in Victorian Britain: Rational Recreations and the Contest for Control, 1830–1885.* London, 1978.

Balmuth, Daniel. *Censorship in Russia, 1865–1905.* Washington, D.C., 1979.

Balukhatyi, S. D. "Dramaturgiia M. Gor'kogo i tsarskaia tsenzura." In *Teatral'noe nasledie. Sbornik pervyi,* 195–252. Leningrad, 1934.

Bardovskii, A. A. *Teatral'nyi zritel' na fronte v kanun oktiabria.* Leningrad, 1928.

Bater, James H. "Between Old and New: St. Petersburg in the Late Imperial Era." In *The City in Late Imperial Russia,* ed. Michael F. Hamm, 43–78. Bloomington, 1986.

———. *St. Petersburg: Industrialization and Change.* London, 1976.

Benedetti, Jean. *Stanislavski: A Biography.* London, 1988.

———. "Stanislavsky and the Moscow Art Theatre, 1898–1938." In *A History of Russian Theatre,* ed. Robert Leach and Victor Borovsky, 254–77. Cambridge, 1999.

Bennett, Susan. *Theatre Audiences: A Theory of Production and Reception.* London, 1990.

Bennett, Tony. *The Birth of the Museum.* London, 1995.

Bennett, Tony, Colin Mercer, and Janet Woollacott, eds., *Popular Culture and Social Relations: History, Theory, Politics.* Milton Keynes, England, 1986.

Berkov, P. N. *Russkaia narodnaia drama XVII–XX vekov.* Moscow, 1953.

Black, Joseph. *Citizens for the Fatherland.* Boulder, 1979.

Bolotnikova, N. I. "Rabochii teatr i ego rol' v kul'turnom stroitel'stve pervykh let sovetskoi vlasti (1917–1920 gg.)." Kandidatskaia dissertatsiia, Moskovskii gosudarstvennyi institut kul'tury. Moscow, 1968.

Booth, Michael. *Victorian Spectacular Theatre, 1850–1910.* London, 1981.

Bonnell, Victoria E. *Roots of Rebellion: Workers' Politics and Organizations in St. Petersburg and Moscow, 1900–1914.* Berkeley, 1983.

Bonnell, Victoria E., ed. *The Russian Worker.* Berkeley, 1983.

Bourdieu, Pierre. *Distinction: A Social Critique of the Judgment of Taste.* Trans. Richard Nice. Cambridge, Mass., 1984.

Bradby, David, and John McCormick, eds. *People's Theatre.* London, 1978.

Bradley, Joseph. *Muzhik and Muscovite: Urbanization in Late Imperial Russia.* Berkeley, 1985.

Braun, Edward. *The Theatre of Meyerhold: Revolution on the Modern Stage.* London, 1979.

Brooks, Jeffrey. "A Changing View of the Autocrat and the Empire." *Russian History/Histoire russe* 14, nos. 1–4 (1987).

———. "Popular Philistinism and the Course of Russian Modernism." In

History and Literature: Theoretical Problems and Russian Case Studies,
ed. Gary Saul Morton. Stanford, 1986.

———. *When Russia Learned To Read: Literacy and Popular Literature,*
1861–1917. Princeton, 1985.

———. "The Zemstvos and the Education of the People." In *The Zemstvo in*
Russia: An Experiment in Local Self-Government, ed. Terence Emmons
and Wayne S. Vucinich, 243–78. Cambridge, 1982.

Brooks, Peter. *The Melodramatic Imagination: Balzac, Henry James, Melo-*
drama, and the Mode of Excess. New Haven, 1976.

Brower, Daniel R. "Labor Violence in Russia in the Late Nineteenth Century."
Slavic Review 41, no. 3 (Fall 1982): 417–31.

———. *The Russian City Between Tradition and Modernity, 1850–1900.*
Berkeley, 1990.

Brown, Frederick. *Theater and Revolution: The Culture of the French Stage.*
New York, 1980.

Certeau, Michel de. *Arts de Faire.* Paris, 1980.

Choldin, Marianna Tax. *A Fence around the Empire: Russian Censorship of*
Western Ideas under the Tsars. Durham, N.C., 1985.

Clark, Katerina. *Petersburg: Crucible of Cultural Revolution.* Cambridge,
Mass., 1995.

Clayton, J. Douglas. *Pierrot in Petrograd: The Commedia dell'Arte/Balagan in*
Twentieth-Century Russian Theatre and Drama. Montreal, 1993.

Clowes, Edith W. "Merchants on Stage and in Life: Theatricality and Public
Consciousness." In *Merchant Moscow: Images of Russia's Vanished*
Bourgeoisie, ed. James L. West and Iurii A. Petrov, 147–59. Princeton, 1998.

———. "Social Discourse in the Moscow Art Theater." In *Between Tsar and*
People: Educated Society and the Quest for Public Identity in Late Imperial
Russia, ed. Edith W. Clowes, Samuel Kassow, and James L. West, 271–78.
Princeton, 1991.

Clowes, Edith W., Samuel Kassow, and James L. West, eds. *Between Tsar and*
People: Educated Society and the Quest for Public Identity in Late Imperial
Russia. Princeton, 1991.

Corbin, Alain. "L'agitation dans les théâtres de province sous la Restauration."
In *Popular Traditions and Learned Culture in France from the Sixteenth to*
the Twentieth Century, ed. Marc Bertrand, 93–114. Saratoga, Calif., 1985.

Cunningham, Hugh. *Leisure in the Industrial Revolution.* London, 1980.

Danilov, S. S. "Materialy po istorii russkogo zakonodatel'stva o teatre." In *O*
teatre. Sbornik statei, ed. S. S. Danilov and S. S. Mokul'skii, 177–83.
Leningrad, 1940.

———. *Ocherki po istorii russkogo dramaticheskogo teatra.* Leningrad, 1948.

Davies, Cecil W. *Theatre for the People: The Story of the Volksbühne.* Austin,
Tex., 1977.

Denning, Michael. "Cheap Stories: Notes on Popular Fiction and Working-
Class Culture in Nineteenth-Century America." *History Workshop*
Journal, no. 22 (Autumn 1986): 1–17.

———. *Mechanic Accents: Dime Novels and Working-Class Culture in America.* New York, 1987.

Dmitriev, Iu. A. *Mikhail Lentovskii.* Moscow, 1978.

———. "Na starom Moskovskom gulianii." *Teatral'nyi almanakh VTO,* book 4. Moscow, 1947.

———. *Tsirk v Rossii.* Moscow, 1977.

Dolinskii, Mikhail, and Semen Chertok. "Kak eto nachinalos'." *Teatr,* no. 2 (February 1963): 139–42.

Drizen, N. V. *Dramaticheskaia tsenzura dvukh epokh, 1825–1881.* Petrograd, 1917.

———. *Materialy k istorii russkogo teatra.* Moscow, 1905.

Dukov, E. V., ed. *Razvlekatel'naia kul'tura Rossii XVIII–XIX vv. Ocherki istorii i teorii.* St. Petersburg, 2000.

Eklof, Ben. *Russian Peasant Schools: Officialdom, Village Culture, and Popular Pedagogy, 1861–1914.* Berkeley, 1986.

Eklof, Ben, John Bushnell, and Larissa Zakharova, eds. *Russia's Great Reforms, 1855–1861.* Bloomington, 1994.

Elias, Norbert. *The Civilizing Process.* Trans. Edmund Jephcott. 2 vols. New York, 1982.

Engel, Barbara, *Between the Fields and the City: Women, Work, and Family in Russia, 1861–1914.* Cambridge, 1994.

Engelstein, Laura. "Combined Underdevelopment: Discipline and Law in Imperial and Soviet Russia." *American Historical Review* 98, no. 2 (April 1993): 338–53.

———. *The Keys to Happiness: Sex and the Search for Modernity in Fin-de-Siècle Russia.* Ithaca, 1992.

———. *Moscow, 1905: Working-Class Organization and Political Conflict.* Stanford, 1982.

Epstein, Barbara L. *The Politics of Domesticity: Women, Emancipation and Temperance in Nineteenth-century America.* Middletown, Conn., 1986.

Evreinov, N. N. *Istoriia russkogo teatra s drevneishikh vremen do 1917 goda.* New York, 1955.

Field, Daniel. *Rebels in the Name of the Tsar.* Boston, 1976.

Filippov, A. M. "Revoliutsionnoe gnezdo." *Sud idet!,* no. 4 (68) (February 1927): 195–96.

Firsov, S. L. "Rabochie i pravoslavnaia tserkov' v Rossii v nachale XX v." In *Rabochie i intelligentsiia v epokhu reform i revoliutsii 1861–fevral' 1917 g.,* ed. S. I. Potolov et al., 327–39. St. Petersburg, 1997.

Fish, Stanley. *Is There a Text in This Class? The Authority of Interpretive Communities.* Cambridge, Mass., 1980.

Fisher, David J. "The Origins of French Popular Theater." *Journal of Contemporary History* 12, no. 3 (July 1977): 461–97.

———. "Romain Rolland and the French People's Theatre." *The Drama Review* (March 1977): 75–90.

———. *Romain Rolland and the Politics of Cultural Engagement.* Berkeley, 1988.

Fiske, John. *Reading the Popular.* Boston, 1989.

——. *Understanding Popular Culture.* Boston, 1989.

Foucault, Michel. *Discipline and Punish: The Birth of the Prison.* Trans. Alan Sheridan. New York, 1977.

——. *The History of Sexuality. Vol. 1. An Introduction.* Trans. Robert Hurley. New York, 1978.

Frame, Murray. "Censorship and Control in the Russian Imperial Theatre during the 1905 Revolution and Its Aftermath." *Revolutionary Russia* 7, no. 2 (December 1994): 164–91.

——. *The St. Petersburg Imperial Theaters: Stage and State in Revolutionary Russia, 1900–1920.* Jefferson, N.C., 2000.

Frank, Stephen P. "Confronting the Domestic Other: Rural Popular Culture and Its Enemies in Fin-de-Siècle Russia." In *Cultures in Flux: Lower-Class Values, Practices, and Resistance in Late Imperial Russia,* ed. Stephen P. Frank and Mark D. Steinberg, 74–107. Princeton, 1994.

——. *Crime, Cultural Conflict, and Justice in Rural Russia, 1856–1914.* Berkeley, 1999.

——. "'Simple Folk, Savage Customs?' Youth, Sociability, and the Dynamics of Culture in Rural Russia, 1856–1914." *Journal of Social History* 25, no. 4 (Summer 1992): 711–36.

Frank, Stephen P., and Mark D. Steinberg, eds. *Cultures in Flux: Lower-Class Values, Practices, and Resistance in Late Imperial Russia.* Princeton, 1994.

Freeze, Gregory. "The Estate (*Soslovie*) Paradigm and Russian Social History." *American Historical Review* 91, no. 1 (January 1986): 11–36.

Freidkina, L. M. *Dni i gody Vl. I. Nemirovicha-Danchenka. Letopis' zhizni i tvorchestva.* Moscow, 1962.

Glickman, Rose. *Russian Factory Women: Workplace and Society, 1880–1914.* Berkeley, 1984.

Golby, J. M., and A. W. Purdue. *The Civilization of the Crowd.* New York, 1984.

Gorzka, Gabriele. *Arbeiterkultur in der Sowjetunion. Industriearbeiter-Klubs 1917–1929: Ein Beitrag zur sowjetischen Kulturgeschicte.* Berlin, 1990.

Gudnovtsev, M. I. *Tserkov' i teatr.* Moscow, 1970.

Gugushvili, E. N., and A. Z. Iufit. *Bol'shevistskaia pechat' i teatr.* Leningrad, 1961.

Gusev, V. E. "Ot obriada k narodnomu teatru (evoliutsiia sviatochnykh igr v pokoinika)." In *Fol'klor i etnografiia: Obriadi i obriadovoi fol'klor,* 49–59. Leningrad, 1974.

——. *Russkii fol'klornyi teatr XVIII–nachala XX veka.* Leningrad, 1980.

Gvozdev, A., and Andrei Piotrovskii. "Teatral'naia 'Gaponovshchina.'" *Teatr i dramaturgiia,* nos. 2–3 (May–June 1933): 54–57.

Haimson, Leopold H. "The Problem of Social Stability in Urban Russia, 1905–1917." Parts 1–2. *Slavic Review* 23, no. 4 (December 1964): 619–42; 24, no. 1 (March 1965): 1–22.

Harrison, Brian. *Drink and the Victorians: The Temperance Question in England, 1815–1872.* London, 1971.

Herlihy, Patricia. "'Joy of the Rus': Rites and Rituals of Russian Drinking." *Russian Review* 50, no. 2 (April 1991): 131–47.

———. "Strategies of Sobriety: Temperance Movements in Russia, 1880–1914." Occasional paper no. 238, Kennan Institute for Advanced Russian Studies. Washington, D.C., 1990.

Herrlinger, Kimberley Page. "Class, Piety, and Politics: Workers, Orthodoxy and the Problem of Religious Identity in Russia." Ph.D. dissertation, University of California, Berkeley, 1996.

Iser, Wolfgang. *The Act of Reading: A Theory of Aesthetic Response.* Baltimore, 1978.

———. *The Implied Reader: Patterns of Communication in Prose Fiction from Bunyan to Beckett.* Baltimore, 1974.

———. "Interaction Between Text and Reader." In *The Reader in the Text: Essays on Audience and Interpretation*, ed. Susan R. Suleiman and Inge Crosman, 106–19. Princeton, 1980.

———. "The Reading Process." In *New Directions in Literary History*, ed. Ralph Cohen. London, 1974.

Istoriia Moskvy. 6 vols. Moscow, 1952–59.

Istoriia rabochikh Leningrada. Ed. V. S. Diakin et al. 2 vols. Leningrad, 1972.

Istoriia russkogo dramaticheskogo teatra v semi tomakh. Ed. E. G. Kholodov et al. 7 vols. Moscow, 1977–87.

Iunisov, M. V. "'Lishnii' teatr: o liubiteliakh i ikh 'gubiteliakh.'" In *Razvleka-tel'naia kul'tura Rossii XVIII–XIX vv. Ocherki istorii i teorii*, ed. E. V. Dukov, 372–93. St. Petersburg, 2000.

———. "Sel'skii liubitel'skii teatr Rossii (1917–1941 gody)." Kandidatskaia dissertatsiia, Rossiiskii institut iskusstvoznaniia, Moscow, 1993.

Ivanov, F. "Iz istorii narodnykh zrelishch." *Narodnoe tvorchestvo*, no. 7 (1937): 37–39.

Ivanov, L. M. "Ideologicheskoe vozdeistvie na proletariat tsarizma i burzhu-azii." In *Rossiiskii proletariat: oblik, bor'ba, gegemoniia*, ed. L. M. Ivanov, 317–54. Moscow, 1970.

———, ed. *Rossiiskii proletariat: oblik, bor'ba, gegemoniia.* Moscow, 1970.

Jahn, Hubertus. *Patriotic Culture in Russia During World War I.* Ithaca, 1995.

Johnson, Robert. *Peasant and Proletarian: The Working Class of Moscow in the Late Nineteenth Century.* New Brunswick, N.J., 1979.

Jones, Gareth Stedman. *Languages of Class: Studies in English Working-Class History, 1832–1982.* Cambridge, 1983.

Kabo, E. A. *Ocherki rabochego byta: Opyt monograficheskogo issledovaniia domashnego rabochego byta.* Vol. 1. Moscow, 1928.

———."Rabochaia kul'tura i rabochii byt," *Prizyv*, no. 3(March 1925).

Kachalov, M. V. "Narodnyi teatr v Moskve na Devich'em pole: Materialy k istorii teatra v XVIII veke." *Istoricheskaia biblioteka*, no. 5 (May 1878): 1–10.

Karlinsky, Simon. *Russian Drama from Its Beginnings to the Age of Pushkin.* Berkeley, 1985.

Kelly, Catriona. *Petrushka: The Russian Carnival Puppet Theatre.* Cambridge, 1990.

———. "Popular, Provincial and Amateur Theatres." In *A History of Russian Theatre,* ed. Robert Leach and Victor Borovsky, 124–45. Cambridge, 1999.

———. "A Stick with Two Ends, or, Misogyny in Popular Culture: A Case Study of the Puppet Text 'Petrushka.'" In *Sexuality and the Body in Russian Culture,* ed. Jane T. Costlow, Stephanie Sandler, and Judith Vowles, 73–96. Stanford, 1993.

Kelly, Catriona, and David Shepherd, eds. *Constructing Russian Culture in the Age of Revolution, 1881–1940.* Oxford, 1998.

Khaichenko, G. A. *Russkii narodnyi teatr kontsa XIX–nachala XX veka.* Moscow, 1975.

King, E. *The People's Palace and Glasgow Green.* Glasgow, 1985.

Kizevetter, A. A. *Pervyi obshchedostupnyi teatr v Rossii.* Petrograd, 1917.

Kleberg, Lars. "'People's Theater' and the Revolution: On the History of a Concept Before and After 1917." In *Art, Society, Revolution: Russia 1917–1921,* ed. N. A. Nilsson, 179–97. Stockholm Studies in Russian Literature, no. 11. Stockholm, 1979.

Klinchin, A. P. "Narodnyi teatr na Politekhnicheskoi vystavke." In *Teatral'noe nasledstvo. Soobshcheniia. Publikatsii,* 347–74. Moscow, 1956.

Koksheneva, K. A. "Zritel' teatra revoliutsionnoi epokhi. 1917–1924." Kandidatskaia dissertatsiia, Gosudarstvennyi institut teatral'nogo iskusstva im. A. V. Lunacharskogo, Moscow, 1985.

Konechnyi, A. M. *Byt i zrelishchnaia kul'tura Sankt-Peterburga-Petrograda, XVII–nachalo XX veka. Materialy k bibliografii.* St. Petersburg, 1997.

———."Garderob peterburgskikh razvlechenii." In *"Garderob." Vystavka sovremennykh karnaval'nykh kostiumov,* 23–27. St. Petersburg, 1992.

———. "Obshchestvennye razvlecheniia i gorodskie zrelishcha v Tsarskom Sele (XVIII–nachalo XX v.)." In *Etnografiia Peterburga-Leningrada. Materialy ezhegodnykh nauchnykh chtenii,* no. 2, ed. N. V. Iukhneva, 13–21. Leningrad, 1988.

———. "Peterburgskie narodnye gulian'ia na maslenoi i paskhal'noi nedeliakh." In *Peterburg i guberniia: Istoriko-etnograficheskie issledovaniia,* ed. N. V. Iukhneva, 21–52. Leningrad, 1989.

———. "Popular Carnivals during Mardi Gras and Easter Week in St. Petersburg." *Russian Studies in History* 35, no. 4 (Spring 1997): 52–91.

———. "Raek: narodnaia zabava." *Dekorativnoe iskusstvo,* no. 9 (1986): 13–15.

———. "Shows for the People: Public Amusement Parks in Nineteenth-Century St. Petersburg." In *Cultures in Flux: Lower-Class Values, Practices, and Resistance in Late Imperial Russia,* ed. Stephen P. Frank and Mark D. Steinberg, 121–30. Princeton, 1994.

———. "Zrelishchnaia kul'tura Peterburga." Paper presented to the American Association for the Advancement of Slavic Studies, Phoenix, Arizona, 20 November 1992.

Konechnyi, A. M., ed. and comp. *Peterburgskie balagany.* St. Petersburg, 2000.

Krupianskaia, V. Iu. "Narodnaia drama *Lodka,* ee genezis i literaturnaia istoriia." In *Kratkie soobshcheniia instituta etnografii Akademii nauk SSSR,* no. 3. Moscow, 1947.

Kruze, E. E. *Peterburgskie rabochie v 1912–1914 godakh.* Leningrad, 1961.

———. *Polozhenie rabochego klassa Rossii v 1900–1914 godakh.* Leningrad, 1976.

Kuz'mina, V. D. *Russkii demokraticheskii teatr XVIII veka.* Moscow, 1958.

Laman, N. "Fabrichnyi teatr v Moskve." *Khudozhestvennaia samodeiatel'-nost',* no. 1 (1963): 30–33.

Lapshin, V. L. *Khudozhestvennaia zhizn' Moskvy i Petrograda v 1917 godu.* Moscow, 1983.

Leach, Robert, and Victor Borovsky, eds. *A History of Russian Theatre.* Cambridge, 1999.

Ledkovsky, Marina, Charlotte Rosenthal, and Mary Zirin, eds. *Dictionary of Russian Women Writers.* Westport, Conn., 1994.

Leikina-Svirskaia, V. R. *Intelligentsiia v Rossii vo vtoroi polovine XIX veka.* Moscow, 1971.

———. *Russkaia intelligentsiia v 1900–1917 godakh.* Moscow, 1981.

Levin, I. V. "Rabochie kluby v Peterburge (1907–1914 gg.)." Parts 1 and 2. In *Materialy po istorii professional'nogo dvizheniia v Rossii,* vol. 3., 88–111, vol. 4, 200–44. Moscow, 1925.

Levine, Lawrence W. *Highbrow/Lowbrow: The Emergence of Cultural Hierarchy in America.* Cambridge, Mass., 1988.

Levinson, A. G. "Razvitie fol'klornykh traditsii russkogo iskusstva na guliani-akh." Kandidatskaia dissertatsiia, Vsesoiuznyi nauchno-issledovatel'skii institut iskusstvoznaniia, Moscow, 1980.

Lidtke, Vernon. *The Alternative Culture: Socialist Labor in Imperial Germany.* New York, 1985.

Lincoln, W. Bruce. *Nicholas I: Emperor and Autocrat of All the Russias.* Bloomington, 1979.

Lindenmeyer, Adele. *Poverty Is Not a Vice: Charity, Society, and the State in Imperial Russia.* Princeton, 1996.

Lotman, L. M., ed. *Istoriia russkoi dramaturgii (vtoraia polovina XIX–nachalo XX veka).* Leningrad, 1987.

Löwe, Heinz-Dietrich. "Political Symbols and Rituals, 1900–1914." *Slavonic and East European Review* 76, no. 3 (July 1998): 441–66.

L'vov-Rogachevskii, V. L. *Ocherki proletarskoi literatury.* Moscow, 1927.

Machan, Helen Whitman. "The Popular-Theater Movement in France: Romain Rolland and the Revue d'Art Dramatique." Ph.D. dissertation, University of Illinois, 1950.

Madariaga, Isabel de. "The Foundation of the Russian Educational System by Catherine II." *Slavonic and East European Review* 57, no. 3 (July 1979): 369–95.

Mally, Lynn. *Culture of the Future: The Proletkult Movement in Revolutionary Russia.* Berkeley, 1990.

————. *Revolutionary Acts: Amateur Theater and the Soviet State, 1917–1939.* Ithaca, 2000.

Mathewson, Rufus W., Jr. *The Positive Hero in Russian Literature.* 2nd ed. Stanford, 1975.

Mazaev, A. *Prazdnik kak sotsial'no-khudozhestvennoe iavlenie.* Moscow, 1978.

McConachie, Bruce A., and Daniel Friedman, eds. *Theatre for Working-Class Audiences in the United States, 1830–1980.* Contributions in Drama and Theatre Studies, no. 14. Westport, Conn., 1985.

McDaniel, Tim. *Autocracy, Capitalism, and Revolution in Russia.* Berkeley, 1988.

McKean, Robert B. *St. Petersburg between the Revolutions: Workers and Revolutionaries, June 1907–February 1917.* New Haven, 1990.

McKee, W. Arthur. "Sobering up the Soul of the People: The Politics of Popular Temperance in Late Imperial Russia." *Russian Review* 58, no. 2 (April 1999): 212–33.

————. "Taming the Green Serpent: Alcoholism, Autocracy, and Russian Society, 1890–1917." Ph.D. dissertation, University of California, Berkeley, 1997.

McReynolds, Louise. *The News under Russia's Old Regime: The Development of a Mass-Circulation Press.* Princeton, 1991.

McReynolds, Louise, and Cathy Popkin. "The Objective Eye and the Common Good." In *Constructing Russian Culture in the Age of Revolution, 1881–1940,* ed. Catriona Kelly and David Shepherd, 57–105. Oxford, 1998.

Medvedev, D. "Narodnyi teatr na Moskovskoi politekhnicheskoi vystavke (K istorii russkogo narodnogo teatra v XIX veke)." *Istoricheskii vestnik* (September 1905): 741–61.

Mikhailova, R. F. "K voprosu o sozdanii narodnogo teatra v Rossii v kontse 60-kh–nachale 70-kh godov XIX veka." In *Vestnik Leningradskogo gosudarstvennogo universiteta,* no. 8, vypusk 2, 67–78. Leningrad, 1961.

Mikhailovskii, V. V. *Dramaturgiia M. Gor'kogo epokhi pervoi russkoi revoliutsii.* 2nd ed. Moscow, 1955.

Mironov, B. N. "Prestupnost' v Rossii v XIX–nachale XX veka." *Otechestvennaia istoriia,* no. 1 (January–February 1998): 24–42.

Monas, Sidney. *The Third Section: Police and Society Under Nicholas I.* Cambridge, Mass., 1961.

Moon, David. "Peasants into Russian Citizens? A Comparative Perspective." *Revolutionary Russia* 9 (June 1996): 43–81.

Mouffe, Chantal. "Hegemony and Ideology in Gramsci." In *Gramsci and Marxist Theory,* ed. Chantal Mouffe. Boston, 1979.

Muzykal'naia entsiklopediia. 6 vols. Moscow, 1973–82.

Nasaw, David. *Going Out: The Rise and Fall of Public Amusements.* New York, 1993.

Nekrylova, A. F. "Ocherki-shestidesiatniki." In *Russkaia literatura i fol'klor (Vtoraia polovina XIX v.),* 131–77. Leningrad, 1982.

————. *Russkie narodnye gorodskie prazdniki, uveseleniia i zrelishcha.* Leningrad, 1988.

Nekrylova, A. F., and N. I. Savushkina, eds. *Fol'klornyi teatr.* Moscow, 1988.

Neuberger, Joan. *Hooliganism: Crime, Culture, and Power in St. Petersburg, 1900–1914.* Berkeley, 1993.

————. "Stories of the Street: Hooliganism in the St. Petersburg Popular Press." *Slavic Review* 48, no. 2 (Summer 1989): 177–94.

Ocherki istorii Leningrada. Ed. M. P. Viatkin. 7 vols. Leningrad, 1955–89.

Orlov, Iu. *Moskovskii khudozhestvennyi teatr. Legendy i fakty (opyt khoziastvovaniia) 1898–1917 gg.* Moscow, 1994.

Ostrovsky, Arkady. "Imperial and Private Theatres, 1882–1905." In *A History of Russian Theatre,* ed. Robert Leach and Victor Borovsky, 218–53. Cambridge, 1999.

Owen, Thomas. *Capitalism and Politics in Russia: A Social History of the Moscow Merchants.* Cambridge, 1981.

Péchoux, P. "L'ombre de Pugacev." In *Le statut des paysans libérés du servage, 1861–1961,* ed. R. Portal, 128–52. Paris, 1962.

Petrovskaia, I. F. *Istochnikovedenie istorii russkogo dramaticheskogo teatra.* Leningrad, 1971.

————. *Materialy k istorii russkogo teatra. Obzory dokumentov. XVII vek–1917 g.* Moscow, 1966.

————. *Teatr i muzyka v Rossii XIX–nachala XX v. Obzor bibliograficheskikh i spravochnykh materialov.* Leningrad, 1984.

————. *Teatr i zritel' rossiiskikh stolits, 1895–1917.* Leningrad, 1990.

Petrovskaia, I. F., and V. Somina. *Teatral'nyi Peterburg. Nachalo XVIII veka–oktiabr' 1917 goda.* St. Petersburg, 1994.

Phillips, Laura L. *Bolsheviks and the Bottle: Drink and Worker Culture in St. Petersburg, 1900–1929.* DeKalb, Ill., 2000.

————. "Everyday Life in Revolutionary Russia: Working-Class Drinking and Taverns in St. Petersburg, 1900–1929." Ph.D. dissertation, University of Illinois, Champaign-Urbana, 1993.

Pick, Daniel. *Faces of Degeneration: A European Disorder.* Cambridge, 1989.

Potolov, S. I., et al., eds. *Rabochie i intelligentsiia v epokhu reform i revoliutsii 1861–fevral' 1917 g.* St. Petersburg, 1997.

Propp, Vladimir. *Russkie agrarnye prazdniki.* Leningrad, 1963.

Prozorova, T A. "A. M. Gor'kii v bor'be za narodnyi teatr (1892–1904). Kandidatskaia dissertatsiia, Gosudarstvennyi institut teatral'nogo iskusstva imeni A. V. Lunacharskogo. Leningrad, 1967.

Pushkareva, I. M. *Rabochee dvizhenie v Rossii v period reaktsii, 1907–1910 gg.* Moscow, 1989.

Pyliaev, M. I. *Staraia Moskva.* St. Petersburg, 1891.

————. *Staryi Peterburg.* St. Petersburg, 1903.

Rabochee dvizhenie v Rossii v XIX veke. Sbornik dokumentov i materialov. Vol. 4, part 1 (1895–1917). Ed. L. M. Ivanov. Moscow, 1961.

Rancière, Jacques. *La nuit des prolétaires: Archives de rêve ouvrier.* Paris, 1981.

Rashin, A. G. *Formirovanie rabochego klassa Rossii: Istoriko-ekonomicheskii ocherk.* Moscow, 1958.

Reid, Douglas A. "Popular Theatre in Victorian Birmingham." In *Performance and Politics in Popular Drama,* ed. David Bradby, 65–90. Cambridge, 1980.

Rieber, Alfred. *Merchants and Entrepreneurs in Imperial Russia.* Chapel Hill, N.C., 1982.

Ritter, Gerhard. "Workers' Culture in Imperial Germany." *Journal of Contemporary History* 13, no. 2 (April 1978): 165–89.

Rolland, Romain. *Le théâtre du peuple.* Paris, 1903.

Rosenthal, Bernice Glatzer. "Theatre as Church: The Vision of the Mystical Anarchists." *Russian History/Histoire russe* 4, no. 2 (Summer 1977): 122–41.

Ruane, Christine. "Clothes Shopping in Imperial Russia: The Development of a Consumer Culture." *Journal of Social History* 28, no. 4 (Summer 1995): 765–82.

Ruckman, Jo Ann. *The Moscow Business Elite: A Social and Cultural Portrait of Two Generations, 1840–1905.* DeKalb, Ill., 1984.

Russell, Robert. "People's Theater and the October Revolution." *Irish Slavonic Studies,* no. 7 (1986): 65–84.

Russkii vodevil'. Leningrad, 1959.

Saccett, Robert Eben. *Popular Entertainment, Class, and Politics in Munich, 1900–1923.* Cambridge, Mass., 1982.

Sady i parki Leningrada. Leningrad, 1981.

Samuel, Raphael, Ewan MacColl, and Stuart Cosgrove, eds. *Theatres of the Left, 1880–1935: Workers' Theatre Movements in Britain and America.* London, 1985.

Sartseva, E. A. "Kafeshantan Sharlia Omona," In *Razvlekatel'naia kul'tura Rossii XVIII–XX vv. Ocherki istorii i teorii,* ed. E. V. Dukov, 350–71. St. Petersburg, 2000.

Savushkina, N. I. *Russkaia narodnaia drama.* Moscow, 1988.

Scascighini, Mario. *La maison du peuple: le temps d'un édifice de classe.* Lausanne, 1991.

Schneiderman, Jeremiah. *Sergei Zubatov and Revolutionary Marxism: The Struggle for the Working Class in Tsarist Russia.* Ithaca, 1976.

Schuler, Catherine A. *Women in Russian Theatre: The Actress in the Silver Age.* London, 1996.

Segal, Boris M. *Russian Drinking: Use and Abuse of Alcohol in Pre-Revolutionary Russia.* New Brunswick, N.J., 1987.

Segal, Harold B. *Turn-of-the-Century Cabaret: Paris, Barcelona, Berlin, Munich, Vienna, Cracow, Moscow, St. Petersburg, Zurich.* New York, 1987.

Semenova, L. N. "Obshchestvennye razvlecheniia v Peterburge v pervoi polovine XVIII v." In *Staryi Peterburg: Istoriko-etnograficheskie issledovaniia,* 147–63. Leningrad, 1982.

Senelick, Lawrence. "Boris Geyer and Cabaretic Playwriting." In *Russian Theatre in the Age of Modernism,* ed. Robert Russell and Andrew Barratt, 33–37. New York, 1990.

Serpoletti, A. Z. "Moskovksie uveselitel'nye sady. Ocherk s 1867 g." Unpublished manuscript, 1928. GTsTM, f. 533, d. 33–34.

Siegelbaum, Lewis H., and Ronald Grigor Suny, eds. *Making Workers Soviet: Power, Class, and Identity.* Ithaca, 1994.

Smith, S. A. "Workers Against Foremen in St. Petersburg, 1905–1917." In *Making Workers Soviet: Power, Class, and Identity,* ed. Lewis H. Siegelbaum and Ronald Grigor Suny, 113–37. Ithaca, 1994.

Smith, Steve. "Citizenship and the Russian Nation during World War I: A Comment." *Slavic Review* 59, no. 2 (Summer 2000): 316–29.

Smith, Steve, and Catriona Kelly. "Commercial Culture and Consumerism." In *Constructing Russian Culture in the Age of Revolution, 1881–1940,* ed. Catriona Kelly and David Shepherd, 106–55. Oxford, 1998.

Snigerev, I. M. *Russkie prostonarodnye prazdniki i suevernye obriadi.* Vypusk 2. Moscow, 1838.

Snow, George E. "Alcoholism in the Russian Military: The Public Sphere and the Temperance Discourse, 1883–1917." *Jahrbücher für Geschichte Osteuropas* 45, no. 3 (1997): 417–31.

———. "Socialism, Alcoholism, and the Russian Working Classes before 1917." In *Drinking: Behavior and Belief in Modern History,* ed. Susanna Barrows and Robin Room, 243–64. Berkeley, 1991.

Sobolev, Iu. *Moskovskii khudozhestvennyi teatr. Ocherki.* Moscow, 1938.

Sochor, Zenovia. *Revolution and Culture: The Bogdanov-Lenin Controversy.* Ithaca, 1988.

Starikova, L. N. *Teatr v Rossii XVIII veka.* Moscow, 1997.

———. *Teatral'naia zhizn' starinnoi Moskvy: Epokha. Byt. Nravy.* Moscow, 1988.

Stavrou, Theophanis, ed. *Art and Culture in Nineteenth-Century Russia.* Bloomington, 1983.

Steinberg, Mark D. *Moral Communities: The Culture of Class Relations in the Russian Printing Industry, 1867–1907.* Berkeley, 1992.

———. "Vanguard Workers and the Morality of Class." In *Making Workers Soviet: Power, Class, and Identity,* ed. Lewis H. Siegelbaum and Ronald Grigor Suny, 66–84. Ithaca, 1994.

———. "Worker-Authors and the Cult of the Person." In *Cultures in Flux: Lower-Class Values, Practices, and Resistance in Late Imperial Russia,* ed. Stephen P. Frank and Mark D. Steinberg, 168–84. Princeton, 1994.

Stephens, John Russell. *The Censorship of English Drama, 1824–1901.* Cambridge, 1980.

Storch, R. D., ed. *Popular Culture and Custom in Nineteenth-Century England.* London, 1982.

Stuart, Mary. "The Ennobling Illusion: The Public Library Movement in Late Imperial Russia," *The Slavonic and East European Review* 76, no. 3 (July 1998): 401–40.

Surh, Gerald D. *1905 in St. Petersburg: Labor, Society, and Revolution.* Stanford, 1989.

Swift, E. Anthony. "Fighting the Germs of Disorder: The Censorship of Russian Popular Theater, 1888–1917." *Russian History/Histoire russe* 18, no. 1 (Spring 1991): 1–49.

———. "Kul'turnoe stroitel'stvo ili kul'turnaia razrukha? Nekotorye aspekty teatral'noi zhizni Moskvy i Petrograda v 1917 g." In *Anatomiia revoliutsii: 1917 god v Rossii. Massy, partii, vlast'*, ed. V. Iu. Chernaev et al., 394–405. Moscow, 1994.

———. "Razvlekatel'naia kul'tura gorodskikh rabochikh kontsa XIX–nachala XX veka." In *Razvlekatel'naia kul'tura Rossii XVIII–XIX vv. Ocherki istorii i teorii*, ed. E. V. Dukov, 372–93. St. Petersburg, 2000.

———. "Workers' Theater and 'Proletarian Culture' in Pre-Revolutionary Russia, 1905–1917." *Russian History/Histoire russe* 23 (1996): 67–94.

Teatral'naia entsiklopediia. 5 vols. and supplement. Moscow, 1961–67.

Thurston, Gary. "The Impact of Russian Popular Theatre, 1886–1915." *Journal of Modern History* 55, no. 2 (June 1983): 237–67.

———. *The Popular Theatre Movement in Russia, 1862–1919.* Evanston, Ill., 1998.

———. "Theatre and Acculturation in Russia from Peasant Emancipation to the First World War." *Journal of Popular Culture* 18, no. 2 (Fall 1984): 3–16.

———. "Theatre in the Village School: The Bunakovs' Discoveries." In *School and Society in Tsarist and Soviet Russia*, ed. Ben Eklof, 70–94. New York, 1993.

Thurston, Robert W. *Liberal City, Conservative State: Moscow and Russia's Urban Crisis, 1906–1914.* New York, 1987.

Tikhonravov, N. S. *Russkie dramaticheskie proizvedeniia 1672–1725 godov.* Vol. 1. St. Petersburg, 1874.

Tikhvinskaia, Liudmilla. *Kabare i teatry miniatiur v Rossii, 1908–1917.* Moscow, 1995.

Tsinkovich, V. A. "Narodnyi teatr i dramaticheskaia tsenzura." In *Teatral'noe nasledstvo. Soobshcheniia. Publikatsii*, 375–401. Moscow, 1956.

Tsivian, Yuri. *Early Cinema in Russia and Its Cultural Reception.* Trans. Alan Bodger. London, 1994.

Tsuchiya, Hiroko. "'Let Them Be Amused': The Industrial Drama Movement, 1910–1929." In *Theatre for Working-Class Audiences in the United States, 1830–1980*, ed. Bruce A. McConachie and Daniel Friedman, 97–110. Contributions in Drama and Theatre Studies, no. 14. Westport, Conn., 1985.

Tsvetkovskii-Prosveshchenskii, A. K. *V gody reaktsii i pod"ema (1907–1910 gg.).* Leningrad, 1926.

Veitch, Norman. *The People's Theatre.* London, 1950.

Viatkin, M. P., ed. *Istoriia Leningrada.* 3 vols. Moscow, 1955–57.

Vinogradskaia, I. N. *Zhizn' i tvorchestvo K. S. Stanislavskogo. Letopis' v chetyrekh tomakh, 1863–1938.* 4 vols. Moscow, 1971–76.

Von Geldern, James. *Bolshevik Festivals, 1917–1920.* Berkeley, 1993.

———. "Life in Between: Migration and Popular Culture in Late Imperial Russia," *Russian Review* 55, no. 3 (July 1996): 365–83.

Vsevolodskii-Gerngross, Vsevolod. *Istoriia russkogo teatra*. Leningrad, 1929.

Walicki, Andrzej. *A History of Russian Thought from the Enlightenment to Marxism*. Trans. Hilda Andrews-Rusiecka. Stanford, 1979.

Warner, Elizabeth, *The Russian Folk Theatre*. The Hague, 1977.

Waters, Chris. *British Socialists and the Politics of Popular Culture, 1884–1914*. Manchester, 1990.

West, James L., and Iurii A. Petrov, eds. *Merchant Moscow: Images of Russia's Vanished Bourgeoisie*. Princeton, 1998.

Wildman, Alan K. *The Making of a Workers' Revolution: Russian Social Democracy, 1891–1903*. Chicago, 1967.

Willis, Paul. *Common Culture: Symbolic Work at Play in the Everyday Life of the Young*. Milton Keynes, England, 1990.

Wortman, Richard. *Scenarios of Power: Myth and Ceremony in Russian Monarchy*. 2 vols. Princeton, 1995–2000.

Wynn, Charters. *Workers, Strikes, and Pogroms: The Donbass-Dnepr Bend in Late Imperial Russia, 1870–1905*. Princeton, 1992.

Youngblood, Denise. *The Magic Mirror: Moviemaking in Russia, 1908–1918*. Madison, 1999.

Zabelin, Ivan E. "Iz khroniki obshchestvennoi zhizni v Moskve v XVIII stoletii." In *Sbornik obshchestva liubitelei rossiiskoi slovesnosti na 1891 god*, 557–82. Moscow, 1891.

Zasosov, D. A., and V. I. Pyzin. *Iz zhizni Peterburga 1890–1910-kh godov*. Leningrad, 1991.

Zelnik, Reginald E. *Labor and Society in Tsarist Russia: The Factory Workers of St. Petersburg, 1855–1870*. Stanford, 1971.

———. "Russian Bebels." Parts 1–2. *Russian Review* 35, no. 3 (July 1976): 249–89; 35, no. 4 (October 1976): 417–47.

———. "The Sunday School Movement in Russia, 1859–1862." *The Journal of Modern History* 27, no. 2 (June 1965): 151–70.

———. "'To the Unaccustomed Eye': Religion and Irreligion in the Experience of St. Petersburg Workers in the 1870s." *Russian History/Histoire russe* 16, nos. 2–4 (1989): 297–326.

———. "*Weber* into *Tkachi*: On a Russian Reading of Gerhart Hauptmann's Play *The Weavers*." In *Self and Story in Russian History*, ed. Laura Engelstein and Stephanie Sandler, 217–41. Ithaca, 2000.

———, ed. *Workers and Intelligentsia in Late Imperial Russia: Realities, Representations, Reflections*. Berkeley, 1999.

Zel'tser, S. *A. A. Briantsev*. Moscow, 1962.

Zguta, Russel. *Russian Minstrels: A History of the Skomorokhi*. Philadelphia, 1978.

Zhislina, S. "Iz istorii narodnogo teatra." *Narodnoe tvorchestvo*, no. 12 (1938): 55–59.

Zorkaia, N. M. *Na rubezhe stoletii. U istokov massovogo iskusstva v Rossii 1900–1910 godov*. Moscow, 1976.

Index

STUDIES ON THE HISTORY OF SOCIETY AND CULTURE

Victoria E. Bonnell and Lynn Hunt, Editors

Compositor:	BookMatters, Berkeley
Text:	11/15 Granjon
Display:	Granjon
Printer and Binder:	Thompson-Shore

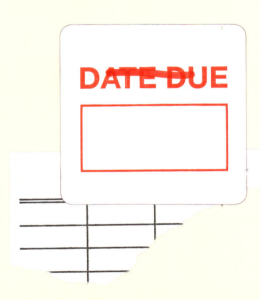

DATE DUE